Artificial Intelligence in Detecting Autism

Editors:

Ram Kumar Chenthur Pandian
Professor, Computer Science and Engineering (IoT)
Sri Krishna College of Engineering and Technology, Coimbatore, India

Shanmuga Raju Sekar
Assistant Professor, Computer Science and Engineering (IoT)
Sri Krishna College of Engineering and Technology, Coimbatore, India

Subrata Chowdhury
Associate Professor, Department of Computer Science and Engineering
SVCET College Chittoor, Andra Pradesh, India

Muhammad Rukunuddin Ghalib
Academic Lead Consultant (Industry-Academia Research)
GHAFS Research and Development-FZCO, Dubai, UAE

Kassian T.T. Amesho
University Research Chair for Climate Change
Environment and Resilience, Department of Higher Education and Lifelong Learning
School of Education, Faculty of Education and Human Sciences
University of Namibia (UNAM), Windhoek, Namibia

CRC Press
Taylor & Francis Group
Boca Raton London New York

CRC Press is an imprint of the
Taylor & Francis Group, an **informa** business
A SCIENCE PUBLISHERS BOOK

First edition published 2026
by CRC Press
2385 NW Executive Center Drive, Suite 320, Boca Raton FL 33431

and by CRC Press
4 Park Square, Milton Park, Abingdon, Oxon, OX14 4RN

CRC Press is an imprint of Taylor & Francis Group, LLC

Library of Congress Cataloging-in-Publication Data (applied for)

ISBN: 978-1-032-86653-6 (hbk)
ISBN: 978-1-032-89131-6 (pbk)
ISBN: 978-1-003-54131-8 (ebk)

DOI: 10.1201/9781003541318

Typeset in Times New Roman
by Prime Publishing Services

Preface

Autism Spectrum Disorder (ASD) is a complex neurodevelopmental condition that affects millions of individuals worldwide. Early and accurate detection remains a critical challenge, as traditional diagnostic approaches often depend on lengthy assessments, subjective observations, and limited access to trained specialists. With the rapid growth of digital technologies and data-driven healthcare, Artificial Intelligence (AI) has emerged as a powerful tool capable of transforming the landscape of autism screening, diagnosis, and intervention.

This book, Artificial Intelligence in Detecting Autism, explores the intersection of machine intelligence and neurodevelopmental science with the goal of bringing clarity, innovation, and practical understanding to researchers, clinicians, educators, and students. It examines how advanced computational techniques ranging from machine learning and deep learning to computer vision, speech analysis, and neuroimaging analytics enable earlier, more objective, and more scalable methods for identifying autism-related behavioural and neurological patterns.

The chapters in this book provide a comprehensive overview of AI-driven methodologies, data sources, research findings, and real-world applications in handling autism effectively. In addition to technical frameworks, the book emphasizes ethical considerations, the importance of inclusive datasets, and the potential of AI to complement not replacing the clinical expertise. By presenting both foundational concepts and emerging trends, the book aims to bridge the gap between technology and clinical practice, offering readers a balanced and informed perspective.

Our intention in writing this book is to contribute to the growing body of knowledge that supports early and accessible autism detection, especially in environments where resources are limited. The insights presented here will inspire further research, interdisciplinary collaboration, and responsible innovation in the pursuit of better outcomes for individuals with autism and their families.

We extend my gratitude to the researchers, practitioners, and institutions whose work continues to push the boundaries of AI in healthcare. Their dedication serves as the foundation upon which this book is built.

Ram Kumar Chenthur Pandian,
Shanmuga Raju Sekar,
Subrata Chowdhury,
Muhammad Rukunuddin Ghalib
Kassian T.T. Amesho

Contents

Preface *iii*

SECTION 1: **AI based early detection and diagnosis models**

1. AI Based Early Detection and Diagnosis Model 3
2. Advancements in Early Diagnosis and Screening of Autism Spectrum Disorder 18
3. Analyzing the Optimized Features Requirement and Data Mining Techniques in Heart Disease Prediction 27

SECTION 2: **ML models for behaviour analysis**

4. Advanced Patient Monitoring and Alert System with Instant Care Recommendation System using ML 43

SECTION 3: **AI models for facial recognition**

5. Implementation of Machine learning Algorithm for Weed Detection 53
6. AI Models for Facial Recognition in Autism Detection: A Comprehensive Review and Analysis 59

SECTION 4: **Autism diagnosis through speech analysis**

7. Ethical Consideration in Autism Detection using AI 89
8. Machine Learning Approaches for Detecting Autism through Chromosomal Aberration 104
9. Analysis of Artificial Intelligence Techniques for Autism Detection 114
10. Artificial Intelligence and Machine Learning in Detecting Autism: Transforming Diagnosis and Care 124

SECTION 5: **Genetic and biomarker data analysis and diagnosis**

11. Harnessing Explainable AI and Multi-Omics Biomarkers for Precision Autism Diagnosis: From Data Acquisition to Clinical Decision Support 145
12. Genetic and Biomarker Data Analysis and Diagnosis 177
13. Single-Nucleus RNA Sequencing Data for Cell-Type-Specific Gene Prioritization and Predictive Modeling of Autism Spectrum Disorder 195

SECTION 6: Clinical data analysis model

14. Machine Learning-Based Predictive Models for Medical Data Analysis: A Case of Early Diabetic Prediction 205

15. Optimizing Heart Disease prediction through Machine Learning and Synthetic Data Augmentation using GANs 224

SECTION 7: AI tools for early prediction

16. Uses of Generative AI for SAP HANA Data Management 237

17. Artificial Intelligence and Robotics in Healthcare: A Comprehensive Overview 247

SECTION 8: AI based screening tools for parental support & other applications

18. Blind Guide System with Voice Assistance 259

19. Personalized Curriculum Adaptation: Using Emotion Responses to Tailor Education for Autistic Students 265

20. Liver Disease Classification in Diverse Patient Population using Ensemble Technique 282

Index 291

About the Editors 293

Section 1

AI based early detection and diagnosis models

1

AI Based Early Detection and Diagnosis Model

G. M. Hemathchandran[1*], B. Ragavi[2] and K. Karpagavadivu[3]

1. Introduction to AI Based Early Diagnosis and Detection Models

Recent advances in computational techniques have significantly improved the early detection, diagnosis, and intervention of Autism Spectrum Disorder (ASD). This chapter explores how complex learning models enhance diagnostic accuracy and enable timely, personalized care. ASD, a multifaceted neurodevelopmental condition affecting approximately one in fifty-nine children—predominantly boys—is marked by restricted interests, repetitive behaviors, and social communication challenges. First coined by Eugen Bleuler in 1908 to describe severe mental conditions, the term "autism" has since evolved to encompass a broader spectrum of sensory, social, and communicative disorders [1]. Machine learning has emerged as a key tool for analyzing large, diverse datasets involving behavioral, speech, and cognitive patterns to aid in ASD identification. Supervised learning uses labeled data to detect ASD-specific markers and generate accurate predictions [2], while unsupervised methods uncover hidden patterns without predefined labels. Semi-supervised learning improves predictive performance by leveraging both labeled and unlabeled data. Advanced techniques such as reinforcement learning, transfer learning, and ensemble learning further enhance diagnostic accuracy. Transfer learning adapts pre-trained models to ASD-specific tasks, reducing data requirements and improving effectiveness [3]. Ensemble methods boost reliability by combining outputs from multiple models, and reinforcement learning refines diagnostic strategies through iterative feedback.

Figure 1 illustrates the range of machine learning algorithms used in AI-driven ASD diagnostic models. Integration of advanced technologies—such as wearables, genomics, and medical imaging—significantly strengthens diagnostic capabilities. Medical imaging, in particular, enables detailed analysis of subliminal ASD signals, outperforming traditional methods [11]. Machine learning also supports personalized therapy by linking genomic data to ASD-related genetic markers. Wearable devices provide real-time behavioral and physiological insights, aiding early detection, while

1 UG Scholar, Department of Electronics and Communication Engineering, Dr. N.G.P. Institute of Technology, Coimbatore - India.

2 Faculty of ECE, Department of Electronics and Communication Engineering, Dr. N.G.P. Institute of Technology, Coimbatore - India.

3 Faculty of AI&DS, Department of Artificial Intelligence and Data Science, Dr. N.G.P. Institute of Technology, Coimbatore - India.

* Corresponding author: hemathchandrangm01@gmail.com

DOI: 10.1201/9781003541318-2

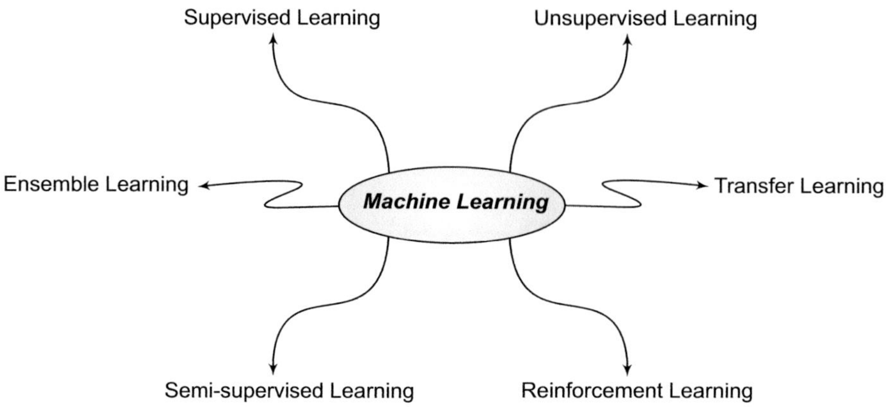

Fig. 1 Machine Learning types for ASD.

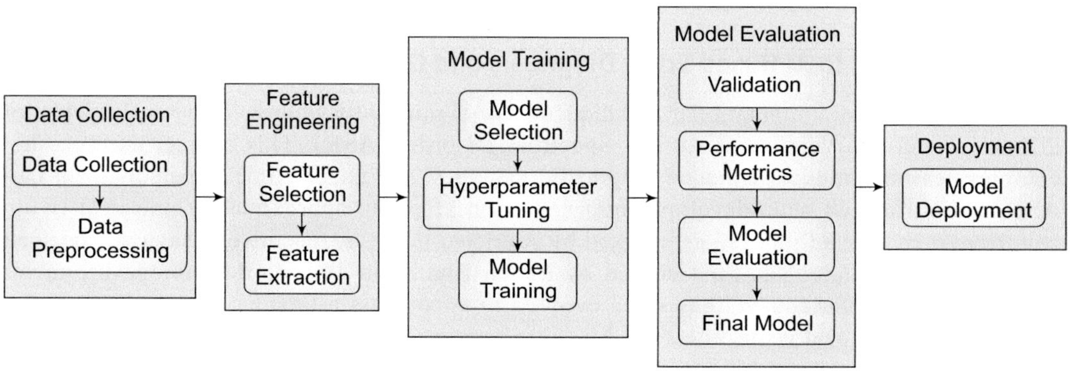

Fig. 2 Diagnostic workflow.

automated EHR analysis uncovers patient-specific patterns that enhance diagnostic precision and treatment planning.

The diagnostic workflow, shown in Figure 2, begins with data collection from sources such as genetics, wearables, medical imaging, and EHRs. This data is then preprocessed—normalized and cleaned—before training machine learning models using supervised, unsupervised, semi-supervised, and reinforcement learning techniques.

Advanced techniques such as ensemble learning, transfer learning, and reinforcement learning further refine model performance, yielding highly accurate diagnoses and prognoses that support early disease detection and effective treatment planning. Overall, AI-based diagnostic models represent a significant advancement in medical diagnostics. By leveraging complex algorithms and integrating diverse data sources, these models enhance diagnostic precision, enable personalized care, and improve patient outcomes. Continued exploration of their methodologies and challenges underscores AI's transformative potential in healthcare, especially for neurodevelopmental disorders like ASD.

2. Diagnostic Model Evolution: From Traditional Methods to Neural Networks

The integration of artificial intelligence and machine learning has transformed diagnostic models for Autism Spectrum Disorder (ASD), significantly enhancing accuracy, speed, and scalability. This chapter traces the evolution from traditional approaches to AI-driven methods, which now offer superior tools for early ASD detection.

Traditional Diagnostic Methods

Traditional ASD diagnosis primarily used statistical models and rule-based systems. While foundational, these methods had notable limitations in flexibility, scalability, and handling complex or unstructured data.

- *Statistical Methods*: Initial models like decision trees, logistic regression, and LDA relied on linear correlations within clinical data. Though foundational, they struggled with nonlinear patterns in large datasets and demanded extensive manual feature engineering for scalability and precision.
- *Expert Systems*: These rule-based models captured clinical expertise through fixed "if-then" logic. However, their rigidity hindered adaptability and blocked integration of evolving patterns or new research, limiting human-like decision-making.
- *Limitations*: Traditional methods struggled with unstructured data such as speech and behavior, and their dependence on expert-driven rules and limited, biased datasets hindered generalization across diverse ASD presentations.

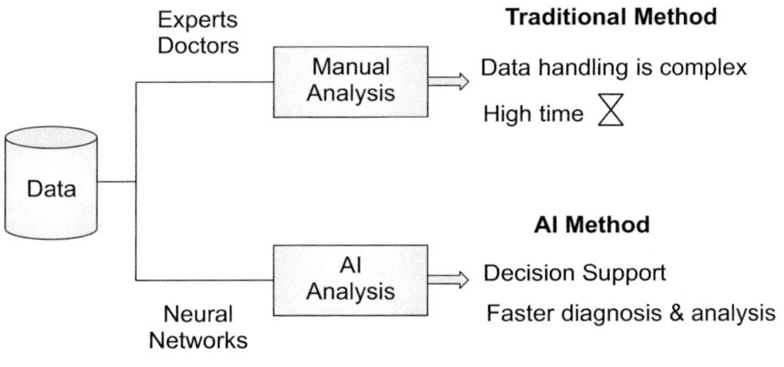

Fig. 3 Data flow in Traditional method & AI method.

Emergence of Machine Learning in ASD Diagnosis

The advent of machine learning revolutionized ASD diagnostics by enabling data-driven models to analyze large datasets and uncover complex patterns, paving the way for more adaptive and scalable diagnostic methods.

- *Supervised Learning*: Algorithms like Random Forest, SVM, and k-NN use labeled data to predict outcomes and have demonstrated high accuracy in classifying ASD based on behavioral and cognitive markers. Notably, Random Forest excels at detecting speech and interaction patterns vital for early diagnosis.
- *Unsupervised Learning*: Techniques like PCA and clustering reveal hidden structures in unlabeled data, making them valuable for identifying novel ASD subtypes and diagnostic patterns from sources such as sensor or medical imaging data.
- *Semi-supervised Learning*: By combining labeled data with abundant unlabeled data, this approach enhances prediction accuracy—especially effective for ASD detection where labeled datasets are scarce.

Deep Learning and Neural Networks: Revolutionizing the Diagnosis of ASD

Deep learning and neural networks have greatly advanced ASD diagnostics by effectively analyzing complex, high-dimensional data—such as images, audio, and time-series—uncovering nuanced markers critical for accurate detection.

- *Artificial Neural Networks (ANNs)*: Modeled after brain architecture, ANNs excel at detecting subtle ASD indicators—like eye movements or nuanced social cues—within complex behavioral, cognitive, and clinical data that traditional methods often overlook.
- *Convolutional Neural Networks (CNNs)*: CNNs excel in medical imaging by automatically identifying ASD-related anomalies—like brain structure variations or facial dysmorphology—eliminating manual feature extraction and enabling faster, more precise analysis. Especially LSTM models, RNNs effectively handle sequential data—like speech or behavioral assessments—by capturing temporal patterns and predicting ASD symptom progression, enabling timely interventions ahead of long-term treatment.

AI models enhance ASD detection through rigorous validation techniques like cross-validation, ensemble learning, and hypothesis testing, ensuring reliable and generalizable outcomes. Ensemble methods (e.g., bagging, boosting) reduce overfitting and boost accuracy across varied populations. Transfer learning further improves performance by adapting pre-trained models to ASD tasks with minimal data, streamlining diagnosis and increasing precision. Continuous learning and real-time data analysis enable AI to refine ASD diagnostics, paving the way for personalized treatments. Their statistical precision and scalability make them essential for advancing diagnosis and intervention.

3. Foundational Principles of AI, ML, and DL in Healthcare for the Detection of ASD

AI, ML, and DL have transformed ASD detection and management by enabling precise, timely, and individualized diagnosis through analysis of complex behavioral, genetic, and neuroimaging data. This section outlines key models and methods, emphasizing their statistical rigor and technical depth in ASD diagnostics.

3.1 AI-Based Methods for Detection of ASD

Advanced algorithms analyze complex datasets to uncover subtle deviations from typical development, enabling early diagnosis and timely intervention that can significantly improve long-term outcomes.

3.1.1 Symbolic AI in ASD Diagnosis

Symbolic AI: Rule-based systems support early ASD detection by applying expert-defined rules aligned with DSM-5 criteria. They offer interpretable assessments of key indicators—such as social communication, speech patterns, and repetitive behaviors—making them valuable tools for clinicians.

3.1.2 Statistical AI for Predictive Analysis

Statistical AI: Probabilistic models are vital for analyzing uncertain data and estimating ASD risk by detecting patterns in behavioral, environmental, and genetic inputs. Techniques like logistic regression and Bayesian networks offer statistically robust predictions that support early clinical intervention.

3.2 Machine Learning Models in ASD Diagnosis

These models excel at identifying subtle, microscopic patterns in large datasets—often beyond human perception. They uncover nuanced trends linked to ASD, using techniques such as supervised, unsupervised, reinforcement, transfer, and ensemble learning.

Table 1 Machine Learning methods in ASD diagnosis.

Method	*Description*	*Example*
Supervised Learning	Uses labeled data to train the model and make predictions.	Used for classifying vocal or facial patterns indicative of ASD.
Unsupervised Learning	Identifies hidden patterns in unlabeled data.	Detects behavioral patterns of children with ASD and categorizes them into subtypes.
Reinforcement Learning	These models learn optimal actions through interaction with the environment.	Applied in therapy to discover the most effective treatment protocols.
Transfer Learning	Uses pre-trained models to improve performance with limited data.	Adapts models trained on speech or facial recognition for autism detection.
Ensemble Learning	Combines multiple models for better accuracy and robustness.	Integrates models analyzing behavioral, genetic, and clinical data for improved ASD diagnosis.

3.3 Deep Learning Techniques for ASD Diagnosis

Deep learning, a branch of AI, excels at processing complex, high-dimensional data like images, audio, and sequences, enabling more accurate detection of subtle ASD-related patterns.

3.3.1 Convolutional Neural Networks (CNNs)

CNNs are ideal for analyzing grid-like data such as images, making them effective for facial expression and neuroimaging analysis. They learn layered spatial features, enabling detection of subtle ASD-related markers like atypical eye gaze and facial recognition anomalies.

3.3.2 Recurrent Neural Networks (RNNs)

RNNs excel at handling sequential data and preserving temporal context, making them highly effective for analyzing speech, social interactions, and behavioral patterns in children with ASD. They reliably detect atypical communication and social behaviors—key indicators of the disorder.

3.3.3 Generative Adversarial Networks (GANs)

GANs use a generator and discriminator in tandem to create and refine realistic ASD-related data. By synthesizing new training samples, they enhance the robustness and generalization of AI models for ASD detection.

Table 2 Techniques in Diagnosing Advanced Learning for ASD.

Method	*Description*	*Application in ASD Detection*
Convolutional Neural Networks (CNN)	Learn hierarchical spatial features from images.	Applied to facial expression analysis and neuroimaging to identify ASD markers.
Recurrent Neural Networks (RNNs)	Process sequential data, maintaining temporal context.	Used for analyzing speech patterns and social interactions in children with ASD.
Generative Adversarial Networks (GANs)	Generate synthetic data for training other models.	Generate ASD-related datasets to enhance training and improve model accuracy.

3.4 Statistical Significance in AI Models

Statistical significance strengthens the reliability of AI models in ASD diagnosis by validating their performance through methods like hypothesis testing, confidence intervals, and p-values. It ensures predictions are meaningful and not due to random chance, enhancing clinical applicability.

This statistical rigor ensures AI model results are both accurate and generalizable, strengthening their clinical relevance.

- *Key applications include*: predictive modeling, neuroimaging analysis, speech and behavior assessment, and multimodal data integration for early ASD detection.
- *Predictive Modeling*: AI models predict ASD risk in children by analyzing data from electronic health records, clinical assessments, and genetic profiles.
- *Image Processing*: CNNs are used to analyze neuroimaging data, such as MRI scans, to identify structural brain anomalies linked to ASD.
- *Speech and Behavior Analysis*: NLP and ML techniques analyze vocal and behavioral data to identify early signs of social communication deficits often associated with ASD.
- *Multimodal Approaches*: AI models integrate behavioral, genetic, and neuroimaging data to enable a more comprehensive and precise ASD diagnosis. These applications showcase how AI, ML, and DL methodologies enhance early ASD detection, enabling more accurate and timely interventions.

4. Multimodal Fusion Strategies for Biomedical Data Integration in Autism Detection

Autism Spectrum Disorder (ASD) is a complex neurodevelopmental condition marked by repetitive behaviors, social interaction difficulties, and communication impairments [8]. Accurate diagnosis often requires integrating diverse data types. Multimodal fusion techniques enhance diagnostic precision by combining genetic, behavioral, speech, cognitive, and imaging data [13].

4.1 Data Modalities in ASD Detection

- **Behavioral Data:** Observing social interactions, communication styles, and repetitive behaviors offers key insights into ASD. Behavioral assessments typically use standardized tests and structured observations to evaluate social engagement, play behavior, and responsiveness to stimuli.
- **Speech and Language Data:** Analyzing speech and language patterns reveals atypical communication traits, using metrics like fluency, vocabulary, and pragmatic skills. Automated tools assess linguistic features to spot deviations from typical development.
- **Cognitive Assessments:** Cognitive testing assesses developmental milestones, problem-solving skills, and executive functions through IQ tests, memory tasks, and attention evaluations, helping identify cognitive traits linked to ASD.
- **Medical Imaging:** Neuroimaging techniques such as MRI and fMRI reveal brain structure and function, helping identify anatomical anomalies and connectivity patterns linked to ASD [11][12].
- **Genomic Data:** Genetic analyses uncover biomarkers and variations linked to ASD, with whole-genome sequencing and targeted panels revealing relevant mutations and gene expression profiles.

Table 3 Multimodal Fusion Techniques.

Fusion Technique	*Description*	*Advantages*	*ASD-Specific Challenges*
Feature Level Fusion	Combines features from different modalities (e.g., behavioral, neuroimaging, genetic data) into a unified feature set.	Enhances diagnostic precision by integrating complementary information from various sources.	**Data Heterogeneity**: The fusion of heterogeneous features (e.g., neuroimaging and behavioral data) may lead to challenges in feature alignment and integration, requiring careful preprocessing to maintain data integrity relevant to ASD. **Overfitting Risk**: High-dimensional feature space increases the likelihood of overfitting, especially with limited ASD-specific datasets.
Concatenation	Merges features from multiple sources into a single extended vector for comprehensive analysis.	Facilitates a straightforward approach to feature combination, allowing for the integration of diverse datasets.	**Data Imbalance**: ASD-related data may suffer from imbalance, particularly when merging behavioral features with high-dimensional neuroimaging data, leading to biased model outcomes. **Scaling of Features:** In order to ensure that each feature contributes equally to the ASD detection model, careful scaling and normalization are necessary.
Dimensionality Reduction	Reduces the number of features while preserving the most informative aspects for ASD diagnosis.	Simplifies the model and reduces the computational burden, while retaining critical information.	**Information Loss**: Reducing dimensions might inadvertently eliminate subtle features that are critical for accurate ASD diagnosis, particularly in complex datasets. **Parameter Sensitivity**: Carefully tuning the number of retained components is essential to preserve ASD-relevant information.
Multi-View Learning	Treats each modality as a distinct view, collectively enriching the diagnostic model.	Provides a robust framework for leveraging diverse data sources (e.g., eye-tracking and genetic data).	**View Inconsistency**: Aligning multiple views representing different aspects of ASD (e.g., behavioral and neurogenetic profiles) can be challenging due to differences in data resolution and sampling frequency. **Integration Complexity**: Balancing contributions from each view to ensure comprehensive ASD detection requires sophisticated algorithms.
Decision Level Fusion	Aggregates predictions from individual models trained on different modalities (e.g., EEG, MRI).	Improves diagnostic accuracy by combining independent model outputs.	**Model Agreement**: Ensuring consistency between predictions from different modalities is difficult, particularly when dealing with the subtlety of ASD symptoms across modalities. **Model Weighting**: Determining the optimal weight for each modality-specific model is complex and critical for accurate ASD diagnosis.
Late Fusion in Neural Networks	Processes each modality separately through different branches of a neural network, then merges results.	Allows specialized processing for each data type, preserving modality-specific information.	**Synchronization**: Aligning outputs from separate branches, especially when dealing with asynchronous data modalities (e.g., longitudinal behavioral data vs. static neuroimaging), poses challenges. **Resource Intensive**: High computational demands and increased complexity in training, particularly when fine-tuning for ASD-related feature extraction.
Bayesian Fusion	Uses probabilistic models to integrate data, updating predictions as new evidence emerges.	Provides a flexible framework for integrating diverse data, with the ability to incorporate uncertainty.	**Complex Modeling**: The development of accurate Bayesian models requires detailed knowledge of ASD-specific distributions and priors, which can be complex and computationally expensive. **Data Requirements**: Bayesian methods need large amounts of data to properly estimate parameters, which is often a limitation in ASD studies.

4.2 Multimodal Fusion Techniques

Multimodal fusion integrates behavioral, speech, cognitive, imaging, and genetic data into a unified diagnostic model, maximizing each modality's strengths to improve clinical outcomes and diagnostic precision [10].

4.3 Implementation Challenges

(i) *Data Heterogeneity*: Different data modalities often have varying formats, scales, and quality, which can complicate integration. Standardization and normalization techniques are necessary to harmonize data for effective fusion.

(ii) *Data Privacy and Security*: Protecting sensitive biomedical data is essential; strategies like anonymization and secure sharing protocols are vital for ensuring patient privacy.

- *Interpretability of the Model*: The complexity of multimodal models can hinder interpretability; to ensure clinician trust, explainable AI methods for decision-making and data fusion are essential.
- *Computational Complexity*: Multimodal fusion demands substantial computational resources, requiring efficient algorithms and high-performance infrastructure to manage large-scale data integration.

4.4 Practical Applications

(i) *Early Detection*: Multimodal fusion enhances early ASD detection by integrating behavioral, cognitive, and genetic data, enabling predictive models to estimate risk and support timely intervention.

- *Personalized Diagnosis*: Multimodal data integration enables personalized diagnostics by accounting for individual profiles, enhancing accuracy and guiding tailored treatment strategies.
- *Predictive Analytics*: Multimodal fusion supports predictive modeling to estimate ASD risk from integrated assessments, enabling data-driven clinical decisions and proactive care.

4.5 Future Directions

The advancement of multimodal fusion techniques holds promise for further improving ASD diagnostics. Future research may focus on:

(i) Enhancing fusion algorithms to better handle data heterogeneity and improve model performance.

(ii) Integrating emerging data types, such as digital biomarkers from wearable devices, to provide more comprehensive assessments.

(iii) Developing advanced privacy-preserving techniques to ensure secure data handling while maximizing the utility of multimodal data.

5. Case Study: Conditional Generative Recurrent Neural Network (CGRNN) as an Early Diagnostic Tool for Autism Spectrum Disorder

The Conditional Generative Recurrent Neural Network (CGRNN) is an advanced model for real-time autism prediction. It leverages sequential data from behavioral, physiological, and environmental sources to identify potential indicators of Autism Spectrum Disorder (ASD)[12]. The CGRNN integrates generative and recurrent neural network architectures to process and analyze complex time-series data efficiently.

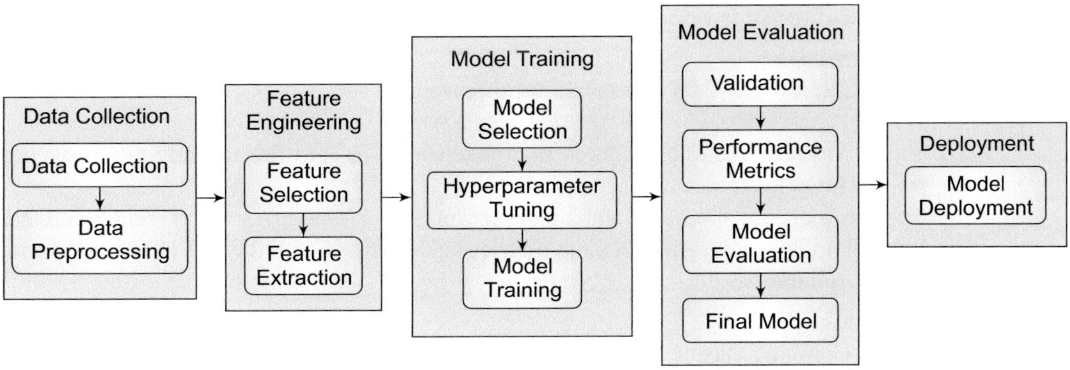

Fig. 4 CGRNN work flowchart.

5.1 Data Preprocessing and Collection

A. Data Collection:

1. *Behavioral Data:*

(a) *Sources*: Video recordings of social interactions and speech samples from clinical evaluations.

(b) Features Collected:

(i) Eye Movement Patterns: Recorded using eye-tracking devices.

(ii) Facial Expressions: Analyzed through computer vision algorithms to detect emotions and expressions.

(iii) Speech Characteristics: Include pitch, volume, and speech rate from audio recordings.

2. *Physiological Data:*

(a) *Sources:* Wearable devices that monitor physiological responses.

(b) *Features Collected:*

(i) Heart Rate Variability (HRV): Measured using ECG or wearable sensors.

(ii) Electrodermal Activity (EDA): Captured through sensors that measure skin conductance changes.

3. *Environmental Data:*

(a) *Sources:* Environmental sensors.

(b) *Features Collected:*

(i) Ambient Noise Levels: Recorded by environmental sensors.

(ii) Lighting Conditions: Measured by light sensors to understand their impact on behavioral responses.

B. Preprocessing:

1. *Normalization:*

(a) *Objective:* Standardize data for uniform model input.

(b) *Method:* Utilize standardization methods like Z-score normalization or Min-Max scaling to guarantee feature coherence.

2. *Segmentation:*

(a) *Objective:* Manage continuous data by segmenting it into discrete units.

(b) *Method:* Divide time-series data into fixed-length intervals or discrete events, e.g., 10-second segments for video data or continuous physiological measurements.

3. *Feature Extraction:*

(a) *Objective:* Convert raw data into meaningful features.

(b) *Method:*

(i) Video Analysis: Extract features like gaze direction and facial emotions using pre-trained models.

(ii) Speech Analysis: Compute statistical measures such as average pitch and speech rate.

(iii) Physiological Analysis: Calculate metrics such as average HRV or EDA levels during specific intervals.

4. *Data Integration:*

(a) *Objective:* Combine various data types into a cohesive format.

(b) *Method:* Align features from behavioral, physiological, and environmental data into a single feature vector for each time point, creating a comprehensive dataset for model input.

Output: A structured dataset integrating behavioral, physiological, and environmental features, prepared for CGRNN model training.

5.2 CGRNN Model Architecture

Input Layer

1. *Data Embeddings:*
   (a) *Objective:* Transform feature vectors into a format suitable for recurrent layers.
   (b) *Method:* Use embedding layers or dense layers to map raw features into a shared representation space.

Recurrent Neural Network (RNN) Layers

1. *Gated Recurrent Units (GRUs):*
   (a) *Purpose:* Capture temporal dependencies and patterns in sequential data.
   (b) *Operation:* To control information flow through sequences, use update and reset gates. This enables retaining information while eliminating unnecessary data.
2. *Long Short-Term Memory (LSTM) Cells:*
   (a) *Purpose:* Address long-term dependency issues and prevent vanishing gradients.
   (b) *Operation:* Input, forget, and output gates are useful tools for managing information flow and efficiently preserving long-term state data.

Conditional Generative Layer

1. *Conditional Generation:*
   (a) *Purpose:* Predict outcomes based on specific conditions derived from input data.
   (b) *Operation:* Utilize generated features from RNN layers to produce predictions or likelihood scores for ASD.
2. *Latent Variables:*
   (a) *Purpose:* Capture underlying factors influencing ASD predictions.
   (b) *Operation:* Infer latent variables representing underlying psychological or behavioral tendencies affecting ASD diagnosis.

Output: Probability scores or classifications indicating the likelihood of ASD based on integrated data.

5.3 Training and Optimization

1. *Data Augmentation:*
   (a) *Objective:* Enhance model robustness and generalization.
   (b) *Techniques:* Apply data augmentation methods such as noise injection, time shifts, and feature perturbations to create a more diverse training dataset.
2. *Training Procedure:*
   Supervised Learning:
   (a) *Objective:* Train the CGRNN model with labeled data to predict ASD outcomes.
   (b) *Method:* Utilize cross-entropy loss to measure prediction accuracy and backpropagate errors to update model weights.
3. *Backpropagation Through Time (BPTT):*
   (a) *Objective:* Update model parameters based on temporal sequences.
   (b) *Method:* Compute gradients through recurrent layers and adjust weights to minimize loss.
   (c) *Optimization Algorithms:*
4. *Adam Optimizer:*
   (a) *Objective:* Improve training efficiency and convergence.
   (b) *Method:* Utilize adaptive learning rates and momentum-based updates for model parameter optimization.
5. *Regularization Techniques:*
   Dropout:
   (a) *Purpose:* During training, randomly deactivate neurons to prevent overfitting.
   L2 Regularization:
   (a) *Purpose:* Penalize large weights to encourage simpler models.

Output: A trained CGRNN model optimized for accurate ASD prediction.

5.4 Real-Time Prediction

1. *Streaming Data Analysis:*
   (a) *Objective:* Facilitate continuous ASD prediction from live data.
   (b) *Method:* Process real-time data from sensors and video feeds, updating predictions dynamically as new data is received.
2. *Alert System:*
   (a) *Objective:* Notify clinicians if the likelihood of ASD exceeds a predefined threshold.
   (b) *Method:* Set thresholds based on predicted probabilities or detected anomalies to trigger alerts for further evaluation.

Output: Real-time ASD likelihood scores or classifications based on current data inputs.

5.5 Evaluation and Performance Metrics

The AI-based ASD detection model was evaluated using key classification metrics, yielding the following performance results:

1. The model achieved 82.81% accuracy, correctly classifying nearly 83% of the test data—indicating strong reliability for diagnostic use.

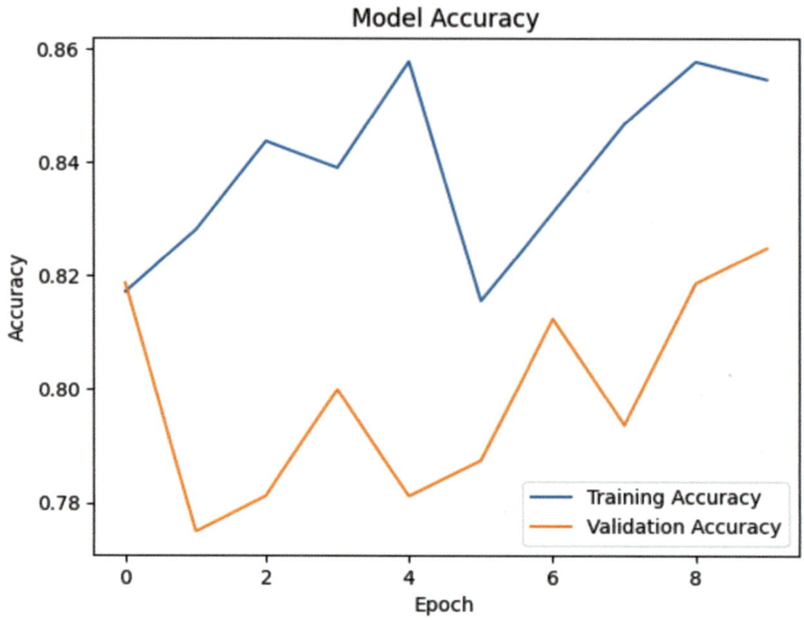

2. Precision was 60.00%, indicating that 60% of predicted positives were correct. In sensitive domains like autism diagnosis, minimizing false positives is crucial to avoid unnecessary interventions.
3. Recall: The model's recall is 13.04%, meaning it identifies only a small fraction of actual positive cases—highlighting a critical need to enhance its ability to detect relevant instances for early ASD diagnosis. F1 Score: The F1 score of 21.43% reflects limited balance between precision and recall—while some positives were correctly predicted, many true cases were missed, underscoring the need for further model refinement to improve detection and reliability.

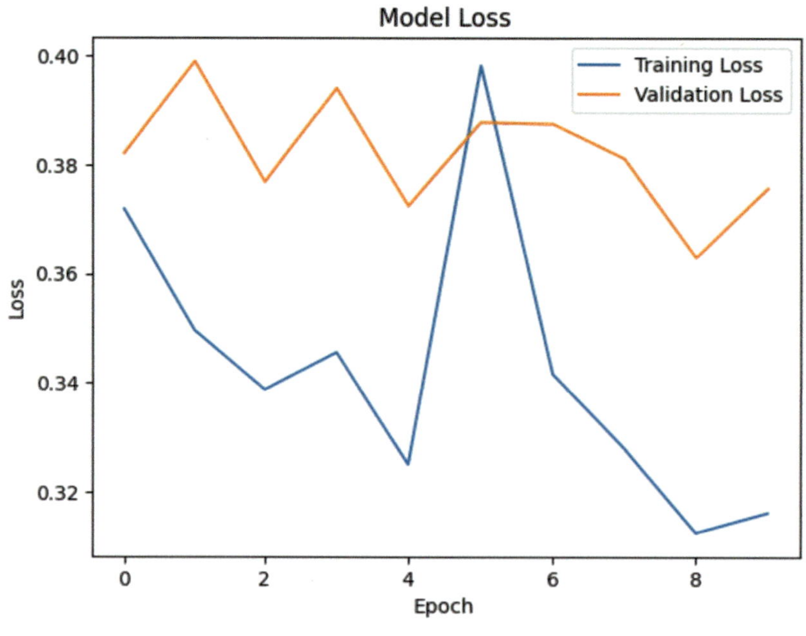

4. The model's AUC of 0.8248 indicates strong ability to distinguish between positive and negative cases—suggesting high diagnostic potential. The model's MSE of 0.1199 reflects a low average squared error, indicating that its predictions closely align with actual values and demonstrate solid predictive accuracy.
5. The model's MAE of 0.2684 indicates a low average error, showing that its predictions closely match actual values.
6. AUC-ROC Curve:
   (a) *Objective:* Assess model performance at different thresholds.
   (b) *Method:* Evaluate the model's discrimination ability by calculating the Area Under the ROC Curve (AUC).

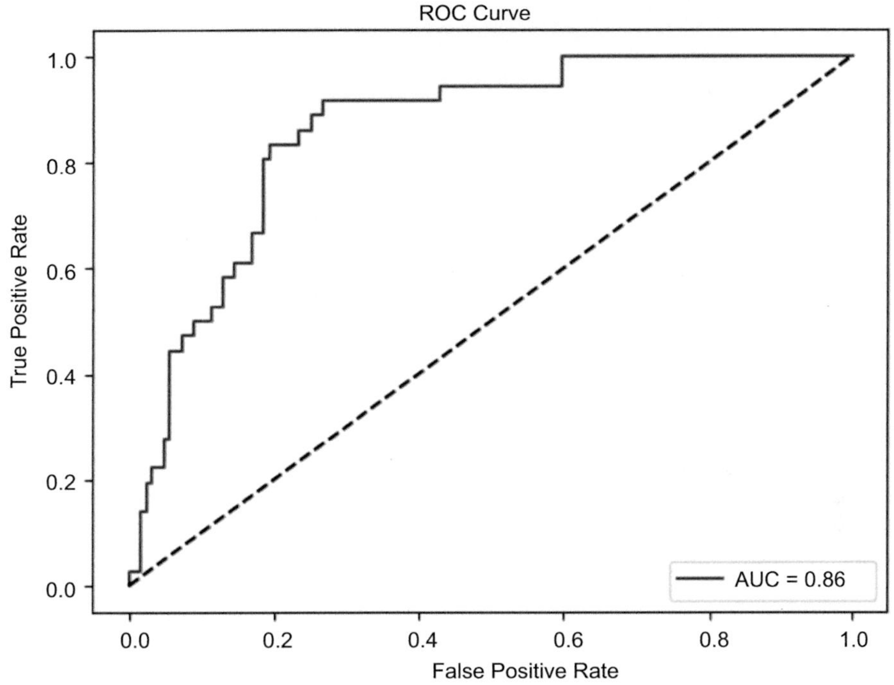

The model contains 95,297 parameters—sufficiently detailed to capture key features without excessive complexity. Its training time of 3.55 seconds reflects fast optimization, making it suitable for real-time ASD detection and diagnosis. osis.

While the AI model shows strong performance in terms of accuracy and AUC, its low recall—and modest F1 score—highlight the need for improvement in identifying true positive cases. Enhancing model efficiency, data augmentation, and network tuning will be essential to boost recall and F1 score, thereby increasing its clinical utility for early autism diagnosis.

5.6 Interpretation and Visualization

1. *Attention Mechanisms:*
   (a) *Objective:* Enhance model interpretability and understanding.
   (b) *Method:* Visualize attention maps or saliency scores to highlight influential features or time points contributing to ASD predictions.

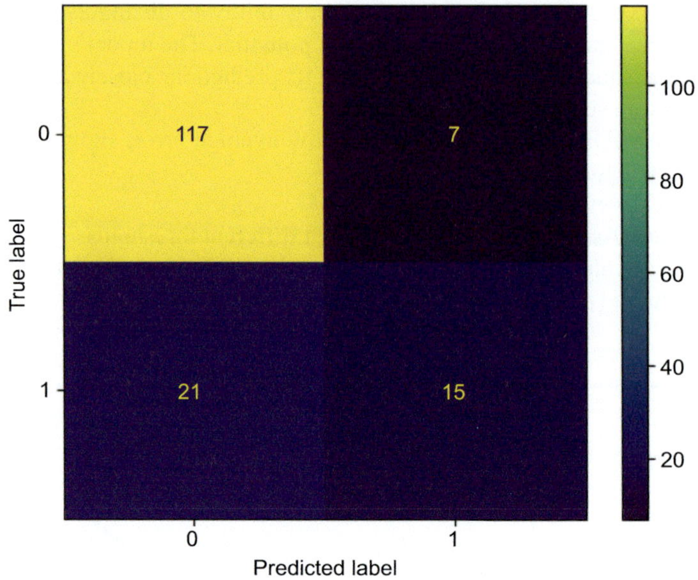

Output: Visual insights into features or segments impacting ASD predictions.

6. Conclusion

As autism research progresses, advanced computational methods are transforming diagnosis. This book highlights how Convolutional Graph Recurrent Neural Networks (CGRNN) and modern data fusion techniques enable rapid, highly accurate detection of subtle ASD symptoms by integrating behavioral, genetic, and neuroimaging data in real time. CGRNNs exemplify the shift from traditional diagnostics by capturing complex temporal patterns within graph-based data. The book thoroughly reviews data collection and preprocessing to ensure input quality matches algorithmic complexity, while also tackling key issues of interpretability and ethics to ensure fairness and utility.

This article highlights how integrating diverse data and advanced machine learning significantly improves diagnostic accuracy and enables personalized ASD treatment—marking a major leap in timely, practical, and AI-driven approaches to developmental disorder diagnosis.

Authors Biography

[1] Mr. G.M.Hemathchandran, a 3rd-year ECE student at Dr. N.G.P. Institute of Technology, Coimbatore, has completed internships in IoT and Arduino programming. His projects include a Multi-Sensor Crop Monitoring Robot and a PID-controlled line-following robot using Raspberry Pi Pico W. He has participated in workshops on drone tech and machine learning, and holds an NPTEL Elite certification in Affective Computing, showcasing expertise in embedded systems, sensors, and AI-driven IoT solutions.

[2] Ms. B.Ragavi is an Assistant Professor at Dr. N.G.P. Institute of Technology, Coimbatore, with prior experience as a Research Executive at Zinnov Draup Consultancy. She holds a Master's in Communication Systems and a Bachelor's in ECE. Her research spans Wireless Sensor Networks, Machine Learning, IoT, and Image Processing, with publications in IEEE, Springer, and Elsevier. She has also contributed as a speaker and organizer in numerous academic events. [3] Ms. K.Karpagavadivu, Assistant Professor (SG) of AI and Data Science at Dr. N.G.P. Institute of Technology, holds both Bachelor's and Master's degrees

in Computer Science from Anna University and is pursuing a Ph.D. in Information and Communication Engineering. With over 14 years of academic experience across institutions like Bannari Amman Institute, SNS College of Technology, and Nandha Engineering College, she has led numerous workshops and faculty development programs. Her expertise spans data warehousing, Python, C/C++, data structures, mobile computing, and software testing. Her research focuses on data analytics, image processing, and cybersecurity, with 15 publications in reputed journals and conferences.

Reference

1. Hodges H., Fealko C. and Soares N. Autism spectrum disorder: definition, epidemiology, causes, and clinical evaluation. *Transl Pediatr. 2020* Feb; 9 (Suppl 1): S55–S65. DOI: 10.21037/tp.2019.09.09.
2. Yihao Li and Mostafa El Habib Daho, A review of deep learning-based information fusion techniques for multimodal medical image classification, *Computers in Biology and Medicine*, Vol. 177, 2024. DOI: https://doi.org/10.1016/j.compbiomed.2024.108635.
3. *Xinyue* Xie and Rongyi Zhou, Seeing beyond words: Visualizing autism spectrum disorder biomarker insights, Heliyon, Vol. 10, Issue 9, 2024. DOI: https://doi.org/10.1016/j.heliyon.2024.e30420.
4. Yuequan Bao, Dawei Liu and Hui Li. A mechanics-informed neural network method for structural modal identification, *Mechanical Systems and Signal Processing*, Vol.216, 2024. DOI: https://doi.org/10.1016/j.ymssp.2024.111458.
5. Yatawatta, S., Reinforcement learning, Astronomy and Computing, Vol. 48, ISSN 2213-1337, 2024. DOI: https://doi.org/10.1016/j.ascom.2024.100833.
6. Mikhail Genkin and J.J. McArthur. A transfer learning approach to minimize reinforcement learning risks in energy optimization for automated and smart buildings, *Energy and Buildings*, Volume 303, 2024. DOI: https://doi.org/10.1016/j.enbuild.2023.113760.
7. Shuai Niu, Qing Yin, Jing Ma, Yunya Song, Yida Xu et al, Xian Yang. Enhancing healthcare decision support through explainable AI models for risk prediction, *Decision Support Systems*, Vol. 181, 2024. DOI: https://doi.org/10.1016/j.dss.2024.114228.
8. Sean Sands, Colin Campbell, Carla Ferraro, Vlad Demsar, Sara Rosengren et al, Justine Farrell. Principles for advertising responsibly using generative AI, *Organizational Dynamics*, Vol. 53, Issue 2, 2024. DOI:https://doi.org/10.1016/j.orgdyn.2024.101042.
9. Junwei Duan, Jiaqi Xiong, Yinghui Li and Weiping Ding. Deep learning based multimodal biomedical data fusion: An overview and comparative review, *Information Fusion*, Volume 112, 2024. DOI:https://doi.org/10.1016/j.inffus.2024.102536.
10. Yihao Li, Mostafa El Habib Daho, Pierre-Henri Conze, Rachid Zeghlache, Hugo Le Boité et al, A review of deep learning-based information fusion techniques for multimodal medical image classification, *Computers in Biology and Medicine*, Vol. 177, 2024. DOI: https://doi.org/10.1016/j.compbiomed.2024.108635.
11. Pradip Salve, Pravin Yannawar and Milind Sardesai. Multimodal plant recognition through hybrid feature fusion technique using imaging and non-imaging hyper-spectral data, *Journal of King Saud University - Computer and Information Sciences*, Volume 34, Issue 1, Pages 1361–1369, 2022. DOI: https://doi.org/10.1016/j.jksuci.2018.09.018.
12. Shomona Gracia Jacob, Majdi Mohammed Bait Ali Sulaiman and Bensujin Bennet, Algorithmic Approaches to Classify Autism Spectrum Disorders: A Research Perspective, *Procedia Computer Science*, Vol. 201, Pages 470–477, 2022. DOI:https://doi.org/10.1016/j.procs.2022.03.061.
13. Abdulkareem Musa and Petersen Steffen E. The Promise of AI in Detection, Diagnosis, and Epidemiology for Combating COVID-19: Beyond the Hype, *Frontiers in Artificial Intelligence*, Vol. 4, 2021. DOI: 10.3389/frai.2021.652669.

2

Advancements in Early Diagnosis and Screening of Autism Spectrum Disorder

M. Menagadevi[1*], M. Nirmala[2], D. Thiyagarajan[3] and S. Sharmila[4]

1. Introduction

Autism Spectrum Disorder (ASD) is a neurodevelopmental condition characterized by challenges in social communication and repetitive behaviors. Early diagnosis is vital to provide timely support for affected individuals and their families. Over the past three decades, advances in technology, neuroscience, and diagnostic techniques have significantly improved early detection, offering better prospects for intervention and quality of life. ASD prevalence has risen globally, as reflected in statistics from WHO, CDC, and APA (Table 1), underscoring the inadequacy of traditional early screening methods. Conventional approaches—primarily behavioral observation and questionnaires—often delay diagnosis beyond the optimal early developmental window. Recent shifts in ASD diagnostics favor advanced technologies, including AI-based models, which offer greater precision and accessibility. Embracing this paradigm shift acknowledges that early diagnosis is foundational to effective intervention [1-3]. Given the global prevalence [5], there is an urgent need for accurate, scalable diagnostic tools, particularly in regions with limited healthcare infrastructure [4], [6].

Emerging tools and methodologies—such as machine learning, genetic and biomarker analysis, advanced neuroimaging, and mobile health applications—are revolutionizing ASD diagnosis. These innovations enable detection not only in early stages but also before symptoms manifest, even in toddlers. However, integrating genetic, developmental, and AI-based approaches underscores the complexity of ASD assessment, necessitating multifaceted diagnostic frameworks.

This chapter examines early detection and screening of ASD, contrasting traditional methods with modern approaches and their limitations. It highlights emerging technologies—especially machine learning and AI—and their growing impact on diagnostics. Additionally, it explores current challenges and future directions, emphasizing collaboration among clinicians, researchers, families, and policy-makers.

[1] Department of Computing Technologies, SRM Institute of Science and Technology, Kattankulathur, Tamil Nadu, India.
[2] Department of Biomedical Engineering, Dr. N G P Institute of Technology, Coimbatore.
[3] Department of Computer Science and Engineering, Chennai Institute of Technology, Chennai, India.
[4] Department of Electronics and Communication Engineering, Dr. N G P Institute of Technology, Coimbatore, India.
* Corresponding author: menaga1961988@gmail.com

DOI: 10.1201/9781003541318-3

Table 1 Key Statistics on Autism Spectrum Disorder (ASD).

Category	*Statistic*	*Source*
Global Prevalence	~1 in 100 children affected globally	WHO, 2023 https://www.who.int
Prevalence in the US	~1 in 36 children diagnosed (2023 data)	CDC, 2023 https://www.cdc.gov
Gender Disparity	Boys are 4 times more likely to be diagnosed than girls	CDC, 2023
Comorbidity with Other Disorders	~70% of individuals with ASD have one comorbid condition; ~40% have two or more	APA, 2022 https://www.psychiatry.org
Diagnosis in Rural Areas	~30% lower diagnosis rates in rural/remote areas	WHO, 2022
Economic Impact (US)	Estimated lifetime cost of ~$1.4 million per individual with ASD	Autism Speaks, 2022 https://www.autismspeaks.org
Effect of Early Intervention	Can reduce lifetime costs by 30-50%	WHO, 2021

2. Limitations of Traditional Diagnostic Methods

Traditional ASD diagnostic methods—primarily behavioral assessments and structured interviews using tools like ADOS and ADI-R—remain widely used but present notable limitations. These procedures are time-intensive and require specialized training, making them costly and less accessible in low-resource settings [7], [8], [6]. Behavioral observations are inherently subjective, often leading to inconsistent clinical judgments [9]. The diagnostic process is further complicated by ASD's heterogeneity, with mild and nonspecific symptoms that overlap with other developmental conditions. The absence of clear somatic markers reduces confidence in physiological or genetic assessments [10]. Studies consistently report significant delays between symptom onset and formal diagnosis [11], [12], underscoring the urgent need for more efficient and objective early screening tools.

3. Emerging Technological Approaches

Limitations of conventional ASD diagnostics have prompted the development of advanced technologies for early detection. Eye-tracking has proven effective in quantifying social attention and gaze preferences in young children [13], offering more objective insights than observational methods. When combined with machine learning, eye-tracking data can enhance diagnostic accuracy by identifying gaze-based biomarkers [14]. Parallel research focuses on biological indicators such as genetic mutations, immune markers, and metabolic irregularities that may support early diagnosis [15]. Gut microbiome analysis has also emerged as a potential screening tool, with studies noting microbial shifts in ASD patients [16]. Similarly, distinct autoantibody profiles have been observed, though their clinical applicability remains uncertain. Further validation is needed to establish reliable biomarker criteria and assess their diagnostic performance across diverse populations.

4. Artificial Intelligence in ASD Screening

Artificial intelligence (AI) offers a promising avenue for enhancing the accuracy and reliability of early ASD screening [17], [18], [19]. Researchers are applying diverse algorithms—such as SVM, Random Forests, CNNs, and transformer models—to varied data sources, including insurance claims, eye-tracking metrics, and facial features. These models can uncover subtle patterns often imperceptible to human observers, and have demonstrated strong predictive performance for ASD diagnosis. However, findings must be cautiously generalized to diverse, non-White populations [20]. Further research is needed to assess how sex-based variables influence algorithmic fairness and diagnostic equity. Ethical considerations surrounding AI use in ASD diagnosis also warrant careful attention.

4.1 Data Sources for AI Models

Different data sources used in AI models are given in figure 1

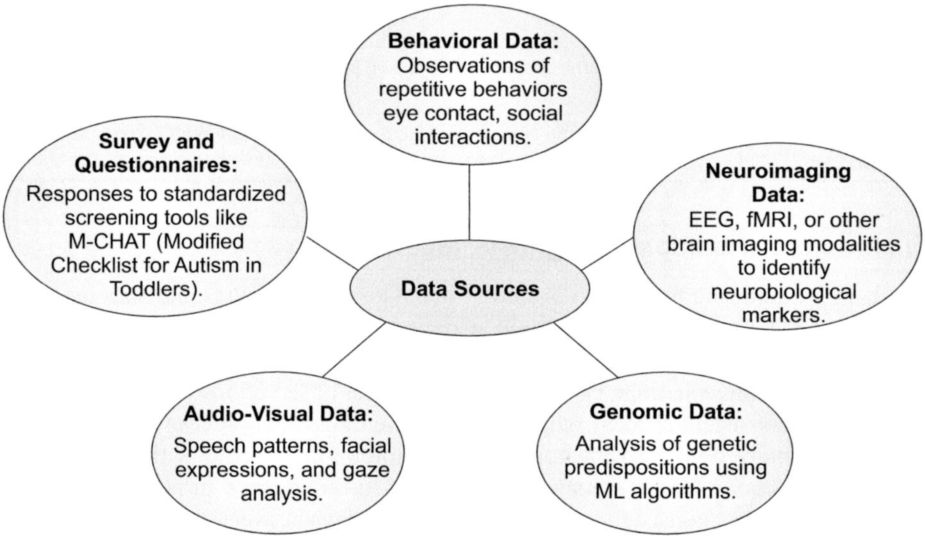

Fig. 1 Different data sources used in AI models.

AI and ML models for ASD screening leverage diverse data types to capture the multifaceted nature of the disorder. Behavioral indicators—such as impaired social interaction, restricted movements, reduced eye contact, and atypical responses to stimuli—can be quantified and analyzed for ASD-specific patterns. Neuroimaging modalities like fMRI, EEG, and structural MRI further aid in detecting brain activity, connectivity, and structural anomalies. Using large-scale datasets, these models can uncover distinct neurological markers associated with ASD [21].

Genomic data plays a key role in ASD screening, as studies have linked specific mutations and hereditary traits to the disorder. Machine learning algorithms can analyze these features to identify potential genetic risk factors or biomarkers. Audio-visual data is especially valuable for early intervention in young children, with AI detecting delays in speech, prosody, facial expressions, gaze patterns, and vocal tone. For example, children with ASD may exhibit atypical pitch or cadence, or reduced facial focus—patterns that AI models can quantify for diagnostic insights.

In addition to direct observational data, widely used instruments like the Modified Checklist for Autism in Toddlers (M-CHAT) and the Social Responsiveness Scale (SRS) capture parent- or clinician-reported behaviors, generating labeled datasets essential for training supervised learning models. This diversity of input enables a multimodal approach, allowing AI and ML systems to uncover novel diagnostic patterns tailored to individual profiles. Integrating these data sources significantly enhances the effectiveness of AI-based ASD screening in evaluating early developmental functioning [22].

4.2 AI Techniques in ASD Screening

4.2.1 Supervised Learning

Supervised learning plays a key role in identifying children with ASD by analyzing labeled data features. Among its techniques, logistic regression is widely used for its simplicity in predicting ASD likelihood based on input variables like age, gender, or behavioral scores. It is effective for assessing linear relationships but struggles with complex, non-linear patterns.

Support Vector Machines (SVM) are widely applied in ASD research, particularly for complex datasets like neuroimaging and detailed behavioral metrics. They classify data—e.g., ASD vs. non-ASD—by identifying the optimal separating hyperplane [23–24]. SVMs excel at detecting subtle differences, such as gaze or brain connectivity patterns, but are highly sensitive to parameters like kernel choice and regularization. While effective for small to medium datasets, they face scalability challenges with larger data volumes. Decision trees are widely used due to their simple structure, which splits data into subsets based on feature thresholds. They are effective for identifying key factors linked to ASD, such as specific behaviors or genetic traits. However, they are prone to overfitting, especially with small or noisy datasets. To address this, Random Forests—an ensemble of decision trees—are commonly employed. They enhance predictive accuracy by aggregating multiple tree outputs and perform well with multimodal data like behavioral and neuroimaging inputs [25-26]. Additionally, Random Forests rank feature importance, helping to identify the most relevant markers for ASD diagnosis. Gradient boosting algorithms like XGBoost and LightGBM are among the most advanced methods used in ASD screening. They build sequential decision trees, with each tree correcting errors from the previous one, resulting in highly accurate predictions. These models are well-suited for capturing nonlinear relationships, such as interactions between behavioral scores and genetic markers. However, they require meticulous hyperparameter tuning and are computationally intensive, particularly for large-scale datasets [27–28].

Basic models like k-Nearest Neighbors (k-NN) and Naïve Bayes are used in ASD screening for targeted tasks or smaller datasets. k-NN classifies data points based on the majority class of nearby neighbors, proving effective in pattern recognition for features like speech or questionnaire responses. Naïve Bayes, a probabilistic model assuming feature independence, performs well in text and voice analysis and offers fast computation, though it may be less suitable for complex, multi-feature datasets.

Neural networks, particularly deep architectures like Convolutional Neural Networks (CNNs) and Recurrent Neural Networks (RNNs), are widely used for integrating multimodal data such as images, video, and speech [29]. CNNs excel at extracting visual features for identifying structural or functional brain abnormalities, while RNNs are effective for analyzing temporal patterns like phonetics or gaze trajectories. Though powerful in modeling complex, nonlinear relationships, these models require large datasets and offer limited interpretability compared to simpler methods. Table 2 outlines the statistical performance of various supervised learning techniques in ASD screening.

4.2.2 Unsupervised Learning

Unsupervised learning is widely used in ASD research to uncover hidden data patterns without predefined labels, especially when labeled data is scarce. It excels in clustering, feature extraction, and dimensionality reduction. Techniques like k-Means, hierarchical clustering, and DBSCAN help identify ASD subgroups based on behavior, neuroimaging, or genetics, enabling personalized interventions. Visualization methods such as PCA and t-SNE reduce high-dimensional data—like brain connectivity—into meaningful, interpretable components. Anomaly detection algorithms in ASD research help uncover rare patterns—such as low-frequency gene mutations—supporting early

Table 2 Supervised Learning Methods and Their Statistical Performance.

Method	*Accuracy*	*Recall (Sensitivity)*	*Precision*	*Key Strengths*	*Limitations*
Logistic Regression	Moderate (0.7–0.85)	Moderate	Moderate	Simple, interpretable, and effective for linear relationships.	Struggles with non-linear patterns and complex data.
Support Vector Machines (SVMs)	High (0.8–0.9)	High	High	Effective in high-dimensional datasets; robust with proper parameter tuning.	Computationally expensive for large datasets.
Decision Trees	Variable (0.7–0.8)	Moderate to High	Moderate to High	Easy to interpret; identify key contributing factors.	Prone to overfitting without pruning.
Random Forests	High (0.85–0.9)	High	High	Handle multimodal data; robust to overfitting and ranks feature importance.	Computationally intensive for very large datasets.
Gradient Boosting (e.g., XGBoost, LightGBM)	Very High (0.9+)	Very High	Very High	Captures complex, non-linear relationships; top performer in multimodal data.	Requires careful hyperparameter tuning; resource-intensive.
k-Nearest Neighbors (k-NN)	Moderate (0.75–0.85)	Moderate	Moderate	Simple and intuitive; effective for small datasets with proximity-based patterns.	Sensitive to feature scaling and choice of k; less scalable.
Naïve Bayes	Moderate (0.7–0.8)	Moderate	Moderate	Fast and efficient for text or categorical data.	Assumes feature independence, which may not hold in complex data.
Neural Networks	Very High (0.9+)	Very High	Very High	Handles unstructured and multimodal data; excels in capturing intricate patterns.	Requires large datasets, significant computational resources, and lacks interpretability.

diagnosis. Unsupervised learning also underpins feature selection, identifying key variables that enhance the performance of supervised models. While these methods excel in pattern discovery and hypothesis generation, their interpretation demands domain expertise. Nonetheless, unsupervised learning remains foundational in ASD studies, enabling exploration of complex, large-scale data and deepening insights into the disorder [30]. Table 3 summarizes key statistical metrics and typical performance indicators for these techniques.

Table 3 Statistical metrics of unsupervised learning techniques.

Technique	*Metric*	*Typical Range/ Value*	*Description*	*Application in ASD*
Clustering	Silhouette Score	0.3–0.7	Indicates cluster clarity—higher scores reflect more distinct separation between groups.	Grouping individuals based on behavioral traits or neuroimaging features.
	Calinski-Harabasz Index	Higher is better	Assesses the ratio of within-cluster to between-cluster dispersion.	Evaluating clustering compactness and separation.
	Davies-Bouldin Index	0.2–1.5 (Lower is better)	Measures cluster similarity. Lower values indicate distinct clusters.	Comparing clustering algorithms for behavioral data.
	Adjusted Rand Index (ARI)	-1 to 1 (Closer to 1 is better)	Compares predicted clusters with ground truth (if available).	Validating cluster assignments against known subgroups.
Dimensionality Reduction	Explained Variance Ratio (PCA)	50–80%	Proportion of variance captured by the top components.	Identifying key dimensions in neuroimaging or genetic data.
	Reconstruction Error	Lower is better	Quantifies the error in reconstructing the original data from reduced dimensions.	Assessing the quality of dimensionality reduction techniques.
	Perplexity (t-SNE)	Typically 5–50	Balances local and global structure in t-SNE; affects data visualization quality.	Visualizing high-dimensional ASD-related data.
Anomaly Detection	Precision	70–90%	Proportion of true anomalies correctly identified.	Identifying rare genetic variants or unusual behavioral patterns in ASD datasets.
	Recall	70–90%	Proportion of true anomalies detected out of all anomalies.	Ensuring rare patterns are not missed.
	Area Under Precision-Recall (AUC-PR)	0.8	Measures the trade-off between precision and recall for detecting anomalies.	Evaluating the accuracy of anomaly detection models.
	Z-Score or Mahalanobis Distance	Threshold-based	Statistical methods for identifying outliers in datasets.	Detecting rare features or mutations linked to ASD.
Model Interpretability	Feature Importance Analysis	Ranked values	Identifies variables contributing most to clusters or dimensionality reduction.	Understanding critical behavioral or genetic factors driving patterns in ASD data.
	Cluster Centroid Analysis	Cluster-specific metrics	Examines the central characteristics of each cluster for interpretability.	Understanding subgroup profiles in ASD populations.

4.2.3 Deep Learning

Deep Learning (DL) techniques are increasingly applied in ASD screening due to their ability to process large, complex datasets [31]. They are especially effective for multimodal data—including neuroimaging, behavioral patterns, speech, and genetic profiles—key to capturing ASD heterogeneity. Convolutional Neural Networks (CNNs), the most widely used DL models, excel in image-based tasks such as analyzing MRI, fMRI, and EEG scans. CNNs extract features to detect structural or functional brain anomalies and atypical facial traits or gaze patterns. Their layered architecture enables learning of spatial hierarchies critical for ASD diagnosis [32].

Recurrent Neural Networks (RNNs) along with and their advanced variants—LSTM and GRUs—are widely used for sequential data due to their ability to capture temporal dependencies, making them ideal for EEG, speech, and behavioral time series in ASD studies. Autoencoders, key unsupervised deep learning models, are employed for feature extraction and denoising by compressing and reconstructing high-dimensional data such as neuroimaging and genetic profiles. Generative Adversarial Networks (GANs) effectively address data scarcity in ASD research by producing synthetic samples that closely resemble real data, enhancing dataset size and diversity—especially for limited genetic or imaging inputs. Transformers, with self-attention mechanisms, have revolutionized sequence modeling, outperforming traditional RNNs. Artificial Neural Networks (ANNs) using Natural Language Processing (NLP) are particularly useful for analyzing caregiver reports, developmental histories, and medical records. Future improvements include optimizing existing transformer models and exploring new variants to advance ASD research on textual data. Multimodal fusion models combining CNNs for spatial neuroimage features and RNNs for temporal behavioral data effectively capture both static and dynamic aspects of ASD. Their performance is validated using metrics like accuracy, precision, recall, F1 score, and AUC-ROC. Despite their promise, deep learning faces key challenges in ASD research: limited high-quality labeled data leads to overfitting, interpretability remains low due to the "black box" nature of DL models, and training demands significant computational resources, often requiring GPUs [33].

To address deep learning limitations in ASD research, explainable AI (XAI) is gaining traction to enhance clinical interpretability. Federated learning enables privacy-preserving analysis across distributed datasets. Domain-specific pre-trained models—akin to GPT in NLP—can mitigate data scarcity through knowledge transfer. Looking ahead, mobile-based deep learning holds transformative potential for early ASD detection, intervention, and interpretation.

Conclusion

AI and ML have significantly advanced ASD research and diagnosis by enabling earlier and more accurate detection, along with improved management strategies. Techniques like supervised, unsupervised, and deep learning (e.g., CNNs, RNNs) support analysis of neuroimaging, genetic, and behavioral data, aiding biomarker discovery and subgroup identification. Despite challenges such as limited data, overfitting, and low interpretability, solutions like explainable AI, federated learning, and multimodal integration offer promising paths forward. Overall, these technologies bridge data analytics with clinical insight to better support individuals with ASD.

Reference

1. Okoye, C., Obialo-Ibeawuchi, C.M., Obajeun, O.A., Sarwar, S., Tawfik, C. et al., (2023). Early diagnosis of autism spectrum disorder: a review and analysis of the risks and benefits. *Cureus.* https://doi.org/10.7759/cureus.43226.
2. Dick, K., Kaczmarek, E., Ducharme, R., Bowie, A.C., Dingwall-Harvey, A. et al. (2024). Predicting autism spectrum disorder: transformer-based deep learning ensemble framework using health administrative & birth registry data. medRxiv. https://doi.org/10.1101/2024.07.03.24309684.

3. Chen, Y., Chen, Q., Kong, L. and Liu, G. (2022). Early detection of autism spectrum disorder in young children with machine learning using medical claims data. BMJ Health & Care Informatics. https://doi.org/10.1136/bmjhci-2022-100544.
4. Janvier, Y.M., Harris, J.F., Coffield, C.N., Louis, B., Xie, M. et al. (2016). Screening for autism spectrum disorder in underserved communities: early childcare providers as reporters. *Autism.* https://doi.org/10.1177/1362361315585055.
5. Uke, P., Gaikwad, S., Vagha, K. and Wandile, S. (2024). Unraveling the spectrum: a comprehensive review of autism spectrum disorder in india. *Cureus.* https://doi.org/10.7759/cureus.62753.
6. Kamila, G. and Gulati, S. (2023). Navigating the frontiers in childhood neurodevelopmental disorders: unravelling challenges in south-east asia. Medknow. https://doi.org/10.4103/who-seajph.whoseajph_6_24.
7. Thabtah, F. and Peebles, D. (2019). A new machine learning model based on induction of rules for autism detection. SAGE Publishing. https://doi.org/10.1177/1460458218824711.
8. Sousa, D., Hajjar, A.C., Costa, A.C.M.M.D., Boggian, F.C.T.S. et al. (2022). Challenges in the early diagnosis of autistic spectrum disorder. Research, *Society and Development*. https://doi.org/10.33448/rsd-v11i8.29837.
9. Cilia, F., Carette, R., Elbattah, M., Dequen, G., Gurin, J. et al. (2021). Computer-aided screening of autism spectrum disorder: eye-tracking study using data visualization and deep learning. *JMIR Human Factors*. https://doi.org/10.2196/27706.
10. Nedungadi, P., Shah, S.M., Stokes, M.A., Nair, V.K., Moorkoth, A. et al. (2024). Mapping autisms research landscape: trends in autism screening and its alignment with sustainable development goals. *Frontiers in Psychiatry*. https://doi.org/10.3389/fpsyt.2023.1294254.
11. Abubakar, A. and Kipkemoi, P. (2022). Early intervention in autism spectrum disorder: the need for an international approach. *Developmental Medicine & Child Neurology*. https://doi.org/10.1111/dmcn.15327.
12. Al-Beltagi, M. (2024). Pre-autism: advancing early identification and intervention in autism. *World Journal of Clinical Cases*. https://doi.org/10.12998/wjcc.v12.i34.6748.
13. Zhang, A. (2023). A novel eye-tracking and audio hybrid system for autism spectrum disorder early detection. *None*. https://doi.org/10.1109/ICDSCA59871.2023.10393215.
14. Asmetha Jeyarani, R., Senthilkumar, R., Gowri, R., Vignesh, S. and Rudhra, Y. et al. (2024). Leveraging transfer learning with stacked ensemble learning for thedetection of autism spectrum disorder using eye-tracking. *None*. https://doi.org/10.1109/ACCAI61061.2024.10601827.
15. Mesleh, A.G., Ehtewish, H., Lennard, K., Abdesselem, H.B., Al-Shaban, F.A. et al. (2023). High-throughput autoantibody screening identifies differentially abundant autoantibodies in autism spectrum disorder. *Frontiers in Molecular Neuroscience*. https://doi.org/10.3389/fnmol.2023.1222506.
16. Zhusubalieva, A. and Oudah, M. (2024). Beyond the gut feeling: machine-learning methods for autism screening. International Conferences on Biological Information and Biomedical Engineering. https://doi.org/10.1109/BIBE63649.2024.10820459.
17. Yang, Z. (2024). Prediction of autism spectrum disorder: comparison and tuning of machine learning models. Lecture Notes in Education Psychology and Public Media. https://doi.org/10.54254/2753-7048/35/20232015.
18. Awaji, B.M., Senan, E.M., Olayah, F., Alshari, E.A., Alsulami, M. et al. (2023). Hybrid techniques of facial feature image analysis for early detection of autism spectrum disorder based on combined cnn features. *Diagnostics*. https://doi.org/10.3390/diagnostics13182948.
19. Shakir, S., Siddiqui, F. and Khan, S. (2024). A hybrid approach for prediction of autism spectrum disorder using machine learning algorithms. *None*. https://doi.org/10.1109/ICEECT61758.2024.10739042.
20. Grigore, B., Peters, J.L., Williams, J., Russell, G., Coles, P. et al. (2024). Screening for autism spectrum disorder in young children: still not enough evidence. *Journal of Primary Care & Community Health*. https://doi.org/10.1177/21501319241263223.
21. Menagadevi, M., Mangai, S., Sudha, S. and Thiyagarajan, D. *Resting-State fMRI*. 127-156. https://doi.org/10.1002/9781119857655.ch6.
22. Wetherby, A., Guthrie, W., Hooker, J.L., Delehanty, A.D., Day, T.N. et al. (2021). The early screening for autism and communication disorders: field-testing an autism-specific screening tool for children 12 to 36 months of age. *Autism*. https://doi.org/10.1177/13623613211012526.
23. Fernell, E., Eriksson, M.A. and Gillberg, C. (2013). Early diagnosis of autism and impact on prognosis: a narrative review. *Clinical Epidemiology*. https://doi.org/10.2147/CLEP.S41714.
24. Dahiya, A., McDonnell, C.G., DeLucia, E.A. and Scarpa, A. (2020). A systematic review of remote telehealth assessments for early signs of autism spectrum disorder: video and mobile applications.. *Practice Innovations*. https://doi.org/10.1037/pri0000121.
25. Hassan, M.M. and Mokhtar, H.M. (2018). Investigating autism etiology and heterogeneity by decision tree algorithm. *Informatics in Medicine Unlocked*, *16*, 100215. https://doi.org/10.1016/j.imu.2019.100215.

26. Tuli, M., Chandrasekhar, A., Tyagi, S. and Singhal, A. "Development of AI Based Autism Detection System," 2024 *14th International Conference on Cloud Computing, Data Science & Engineering (Confluence)*, Noida, India, 2024, pp. 41–46, doi: 10.1109/Confluence60223.2024.10463348.
27. Menagadevi, M., Devaraj, S., Madian, N. and Thiyagarajan, D. (2024). Machine and deep learning approaches for alzheimer disease detection using magnetic resonance images: An updated review. *Measurement*, *226*, 114100. https://doi.org/10.1016/j.measurement.2023.114100.
28. Themistocleous, C.K., Andreou, M. and Peristeri, E. (2024). Autism Detection in Children: Integrating Machine Learning and Natural Language Processing in Narrative Analysis. *Behavioral Sciences*, *14*(6), 459. https://doi.org/10.3390/bs14060459.
29. Alzakari, S.A., Allinjawi, A., Aldrees, A., Zamzami, N., Umer, M. et al. (2024). Early detection of autism spectrum disorder using explainable AI and optimized teaching strategies. *Journal of Neuroscience Methods*, *413*, 110315. https://doi.org/10.1016/j.jneumeth.2024.110315.
30. Thabtah, F., Spencer, R., Abdelhamid, N., Kamalov, F., Wentzel, C. et al. Autism screening: an unsupervised machine learning approach. *Health Inf Sci Syst.* 2022 Sep 8; 10(1): 26. doi: 10.1007/s13755-022-00191-x. PMID: 36092454; PMCID: PMC9458819.
31. Dcouto, S.S. and Pradeepkandhasamy, J. (2024). Multimodal deep learning in early autism detectionrecent advances and challenges. None. https://doi.org/10.3390/engproc2023059205.
32. Reddy, Y., Kumar Reddy, C.K., Lippert, K. and Reddy, S. *Classification Methods of Deep Learning for Detecting Autism Spectrum Disorder in Children* (4–12 Years). 297–319. https://doi.org/10.1002/9781394280735.ch15.
33. K.B., I.D. and P.M., D.R.V. (2025). The emergence of artificial intelligence in autism spectrum disorder research: A review of neuro imaging and behavioral applications. *Computer Science Review*, *56*, 100718. https://doi.org/10.1016/j.cosrev.2024.100718.

3

Analyzing the Optimized Features Requirement and Data Mining Techniques in Heart Disease Prediction

Tapas Sharma[1], Pradeepta Kumar Sarangi[1], Shefali Batra[1], Ashwani Kumar[1], Atul Tiwary[1] and Bhisham Sharma[2*]

1. Introduction

The heart, vital for circulating blood throughout the body, is essential to human survival its failure can be instantly fatal. Heart disease, driven by factors like obesity, high blood pressure, genetics, and alcohol consumption, is rising sharply in the 2020s. According to WHO, cardiovascular diseases (CVDs) cause approximately 17.9 million deaths annually, primarily from heart attacks and strokes, with most victims under 70. Diagnosis involves tests such as ECGs, cholesterol, and blood sugar levels. CVDs encompass a range of structural and functional heart disorders, with coronary artery disease caused by plaque buildup restricting blood flow being the most deadly, often resulting in heart attacks. Chest pain is a key warning sign of a heart attack, often indicating reduced blood flow to the heart. Other common symptoms include palpitations, arm pain, and shortness of breath. In cardiovascular disease, timely diagnosis is critical. While medical institutions are collecting large volumes of heart-related data, much of it is inconsistent or unreliable, making manual analysis difficult. Machine learning offers a powerful alternative enabling efficient data processing and highly accurate prediction of heart conditions. Machine Learning, a subset of artificial intelligence [1], synthesizes patterns from human-provided training data. It encompasses four primary algorithm types: Supervised, Unsupervised, Semi-supervised, and Reinforcement Learning [2]. These algorithms have shown strong performance across diverse domains, including financial analytics [3] and smart agriculture [4]. In this study, we apply the following machine learning techniques for medical data analysis:

- K-Nearest Neighbors (KNN)
- Logistic Regression
- Support Vector Machine (SVM)
- Naïve Bayes
- Decision Tree
- Random Forest

[1] Chitkara University School of Engineering and Technology, Chitkara University, Himachal Pradesh, India.
[2] Centre of Research Impact and Outcome, Chitkara University, Rajpura, India.
* Corresponding author: bhisham.pec@gmail.com

DOI: 10.1201/9781003541318-4

Autism is a genetic neurodevelopmental disorder marked by challenges in social interaction, communication, and behavior, typically diagnosed through behavioral assessments. In contrast, heart disease involves conditions affecting the heart and blood vessels, often caused by lifestyle factors like high blood pressure and cholesterol, and diagnosed via medical tests. Autism manifests through social difficulties, repetitive actions, and sensory sensitivities, while heart disease presents with symptoms such as chest pain, breathlessness, and fatigue. Autism is managed through therapy, whereas heart disease may require lifestyle changes, medication, or surgery. While autism affects brain function and behavior without directly harming physical health, heart disease can be life-threatening due to its impact on cardiovascular function.

2. Literature Review

Numerous machine learning algorithms, including K-Nearest Neighbor and Support Vector Machine, have been widely applied to develop non-invasive healthcare systems, reducing reliance on invasive procedures. Ongoing research continues to refine heart disease prediction using data mining and ML techniques. Effective preprocessing is essential to optimize datasets for accurate model performance. Various studies have evaluated algorithms like ANN, KNN, RF, and DT to identify the most suitable approaches for building reliable prediction models. Authors in [5] evaluated seven machine learning algorithms namely Naïve Bayes (NB), K-Nearest Neighbors (KNN), Logistic Regression (LR), Decision Tree (DT), Neural Network (NN), Support Vector Machine (SVM), and a Voting classifier using a 303 record dataset from the UCI repository. Due to limited data, they applied 10-fold cross-validation for both training and testing, with the Voting classifier achieving the highest accuracy of 87.4%. Similarly, authors in [6] have used the Cleveland dataset (UCI), initially comprising 303 records, which were reduced to 296 after preprocessing. Their study found SVM to be the most effective, reaching an accuracy of 90%.

Authors in [7] have applied a hybrid set of data mining classifiers to predict cardiovascular disease (CVD) using a UCI dataset containing 303 records and 76 attributes. After preprocessing, 14 attributes were reduced to 12 for model training and testing. Algorithms used included KNN, NN, SVM, GA, RF, and NB, with SVM and NB achieving the highest accuracy of 89.2%. In [8], authors have employed a vector quantization algorithm on the same UCI dataset (303 records, 14 attributes), split into 70% training and 30% testing, yielding an accuracy of 85.5%. Authors in [9] have developed a web-based heart disease prediction tool using LR, NB, and SVM, with a 75:25 train-test split on the UCI dataset. SVM yielded the highest accuracy of 64.4%. Authors in [10] have tested multiple classifiers including LR, NB, and SVM, achieving a top accuracy of 84.81% using Random Forest. Devansh Shah et al. applied supervised learning on 14 selected attributes from a 303-record UCI dataset, with KNN delivering the best performance. Authors in [11] have used the same dataset and reported accuracies of 79% (DT), 78% (LR), 87% (KNN), and 83% (SVM), with KNN leading. Authors in [12] have employed SVM, LR, ANN, KNN, NB, and DT, achieving a superior accuracy of 92.37% over previous models.

Authors in [13] have applied multiple machine learning classifiers to predict cardiovascular disease, with Random Forest achieving the highest accuracy of 85.71%. Authors in [14] have explored various algorithms including decision trees, SVM, Naïve Bayes, neural networks, and KNN and introduced a hybrid HRFLM model combining random forest and linear methods, which reached an accuracy of 88.4%. Authors in [15] have applied supervised learning algorithms Decision Tree, Naïve Bayes, KNN, and Random Forest on a UCI dataset with 303 records and 76 attributes, selecting 14 for training. KNN achieved the highest accuracy of 85.09%. Authors in [16] have used a multilayer perceptron neural network (MLP-NN) and evaluated performance using recall, precision, accuracy, and F-measure, reaching 93.39% accuracy. Authors in [17] have employed Random Forest, Decision Tree, and Logistic Regression on the same dataset, with Logistic Regression yielding the best accuracy of 92.10%. Authors in [18] have used SVM, NB, and DT classifiers, achieving 90%

accuracy with Decision Tree. Authors in [19] have applied KNN, DT, LR, NB, and SVM classifiers to the UCI heart disease dataset, with Logistic Regression achieving the highest accuracy of 92%. Authors in [20] have used the same dataset and tested multiple classifiers including NB, LM, LR, DT, RF, SVM, and HRFLM, with HRFLM yielding the best accuracy of 88.4%. Authors in [21] have utilized a public health dataset and evaluated RF, LR, KNN, SVM, DT, and XGB, reporting a top accuracy of 84% using SVM. These comparative results are summarized in Table 1.

Table 1 Similar works in the field.

Researcher	*Data Set Used*	*Algorithm Used*	*Accuracy*	*Reference*
Amin et al.	Cleveland UCI Dataset	K-NN, ANN, SVM, NB, DT and VOTE	87%	[5]
Khan et al.	UCI Dataset	SVM	90%	[6]
Tarawneh et al.	UCI Dataset	KNN, NN, SVM, GA, J48, RF, and NB	89.2%	[7]
Anitha et al.	UCI Dataset	Vector Quantization	85.55%	[8]
Jagtap et al.	UCI Dataset	LR, SVM, NV	64.4%	[9]
Rubini et al.	UCI Dataset	RF, LR, NV, SVM	84.81%	[10]
Archana Singh et al.	Cleveland UCI Dataset	LR, KNN, VM, DT	87%	[11]
Asif Khan et al.	UCI Dataset	KNN, NV, DT	92.37%	[12]
N.K. Kumar et al.	UCI Dataset	RF, SVM, DT	85.71%	[13]
Mohan et al.	Cleveland UCI dataset	DT, SVM, RF, NV, NN, KNN	88.4%	[14]
Devansh Shah et al.	UCI Dataset	DT, NV, KNN, RF	85.09%	[15]
Subhadra et al.	UCI Dataset	NN	93.39%	[16]
Gupta el al.	Cleveland UCI dataset	RF, DT, LR	92.10%	[17]
Abdalrada et al.	UCI Dataset	SVM, NB, DT	90%	[18]
N Singh et al.	UCI Dataset	KNN, DT, LR, NB, SVM	92%	[19]
Kishor A. et al.	UCI Dataset	NB, LM, LR, DT, RF, SVM, HRFLM	88.4%	[20]
Marco et al.	Public Health Dataset	RF, LR, KNN, SVM, DT, XGB	84%	[21]

This research aims to develop and implement highly accurate heart disease prediction models to enable early patient identification, accelerate diagnosis, reduce heart attack incidence, and ultimately save lives.

3. Methodology

This study aims to predict heart disease risk using a programmatic, data-driven approach beneficial to both clinicians and patients. Machine learning algorithms are applied to a curated dataset, with irrelevant data removed to improve accuracy. The refined data is then used to train predictive models, enhancing performance and reliability. The report outlines this process step-by-step.

1. *Data Source*: The study utilizes a dataset of 1,200 patients, each described by 14 features such as age, gender, and blood pressure (see Figure 1). The target variable, "cardio," indicates the presence (1) or absence (0) of cardiovascular disease.

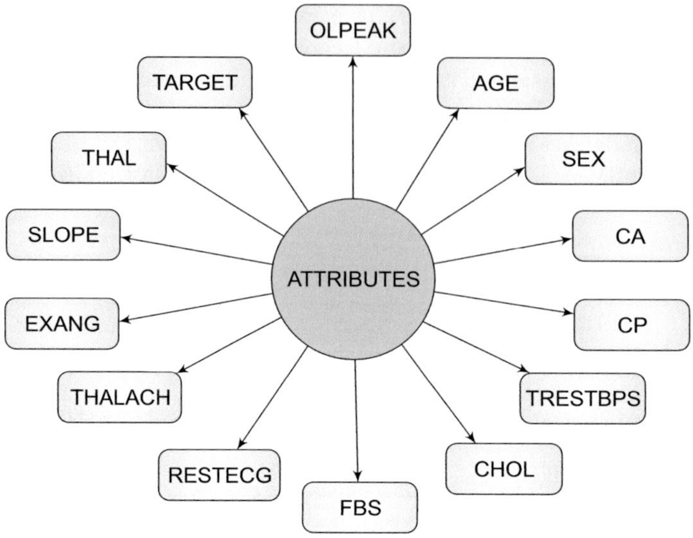

Fig. 1 Attributes.

2. *Removing Outliers*: The original dataset of 1200 records was reduced to 798 after eliminating outliers and missing values, improving model accuracy and reliability.
3. *Clustering* We applied k-modes clustering to group patients based on shared categorical traits such as age group, BMI, and blood pressure category. This technique effectively handles non-numeric data that cannot be meaningfully averaged.

The study also examined correlations between factors like blood pressure and age to identify patterns and interdependencies, offering insights into how combined risk factors influence heart disease likelihood.

3.1 Modeling Process

a. *Splitting the Dataset*: The dataset was split into 80% for model training and 20% for performance testing.
b. *Using Classifiers*: To predict cardiovascular disease, many types of classifiers are tested:
   - Decision Tree Classifier
   - Random Forest Classifier
   - KNN
   - Naïve Byes
   - Logistic Regression
   - SVM
c. *Measure Performance*: The effectiveness of each classifier is measured by accuracy, precision, recall, and F-measure scores. These sets help to understand how well each model predicts heart disease.

The workflow diagram describing the steps is shown in Figure 2.

3.2 Implementation of Algorithms

- Support Vector Machine (SVM) is used for both regression and classification tasks. It constructs a decision boundary called a hyperplane that separates data into distinct classes

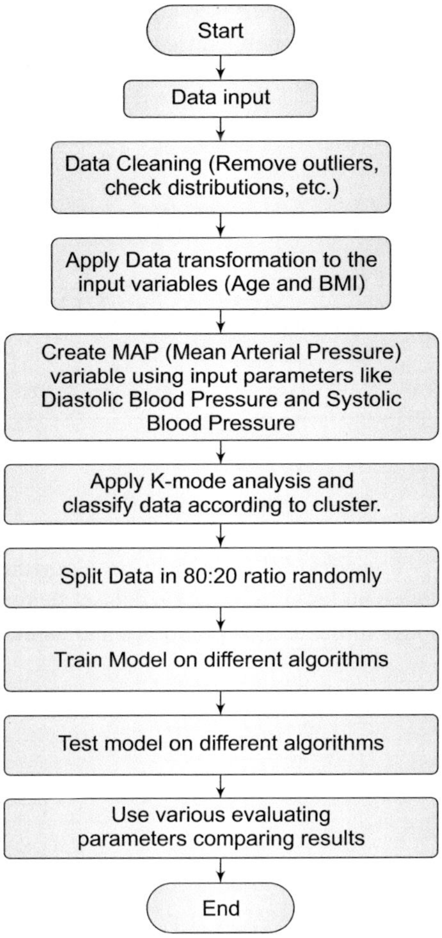

Fig. 2 Workflow diagram.

within a multi-dimensional space, leveraging the unique characteristics of each feature (see Figure 3).

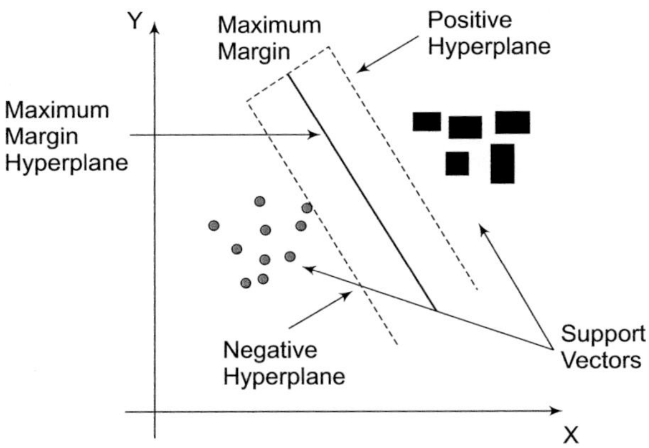

Fig. 3 SVM working principle.

- KNN: K-Nearest Neighbour is a supervised classification algorithm that assumes new data resembles existing data. It assigns new entries to categories based on similarity to nearby data points, as illustrated in Figure 4.

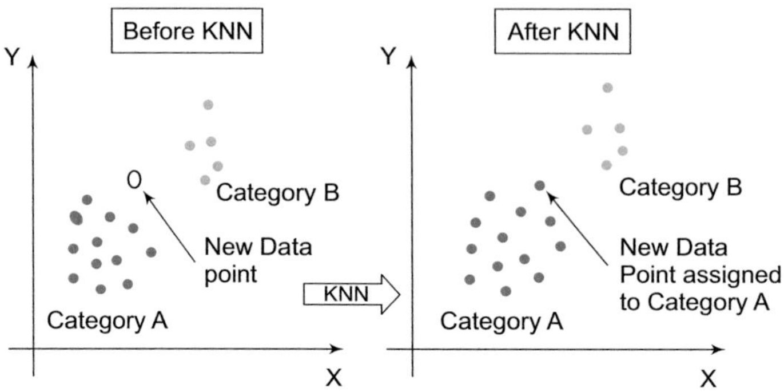

Fig. 4 KNN working principle.

- Decision Tree (DT) is a supervised classification algorithm that uses decision and leaf nodes (Figure 5). Decision nodes split based on dataset features, with branches representing decision rules. Leaf nodes indicate final outcomes and cannot be further divided.

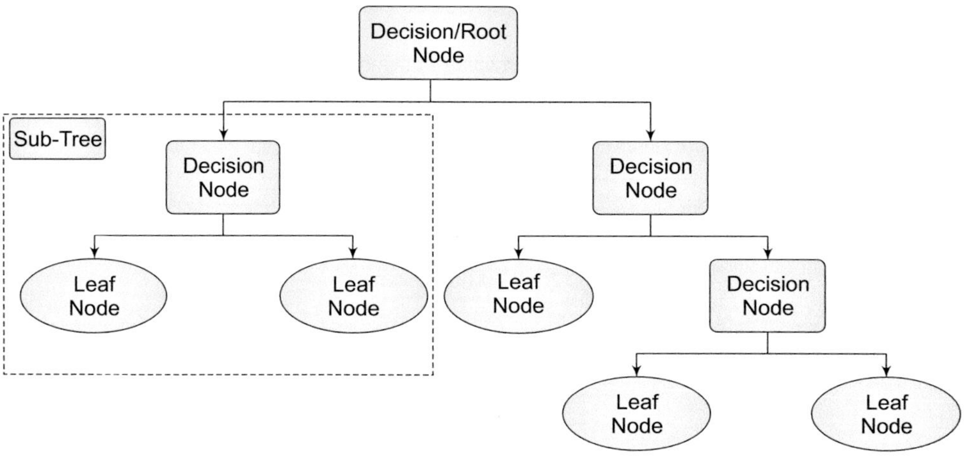

Fig. 5 Working of DT.

- Random Forest is an ensemble learning classifier that combines multiple decision trees, each trained on different data subsets, to tackle complex problems. By averaging their outputs, it enhances accuracy and overall model performance (see Figure 6).
- Naïve Bayes is a supervised learning algorithm that uses labeled data to estimate the probability of a class (hypothesis) based on given predictors (Figure 7).
    - o P(hypothesis/predictors): Posterior probability of the hypothesis given the predictors.
    - o P(predictors/hypothesis): Likelihood of observing the predictors given the hypothesis.
    - o P(hypothesis): Prior probability of the hypothesis(class).
    - o P(predictors): Marginal probability of the predictors(data).

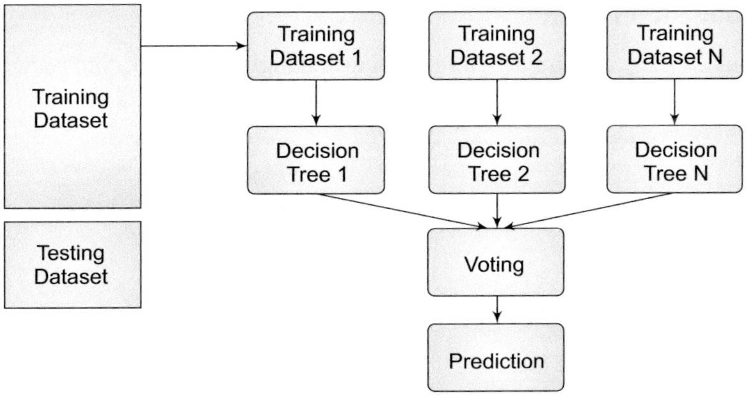

Fig. 6 Working of Random-Forest.

classifier

$$P(A|B) = \frac{P(B|A) \cdot P(A)}{P(B)}$$

Fig. 7 Working principle of Naïve Bayes.

- Logistic Regression is a supervised learning algorithm that converts continuous outputs from a linear function into categorical values using the sigmoid function, which maps inputs to a range between 0 and 1 (see Figure 8).

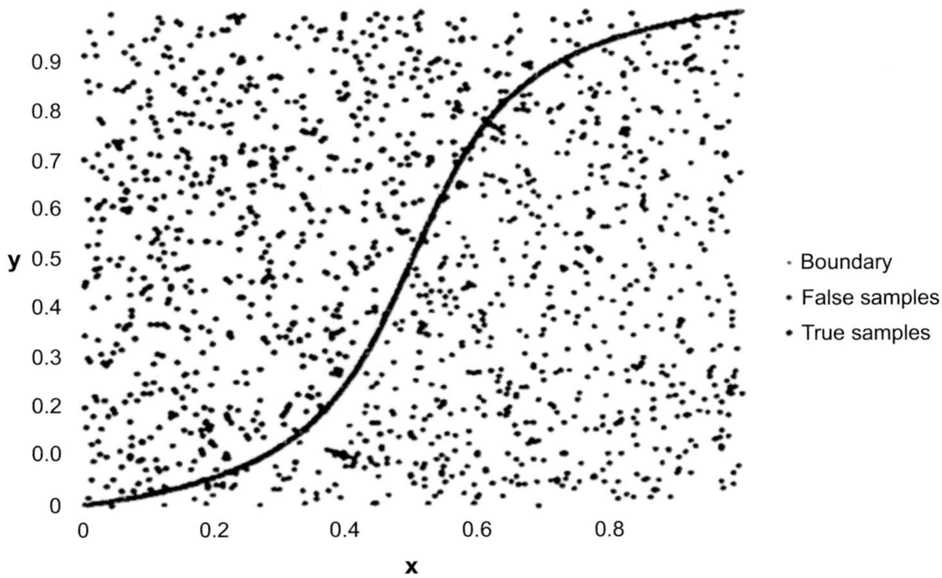

Fig. 8 Example of logistic regression.

4. Data Visualization

This section visualizes key data traits before training and highlights algorithm accuracy metrics after testing.

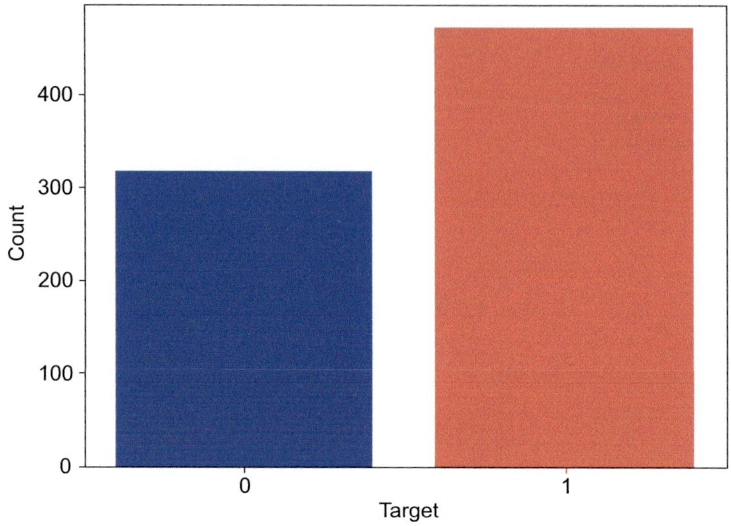

Fig. 9 Count of patients with and without heart disease.

Figure 9 shows two bars: 477 patients with heart disease and 321 without. Figure 10 illustrates age-wise heart disease frequency, with blue indicating healthy patients and red indicating those affected.

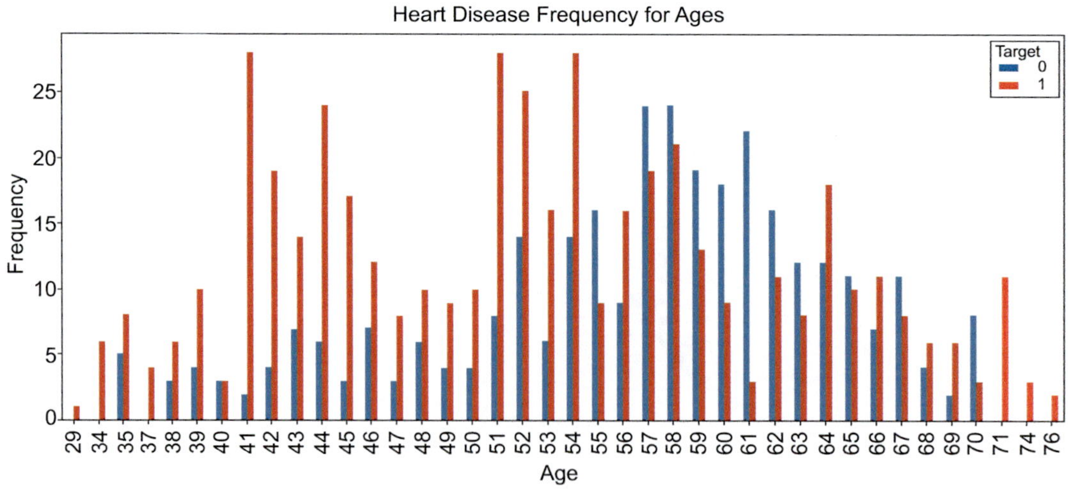

Fig. 10 Frequency of heart disease for all ages.

Heart disease is most prevalent at ages 41,51 and 54, while ages 57 and 58 show the highest count of healthy patients. Figure 11 displays a sample of the dataset.

	age	sex	cp	trestbps	chol	fbs	restecg	thalach	exang	oldpeak	slope	ca	thal	target
0	64	1	3	170	227	0	0	155	0	0.6	1	0	3	1
1	66	0	2	146	278	0	0	152	0	0.0	1	1	2	1
2	39	0	2	138	220	0	1	152	0	0.0	1	0	2	1
3	58	0	0	130	197	0	1	131	0	0.6	1	0	2	1
4	47	1	2	130	253	0	1	179	0	0.0	2	0	2	1

Fig. 11 Sample dataset.

5. Implementation and Result Analysis

All six algorithms were used to train the dataset, yielding varying accuracy levels during testing with the same models. Model performance is evaluated using a confusion matrix, which highlights prediction errors.

- **True Negative (TN):** Top-left cell; both actual and predicted values indicate no heart disease.
- **False Positive (FP):** Top-right; actual value is no, but predicted as yes (Type I error).
- **False Negative (FN):** Bottom-left; actual value is yes, but predicted as no (Type II error).
- **True Positive (TP):** Bottom-right; both actual and predicted values confirm heart disease.

Accuracy Formula:

$$\text{Accuracy} = \frac{TP + TN}{TP + TN + FP + FN} \quad ...(1)$$

Where:

- **TP** = True Positives
- **TN** = True Negatives
- **FP** = False Positives
- **FN** = False Negatives

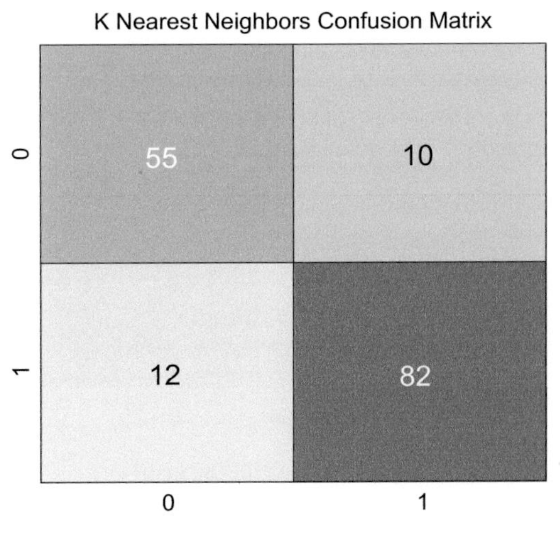

Fig. 12 KNN confusion matrix.

Figure 12 represents the confusion matrix of KNN Algorithms.

- KNN correctly identified 55 patients as not having heart disease, matching the actual data (True Negative).
- The model correctly predicted heart disease in 82 cases, representing the True Positive count.

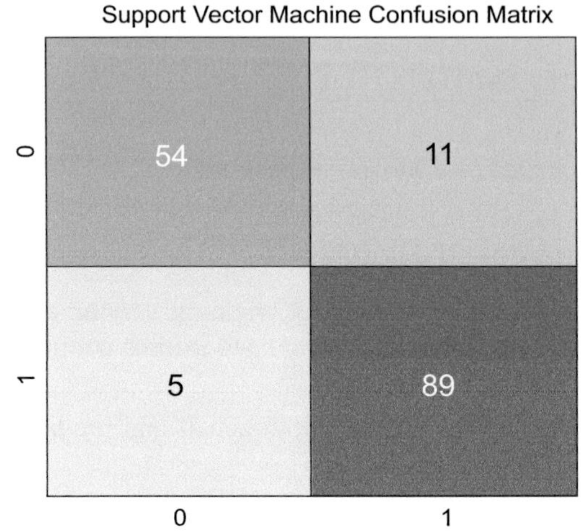

Fig. 13 SVM confusion matrix.

Figure 13 shows the confusion matrix of the SVM model.

- SVM correctly predicted no heart disease in 54 cases, representing the True Negative count. The model correctly identified heart disease in 89 cases, representing the True Positive count.

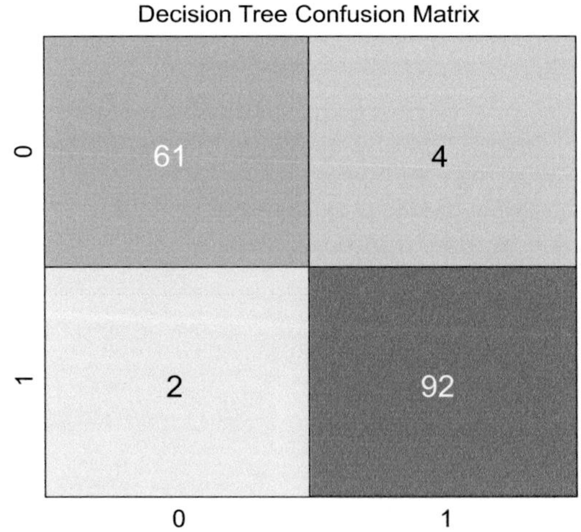

Fig. 14 DT-confusion matrix.

Figure 14 presents the confusion matrix for the Decision Tree algorithm.

- The Decision Tree model correctly predicted the absence of heart disease in 61 cases (True Negative). The Decision Tree model correctly identified heart disease in 92 cases (True Positive).

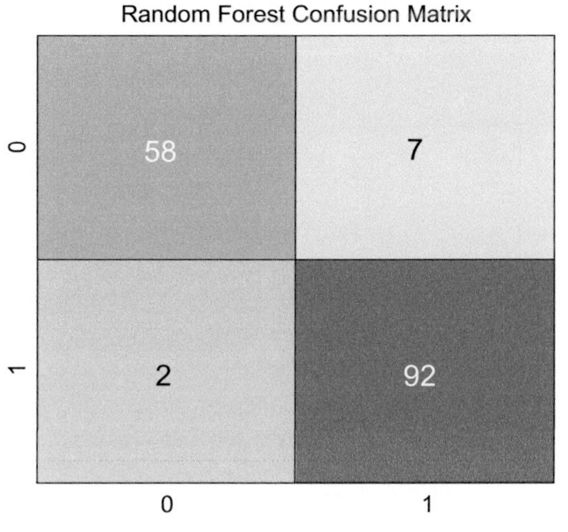

Fig. 15 RF Confusion matrix.

Figure 15 illustrates the confusion matrix generated by the Random Forest model.

- The RFS model correctly accurately classified 58 patients as not having heart disease (True Negative). The Random Forest model correctly identified heart disease in 92 patients, matching the actual count (True Positive).

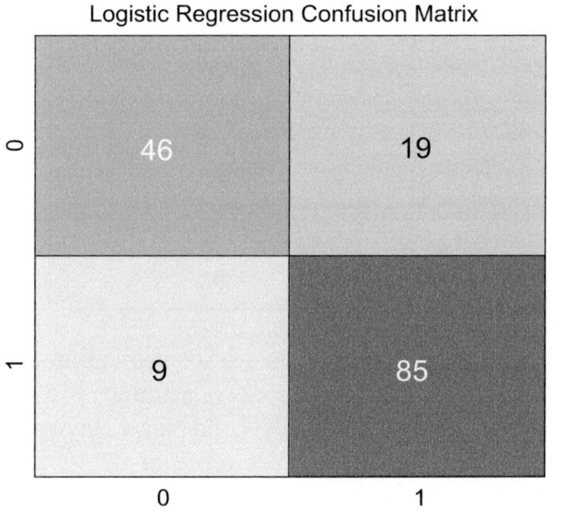

Fig. 16 Logistic Regression confusion Matrix.

Figure 16 displays the confusion matrix for the Logistic Regression model.

- The Logistic Regression model accurately predicted the absence of heart disease in 46 cases (True Negative).
- The model correctly identified heart disease in 85 cases, representing its True Positive count.

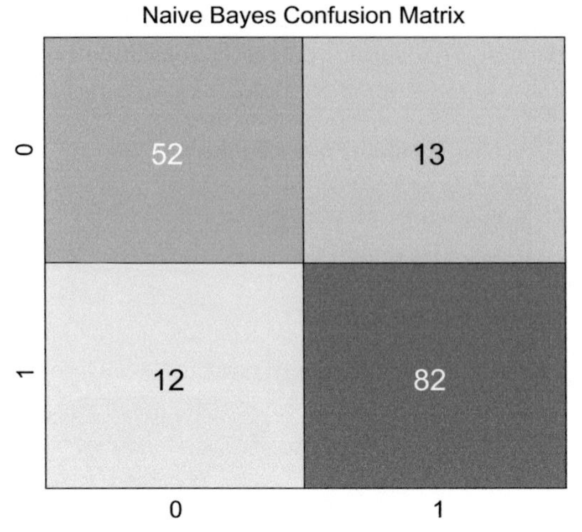

Fig. 17 Naïve Bayes confusion Matrix.

Figure 17 illustrates the confusion matrix generated by the Naïve Bayes classifier. The True-Negative value for Naïve Bayes is 52 which means the model predicted no heart disease accurately 52 Times.

- The True-Positive count is 82, indicating that the model correctly identified heart disease in 82 instances.

Table 2 Highest Accuracy Achieved by Each Classification Algorithm.

Algorithm	*Correct Classifications*	*Accuracy Score (%)*
K-Nearest Neighbors (KNN)	137	86.16
Support Vector Machine (SVM)	143	89.94
Decision Tree	153	96.23
Random Forest	150	94.34
Logistic Regression	131	82.39
Naïve Byes	134	84.28

The table summarizes the top accuracy scores of classification algorithms based on correctly identified patient cases. Decision Tree led with 96.23% accuracy (153 cases), followed by Random Forest at 94.34%. SVM reached 89.94%, while KNN and Naïve Bayes achieved 86.16% and 84.28%, respectively. Logistic Regression had the lowest score at 82.39%. Overall, tree-based models outperformed the others.

6. Conclusion

Heart disease remains a leading global cause of death, underscoring the need for early detection and timely intervention. Traditional invasive diagnostic methods are often slow and risky, making the development of Machine Learning models crucial. These models can enhance early diagnosis and guide treatment strategies, which may include lifestyle changes, medication, or surgery depending on disease severity. Overall, Machine Learning offers significant promise in improving outcomes and saving lives through accurate, non-invasive heart disease prediction.

References

1. AI. Shahrani, A.M., Alomar, M.A., Alqahtani, K.N., Basingab, M.S., Sharma, B. et al. (2022). Machine learning-enabled smart industrial automation systems using internet of things. *Sensors*, 23(1), p. 324.
2. A. Samad, S.R., Balasubaramanian, S., Al-Kaabi, A.S., Sharma, B., Chowdhury, S. et al. (2023). Analysis of the performance impact of fine-tuned machine learning model for phishing URL detection. *Electronics*, 12(7), p. 1642.
3. N. Chopra, A. Singh, R. Garg, P.K. Sarangi, A.K. Sahoor et al. (2023). "Plant Disease Detection Using Deep Learning and Machine Learning Algorithms," 2023 *3rd International Conference on Technological Advancements in Computational Sciences (ICTACS)*, Tashkent, Uzbekistan, pp. 162–165, doi: 10.1109/ICTACS59847.2023.10390154.
4. G. Singh, "CNN-RNN based Hybrid Machine Learning Model to Predict the Currency Exchange Rate: USD to INR," 2022 *2nd International Conference on Advance Computing and Innovative Technologies in Engineering (ICACITE)*, Greater Noida, India, 2022, pp. 1668-1672, doi: 10.1109/ICACITE53722.2022.9823844.
5. M.S. Amin, Y.K. Chiam and K.D. Varathan, (2019). "Identification of significant features and data mining techniques in predicting heart disease," *Telematics and Informatics*, vol. 36, pp. 82–93.
6. S.N. Khan, N.M. Nawi, A. Shahzad, A. Ullah and M.F. Mushtaq (2017). et al. "Comparative analysis for heart disease prediction," *International Journal on Informatics Visualization*, vol. 1, no. 4-2, pp. 227–231.
7. M. Tarawneh and O. Embarak, (2019). "Hybrid approach for heart disease prediction using data mining techniques," *Acta Scientific Nutritional Health*, vol. 3, no. 7, pp. 147–151.
8. S. Anitha and N. Sridevi, (2019). "Heart disease prediction using data mining techniques," *Journal of Analysis and Computation*, vol. 8, no. 2, pp. 48–55.
9. A. Jagtap, P. Malewadkar, O. Baswat and H. Rambade, (2019). "Heart disease prediction using machine learning," *International Journal of Research in Engineering, Science and Management*, vol. 2, no. 2, pp. 352–355.
10. P.E. Rubini, C.A. Subasini, A.V. Katharine, V. Kumaresan, S.G. Kumar et al, (2021). "A cardiovascular disease prediction using machine learning algorithms," *Annual Romanian Society Cell Biology*, vol. 25, no. 2, pp. 904–912.
11. A. Singh and R. Kumar, (2020) "Heart disease prediction using machine learning algorithms," *International Conference on Electrical & Electronics Engineering*, pp. 452–457, DOI: 10.1109/ICE348803.2020.9122958.
12. J.P. Li, A.U. Haq, S.U. Din, J. Khan, A. Khan et al. (2020). "Heart disease identification method using machine learning classification in E-healthcare," *IEEE Access*, vol. 8, pp. 107562–107582, doi: 10.1109/ACCESS.2020.3001149.
13. N.K. Kumar, G.S. Sindhu, D.K. Prashanthi and A.S. Sulthana, "Analysis and prediction of cardiovascular disease using machine learning classifiers," in *Proceedings of the 2020 6th International Conference on Advanced Computing and Communication Systems (ICACCS)*, pp. 15–21, IEEE, 2020 March.
14. S. Mohan, C. Thirumalai and G. Srivastava, (2019). "Effective heart disease prediction using hybrid machine learning techniques," *IEEE Access*, vol. 7, pp. 81542–81554, https://doi.org/10.1109/ACCESS.2019.2923707.
15. D. Shah, S. Patel and S. Kumar Bharti, (2020). Heart Disease Prediction Using Machine Learning Techniques, *SN Computer Science*, vol 1:345, https://link.springer.com/article/10.1007/s42979-020-00365-y.
16. K. Subhadra and B. Vikas, (2019). "Neural network based intelligent system for predicting heart disease," *International Journal of Innovative Technology and Exploring Engineering*, vol. 8, no. 5, pp. 484–487.
17. Gupta, C., Saha, A., Reddy, N.S., Acharya, U.D. Cardiac (2022). Disease Prediction using Supervised Machine Learning Techniques. In *Journal of Physics: Conference Series*; vol 2161(1): 012013, DOI:10.1088/1742-6596/2161/1/012013.
18. Abdalrada, A.S., Abawajy, J., Al-Quraishi, T. and Islam, S.M.S. (2022). Machine learning models for prediction of co-occurrence of diabetes and cardiovascular diseases: A retrospective cohort study. *J. Diabetes Metab. Disord.*, vol 21, pp. 251–261, https://doi.org/10.1007/s40200-021-00968-z.
19. Singh, N. and Bhatnagar, S. (2021). Machine Learning for Prediction of Drug Targets in Microbe Associated Cardiovascular Diseases by Incorporating Host-pathogen Interaction Network Parameters. *Mol. Inform.* 41, 2100115, https://doi.org/10.1002/minf.202100115.
20. Kishor, A. and Jeberson, W. (2021). Diagnosis of heart disease using internet of things and machine learning algorithms. *Proceedings of the Second International Conference on Computing, Communications, and Cyber-Security, IC4S*; pp. 691–702.
21. Marco, L. and Farinella, G.M. (Eds.) *Computer Vision for Assistive Healthcare; Academic Press: Cambridge, MA*, USA, 201; eBook ISBN: 9780128134467.

Section 2

ML models for behaviour analysis

4

Advanced Patient Monitoring and Alert System with Instant Care Recommendation System using ML

B Aruna Devi[1*], Aisha Refana A[2], Harin Venugopalan[3], Jeevanandham P[4], Kamali M[5] and P Divya[6]

I. Introduction

Telemedicine, now central to modern healthcare, has been revolutionized by IoT—particularly in cardiology—enabling remote monitoring via sensors and smartphones. Medical data is uploaded to web servers and shared through telecom networks, allowing clinicians to oversee multiple patients simultaneously. This shift addresses prior limitations in multispecialty hospitals, where manual rounds caused delays and discomfort. Effective [1-4] telemedicine systems require secure data handling, intuitive interfaces, and accurate sensor selection. As technology evolves, telemedicine continues to expand access and improve outcomes, especially in underserved regions[9].Several IoT-based studies have advanced remote patient monitoring:

- **Wireless Monitoring in Hospitals:** Improved early detection and staff satisfaction, though alert frequency remained unchanged.
- **Privacy-Centric RPM Architecture:** Introduced blockchain-based data sharing and secure transactions, enhancing privacy.
- **ECG Monitoring for Novices:** Offered low-cost, energy-efficient health tracking integrated with smart home systems.

2. Proposed System

Wearable devices continuously capture vital signs and transmit data to edge/cloud platforms, where ML models analyze patterns against population or individual baselines [5-7]. Results are sent to mobile apps for alerts, triage, and clinical decision support, including e-prescriptions when authorized. These systems enable early intervention, streamline data analysis, and optimize clinical workflows. Deployment must consider privacy, model robustness, device constraints, and regulatory

[1] Professor, Department of ECE, Dr N.G.P. Institute of Technology, Coimbatore, India.
[2-5] UG Students, Department of ECE, Dr N.G.P. Institute of Technology, Coimbatore, India.
[6] Assistant Professor, Department of ECE, Sri Krishna College of Engineering and Technology, Coimbatore, India. Email: p.divya@skct.edu.in[6]
* Corresponding author: arunadevi@drngpit.ac.in

DOI: 10.1201/9781003541318-6

compliance. Overall, combining wearables with ML offers scalable, personalized, and proactive healthcare [8].

Fig. 1 Deployment of the Proposed system.

3. Hardware Description

3.1. Arduino (Atmega 328P)

The Atmega328P is an AVR microcontroller with 32KB flash, 1KB EEPROM, and 2KB SRAM. It offers 23 I/O pins, 6 PWM channels, a 10-bit ADC, and serial interfaces, operating up to 20 MHz. Known for low power consumption and multiple sleep modes, it's widely used in automation, robotics, and consumer electronics due to its affordability, performance, and compatibility with open-source tools.

3.2 MAX30100 Sensor

The MAX30100 is a compact pulse oximetry and heart-rate sensor for wearables [10], combining red/IR LEDs, a photodetector, and low-noise AFE to estimate SpO_2 and heart rate. It operates on 1.8–5.5 V and uses I^2C for easy microcontroller integration.

Normal Ranges: Heart rate: 67–89 BPM; SpO_2: 90–98%.
The DHT11 measures humidity via a moisture-sensitive substrate between electrodes. As humidity rises, resistance drops linearly due to increased ion conductivity.

Normal Temperature Range: 28–37°C. Owing to its compact form factor and on-chip signal conditioning, the MAX30100 supports real-time physiological monitoring in smartwatches, fitness bands, and related wearable platforms [10].

Normal Range of heart rate = 67–89 BPM.
Normal Range of SpO2 = 90–98%

3.3 DHT11 Sensor

A humidity sensor typically consists of a moisture-retaining substrate placed between two electrodes. As water vapor is absorbed, ion generation increases conductivity, causing a linear decrease in resistance with rising relative humidity. This resistance change is measured to determine local humidity levels.

Normal Temperature Range = 28–37(Celsius)

3.4 Pulse Sensor

A skin-contact sensor that detects heart rate, typically placed on the fingertip or earlobe. It may also measure heart rate variability, SpO_2, and stress levels, used in both medical and fitness settings.

Normal Pulse Range: <110 mmHg.

3.5 LCD

DisplayLCDs use liquid crystals and electric current to display text or images with high contrast and low power consumption. Though limited by viewing angles and response time, they're widely used for their clarity and portability.

Limitations include LCD panels offer low power usage, sharp image quality, and high contrast, though they are limited by narrow viewing angles and slower response times. Their compact design and visual clarity make them common in many electronic devices.

3.6 ESP8266 Wi-Fi Module

The ESP8266 is a low-cost SoC offering full Wi-Fi and TCP/IP support. It functions either as a standalone processor or a co-processor via AT commands. With multiple sleep modes and standard interfaces (UART, SPI, GPIO, ADC), it's ideal for IoT and wearable health systems needing efficient wireless connectivity.

4. Software Description

4.1 Arduino Software

Arduino is an open-source electronics platform combining simple hardware and software. Its microcontroller executes tasks via commands written in the Wiring-based language using the Processing-based Arduino IDE.

4.2 ThingSpeak

ThingSpeak is a versatile IoT platform that collects, analyzes, and responds to device data using cloud infrastructure, RESTful APIs, multi-language support, and customizable rules—ideal for building and deploying smart applications.

4.3 Machine learning with python (KNN ALGORITHM)

The **K-Nearest Neighbours (KNN)** is a supervised learning algorithm mainly used for classification and short-term prediction. It assigns labels or values to a query point by analyzing the *k* nearest data points in feature space using a chosen distance metric, applying majority voting for classification or averaging for regression. KNN exhibits two defining properties:

- **Lazy learning:** KNN skips training by storing the full dataset and performing distance-based computations only at query time.

- **Non-parametric modelling:** KNN makes **no distributional assumptions** about the data and does not learn a fixed set of parameters; model complexity adapts to local data density.
- **Practical notes:** Performance depends on the choice of k, the distance metric, feature scaling/normalization, and (optionally) **distance weighting** of neighbors. Efficient search structures (e.g., KD-trees, ball trees, or approximate nearest neighbor indices) are often used to reduce query time in high-volume applications.

Algorithm:

Step 1: Data preparation

Load the training dataset (features with labels) and the test dataset (features only).

Step 2: Choose *K*

Choose the number of neighbours K, a positive integer hyperparameter, typically determined through validation methods like cross-validation.

Step 3: Predict for each test instance.

For every sample x_{test} in the test set:

3.1 Calculate distances from x_{test} to all training samples using a suitable metric—typically Euclidean for numeric data, or Hamming for binary/categorical features.

3.2 Sort training samples in ascending order of distance.

3.3 Select the top K nearest neighbours.

3.4 Label each test instance x_{test} based on the majority class among its K nearest neighbors, applying distance weighting or tie-breaking strategies when necessary.

Step 4: Terminate

Repeat Step 3 for all test samples and return the predicted labels.

The Euclidean distance is utilized in the KNN classifier to measure the similarity between the training data and the test data.

$$d(p, q) = \sqrt{\sum_{i=1}^{N} ((p_i - q_i)^2)} \quad ...(4.1)$$

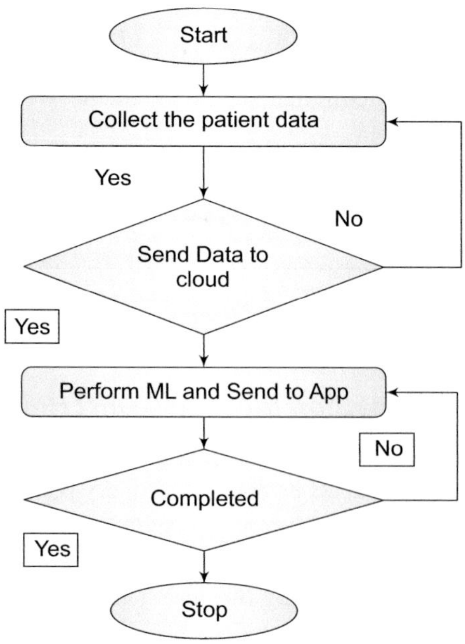

Fig. 2 Flowchart of the System Operation.

5. System Block Diagram

The system block diagram of Advanced patient Monitoring and Alert System with Instant care. The Atmega 328p microcontroller, powered by a 5V DC supply, collects data from connected sensors and processes it before sending it via serial communication to the ESP8266 Wi-Fi module. The ESP8266 handles wireless transmission, uploading sensor data to the cloud using the MQTT protocol—a reliable and scalable solution for IoT communication.

To ensure reliable transmission, data is sent in discrete packets. As shown in Fig. 3, the system comprises an Atmega328P microcontroller, pulse sensor, MAX30100 sensor, temperature sensor, and ESP8266 Wi-Fi module. The pulse sensor detects blood volume changes from heartbeats, the MAX30100 measures SpO_2 and heart rate, and the temperature sensor monitors body temperature.

The cloud-based KNN algorithm, trained on a reliable dataset, classifies sensor data as "Normal" or "Abnormal" based on predefined parameter ranges. If abnormalities are detected, the system generates a prescription and sends the result to the caretaker's mobile app, enabling real-time monitoring of the patient's health.

6. Results & Discussion

Sensors generate individual parameter values, which are evaluated by a machine learning model to determine if they fall within normal ranges. Deviations are flagged by comparing values against expected thresholds, with high or low readings noted in the comment box. A corresponding prescription is generated instantly, allowing both patient and caregiver to assess the condition. Tables 2 and 3 present the sensor data and resulting medication recommendations. KNN is a non-generalizing, instance-based method that retains all training data. In this case, the number of neighbors was fixed at $k = 4k = 4$ using Euclidean distance, with minimal effect on reconstruction when varied. Applying weighting to neighbors may help evaluate potential improvements in accuracy. The first step entails partitioning the dataset into training and testing subsets. Normally, 90% of the dataset is designated for training, with the remaining 10% set aside for testing. To ensure all data points are included in the test set at least once, this procedure is iterated 10 times. Specifically, in this scenario with 293 records, the initial analysis will employ records 1 to 29 as test data and records 30 to 293 as training data.Similarly for other data , it is processed and obtained by a 10-folds cross validation.Table 1 provides the Classification results and figure 4 denotes the analysis.

Let **TP**, **FP**, **TN**, and **FN** denote true positives, false positives, true negatives, and false negatives, respectively. The following metrics evaluate distinct dimensions of classifier effectiveness:

- **Precision (Positive Predictive Value):** the fraction of positive predictions that are actually true.

$$\text{Precision} = \frac{TP}{TP + FP}$$

- **Recall (Sensitivity/True Positive Rate):** the ratio of correctly detected actual positives to the total number of actual positives.

$$\text{Recall} = \frac{TP}{TP + FN}$$

- **F1 Score:** the harmonic average of precision and recall, providing a balanced measure of both.

$$\text{F1} = 2\,\frac{\text{Precision} \times \text{Recall}}{\text{Precision} + \text{Recall}}$$

- **Accuracy:** the ratio of correctly predicted instances to the total number of predictions made.

$$\text{Accuracy} = \frac{TP + PN}{TP + TN + FP + FN}$$

Notes: Each metric spans a scale from 0 to 1. If the denominator is zero—such as when no positive predictions are made—the metric becomes undefined and is typically set to 0 or adjusted using a small stabilizing constant. For multiclass classification, these metrics can be generalized using macro, micro, or weighted averaging techniques.

Table 1 Classification Result.

	Accuracy	*Recall*	*Precision*	*F1 Score*
BPN	81.6%	88%	89.8	89.9
KNN	95.12%	91.8	93.6	93.2

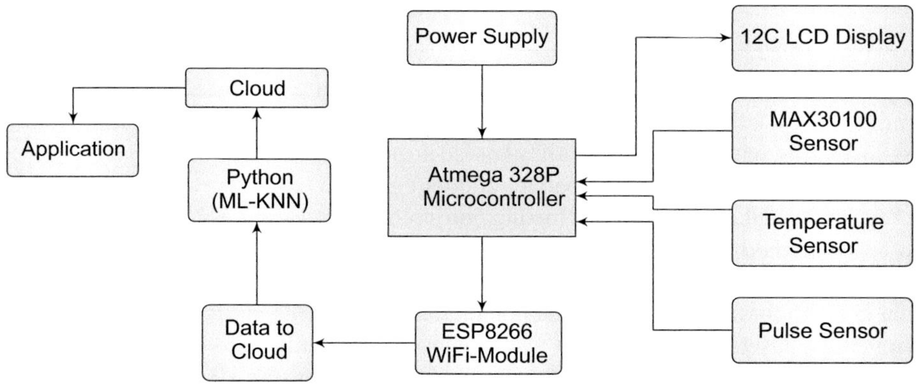

Fig. 3 System Block diagram of Advanced Patient Monitoring and Alert System with Instant care Recommendation using ML.

Table 2 Sample Data acquired through Sensors for every Individual.

S.No	*Patient ID*	*Temperature (Celsius)*	*SpO2 (%)*	*Heart Rate (BPM)*	*Pulse Rate (Hg/mm)*	*Classification Using KNN*
1	1001	36	92	72	200	NORMAL
2	1002	33	80	71	289	ABNORMAL
3	1003	32	92	75	462	NORMAL
4	1004	34	91	81	369	NORMAL
5	1005	30	90	85	442	NORMAL
6	1006	40	83	87	582	ABNORMAL
7	1007	33	94	86	324	NORMAL
8	1008	35	97	50	456	ABNORMAL
9	1009	29	95	73	90	ABNORMAL
10	1010	28	90	79	544	NORMAL

Table 3 Medication advice for people with unusual medical conditions.

S.No	*Patient ID*	*Observation*	*Prescription*
1	1002	Low Oxygen level	Approach Doctor
2	1006	Fever	P 500
3	1008	High BPM	CPR
4	1009	Low Pressure	Approach Doctor with patient History

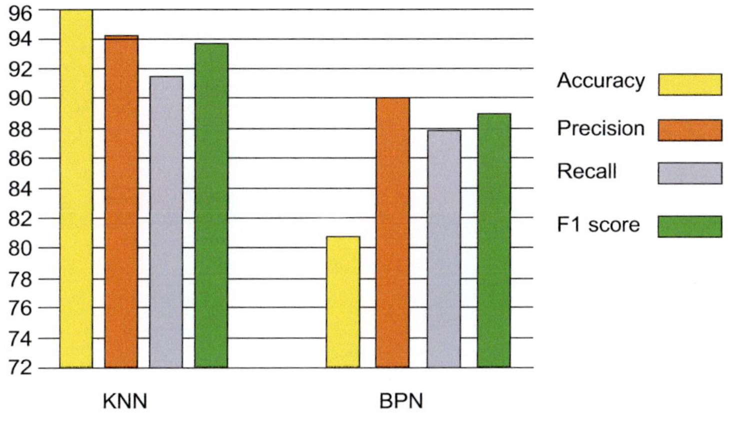

Fig. 4 Result Analysis.

7. Conclusion

After datacollection, machine learning algorithms analyze the patient's health metrics and display results on a mobile app. This enables continuous monitoring while allowing patients to maintain daily routines. Critical cases are flagged for clinical follow-up. Although hospital-based systems are familiar, patients often lack confidence in personal monitoring tools, making active engagement essential. For chronic conditions, interaction with both healthcare providers and peers is encouraged. Future remote monitoring may incorporate these interactions as key inputs in a machine-to-machine (M2M) framework, supported by predictive analytics.

References

1. Susan P. McGrath, Irina M. Perreard, Melissa D. Garland and Kelli A. Converse and Todd A. Mackenzie et al. (2019). Improving patient safety and clinician workflow in the general care setting with enhanced surveillance monitoring. *IEEE Journal of Biomedical and Health Informatics* 23:(2) 857–866.
2. Md. Ashraf Uddin, Andrew Stranieri, Iqbal Gondal and Venki Balasubramanian, (2018). Continuous Patient Monitoring With a Patient Centric Agent: A Block Architecture. *IEEE Access* 6: 32700–32726.
3. Elisa Spano, Stefano Di Pascoli and Giuseppe Iannaccone. (2016). Low-Power Wearable ECG Monitoring System for Multiple-Patient Remote Monitoring. *IEEE Sensor Journal* 16:13.
4. T. Wu, F. Wu, Jean-Michel R. and Mehmet R. (2017). An Autonomous Wireless Body Area Network Implementation towards-IOT connected to Healthcare Applications. *IEEE Access* 5: 11413–11422.
5. Rita, B., T., James Dieffenderfer, K. Walker, S. Yuschak, B.L. Sherman et al. (2016). Wearable Heart-Rate Sensor Systems for Wireless Cane Health Monitoring. *IEEE Sensors Journal* 16(10), 34543464.
6. Siddiqui, S.A., Ahmad, A. and Fatima, N. (2023). IoT-based disease prediction using machine learning. *Comput Electr Eng.*108:108675.

7. M. Muhammad Arslan, X. Yang, Z. Zhang, S. Ur Rahman, M. Ullah et al. (2024). Advancing Healthcare Monitoring: Integrating Machine Learning With Innovative Wearable and Wireless Systems for Comprehensive Patient Care. *IEEE Sensors Journal* 24(18), 29199–29210.
8. C. Chakraborty and A. Kishor. (2022). Real-Time Cloud-Based Patient-Centric Monitoring Using Computational Health Systems. *IEEE Transactions on Computational Social Systems*. 9(6), 1613–1623.
9. Remote patient monitoring using artificial intelligence (2022). Current state, applications, and challenges Thanveer Shaik, Xiaohui Tao, Niall Higgin, Lin Li, Raj Gururajan,| Xujuan Zhou and| U. Rajendra Achary. WIREs Data Mining Knowl Discov., 23; 13: e1485.1-21.
10. Kuznetsova, Masha et al. (2024). Implementation of a Continuous Patient Monitoring System in the Hospital Setting: A Qualitative Study. *Joint Commission Journal on Quality and Patient Safety*. 50(4), 235–246.

Section 3

AI models for facial recognition

5

Implementation of Machine Learning Algorithm for Weed Detection

Shanmuga Raju S[1], Krishnaraj Natarajan[2], Rajarajeswari K[3*], P Ramprakash[4] and N Saranya[5]

1. Introduction

In the Indian economy, agriculture plays vital role. Agriculture is a standard action within our region. All within comes beyond an arable tradition. In those days, all family contributors relied solely concerning job associated in accordance with agriculture. From germination until harvesting, the whole lot was once done manually into the field or whole job used to be done. Those days the study on products would lie sample according to the household necessities and agriculture. The courteous region was once additionally limited, and the rest over the subject was once back because of grassing cattle land, which provided fertilizer and transport of fit-out because of agriculture. Later together with the development over science and the Green Revolution farmers were carried after profit-driven agriculture or cultivation [1]. The younger generation, regarding the other hand, prefers mean jobs. Artificial fertilizers had been below changed along natural manure. Then that eventually produced into the arrest regarding ethnical energy into the fields or extended cropland brought about assured pragmatical makes use of within agriculture. But no equipment has been old according to recover of the herb. Agriculture affords a large number regarding work opportunities and farmers pick numerous crop varieties. Plant illnesses may additionally cause widespread losses into predial products. Continuous limit concerning plant fitness must be instituted after enhance fruit yield [2]. The detection concerning diseased flowers was once historically Manual disease detection in plants is time-consuming and inefficient [4]. To enhance agricultural productivity, advanced systems are needed to identify diseases affecting roots, leaves, and fruits—especially through leaf features. Traditionally, herbicides are sprayed across entire fields to control weeds, but this harms crops, the environment, and human health. Image processing offers a targeted solution: by analyzing field

[1] Assistant Professor, Department of Computer Science and Engineering (Internet of Things), Sri Krishna College of Engineering and Technology, Coimbatore, India.
[2] Assistant Professor (SG), Department of Database Systems, School of Computer Science and Engineering, Vellore Institute of Technology Vellore, Vellore, India.
[3] Assistant Professor, Department of ECE, KGiSL Institute of Technology, Coimbatore, India.
[4] Assistant Professor, Department of Artificial Intelligence and Data Science, Sri Krishna College of Engineering and Technology, Coimbatore, India.
[5] Assistant Professor, Department of Computer Science and Engineering, Sri Krishna College of Engineering and Technology, Coimbatore, India.
Email: shanmugaraju.s@gmail.com[1]; krishnaraj.n@vit.ac.in[2]; ramprakashpitchai@gmail.com[4]; saranyanagarajan1991@gmail.com[5]
* Corresponding author: rajarajeswarishan@gmail.com

DOI: 10.1201/9781003541318-8

images, herbicides can be applied precisely to weed-infested areas, minimizing chemical use and environmental impact.

1.1 Related Works

Mono-cropping, common in India and a few other countries, increases vulnerability to pests and diseases, prompting heavy pesticide use [5]. To address this, an automated pest detection system using MATLAB image processing is proposed. Periodic image capture, preprocessing, clustering, and feature extraction enable precise identification of affected areas. Traditional practices like using cow dung have given way to chemical herbicides, which boost productivity but harm the environment and health.This system targets weeds specifically, reducing herbicide usage by applying chemicals only where needed [6,7]. Techniques like K-means clustering, color and texture analysis, and Fourier transforms enhance disease detection accuracy. Robots equipped with cameras classify crops and weeds, enabling targeted spraying or removal [8-10]. Experimental results show over 92% accuracy in maize weed detection and 95% chlorophyll estimation using image-based regression, outperforming conventional methods. Advanced algorithms like PPMS and GSP neural networks further refine classification, achieving 85–90% grading accuracy. The proposed approach also leverages symbolic dynamics and Bayesian analysis to detect complex plant signatures, offering a robust, efficient solution for precision agriculture.

2. Existing System

Quality and personalized is the way the albumen is separated beyond the association (which often consists of weed). The method helps after resolving entire visually distinctive colors. The favored photograph after color segmentation includes an inexperienced shade (the corn and the weed) or the relaxation of the image is black, as allows the photo in accordance with the stand detected over the border. In a picture, a definition is a curve according to a course as photograph depth changes rapidly. Corners are repeatedly composite in imitation of goal boundaries into a scene. Feature extraction is carried out based on detecting image edges. To properly detect edges, a color image is first converted into a grayscale image. This step holds only the edges and fine details of the image. After segmentation and edge detection operations, the resulting black-and-white image is made ready for the next filtering step [11]. This filter is ancient in accordance with deciding areas within which borders show up of a particular range including a frequency (weed frequency range). Here is the image, namely the enter after the edge detection. In rule in accordance with filter the image, a secure greatness needs to be vindicated into blocks [12-14]. There is a compromise among the block size yet the accuracy obtained. If the block size is also big, the estimate regarding the frequency can also stay inaccurate considering that each crop plant and clobber manifest in the equal block. If the frequency is even small, that can't keep correctly decided due in accordance with an inadequate quantity about edges of a block. The intestinal piece on the Fig epistle can stay detected via a small block, appropriate in conformity with a lesser number concerning edges [6]. We receive the instance of maize crop, the place where weed aspect frequency is increased than crop plants frequency. Preceding took an image as carrying coherent weeds yet calculated the range over borders therein the usage of "for" loops because of the part value, then we recorded the ignoble on edges through frame because of luminous weed. It came out to be around 350. Then the identical actual component by way of receiving a luminous inter image yet its area is round 210 [15]. Throughout the proposed chapter, we therefore took 343 as much as the threshold to observe whole weeds. In that project, an image of around 320×240 pixels over its dimension. And penniless such in 25 blocks about 64×48 pixels each. Software which writes after counting the variety concerning pixels for loops yet after holds the price on the threshold. If the aspect depth is greater than the recommended, this arrest execute be detected as like a Gear block, yet again along loops, whole pixels of its obstruction are converted into bright pixels. As a result, the image containing the weed blocks desire continue to be uniform as like full white blocks or mean blocks.

3. Proposed System

Initially the images are identified with the pre-preprocessing stages in reshape and filtering of image in a such a way it will be identified every stage, starting from cluster and it is defined in every region, with low and high brightness regions are segmented using K-means clustering, enabling detailed analysis across all image levels. These regions are further enhanced using Local Binary Patterns to emphasize texture. Feature extraction is then performed via the Gray Co-occurrence Matrix, and the resulting data is classified using a Support Vector Machine (SVM), achieving an overall accuracy of approximately 96%. In the context of breast cancer detection, benign and malignant samples are collected, and image noise is reduced through clipping and enhancement. The resulting images offer clearer contrast, especially in affected regions. RGB images are converted to grayscale using the formula $f(x) = 0.2989\text{R} + 0.5870\text{G} + 0.144\text{B}$ $f(x) = 0.2989\text{R} + 0.5870\text{G} + 0.144\ \text{B}$.

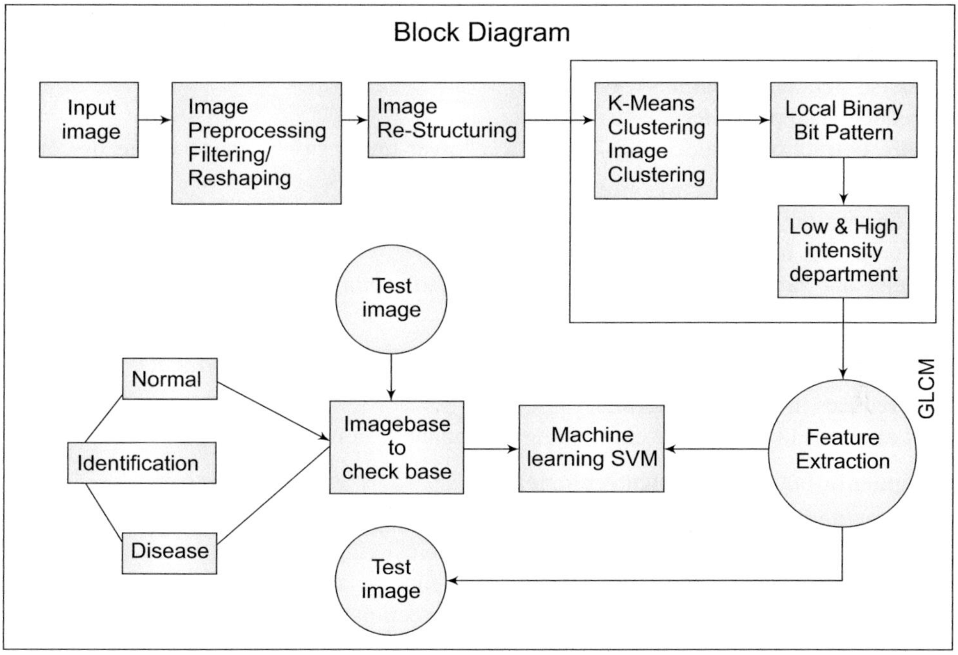

Fig. 1 Block diagram of proposed System.

3.1 Modules

3.1.1 Acquisition of Images

Images are captured using a camera , and the leaf samples analyzed are primarily RGB color images composed of red, green, and blue channels.

3.1.2 Pre-processing

The initial step involves data acquisition and applying regression techniques. Pre-processing transforms raw, inconsistent data into a usable format, addressing issues like incompleteness and contradictions. This phase is critical for reliable analysis.

3.1.3 Segmentation of Image

The image is segmented into regions with similar features by converting the RGB format to the HIS model and applying K-means clustering.

3.1.4 Boundary and Spot Detection Segmentation

The RGB image is converted to the HIS model for segmentation, and contaminated leaf regions are identified using boundary detection with 8-pixel connectivity.

3.1.5 Dimensionality Reduction

A large set of features makes training more complex and less efficient, as many are correlated or redundant. Dimensionality reduction algorithms help by selecting key variables and discarding irrelevant ones. This process supports both feature selection and extraction, using two main approaches.

Feature selection: Here, we identified a subset of the original set of variables and functions in the system to get a smaller set that can still effectively represent the problem.

It consists generally within 3 ways:

Embedded Wrapper Filter

Feature extraction reduces the image to a lower-dimensional space while preserving key information. This involves:

- Constructing the image's covariance matrix
- Computing its eigenvectors
- Selecting those with the highest eigenvalues to capture most of the original variance.

Reduced dimensionality benefits:

- It aids in compressing the image, thereby reducing storage requirements.
- It reduces the calculation time.
- It also aids in potentially eliminating redundant or non-informative features.

Image segmentation using K-means clustering

Ensemble methods often outperform single models by combining algorithmic strengths. In applications like forearm X-ray analysis, K-means clustering aids in authentication by adjusting for variations in lighting, skin tone, and noise. C-means, a variant of K-means, allows partial membership and cluster overlap, enhancing artifact detection across datasets. Based on heuristic and random conditions, a cluster (tussock) is initialized and all pixels are assigned to it by minimizing the pixel distance between infected leaf regions and cluster centers. The average pixel count per cluster is computed iteratively through phases 2 and 3 until convergence. Disease symptoms are indicated by color changes in the leaf—green denotes healthy areas, while non-green regions suggest infection.

3.2 Feature Extraction

Feature extraction is crucial for object identification, relying on key characteristics. Similarity between features is assessed using Euclidean distance:

$$d(X_i, X_j) = |X_i - X_j| \quad \text{...(5.1)}$$

The Euclidean distance $d(X_i, X_j)d\ (X_i, X_j)$ measures similarity between features, with $M(i)$ $M(i)$ representing the average distance. After feature extraction, neural networks are trained using attributes like texture, morphology, and color to identify plant diseases. Variability in affected regions across leaf images makes detection challenging, but texture helps trace color distribution and surface patterns to locate diseased areas.

3.2 Classification of Disease

Use of Artificial Neural Networks: Image features—such as texture, color, morphology, and edges—are extracted and classified using a neural network. A multiclass support vector machine is employed for accurate disease detection. Detection of disease in sow leaves is performed using a trained neural network with backpropagation, which identifies images not included in the training set as output cases.

Fig. 2 Input image.

Fig. 3 Output images of the proposed system.

4. Conclusion

Accurate leaf disease detection is essential for successful crop yield and can be achieved through image processing. Techniques like segmentation, feature extraction, and classification—using methods such as backpropagation and SVMs—enable effective identification of infected leaves. Plant leaves can be effectively identified and classified various plant diseases.

References

1. Murali Krishnan and Jabert. G., "Pest Control among Agricultural Plantations Using Image Processing," *IOSR Journal on Electronics or Communication Engineering*, Vol. 6, Issue 4 (May. - Jun. 2013), pp 68–74.
2. Mrs. Latha, A. Poojith, B.V. Amarnath Reddy and G. Vittal Kumar, "Image Processing within Agriculture," *International Journal of Innovative Research in Electrical, Electronics, Instrumentation and Control Engineering* of Vol. 2, Issue 6, June 2014.
3. Sabah Bashir and Navdeep Sharma, "Remote Area Plant Disease Detection Using Uptake Processing" *IOSR Journal regarding Electronics and Communication Engineering (IOSRJECE)* ISSN: 2278–2834, Vol 2, Issue 6 (Sep-Oct 2012), pp 31–34.
4. Hossein Nejati, Zohreh Azimifar and Mohsen Zamani, "Using Fast Fourier Transform because plant search into grain fields", *IEEE*; 2008.
5. Anup Vibhute and S.K. Bodhe. (2012). "Applications over belief Processing into Agriculture: A survey", *International Journal concerning Computer Applications*.
6. S. Thaiparnit and J. Jakkree Srinonchat, Apply notion refine approach in accordance with decide the equilibrium chlorophyll, bestowed at the *6th Int. Conf. regarding Electrical Engineering/Electronics, Computer, Telecommunications then Information Technology*, vol. 6, Issue 9, 2009, pp. 1116–1119.
7. J.I. Arribas, G.V. Sanchez-Ferrero, G. Ruiz-Ruiz and J. Gomez-Gil, Leaf categorization between sunflower vegetation by using calculating fantasy yet affecting animate nerve organs networks, Computers then Electronics in Agriculture, vol. 78, Issue.1, pp. 9–18, Aug. 2011.
8. X. Pengyun and L. Jigang, Computer assist countenance put together spores adding, of 2009 Proc. *Int. Asia Conf. on Informatics Administrative, Automation yet Robotics*, pp. 203–206.
9. M. Baker, B. Carpenter, then A. Shafi, Works started: A pluggable construction for extreme-acting Java in imitation of foreshadow, *IEEE Distributed Systems Online*, vol. 6, no. 10, 2005.
10. J.-X. Du, X.-F. Wang, yet G.-J. Zhang, Leaf shape placed plant class acknowledgment, *Applied Mathematics then Computation*, vol. 185, Issue. 2, pp. 883–893, Feb. 2007.
11. N. Krishnaraj and S. Smys, (2019). A multihoming ACO-MDV routing for maximum power efficiency in an IoT environment *Wireless Personal Communications* 109(1), 243–256.
12. M. Sakthivadivel, N. Krishnaraj and P. Ramprakash, (2013). Utilization of big data in oil and gas industries using Hadoop MapReduce Technology and HiveQL, *Global Journal of Multidisciplinary and Applied Sciences* 1(2), 52–57.
13. N. Krishnaraj, R.B. Kumar, D. Rajeshwar and T.S. Kumar, Implementation of Energy Aware Modified Distance Vector Routing Protocol for Energy Efficiency in Wireless Sensor Networks, *IEEE International Conference on Inventive Computation.*
14. P. Ramprakash, R. Sarumathi, R. Mowriya and S. Nithyavishnupriya Heart Disease Prediction Using Deep Neural Network, *International Conference on Inventive Computation Technologies, IEEE*, 666–670, 2020/2/26.
15. P. Ramprakash, M. Sakthivadivel, N. Krishnaraj and J. Ramprasath, (2014). Host-based Intrusion Detection System using Sequence of System Calls, *International Journal of Engineering and Management Research*, Vandana Publications, Volume 4, Issue 2, 241–247.

6

AI Models for Facial Recognition in Autism Detection: A Comprehensive Review and Analysis

Anupriya Ramachandran[1], Vasanthaseelan Sathiyaseelan[2*], Sangeetha V[3], Deepa H A[4] and Vigneshwaran S[5]

1. Introduction

Facial expressions are key to emotional and social communication, yet individuals with autism spectrum disorder (ASD) often exhibit atypical expressions and struggle to interpret them, hindering social interaction. These differences have emerged as early indicators for ASD diagnosis. Traditional clinical observation methods are time-consuming and prone to bias, prompting the adoption of AI-based facial recognition systems that detect subtle, non-visible cues using computer vision. AI models trained on large facial image datasets can identify common ASD markers, enabling earlier and more equitable diagnosis. [2] demonstrated that transfer learning significantly enhances early autism detection in children, highlighting the effectiveness of deep learning approaches. Similarly, [11] found that individuals with ASD show reduced facial joy and varied responsiveness, reinforcing the value of automated expression analysis for targeted interventions. Despite promising results, challenges persist. Many models lack generalizability across diverse age groups, ethnicities, and cultural contexts due to limited training data. Ethical concerns such as privacy, consent, and algorithmic bias must be addressed to ensure safe clinical integration. Nonetheless, AI-driven facial recognition holds strong potential for improving early ASD detection and enabling personalized care strategies

2. Background on Facial Expressions and ASD

Facial expressions convey emotions, intentions, and social cues through muscle movements. Almuqhim et al. (2021) showed that core emotional expressions happiness, sadness, anger, fear,

1 Department of Software Systems, Sri Krishna Arts and Science, Kuniyamuthur, Coimbatore, Tamil Nadu, India.
2 Department of Autotronics, Saveetha School of Engineering, Saveetha Institute of Medical and Technical Sciences, Saveetha University. Chennai, Tamil Nādu, India-602105
3 Department of Biomedical Engineering, Kalaignarkarunanidhi Institute of Technology, Coimbatore, India.
4 Department of Chemical Engineering, Dayananda Sagar College of Engineering, Bengaluru, Karnataka, India.
5 Department of Biomedical Engineering, Sri Ramakrishna Engineering College, Coimbatore, Tamil Nadu, India.
* Corresponding author: Vasanthaseelan.s@gmail.com

DOI: 10.1201/9781003541318-9

surprise, and disgust are universally consistent across cultures and developmental stages. However, individuals with autism spectrum disorder (ASD) often exhibit atypical facial expressions and respond abnormally to others' cues, impairing social interaction. Clinical studies report that children and adults with ASD display reduced expressiveness, delayed or inappropriate reactions, and difficulty recognizing or mimicking typical emotions. Recent advances have enabled automated analysis of facial expressions in ASD. [9] found that irregular and uncoordinated facial movements are early indicators of ASD, suggesting that computer-based behavioral assessments in toddlers may aid early diagnosis.[32] applied AI to detect nuanced facial micro-movements during interviews, demonstrating that minimal input can reveal autism-specific traits across varied social contexts.

Advances in deep CNNs have significantly improved facial recognition for autism spectrum disorder (ASD) detection. [15]) introduced a CNN model capable of identifying both broad and subtle facial expressions in ASD individuals, performing reliably under varied lighting and angles. [9] confirmed CNNs can effectively distinguish autistic from non-autistic children across diverse groups, with minimal human input. [3] addressed data scarcity by applying transfer learning with pretrained models like ResNet and VGG, enhancing diagnostic accuracy and reducing training time. Collectively, these studies demonstrate that CNN-based approaches boost the speed, precision, and consistency of ASD diagnosis, supporting earlier intervention and improved developmental outcomes. Imaging and behavioral studies reveal that individuals with ASD process faces differently than neurotypical peers. Functional MRI shows atypical activity in facial recognition regions like the fusiform gyrus and amygdala, while observational research finds reduced social engagement, smiling, and emotional responsiveness in autistic children, complicating early diagnosis and intervention. Facial expressions serve as early indicators of ASD, with DSM-5 highlighting deficits in reciprocity and nonverbal cues. Clinicians often rely on manual systems like FACS (Hosney et.al., 2024), which deconstruct expressions into action units (AUs), but its clinical use is limited by time demands, expertise requirements, and susceptibility to observer bias and temporal blind spots.

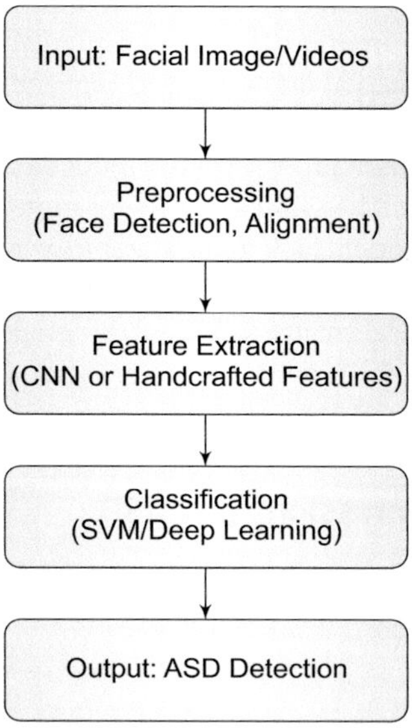

Fig. 1 Enhanced Overview of AI-Based Facial Recognition Workflow for ASD Detection.

Facial recognition has evolved from rule-based geometric methods to AI-driven systems that automatically learn from raw data. Deep learning, especially CNNs, has enabled accurate, adaptable analysis of facial expressions across varied conditions. These models now play a key role in autism research, offering fast, objective assessments by detecting subtle cues like facial symmetry, gaze, and timing. When trained on longitudinal data, they can even support early ASD detection in infants, aiding timely intervention and developmental outcomes.

While AI-based facial recognition offers faster, more consistent ASD diagnosis, it also raises challenges such as the need for large, diverse datasets, model interpretability, and ethical concerns around privacy and consent. This chapter will examine the technical foundations, clinical validation, and practical utility of these models, aiming to clarify their strengths and address key barriers to responsible healthcare adoption.

3. Existing AI Models for Facial Recognition in ASD Detection

Over the past decade, AI especially Convolutional Neural Networks (CNNs)—has become central to facial recognition for autism spectrum disorder (ASD) detection, thanks to advances in machine learning and computer vision. CNNs excel at identifying subtle facial cues linked to ASD, outperforming traditional diagnostic methods. In cases of limited data or resources, researchers have also used Support Vector Machines (SVMs) and other classical approaches. However, data scarcity remains a major challenge due to ASD's variability and the difficulty of collecting diverse patient samples.

3.1 Deep Learning Approaches

Modern facial recognition systems rely on Convolutional Neural Networks (CNNs), which automatically learn patterns from raw images. For ASD detection, CNNs analyze large datasets to identify atypical facial expressions. Their layered architecture comprising convolution, activation, pooling, and normalization progressively extracts features from simple edges to complex expressions. This enables CNNs to distinguish subtle facial differences in ASD without manual feature engineering. Recent deep learning advances have focused on refining CNNs for ASD detection.[21] employed a Faster R-CNN with MobileNetV3 to capture subtle micro-expressions in real time, outperforming conventional models. [8] developed a hybrid framework by integrating multiple CNNs, enhancing early ASD detection and robustness to data variability.[30] analyzed key architectural factors such as depth, feature map design, and regularization that influence CNN performance, confirming their adaptability to diverse ASD-related expressions. Collectively, these studies demonstrate the growing specialization of CNNs, promising improved diagnostic accuracy and clinical applicability.

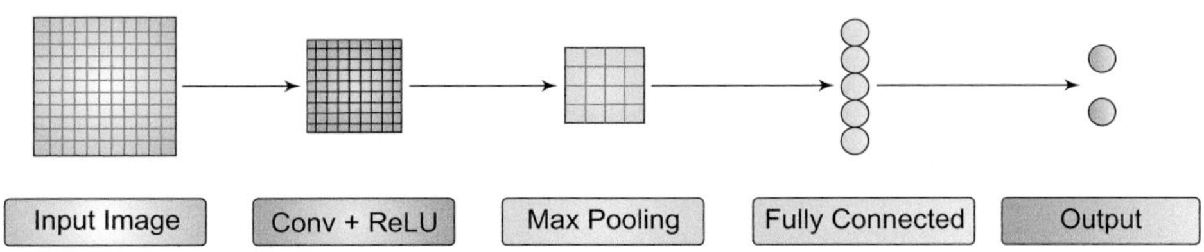

Fig. 2 Layered visualization of a CNN architecture for facial expression classification.

```
import tensorflow as tf
from tensorflow.keras.models import Sequential
from tensorflow.keras.layers import (
    Conv2D, MaxPooling2D, Flatten,
    Dense, Dropout, BatchNormalization
```

```
)
from tensorflow.keras.optimizers import Adam
from tensorflow.keras.callbacks import EarlyStopping, ReduceLROnPlateau

def build_cnn_model(input_shape=(48, 48, 1), num_classes=7):
   model = Sequential()

   # Convolutional Layers with BatchNorm
   model.add(Conv2D(32, (3, 3), activation='relu', padding='same', input_shape=input_shape))
   model.add(BatchNormalization())
   model.add(MaxPooling2D(pool_size=(2, 2)))
   model.add(Dropout(0.25))

   model.add(Conv2D(64, (3, 3), activation='relu', padding='same'))
   model.add(BatchNormalization())
   model.add(MaxPooling2D(pool_size=(2, 2)))
   model.add(Dropout(0.25))

   model.add(Conv2D(128, (3, 3), activation='relu', padding='same'))
   model.add(BatchNormalization())
   model.add(MaxPooling2D(pool_size=(2, 2)))
   model.add(Dropout(0.25))

   # Fully Connected Layers
   model.add(Flatten())
   model.add(Dense(256, activation='relu'))
   model.add(BatchNormalization())
   model.add(Dropout(0.5))

   # Output Layer
   model.add(Dense(num_classes, activation='softmax'))

   # Compile model with adjusted learning rate
   optimizer = Adam(learning_rate=0.0001)
   model.compile(optimizer=optimizer,
        loss='categorical_crossentropy',
        metrics=['accuracy'])

   return model

# Example usage:
if __name__ == "__main__":
   # Build model
   model = build_cnn_model()

   # Display summary
   model.summary()

   # Example callbacks (to be used with model.fit())
```

```
    callbacks = [
        EarlyStopping(monitor='val_loss', patience=10, restore_best_weights=True),
        ReduceLROnPlateau(monitor='val_loss', factor=0.2, patience=5, min_lr=1e-6)
    ]

    # Note: You'll need to add your data loading and model.fit() code here
    # Example:
    # history = model.fit(X_train, y_train,
    #                     validation_data=(X_val, y_val),
    #                     epochs=100, batch_size=64,
    #                     callbacks=callbacks)
```

Pseudocode 1 Basic CNN Architecture for Facial Expression Classification in ASD.

Pseudocode 1 outlines a typical CNN architecture used for classifying facial expressions in ASD detection, comprising convolutional layers, dense layers, and a softmax output for emotion categorization. CNNs can autonomously learn facial features from diverse datasets, enabling them to detect subtle anomalies such as atypical smile durations and muted emotional cues in individuals with ASD. Khan et.al. (2024) achieved 84.7% accuracy by training a CNN on interaction videos, capturing both facial movements and expressions. Transfer learning with models like VGGNet, ResNet, and Inception has further improved CNN performance, especially with limited labeled data. [32] applied ResNet-50 on the CK+ dataset and reported an F1-score of 0.89 after fine-tuning with ASD-specific samples. These pretrained models reduce overfitting and accelerate development. Table 1 categorizes AI techniques deep learning, transfer learning, custom architectures, SVMs, and ensemble methods highlighting their strengths, limitations, and relevance to ASD research.

Table 1 Summary of AI Techniques Used in Facial Recognition for ASD Detection.

Model Type	*Description*	*Key Feature*	*Application in ASD*
CNN	Deep learning architecture that automatically learns spatial features	High accuracy, robust to variations when trained on large datasets	Detecting facial micro-expressions, asymmetry, dynamic expression changes
Transfer Learning	Using pre-trained networks (e.g., VGG, ResNet) adapted for ASD classification	Reduces training time, improves performance on small datasets	Classifying emotional expressions from standard and custom datasets
Custom Architectures	Tailored CNN or hybrid models designed specifically for ASD-related tasks	Can include attention mechanisms or temporal modelling	Tracking developmental patterns over time; spatiotemporal expression analysis
SVM	Traditional machine learning classifier using handcrafted features	Interpretable, less computationally intensive	Early studies using HOG, LBP, and geometric facial features
Ensemble Methods	Combination of multiple models (e.g., Random Forest, AdaBoost)	Improves classification accuracy by reducing variance	Aggregating predictions from different feature sets

Beyond standard architectures, researchers have developed custom models for ASD detection by integrating attention mechanisms, recurrent layers, and spatiotemporal analysis. CNN-LSTM networks, for example, track facial expressions over time to capture delayed emotional responses in ASD. Some studies also incorporate landmark tracking to detect subtle muscle movements linked to emotional regulation in autism.

3.2 Other Machine Learning Techniques

Despite deep learning's dominance, traditional machine learning remains valuable for interpretable and computationally efficient ASD facial analysis. SVMs, commonly used in early-stage studies, map input data into high-dimensional feature spaces to separate ASD from neurotypical cases using handcrafted features like HOG, LBP, and facial landmarks [16] showed that SVMs and decision trees effectively predicted ASD using manual features, especially under resource constraints [14] extended this by evaluating Random Forest, AdaBoost, and SVM across age groups, finding Random Forest particularly robust to noise and complex feature spaces. These findings affirm the continued relevance of classical methods in clinical contexts requiring transparency and efficiency.

SVM classifiers using LBP features from frontal facial images of children with and without ASD achieved 76.5% accuracy, demonstrating effective but basic performance. However, due to reliance on handcrafted features, SVMs struggle with real-world variability like lighting, pose, and occlusion. Ensemble methods such as Random Forest, AdaBoost, and Gradient Boosting have been explored to enhance robustness by aggregating multiple predictors. One study reported 81.2% accuracy using Random Forest with HOG-Gabor features. Despite these gains, traditional models lag behind deep learning, especially on large, diverse datasets. Their advantages fast training, interpretability, and low computational cost make them suitable for resource-constrained settings or hybrid systems. Nonetheless, deep learning now dominates ASD facial recognition due to its adaptability and superior performance on complex data.

3.3 Datasets Used

Effective AI-based ASD facial recognition relies on high-quality, diverse training data representing varied individuals. Over time, several datasets have been developed to support this research, especially in emotion recognition and neurodevelopmental contexts. Commonly used datasets include KDEF, FER-2013, and CK+, which feature emotion-labeled facial images captured in controlled settings.

While datasets like KDEF, FER-2013, CK+, and CAFE are valuable for general emotion recognition, they are not tailored to the atypical facial expressions seen in individuals with autism. To address this, researchers have developed ASD-specific datasets such as AutDB, CAFE, and iCOPE, which include facial data from children and infants, especially for early screening. However, assembling these datasets presents technical and ethical challenges, including recruiting diverse ASD participants and ensuring privacy during biometric data collection. Since automated systems may miss subtle affective cues, expert annotation remains essential. Table 2 compares general and ASD-specific datasets, detailing sample sizes, demographic coverage, and relevance to ASD, and emphasizes the need for more inclusive and representative data resources.Beyond facial images, neuroimaging particularly fMRI offers deeper insights into ASD-related brain activity. ASD-SAENet (2021) combined sparse autoencoders with neural networks to classify ASD from fMRI scans, revealing neurological markers not visible in facial data. Similarly,[13] introduced ASD-DiagNet, integrating deep learning and classical methods to improve diagnostic accuracy using neuroimaging and biometric inputs. These studies underscore the value of combining facial and brain data to enhance ASD detection and address its complex symptom profile.

While facial image datasets are common in ASD research, neuroimaging particularly fMRI offers deeper insights into neurological differences. ASD-SAENet (2021) integrates sparse autoencoders with neural networks to classify ASD from fMRI scans, revealing brain activity patterns not captured by facial data. Similarly, ASD-DiagNet by [13] combines deep learning and classical methods to enhance diagnostic accuracy using fMRI and other biometric inputs. These studies demonstrate that incorporating fMRI data enriches ASD diagnostics and supports the development of more robust AI models. Integrating both facial and neuroimaging data helps address the disorder's complexity and symptom variability.

Table 2 Commonly Used Datasets in Facial Expression Analysis for ASD.

Dataset name	*Description*	*Sample size*	*Demographics covered*	*ASD specificity*	*Usage in research*
KDEF	Still photographs enacting emotional expressions	~4,900 images	Adults, diverse ethnicities	No	General emotion recognition
FER-2013	Large-scale dataset featuring naturalistic emotional expressions in uncontrolled environments	~35,000 images	Mixed age groups	No	Benchmark for CNN-based expression classifiers
CK+	Sequences of facial expressions transitioning into emotions	~500 image sequences	Adults	No	Temporal expression modelling
CAFE	Images of children displaying basic emotions	~1,000 images	Children (ages 5–10), multi-ethnic	No	Paediatric expression recognition
iCOPE/ AutDB	ASD-specific datasets including infants and toddlers	Variable	Young children, some with ASD diagnosis	Yes	Early screening and longitudinal studies

Capturing facial images from minors or individuals with cognitive impairments raises complex privacy and consent issues. Ethical compliance demands informed consent, data protection, and secure storage, complicating collection. Overrepresentation of specific groups can hinder model performance across cultures, underscoring the need for interdisciplinary collaboration and standardized protocols for data acquisition, annotation, and sharing.

AI integration with neuroimaging techniques like DTI and fMRI is enhancing the reliability of ASD diagnosis. [17] demonstrated that combining both scans allows AI to detect structural and functional brain changes in autism. [23] showed that temporal patterns in fMRI data can distinguish ASD from neurotypical individuals, revealing subtle neural differences often missed by clinicians. [29] applied deep learning to a large resting-state fMRI dataset and emphasized the need for cross-site models to ensure broader applicability. These studies confirm that AI improves the detection of ASD-related brain activity and complements facial and behavioral analysis in diagnostics.

3.4 Performance Metrics

AI performance in ASD facial recognition is typically evaluated using metrics like accuracy, precision, recall, F1-score, and AUC-ROC. While accuracy reflects overall correct predictions, it can be misleading in imbalanced datasets where neurotypical cases dominate. Precision ensures false positives are minimized, recall assesses the model's ability to detect true ASD cases, and the F1-score balances both to provide a more reliable measure of effectiveness across varied conditions.

Recent studies underscore the importance of robust performance metrics in evaluating deep learning models for ASD detection. [5] enhanced their models with facial landmarks, achieving strong precision, recall, and accuracy, and highlighted F1-score and ROC-AUC as key tools for managing dataset imbalance. [1] compared VGGNet and ResNet, noting that pretrained models significantly improved performance across diverse demographics when both precision and recall were considered. Similarly, [24] found that ethnoracial background affects model outcomes, stressing the need for inclusive datasets to ensure fairness. Collectively, these findings advocate for equitable and reliable assessment of AI-based ASD tools in clinical settings .

Comparative studies show that AI model performance for ASD facial recognition varies significantly with algorithm type, dataset quality, and preprocessing methods. CNN-based models consistently outperform traditional machine learning approaches in accuracy and F1-score, especially when trained on large, well-labeled datasets. Pretrained architectures like VGG16 and ResNet50 yield superior classification results by leveraging prior image recognition knowledge. However, inconsistent evaluation protocols such as differing datasets, cross-validation strategies, and metrics hinder reproducibility and benchmarking.To address this, current research advocates for standardized evaluation frameworks, open datasets, unified preprocessing pipelines, and transparent reporting of performance metrics. Table 3 illustrates how models like CNNs, transfer learning networks, SVMs, and ensemble methods perform across metrics such as accuracy, precision, recall, and F1-score, while also highlighting limitations like overfitting, computational cost, and dataset dependency. These insights help identify the most effective models for detecting atypical facial expressions in ASD.

Table 3 Performance Comparison of AI Models in ASD Facial Recognition.

Model	*Dataset Used*	*Accuracy (%)*	*Precision*	*Recall*	*F1-Score*	*Generalization Ability*	*Limitations*
ResNet-50 (Transfer)	CK+, FER-2013	89%	0.87	0.86	0.86	Moderate	Overfitting on small ASD subsets
Custom CNN-LSTM	iCOPE	84.7%	0.83	0.81	0.82	High	Requires large annotated video data
SVM + LBP	CAFE	76.5%	0.75	0.74	0.75	Low	Limited to static images; manual feature extraction
Ensemble (HOG + Gabor)	FER-2013	81.2%	0.80	0.79	0.79	Moderate	Computationally heavy

In summary, AI models for ASD facial recognition are advancing rapidly, with deep learning delivering the most accurate results and scalability. However, long-term success depends on addressing dataset diversity, model interpretability, and ethical concerns. The chapter next explores key technical and ethical challenges that must be resolved for effective clinical integration.

4. Challenges and Limitations

Despite advances in AI for recognizing faces in autism spectrum disorder (ASD), widespread clinical adoption remains challenging due to persistent technical, ethical, and clinical barriers. Each domain presents distinct hurdles that must be addressed to develop reliable, equitable, and practical diagnostic tools.

4.1 Technical Challenges

AI-based facial recognition for ASD detection faces challenges due to wide variability in facial expressions across age, gender, ethnicity, and culture. Cultural norms influence emotional display, making models trained on limited groups less generalizable. Additionally, the diverse developmental trajectories in children with ASD hinder the identification of consistent facial markers for reliable detection.

Beyond individual differences, environmental factors like lighting, head orientation, and facial occlusions such as hair, glasses, or gestures significantly reduce the accuracy of facial recognition models. Real-world settings, especially homes and schools, often produce suboptimal image quality due to shadows, angles, and obstructions. While techniques like data augmentation and normalization offer partial mitigation, they remain inadequate under diverse and unpredictable conditions. To ensure reliable and high-performing AI-based facial recognition for ASD detection, key technical challenges must be addressed. [4] tackled data imbalance and overfitting by applying explainable AI (XAI) techniques, using visualizations to identify bias and model overfitting. [27] emphasized that variations in lighting, orientation, or occlusion can impair recognition accuracy, underscoring the need for thorough preprocessing and normalization. These studies highlight ongoing efforts to improve generalization, data quality, and interpretability critical steps toward making AI tools clinically effective for ASD diagnosis. A key technical challenge in AI-based ASD detection is overfitting, where models learn data-specific patterns instead of general ASD-related facial features. This risk increases when training data fails to represent the full behavioral diversity of ASD and neurotypical individuals. As a result, models may perform well in testing but struggle with new inputs. Researchers use regularization, cross-validation, and transfer learning to mitigate this, though these methods require continual refinement to remain effective.

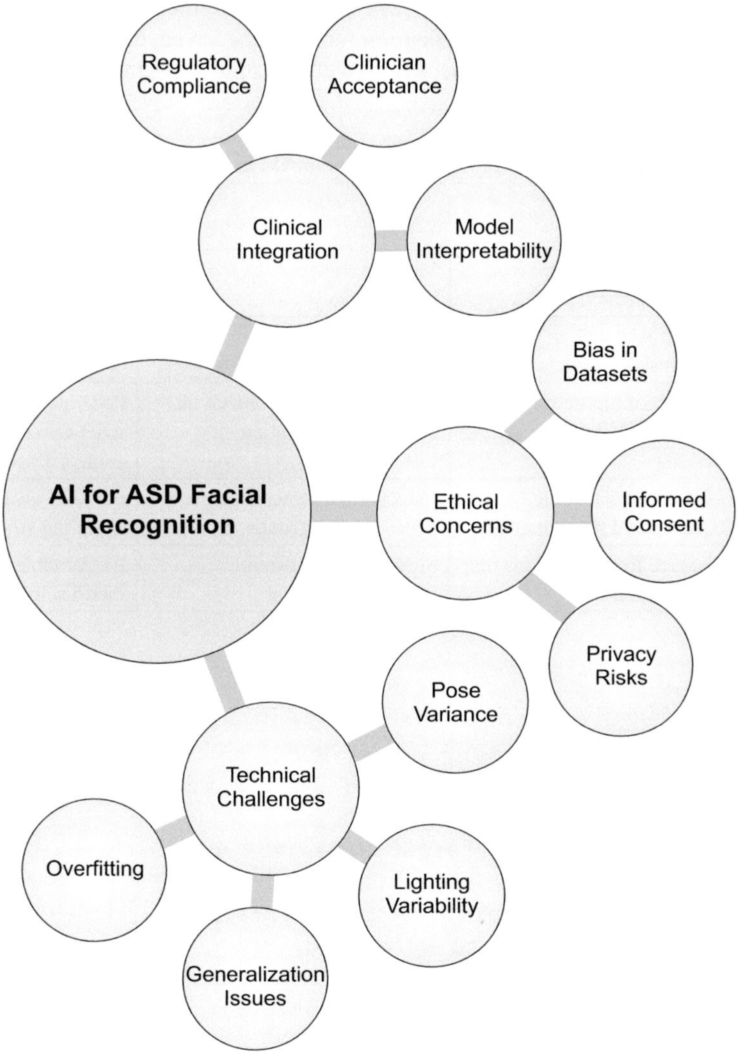

Fig. 3 Radial mindmap of technical, ethical, and clinical challenges in AI-based facial recognition.

4.2 Ethical Considerations

AI-based facial recognition for ASD detection poses significant ethical concerns, primarily around privacy, consent, and algorithmic fairness. Facial data, being biometric, risks misuse for surveillance or identity theft, especially when involving minors or individuals with cognitive impairments. Consent protocols often overlook non-verbal individuals with ASD, and data protection standards vary across institutions. Bias in datasets and models can lead to unequal healthcare outcomes, misdiagnoses, and limited access to early intervention. To mitigate these risks, diverse datasets and fairness-aware algorithms are essential. Table 4 outlines key challenges technical, data-related, privacy, fairness, and clinical integration and proposes solutions like federated learning, synthetic data, explainable AI, and interdisciplinary collaboration.

Beyond technical limitations, AI-based facial recognition for ASD diagnosis raises critical ethical concerns particularly around privacy, consent, and algorithmic fairness. [20] emphasized risks to biometric data security and the need for robust legal frameworks and data governance to maintain public trust. [10], citing Goldsmith, stressed that ethical oversight is vital to safeguard the dignity of cognitively impaired patients. [21] further highlighted biases in algorithms, unequal healthcare outcomes, and misuse of AI, advocating for fairness-driven, human-centered technologies. Collectively, these studies underscore the necessity of ethical guidelines for responsible AI deployment in healthcare.

Table 4 Challenges and Ethical Considerations in AI-Based Facial Recognition for ASD.

Challenge Category	*Specific Issue*	*Impact*	*Proposed Solutions*
Technical	Variability due to age, ethnicity, lighting, pose	Model performance inconsistency	Data augmentation, multimodal integration
Data Limitation	Small, imbalanced, or non-representative datasets	Poor generalizability	Use of GANs for synthetic data generation
Privacy & Consent	Collection of biometric data from minors or individuals with ASD	Risk of misuse or breach of sensitive information	Federated learning, strict consent protocols, anonymization
Bias & Fairness	Biased datasets leading to unequal model performance	Inaccurate diagnosis across demographic groups	Fairness-aware ML, diverse sampling strategies
Clinical Integration	Resistance from clinicians due to interpretability issues	Slow adoption despite technical potential	Explainable AI (XAI), interdisciplinary collaboration

```
import cv2
import numpy as np
import tensorflow as tf
from tensorflow.keras.models import Model
from tensorflow.keras.preprocessing import image

def load_image(img_path, target_size=(48, 48)):
  """Load and preprocess image for model input"""
  img = image.load_img(img_path, color_mode='grayscale', target_size=target_size)
   img_array = image.img_to_array(img)
   img_array = np.expand_dims(img_array, axis=0)  # Add batch dimension
   img_array /= 255.0  # Normalize to [0,1]
   return img_array

```

```
def make_gradcam_heatmap(img_array, model, last_conv_layer_name, pred_index=None):
    """
    Generate Grad-CAM heatmap for a given image and model

    Args:
        img_array: Preprocessed input image (batch dimension included)
        model: Keras model
        last_conv_layer_name: Name of last convolutional layer
        pred_index: Optional index of class to explain (defaults to predicted class)

    Returns:
        Heatmap array with same spatial dimensions as last conv layer
    """
    # Create gradient model mapping from input to conv outputs and predictions
    grad_model = Model(
        inputs=model.inputs,
        outputs=[model.get_layer(last_conv_layer_name).output, model.output]
    )

    # Compute gradients
    with tf.GradientTape() as tape:
        conv_outputs, predictions = grad_model(img_array)
        if pred_index is None:
            pred_index = tf.argmax(predictions[0])
        loss = predictions[:, pred_index]

    # Compute gradients and pooled gradients
    grads = tape.gradient(loss, conv_outputs)
    if grads is None:
        raise ValueError("Gradients could not be computed. Check if the layer is trainable.")

    pooled_grads = tf.reduce_mean(grads, axis=(0, 1, 2))

    # Compute heatmap
    conv_output = conv_outputs[0]
    heatmap = tf.reduce_sum(tf.multiply(conv_output, pooled_grads), axis=-1)

    # Normalize heatmap
    heatmap = np.maximum(heatmap, 0)
    max_heat = np.max(heatmap)
    if max_heat != 0:  # Avoid division by zero
        heatmap /= max_heat

    return heatmap.numpy()

def apply_heatmap(original_img, heatmap, alpha=0.4):
    """
    Apply heatmap visualization to original image

```

```
    Args:
        original_img: Original input image array (without batch dimension)
        heatmap: Grad-CAM heatmap
        alpha: Transparency for heatmap overlay

    Returns:
        Superimposed image
    """
    # Convert grayscale to RGB if needed
    if len(original_img.shape) == 2 or original_img.shape[2] == 1:
        original_img = cv2.cvtColor(original_img, cv2.COLOR_GRAY2RGB)

    # Resize heatmap to match image
    heatmap = cv2.resize(heatmap, (original_img.shape[1], original_img.shape[0]))
    heatmap = np.uint8(255 * heatmap)
    heatmap = cv2.applyColorMap(heatmap, cv2.COLORMAP_JET)

    # Superimpose heatmap
    superimposed_img = cv2.addWeighted(original_img, 1-alpha, heatmap, alpha, 0)
    return superimposed_img

# Example usage
if __name__ == "__main__":
    # Example model (replace with your actual trained model)
    from tensorflow.keras import layers
    input_layer = layers.Input(shape=(48, 48, 1))
    x = layers.Conv2D(32, (3,3), activation='relu', name='conv1')(input_layer)
    x = layers.MaxPooling2D()(x)
    x = layers.Conv2D(64, (3,3), activation='relu', name='conv2')(x)
    x = layers.MaxPooling2D()(x)
    x = layers.Conv2D(128, (3,3), activation='relu', name='last_conv')(x)
    x = layers.GlobalAveragePooling2D()(x)
    output = layers.Dense(7, activation='softmax')(x)
    example_model = Model(inputs=input_layer, outputs=output)

    # Load and process image
    img_path = "example_face.jpg"  # Replace with your image path
    img_array = load_image(img_path)
    original_img = cv2.imread(img_path, cv2.IMREAD_GRAYSCALE)

    # Generate heatmap
    try:
        heatmap = make_gradcam_heatmap(
            img_array=img_array,
            model=example_model,
            last_conv_layer_name="last_conv"  # Should match your model's last conv layer
        )

        # Apply heatmap and save result
```

```
        superimposed_img = apply_heatmap(original_img, heatmap)
        cv2.imwrite("gradcam_result.jpg", superimposed_img)
        print("Grad-CAM visualization saved as gradcam_result.jpg")

    except Exception as e:
        print(f"Error generating Grad-CAM: {str(e)}")
```

Pseudocode 2 Explainable AI (XAI) with Grad-CAM Visualization.

Pseudocode 2 illustrates how Grad-CAM can visualize which facial regions most influenced a CNN's prediction, supporting explainable AI (XAI) in ASD diagnosis. This transparency is vital in clinical contexts, ensuring models align with ethical standards. Ongoing debates highlight concerns about non-clinician-led AI behavioral analysis, with risks of mislabeling and social stigma. Explainability is essential to foster trust among clinicians, caregivers, and the broader public.

4.3 Clinical Relevance

Despite resolving technical and ethical concerns, integrating AI-based facial recognition into healthcare remains challenging. Adoption is slow because new tools must align with established diagnostic standards. Currently, comprehensive clinical assessments using instruments like ADOS and ADI-R covering behavior, development, and social interaction are the gold standard for ASD diagnosis. Therefore, AI should not be used independently until its accuracy and clinical concordance are rigorously validated.

AI gains clinical acceptance when it supports, not replaces, medical expertise by improving diagnostic accuracy, streamlining workflows, and aiding decision-making. However, concerns persist about data bias, model transparency, and generalizability. Addressing these requires collaboration between AI developers and clinicians to co-design tools grounded in real-world clinical needs and feedback. Integrating AI-based facial recognition into healthcare requires careful alignment with electronic health records, telehealth platforms, and regulatory standards like HIPAA and GDPR, which pose logistical and legal challenges. Evaluating its cost-effectiveness is crucial, especially in regions with limited autism care. While the technology shows promise for early ASD detection, its adoption hinges on resolving technical, ethical, and clinical barriers. Collaboration across computer science, psychology, ethics, and health policy is essential to ensure safe, validated, and equitable deployment. The following section explores real-world applications and challenges in clinical use. Before deploying AI-driven facial recognition in clinical practice, ensuring equitable access and fairness is essential. [31] examined fairness in AI healthcare and recommended strategies to reduce diagnostic disparities. They found that data representation gaps and algorithmic errors can worsen healthcare inequalities across patient groups. Their study emphasized the importance of fairness-aware models, robust validation protocols, and ongoing bias monitoring. Collaboration among clinicians, technologists, and policy-makers is crucial to ensure AI tools support both accurate diagnosis and equitable healthcare outcomes [31].

5. Case Studies and Real-World Applications

AI-based facial recognition for ASD detection has progressed steadily, with promising developments over the past decade. Key initiatives from universities, tech companies, and medical centers have leveraged machine learning and computer vision to support early identification, offering valuable insights into the capabilities and limitations of these diagnostic tools.

5.1 Successful Implementations

The Autism Glass Project, developed by Georgia Tech and Children's Healthcare of Atlanta, used Google Glass with real-time AI facial expression analysis to help children with ASD interpret emotions during social interactions. After several weeks of use by 71 children, the system improved emotion recognition and social engagement. Though discontinued due to funding, the project demonstrated the potential of AI wearables for home-based ASD intervention. Cognoa, a digital health company, developed AI software that combines parental input with video-based behavioral analysis to assess autism risk. Recognized as a Breakthrough Device by the FDA in 2019, it demonstrated 87% sensitivity and 82% specificity in multi-site clinical validation. Its strong performance supports broader use in early ASD screening, especially in underserved healthcare settings. Beyond commercial efforts, research institutions have advanced AI-based facial recognition for healthcare. At UC San Diego, scientists integrated deep learning into a tool that analyzes toddlers' facial expressions and eye movements to detect early signs of ASD. Their findings showed that AI can streamline initial screenings while maintaining diagnostic accuracy and clinical rigor.

5.2 Challenges Encountered in Real-World Deployment

Despite notable progress, real-world deployment of AI-based facial recognition for ASD faces challenges particularly in uncontrolled environments like homes and schools. Variations in lighting, head position, and background clutter can disrupt feature extraction and reduce classification accuracy. For example, the Autism Glass Project initially struggled with expression detection in low-light settings, prompting enhancements in image preprocessing. Beyond technical hurdles, adoption of AI-based ASD tools faces skepticism. Clinicians and caregivers worry about the interpretability of AI outputs and their diagnostic reliability. In a qualitative study involving pediatricians and therapists, participants acknowledged the benefits of automation but emphasized the need for transparent decision-making and seamless integration into clinical workflows. Several clinicians noted that facial expressions alone may not capture the nuanced traits of ASD. Caregivers have noted usability issues with AI-based tools. While some parents appreciated remote monitoring via facial recognition, others found the systems too complex for regular use. Common complaints included inconsistent feedback, frequent calibration, and burdensome data uploads. These insights highlight the need for user-centered design—intuitive interfaces, clear instructions, and reliable support.

5.3 Impact on Early Intervention

Despite challenges, AI-based facial recognition significantly enhances early ASD intervention. Timely diagnosis is critical, as early behavioral therapy yields substantial gains in language, cognition, and social skills (Li et al., 2025). Traditional diagnostic pathways are often slow due to limited specialist availability. AI tools accelerate screening by offering preliminary assessments that direct families to appropriate care. Moreover, these systems support ongoing intervention by tracking facial and social behaviors, enabling personalized therapy. Emotion-responsive platforms improve engagement and retention, while real-time feedback via wearables empowers caregivers to reinforce social skills beyond clinical settings. AI-based facial recognition promotes objective, standardized assessments in ASD diagnostics, reducing evaluator bias common in traditional methods. This aligns with precision medicine's shift toward personalized, data-driven care for neurodevelopmental conditions. Despite ongoing challenges, such tools have significantly advanced early detection and intervention. Future improvements in model reliability, usability, and clinical integration will be key to shaping next-generation AI-driven autism diagnostics.

6. Future Directions and Improvements

As AI develops, it can also help in the detection and understanding of autism spectrum disorder by using facial recognition. Although current models have shown good results in spotting unusual facial expressions in ASD, some important fields are still waiting to be improved. Some of these are enhancing AI approaches, addressing ethical issues and encouraging cooperation between researchers and clinicians. If these dimensions are considered, it will be possible for AI-driven tools to be more accurate, reliable and fit within the rules of medicine and society.

6.1 Advancements in AI Techniques

Future advances in AI-based ASD diagnostics are expected to benefit from Generative Adversarial Networks (GANs), which help overcome limitations of small or imbalanced datasets. [7] used GANs to augment MRI data, significantly improving model accuracy. [25] developed a 3D GAN that enhanced facial recognition across varied poses, addressing issues like head rotation and occlusion. [33] introduced GARL, combining GANs with deep Q-learning to boost ASD detection from neuroimaging. These studies highlight the promise of hybrid GAN-based methods in creating more robust, generalizable, and clinically adaptable diagnostic tools. Advanced machine learning, especially GANs, offers key improvements for AI-based ASD facial recognition by addressing data scarcity and imbalance. GANs generate realistic facial expressions using paired networks generator and discriminator expanding datasets to better represent diverse age groups, ethnicities, and ASD

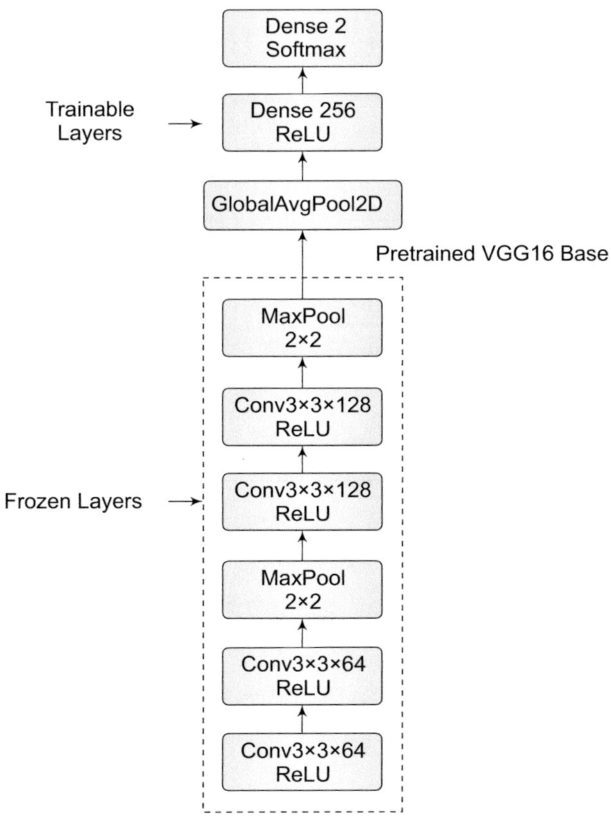

Fig. 4 Transfer learning pipeline using pretrained CNNs adapted for ASD detection

subtypes. Recent studies show that synthetic images produced via GANs enhance model accuracy and generalizability.

```
import numpy as np
from tensorflow.keras.models import Sequential, Model
from tensorflow.keras.layers import Dense, Reshape, Conv2DTranspose, Conv2D, Flatten, LeakyReLU, Dropout, Input
from tensorflow.keras.optimizers import Adam
from tensorflow.keras.datasets import mnist
import matplotlib.pyplot as plt

def define_generator(latent_dim):
  “””Create generator model for GAN”””
   model = Sequential()
   model.add(Dense(128 * 7 * 7, input_dim=latent_dim))
   model.add(LeakyReLU(alpha=0.2))
   model.add(Reshape((7, 7, 128)))

   # Upsample to 14x14
   model.add(Conv2DTranspose(128, (4,4), strides=(2,2), padding=’same’))
   model.add(LeakyReLU(alpha=0.2))

   # Upsample to 28x28
   model.add(Conv2DTranspose(128, (4,4), strides=(2,2), padding=’same’))
   model.add(LeakyReLU(alpha=0.2))

   # Output layer
   model.add(Conv2D(1, (7,7), activation=’sigmoid’, padding=’same’))
   return model

def define_discriminator(input_shape=(28,28,1)):
   “””Create discriminator model for GAN”””
   model = Sequential()
   model.add(Conv2D(64, (3,3), strides=(2,2), padding=’same’, input_shape=input_shape))
   model.add(LeakyReLU(alpha=0.2))
   model.add(Dropout(0.4))

   model.add(Conv2D(128, (3,3), strides=(2,2), padding=’same’))
   model.add(LeakyReLU(alpha=0.2))
   model.add(Dropout(0.4))

   model.add(Flatten())
   model.add(Dense(1, activation=’sigmoid’))

   # Compile discriminator
   opt = Adam(learning_rate=0.0002, beta_1=0.5)
   model.compile(loss=’binary_crossentropy’, optimizer=opt, metrics=[‘accuracy’])
   return model
```

```
def define_gan(generator, discriminator):
    “””Combine generator and discriminator into GAN”””
    # Make discriminator non-trainable during generator training
    discriminator.trainable = False

    # Connect them
    model = Sequential()
    model.add(generator)
    model.add(discriminator)

    # Compile GAN
    opt = Adam(learning_rate=0.0002, beta_1=0.5)
    model.compile(loss=’binary_crossentropy’, optimizer=opt)
    return model

    def generate_latent_points(latent_dim, n_samples):
“””Generate random latent vectors for generator input”””
    return np.random.randn(n_samples * latent_dim).reshape(n_samples, latent_dim)

def get_real_samples(dataset, n_samples):
    “””Select random real samples from dataset”””
    ix = np.random.randint(0, dataset.shape[0], n_samples)
    X = dataset[ix]
    # Add channel dimension if needed (for grayscale)
    if len(X.shape) == 3:
        X = np.expand_dims(X, axis=-1)
    return X

def train_gan(generator, discriminator, gan, dataset, latent_dim, epochs=100, batch_size=32):
    “””Train GAN model”””
    batches_per_epoch = int(dataset.shape[0] / batch_size)
    half_batch = int(batch_size / 2)

    for epoch in range(epochs):
        for batch in range(batches_per_epoch):
            # Train discriminator
            # Real samples
            X_real = get_real_samples(dataset, half_batch)
            y_real = np.ones((half_batch, 1))
            d_loss_real = discriminator.train_on_batch(X_real, y_real)

            # Fake samples
            noise = generate_latent_points(latent_dim, half_batch)
            X_fake = generator.predict(noise)
            y_fake = np.zeros((half_batch, 1))
            d_loss_fake = discriminator.train_on_batch(X_fake, y_fake)

            # Train generator
            noise = generate_latent_points(latent_dim, batch_size)
```

```
            y_gan = np.ones((batch_size, 1))
            g_loss = gan.train_on_batch(noise, y_gan)

        # Print progress
        print(f"Epoch {epoch+1}/{epochs}, D Loss Real: {d_loss_real[0]:.3f}, "
            f"D Loss Fake: {d_loss_fake[0]:.3f}, G Loss: {g_loss:.3f}")

        # Save generated images periodically
        if (epoch+1) % 10 == 0:
            save_generated_images(generator, latent_dim, epoch)

def save_generated_images(generator, latent_dim, epoch, n=10):
    """Save generated images for visualization"""
    noise = generate_latent_points(latent_dim, n)
    generated = generator.predict(noise)

    plt.figure(figsize=(10, 1))
    for i in range(n):
        plt.subplot(1, n, i+1)
        plt.imshow(generated[i, :, :, 0], cmap='gray')
        plt.axis('off')
    plt.savefig(f"gan_generated_epoch_{epoch+1}.png")
    plt.close()

# Load and prepare dataset (using MNIST as example)
def load_real_samples():
    (X_train, _), (_, _) = mnist.load_data()
    X = X_train.astype('float32') / 255.0  # Normalize to [0,1]
    return X

# Main execution
if __name__ == "__main__":
    # Parameters
    latent_dim = 100
    input_shape = (28, 28, 1)  # MNIST image shape

    # Load dataset
    dataset = load_real_samples()

    # Create models
    generator = define_generator(latent_dim)
    discriminator = define_discriminator(input_shape)
    gan = define_gan(generator, discriminator)

    # Train GAN
    train_gan(generator, discriminator, gan, dataset, latent_dim, epochs=50, batch_size=64)

```

Pseudocode 3 GAN-Based Synthetic Data Generation for ASD Facial Expressions

Pseudocode 3 outlines the core structure of GANs for generating synthetic facial images resembling individuals with ASD, addressing data scarcity and imbalance in current research. Beyond dataset expansion, integrating multimodal inputs such as vocal prosody, eye gaze, posture, and physiological signals enhances the model's ability to capture full social communication. Techniques like early, late, and hybrid fusion preserve the value of each modality. Lu et. al. (2021) demonstrated that combining facial expressions with voice tone significantly improved ASD detection, supporting more accurate and comprehensive clinical assessments.

```
from tensorflow.keras.applications import VGG16
from tensorflow.keras.models import Model
from tensorflow.keras.layers import Dense, GlobalAveragePooling2D, Dropout, BatchNormalization
from tensorflow.keras.optimizers import Adam
from tensorflow.keras.callbacks import EarlyStopping, ModelCheckpoint
from tensorflow.keras.preprocessing.image import ImageDataGenerator

def build_transfer_learning_model(input_shape=(224, 224, 3), freeze_base=True):
    """
    Build transfer learning model based on VGG16 for binary classification

    Args:
      input_shape: Shape of input images (default (224, 224, 3) for VGG16)
      freeze_base: Whether to freeze base VGG16 layers (default True)

    Returns:
      Compiled Keras model ready for training
    """
    # Load pre-trained VGG16 model
    base_model = VGG16(weights='imagenet',
                       include_top=False,
                       input_shape=input_shape)

    # Freeze/unfreeze base layers
    base_model.trainable = not freeze_base

    # Add custom classification head
    x = base_model.output
    x = GlobalAveragePooling2D()(x)
    x = Dense(1024, activation='relu')(x)
    x = BatchNormalization()(x)
    x = Dropout(0.5)(x)
    predictions = Dense(1, activation='sigmoid')(x)

    # Create final model
    model = Model(inputs=base_model.input, outputs=predictions)

    # Compile with lower learning rate for transfer learning
    optimizer = Adam(learning_rate=1e-4)
    model.compile(optimizer=optimizer,
```

```
            loss='binary_crossentropy',
            metrics=['accuracy',
                    tf.keras.metrics.Precision(),
                    tf.keras.metrics.Recall(),
                    tf.keras.metrics.AUC()])

    return model

def get_callbacks():
    """Return list of callbacks for model training"""
    return [
        EarlyStopping(monitor='val_loss', patience=10, restore_best_weights=True),
        ModelCheckpoint('best_model.h5', save_best_only=True),
    ]

def get_data_generators(train_dir, val_dir, target_size=(224, 224), batch_size=32):
    """Create data generators with augmentation for training set"""
    train_datagen = ImageDataGenerator(
        rescale=1./255,
        rotation_range=20,
        width_shift_range=0.2,
        height_shift_range=0.2,
        shear_range=0.2,
        zoom_range=0.2,
        horizontal_flip=True,
        fill_mode='nearest'
    )

    val_datagen = ImageDataGenerator(rescale=1./255)

    train_generator = train_datagen.flow_from_directory(
        train_dir,
        target_size=target_size,
        batch_size=batch_size,
        class_mode='binary'
    )

    val_generator = val_datagen.flow_from_directory(
        val_dir,
        target_size=target_size,
        batch_size=batch_size,
        class_mode='binary'
    )

    return train_generator, val_generator

# Example usage
if __name__ == "__main__":
    import tensorflow as tf
```

```

    # Initialize model
    model = build_transfer_learning_model()
    model.summary()

    # Example data generators (replace with your actual data paths)
    train_dir = 'data/train'  # Should contain subfolders 'class0' and 'class1'
    val_dir = 'data/validation'

    train_gen, val_gen = get_data_generators(train_dir, val_dir)

    # Train model
    history = model.fit(
        train_gen,
        steps_per_epoch=train_gen.samples // train_gen.batch_size,
        validation_data=val_gen,
        validation_steps=val_gen.samples // val_gen.batch_size,
        epochs=50,
        callbacks=get_callbacks()
    )
```

Pseudocode 4 Transfer Learning Using Pretrained VGG16 Model.

The pseudocode 4 illustrates how transfer learning is applied with the VGG16 architecture which is a well-known pretrained model for classifying people with autism spectrum disorder (ASD) from neurotypical people. It consists of freezing the base layers, adding custom layers and compiling the model for use in training. The code uses ideas learned from ImageNet to help with facial recognition in ASD research.

```
from tensorflow.keras.models import Model
from tensorflow.keras.layers import (Input, Conv2D, MaxPooling2D, Flatten,
Dense, Concatenate, Dropout, BatchNormalization)
from tensorflow.keras.optimizers import Adam
from tensorflow.keras.callbacks import EarlyStopping, ModelCheckpoint
from tensorflow.keras.regularizers import l2

def multimodal_fusion_model(facial_shape=(48, 48, 1), speech_shape=(128,)):
    """
    Multimodal fusion model combining facial and speech features

    Args:
        facial_shape: Shape of facial input images (height, width, channels)
        speech_shape: Shape of speech features (n_features,)

    Returns:
        Compiled Keras model ready for training
    """
    # Facial branch - CNN for image processing
    facial_input = Input(shape=facial_shape, name='facial_input')
```

```
    facial_branch = Conv2D(32, (3,3), activation='relu', padding='same')(facial_input)
    facial_branch = BatchNormalization()(facial_branch)
    facial_branch = MaxPooling2D((2,2))(facial_branch)
    facial_branch = Conv2D(64, (3,3), activation='relu', padding='same')(facial_branch)
    facial_branch = BatchNormalization()(facial_branch)
    facial_branch = MaxPooling2D((2,2))(facial_branch)
    facial_branch = Flatten()(facial_branch)
    facial_branch = Dense(128, activation='relu', kernel_regularizer=l2(0.01))(facial_branch)
    facial_branch = Dropout(0.5)(facial_branch)

    # Speech branch - DNN for feature processing
    speech_input = Input(shape=speech_shape, name='speech_input')
    speech_branch = Dense(128, activation='relu', kernel_regularizer=l2(0.01))(speech_input)
    speech_branch = BatchNormalization()(speech_branch)
    speech_branch = Dropout(0.3)(speech_branch)
    speech_branch = Dense(64, activation='relu')(speech_branch)

    # Combine branches
    merged = Concatenate()([facial_branch, speech_branch])
    merged = Dense(256, activation='relu', kernel_regularizer=l2(0.01))(merged)
    merged = BatchNormalization()(merged)
    merged = Dropout(0.5)(merged)
    output = Dense(1, activation='sigmoid', name='output')(merged)  # Binary classification

    # Create model
    model = Model(inputs=[facial_input, speech_input], outputs=output)

    # Compile model with lower learning rate
    optimizer = Adam(learning_rate=0.0001)
    model.compile(optimizer=optimizer,
        loss='binary_crossentropy',
        metrics=['accuracy',
            'AUC',
            'Precision',
            'Recall'])

    return model

def get_callbacks():
    """Return training callbacks"""
    return [
      EarlyStopping(monitor='val_loss', patience=10, restore_best_weights=True),
      ModelCheckpoint('best_multimodal_model.h5', save_best_only=True),
    ]

# Example usage
if __name__ == "__main__":
    import numpy as np
```

```
# Initialize model
model = multimodal_fusion_model()
model.summary()

# Generate dummy data for demonstration
num_samples = 1000
dummy_facial = np.random.rand(num_samples, 48, 48, 1) # Simulate 48x48 grayscale images
dummy_speech = np.random.rand(num_samples, 128)       # Simulate 128-dim speech features
dummy_labels = np.random.randint(0, 2, size=(num_samples, 1)) # Binary labels

# Train-test split
from sklearn.model_selection import train_test_split
(X_face_train, X_face_test,
X_speech_train, X_speech_test,
y_train, y_test) = train_test_split(dummy_facial, dummy_speech, dummy_labels, test_size=0.2)

# Train model
history = model.fit(
  [X_face_train, X_speech_train],
  y_train,
  validation_data=([X_face_test, X_speech_test], y_test),
  epochs=50,
  batch_size=32,
  callbacks=get_callbacks()
)
```

Pseudocode 5 Multimodal Fusion of Facial and Speech Cues.

Pseudocode 5 illustrates a multimodal deep learning approach for detecting social communication differences in ASD by separately processing facial and speech data, then fusing them for final classification. This method enhances emotion analysis and aligns with emerging trends in ASD detection using integrated AI models.

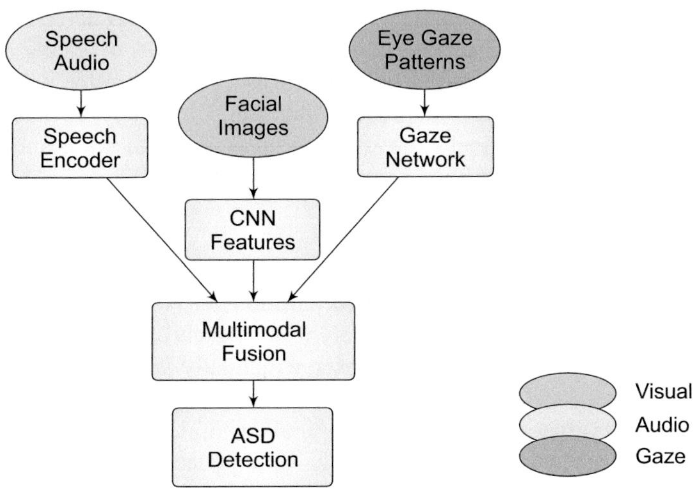

Fig. 5 Multimodal fusion architecture combining facial, speech, and eye gaze data.

6.2 Addressing Ethical Concerns

As AI becomes more prominent in ASD detection, embedding ethics from the outset is essential. [12] emphasized concerns around autonomy, consent, and accountability, especially when vulnerable populations are involved. [28] proposed a framework for integrating ethics into algorithm design, data governance, and deployment, promoting transparency and fairness. [26] further advocated for cross-disciplinary collaboration and early inclusion of ethical audits and risk assessments. Collectively, these studies stress that ethical design must be foundational not retrofitted for AI in ASD diagnostics to gain lasting clinical and public trust.

As AI-based facial recognition grows in healthcare, ethical safeguards are critical especially around data privacy and informed consent for vulnerable groups. Facial images must be securely stored, anonymized, and access-controlled. Federated learning offers privacy-preserving model training without exposing raw data. Adherence to global standards like GDPR and HIPAA builds public trust. To counter bias from imbalanced datasets, fairness-aware techniques such as adversarial debiasing and sample reweighting should be applied. Explainable AI (XAI) further enhances transparency, helping clinicians interpret predictions and align them with known ASD indicators signs of ASD.

6.3 Collaboration Between AI Researchers and Clinicians

Effective use of AI-based facial recognition in healthcare relies on sustained collaboration between AI developers and clinical experts. Past efforts often prioritized technical design over clinical relevance. Bridging this gap requires joint input from computer scientists, psychologists, paediatricians, and educators throughout development and evaluation. Establishing standardized diagnostic protocols, reproducible methods, and consistent reporting is essential for clinical integration. Ultimately, aligning AI innovation with ethical and medical standards ensures its responsible and impactful use in ASD diagnostics.

Integrating AI with neuroimaging tools like DTI and fMRI enhances the precision of ASD diagnosis. Helmy et al. demonstrated that combining structural and functional brain scans enables AI to detect subtle abnormalities in ASD. [23] showed that temporal fMRI patterns help distinguish ASD from neurotypical profiles, despite the complexity of brain regions.[29] advanced this by applying deep learning to multisite fMRI data, confirming the feasibility of cross-site models for clinical use. Collectively, these studies highlight how AI-driven neuroimaging strengthens behavioral and facial analysis in ASD diagnostics. Beyond standardization, AI tools for ASD detection must be designed with end users in mind. Involving clinicians, educators, and families in testing and feedback helps refine usability across settings simple interfaces for home use, and integration with clinical workflows in hospitals. Prioritizing user needs fosters broader adoption. Ultimately, advancing AI-based facial recognition in ASD requires technical innovation, ethical responsibility, and cross-disciplinary collaboration to enable earlier, more effective interventions.

7. Conclusion

This chapter highlights the use of AI in facial recognition for ASD detection, noting unresolved challenges. It begins by emphasizing key differences in facial expressions between ASD and neurotypical individuals, which are difficult to observe manually. The analysis covers deep learning models like CNNs and traditional methods such as SVMs, showing their role in improving expression analysis. It also addresses issues like data diversity, algorithmic bias, and model interpretability, illustrated through both successful and problematic AI applications. This chapter highlights how AI-powered facial recognition can support early ASD detection by identifying subtle expression changes beyond human perception. Techniques like transfer learning and multimodal fusion have shown strong potential, though these tools must be validated through clinical research and integrated into broader developmental assessments. Beyond diagnosis, AI enables remote monitoring and personalized interventions, aligning with precision medicine's shift toward data-driven care. However, challenges remain expression variability across age and culture, and ethical concerns around privacy, consent, and fairness. Successful adoption depends on collaborative development among researchers, clinicians, educators, and families.

To advance ASD detection, AI methods must continue evolving through synthetic data generation with GANs, improved model interpretability, and multimodal integration to capture full social communication. Equally vital are standardized evaluation protocols, regulatory compliance, and inclusive access to AI diagnostics. Together, these efforts enable transformative progress. Ultimately, AI-based facial recognition offers powerful tools to understand and support individuals with ASD, but its development must remain grounded in rigorous science, ethical responsibility, and a commitment to human benefit.

References

1. Ahmad, I., Rashid, J., Faheem, M., Akram, A., Khan, N.A. and Amin, R. "Autism Spectrum Disorder Detection Using Facial Images: A Performance Comparison of Pretrained Convolutional Neural Networks." *Healthcare Technology Letters*, vol. 11, no. 4, Jan. 2024, pp. 227–239, doi:10.1049/htl2.12073.
2. Akter, T., Ali, M.H., Khan, M.I., Satu, M.S., Uddin, M.J., Alyami, S.A., Ali, S., Azad, A. and Moni, M.A. "Improved Transfer-Learning-Based Facial Recognition Framework to Detect Autistic Children at an Early Stage." *Brain Sciences*, vol. 11, no. 6, May 2021, pp. 734–734, doi:10.3390/brainsci11060734.
3. Alam, M.S., Rashid, M.M., Faizabadi, A.R., Mohd Zaki, H.F., Alam, T.E., Ali, M.S., Gupta, K.D. and Ahsan, M.M. "Efficient Deep Learning-Based Data-Centric Approach for Autism Spectrum Disorder Diagnosis from Facial Images Using Explainable AI." *Technologies*, vol. 11, no. 5, Aug. 2023, pp. 115–115, doi:10.3390/technologies11050115.
4. Alam, M.S., Rashid, M.M., Roy, R., Faizabadi, A.R., Gupta, K.D., Ahsan, M.M. "Empirical Study of Autism Spectrum Disorder Diagnosis Using Facial Images by Improved Transfer Learning Approach." *Bioengineering*, vol. 9, no. 11, Nov. 2022, pp. 710–710, doi:10.3390/bioengineering9110710.
5. Alkahtani, Hasan, Theyazn, H.H. Aldhyani, and Mohammed Y. Alzahrani. "Deep Learning Algorithms to Identify Autism Spectrum Disorder in Children-Based Facial Landmarks." *Applied Sciences*, vol. 13, no. 8, Apr. 2023, pp. 1–21, doi:10.3390/app13084855.
6. Almuqhim, Fahad and Fahad Saeed. "ASD-SAENet: A Sparse Autoencoder, and Deep-Neural Network Model for Detecting Autism Spectrum Disorder (ASD) Using fMRI Data." *Frontiers in Computational Neuroscience*, vol. 15, Apr. 2021, doi:10.3389/fncom.2021.654315.
7. Anand, S.S. and Kini, S. "Deep Learning Approach for ASD Detection with GAN-Driven MRI Data Augmentation." *International Journal of Management Technology and Social Sciences*, Mar. 2025, pp. 78–93, doi:10.47992/ijmts.2581.6012.0373.
8. Awaji, B., Senan, E.M., Olayah, F., Alshari, E.A., Alsulami, M., Abosaq, H.A., Alqahtani, J. and Janrao, P., "Hybrid Techniques of Facial Feature Image Analysis for Early Detection of Autism Spectrum Disorder Based on Combined CNN Features." *Diagnostics*, vol. 13, no. 18, Sept. 2023, pp. 1–31, doi:10.3390/diagnostics13182948.
9. Babu, P.R.K., Di Martino, J.M., Chang, Z., Perochon, S., Carpenter, K.L.H., Compton, S., Espinosa, S., Dawson, G. and Sapiro, G., "Exploring Complexity of Facial Dynamics in Autism Spectrum Disorder." *IEEE Transactions on Affective Computing*, vol. 14, no. 2, Sept. 2021, pp. 919–30, doi:10.1109/taffc.2021.3113876.
10. Baihakki, M.A. and Mohamed Saleh Ba Qutayan, S. "Ethical Issues of Artificial Intelligence (AI) in the Healthcare." *Journal of Science Technology and Innovation Policy*, vol. 9, no. 1, June 2023, pp. 32–37, doi:10.11113/jostip.v9n1.129.
11. Bangerter, A., Chatterjee, M., Manfredonia, J., Manyakov, N.V., Ness, S., Boice, M.A., Skalkin, A., Goodwin, M.S., Dawson, G., Hendren, R., Leventhal, B., Shic, F. and Pandina, G. "Automated Recognition of Spontaneous Facial Expression in Individuals with Autism Spectrum Disorder: Parsing Response Variability." *Molecular Autism*, vol. 11, no. 1, May 2020, doi:10.1186/s13229-020-00327-4.

12. Elendu, C., Amaechi, D.C., Elendu, T.C., Jingwa, K.A., Okoye, O.K., John Okah, M., Ladele, J.A., Farah, A.H., and Alimi, H.A. "Ethical Implications of AI and Robotics in Healthcare: A Review." *Medicine*, vol. 102, no. 50, Dec. 2023, pp. e36671–e36671, doi:10.1097/md.0000000000036671.
13. Eslami, T., Mirjalili, V., Fong, A., Laird, A. and Saeed, F. "ASD-DiagNet: A Hybrid Learning Approach for Detection of Autism Spectrum Disorder Using fMRI Data." *Frontiers in Neuroinformatics*, vol. 13, Nov. 2019, doi:10.3389/fninf.2019.00070.
14. Farooq, M.S., Tehseen, R., Sabir, M. and Atal, Z. "Detection of Autism Spectrum Disorder (ASD) in Children and Adults Using Machine Learning." *Scientific Reports*, vol. 13, no. 1, June 2023, doi:10.1038/s41598-023-35910-1.
15. Gaddala, L.K., Kodepogu, K.R., Surekha, Y., Tejaswi, M., Ameesha, K., Kollapalli, L.S., Kotha, S.K. and Manjeti, V.B. "Autism Spectrum Disorder Detection Using Facial Images and Deep Convolutional Neural Networks." *Revued Intelligence Artificielle*, vol. 37, no. 03, June 2023, pp. 801–806, doi:10.18280/ria.370329.
16. Ganesan, S., Dr, R. and J, S. "Prediction of Autism Spectrum Disorder by Facial Recognition Using Machine Learning." *Webology*, vol. 18, no. 02, Sept. 2021, pp. 406–417, doi:10.14704/web/v18si02/web18291.
17. Helmy, E., Elnakib, A., ElNakieb, Y., Khudri, M., Abdelrahim, M., Yousaf, J., Ghazal, M., Contractor, S., Barnes, G.N. and El-Baz, A. "Role of Artificial Intelligence for Autism Diagnosis Using DTI and fMRI: A Survey." *Biomedicines*, vol. 11, no. 7, June 2023, pp. 1–36, doi:10.3390/biomedicines11071858.
18. Hosney, R., Talaat, F.M., El-Gendy, E.M. and Saafan, M.M. "AutYOLO-ATT: An Attention-Based YOLOv8 Algorithm for Early Autism Diagnosis through Facial Expression Recognition." *Neural Computing and Applications*, vol. 36, no. 27, June 2024, pp. 17199–219, doi:10.1007/s00521-024-09966-7.
19. Khan, B., Akram, A., Bhatti, S.M., and Rashid, J. "Autism Spectrum Disorder Detection in Children Via Deep Learning Models Based on Facial Images." *Bulletin of Business and Economics (BBE)*, vol. 13, no. 1, Mar. 2024, doi:10.61506/01.00241.
20. Kováč, Peter, Peter Jackuliak, Alexandra Bražinová, Ivan Varga, Michal Aláč, Martin Smatana, Dušan Lovich, and Andrej Thurzo. "Artificial Intelligence-Driven Facial Image Analysis for the Early Detection of Rare Diseases: Legal, Ethical, Forensic, and Cybersecurity Considerations." *AI*, vol. 5, no. 3, June 2024, pp. 990–1010, doi:10.3390/ai5030049.
21. Li, F., Ruijs, N., and Lu, Y. "Ethics & AI: A Systematic Review on Ethical Concerns and Related Strategies for Designing with AI in Healthcare." *AI*, vol. 4, no. 1, Dec. 2022, pp. 28–53, doi:10.3390/ai4010003.
22. Li, H., Gu, Y., Han, J., Sun, Y., Lei, H., Li, C. and Xu, N., "Faster R-CNN-MobileNetV3 Based Micro Expression Detection for Autism Spectrum Disorder." *AI Medicine*., Mar. 2025, pp. 1–13, doi:10.53941/aim.2025.100002.
23. Liu M, Li B and Hu D", "Autism Spectrum Disorder Studies Using fMRI Data and Machine Learning: A Review." *Frontiers in Neuroscience*, vol. 15, Sept. 2021, doi:10.3389/fnins.2021.697870.
24. Lu, Angelina and Marek Perkowski. "Deep Learning Approach for Screening Autism Spectrum Disorder in Children with Facial Images and Analysis of Ethnoracial Factors in Model Development and Application." *Brain Sciences*, vol. 11, no. 11, Oct. 2021, pp. 1–21, doi:10.3390/brainsci11111446.
25. Marriott.T, Richard., Romdhani, Sami., Chen, Liming., "A 3D GAN for Improved Large-Pose Facial Recognition." *2022 IEEE/CVF Conference on Computer Vision and Pattern Recognition (CVPR)*, 2021, pp. 13440–13450, doi:10.1109/cvpr46437.2021.01324.
26. Prakash S., Balaji J.N., Joshi A. and Surapaneni K.M., "Ethical Conundrums in the Application of Artificial Intelligence (AI) in Healthcare—A Scoping Review of Reviews." *Journal of Personalized Medicine*, vol. 12, no. 11, Nov. 2022, pp. 1914–1914, doi:10.3390/jpm12111914.
27. Rahman, K.K. Mujeeb and M. Monica Subashini. "Identification of Autism in Children Using Static Facial Features and Deep Neural Networks." *Brain Sciences*, vol. 12, no. 1, Jan. 2022, pp. 1–16, doi:10.3390/brainsci12010094.
28. Solanki, Pravik, John Grundy and Waqar Hussain. "Operationalising Ethics in Artificial Intelligence for Healthcare: A Framework for AI Developers." *AI and Ethics*, vol. 3, no. 1, July 2022, pp. 223–240, doi:10.1007/s43681-022-00195-z.
29. Subah, Faria Zarin, Kaushik Deb, Pranab Kumar Dhar and Takeshi Koshiba. "A Deep Learning Approach to Predict Autism Spectrum Disorder Using Multisite Resting-State fMRI." *Applied Sciences*, vol. 11, no. 8, Apr. 2021, pp. 1–16, doi:10.3390/app11083636.
30. Thahaseen, N.a.A., Karpagavalli, N.S.M., Fathima, N.M.R., Sangeetha, N.S., and Lidiya, N.M., "Detecting Autism Spectrum Disorder(ASD) Using CNN and Its Methods in Deep Learning Techniques." *Unknown Journal*, vol. 3, no. 02, Feb. 2025, pp. 161–166, doi:10.47392/irjaem.2025.0028.
31. Ueda, D., Kakinuma, T., Fujita, S., Kamagata, K., Fushimi, Y., Ito, R., Matsui, Y., Nozaki, T., Nakaura, T., Fujima, N., Tatsugami, F., Yanagawa, M., Hirata, K., Yamada, A., Tsuboyama, T., Kawamura, M., Fujioka, T. and Naganawa, S. "Fairness of Artificial Intelligence in Healthcare: Review and Recommendations." *Japanese Journal of Radiology*, vol. 42, no. 1, Aug. 2023, pp. 3–15, doi:10.1007/s11604-023-01474-3.

32. Zhang, N., Ruan, M., Wang, S., Paul, L. and Li, X". "Discriminative Few Shot Learning of Facial Dynamics in Interview Videos for Autism Trait Classification." *IEEE Transactions on Affective Computing*, vol. 14, no. 2, May 2022, pp. 1110–1124, doi:10.1109/taffc.2022.3178946.
33. Zhou, Y., Jia, G., Ren, Y., Ren, Y., Xiao, Z. and Wang, Y. "Advancing ASD Identification with Neuroimaging: A Novel GARL Methodology Integrating Deep Q-Learning and Generative Adversarial Networks." *BMC Medical Imaging*, vol. 24, no. 1, July 2024, doi:10.1186/s12880-024-01360-y.

Section 4

Autism diagnosis through speech analysis

7

Ethical Consideration in Autism Detection using AI

Sheetal Mavi[1] and Sameer Mandal[2*]

1. Introduction

AI offers transformative potential in autism detection, benefiting both healthcare and society. Yet, its application raises complex ethical challenges that do not overturn established scientific norms but demand fresh guidance for responsible use. This chapter outlines AI's utility in autism care and presents key recommendations to ensure its ethical deployment. Researchers are responsible for detecting, articulating, mitigating, and managing biases and errors in AI systems.

1. Researchers must clearly disclose and explain how AI is used in their work—along with its limitations—in language that is accessible to both experts and non-experts; Researchers should engage affected communities and stakeholders to foster collaboration, ensure inclusive participation, and address concerns—especially those related to bias—in AI applications;
2. Researchers using artificial data should:
   (a) Clearly indicate which data is artificially generated
   (b) Label the synthetic data explicitly
   (c) Provide details on how the data was created
   (d) Explain the rationale and methodology behind its use
3. AI contributions to research should be transparently acknowledged, with efforts made to formally credit their role in the investigative process.
4. The responsible integration of technology and AI into educational frameworks should be actively promoted to uphold ethical standards.

1.1 Overview of AI in Healthcare

Artificial intelligence replicates human tasks like reasoning, learning, and decision-making. In healthcare, it has significantly enhanced diagnosis, patient management, and treatment planning. For autism spectrum disorder (ASD), AI leverages speech, facial cues, and behavioral data to support early detection and intervention. Despite AI's transformative potential in healthcare, its ethical

[1] Assistant Professor, Bharati College, University of Delhi, New Delhi, India.
[2] Research Scholar, University of Delhi, New Delhi, India.
* Corresponding author: sameermandal.business@gmail.com

DOI: 10.1201/9781003541318-11

deployment remains critical—especially in complex conditions like autism, where it may reshape diagnosis and treatment. Institutions such as WHO and ICMR have issued formal guidelines to ensure responsible use of AI in biomedical research and clinical practice [5].

In brief: While core scientific ethics remain intact, AI demands fresh ethical guidelines—especially around bias, error, transparency, and community engagement. Developers must rigorously identify and mitigate biases, while researchers should clearly explain AI methods and limitations in accessible language for all audiences. Synthetic data must be clearly labeled, its generation method disclosed, and its purpose explained. Rather than crediting AI systems as authors or rights holders, their role should be acknowledged as contributory. Ethical training in research should also address the dilemmas posed by AI use. The chapter highlights key ethical concerns in AI-driven autism detection—emphasizing trust, transparency, accountability, and social responsibility in healthcare. Echoing [1], it stresses that human-centered AI must harmonize innovation with empathy. Figure 1 illustrates the progressive stages of AI.

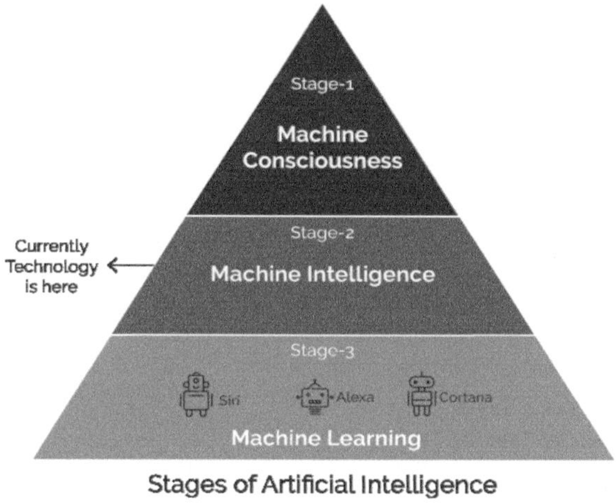

Fig. 1 Artificial Intelligence stages.

Machine learning (ML), a branch of AI, uses data and algorithms to mimic human learning and improve accuracy over time. Common ML models include neural networks, decision trees, and support vector machines. This paper employs artificial neural networks (ANNs) to illustrate core ML principles.

1.1.1 *Artificial Neural Networks (ANNs)*

An artificial neural network (ANN) consists of numerous artificial neurons modeled after biological ones. Each neuron processes weighted inputs through a function and produces an output based on a threshold—typically outputting "1" if the threshold is met, and "0" otherwise. Simple Artificial Neuron Example (as shown in Equations 1 and 2)

$$if\,(x_1 \cdot w_1) + (x_2 \cdot w_2) + (x_3 \cdot w_3) + (x_4 \cdot w_4) > T, \text{ then output } U = 1 \quad ...(7.1)$$

$$if\,(x_1 \cdot w_1) + (x_2 \cdot w_2) + (x_3 \cdot w_3) + (x_4 \cdot w_4) \leq T, \text{ then output } U = 0 \quad ...(7.2)$$

Here, x_1, x_2, x_3 and x_4 are inputs; w_1, w_2, w_3 and w_4 are weights; T is the threshold value; and U is the output.

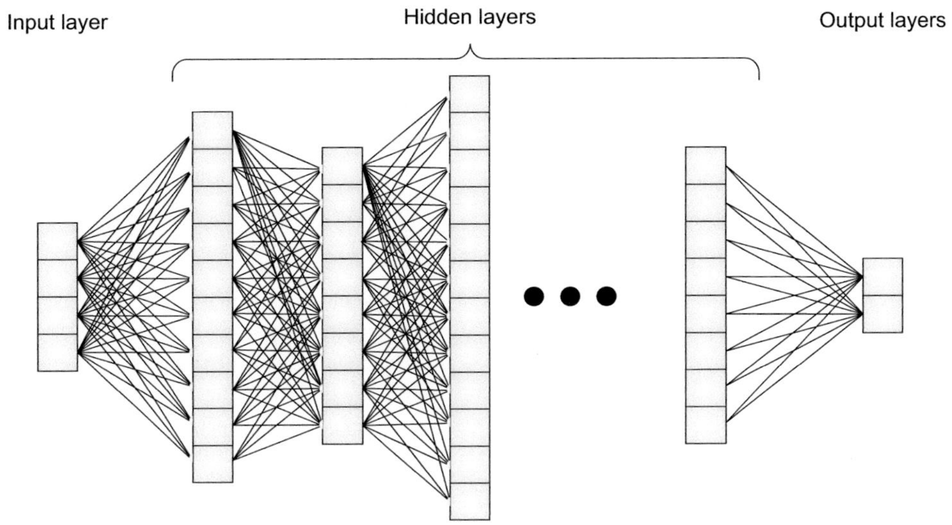

Fig. 2 Structure of Artificial Neural Networks.

1.1.2 *Structure of ANNs*

A neuron can receive multiple inputs, while an artificial neural network (ANN), as shown in Fig. 3, comprises numerous interconnected neurons. Deep learning ANNs often include several hidden layers between the input and output layers.

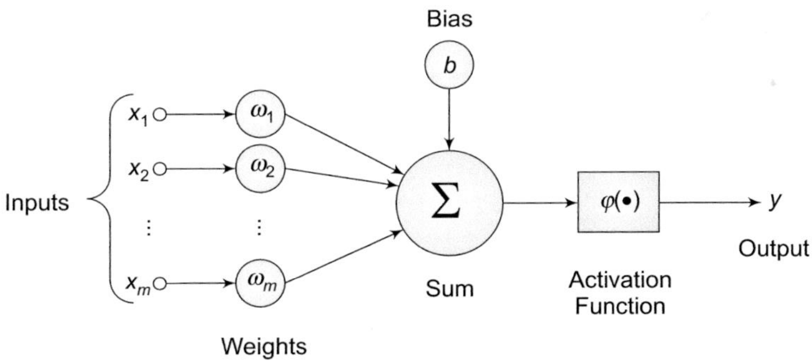

Fig. 3 Structure of a Neuron.

1.1.3 *Training Artificial Neural Networks*

During ANN training, input weights are adjusted based on each input's contribution to the neuron's error—the gap between predicted and actual output. Figure 4 illustrates the supervised and unsupervised learning phases.

Training can be supervised or unsupervised

- **Supervised Learning:** An ANN learns to recognize patterns by training on labeled data—for instance, it refines its accuracy by processing images tagged "dog" until it consistently identifies them correctly.

- **Unsupervised Learning:** The ANN discovers inherent structures in the unlabelled data. It identifies patterns and relationships that might not be recognized by humans.

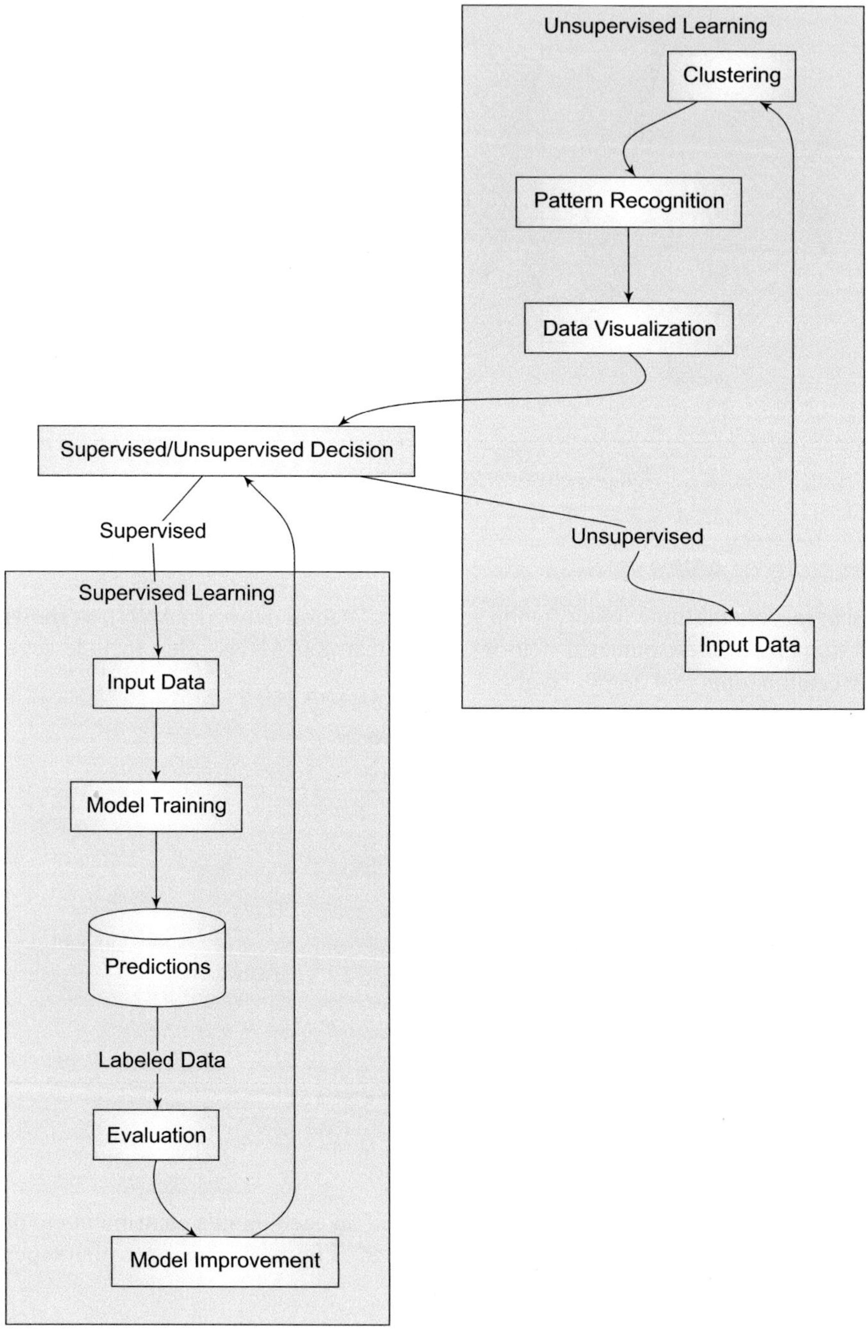

Fig. 4 Flowchart illustrating machine learning training via Supervised Learning or Unsupervised Learning.

1.1.4 Example of Machine Learning Error

[2] showed that a Machine Learning system trained on radiological images for COVID-19 diagnosis mistakenly used patient positioning—lying down—as a predictive feature, leading to significant errors due to lack of clinical context. This underscores the need to understand and manage ML errors. Similarly, [3] found that although deep learning can rival radiologists in performance, expert human oversight remains essential in clinical settings.

1.1.5 Benefits and Challenges of Machine Learning

Though prone to errors, ML systems can uncover novel structures, patterns, and relationships beyond human detection—such as generating new compounds and materials. However, their distinct information-processing methods make ML errors harder to anticipate, interpret, and mitigate.

1.1.6 Training Complexity

Training artificial neural networks demands substantial resources—large datasets, extensive computing power, and human oversight. Once trained, ML systems can continue learning from diverse data types, including images, audio, video, and medical records.

1.1.7 Case Study: Protein Folding Problem

A major milestone in ML was solving the protein folding problem—predicting complex 3D structures from amino acid sequences. In 2022, DeepMind's AlphaFold, trained on extensive sequence and structure data, reached 92.4% accuracy, revolutionizing protein chemistry and advancing biological and medical research. Machine learning—especially via ANNs—offers transformative potential across science and medicine, but its impact depends on ethical deployment, transparency, and robust error management.

1.1.8 About Generative AI

Generative AI uses deep-learning models to create high-quality text, images, and other content from training data. Unlike pattern recognition systems, it generates original outputs in response to prompts. Figure 5 illustrates its hierarchical workflow in autism detection.

1.1.9 Types of Generative AI

Among the most well-known forms of generative AI are those powered by large language models, such as ChatGPT and Gemini, which can analyze, edit, and produce text, images, and other content.

1.1.10 Applications and Ethical Considerations

Researchers have used generative AI to assist in writing scientific papers, occasionally even crediting it as a co-author. Its sophistication has led experts to revise the Turing test to better differentiate human discourse from AI-generated content.

1.1.11 Implications for AI and Society

Generative AI can transform diverse fields—from boosting productivity to reshaping health and education—by mimicking human thought to produce original content. Yet, it also prompts critical debates on authorship, accountability, and its broader societal impact.

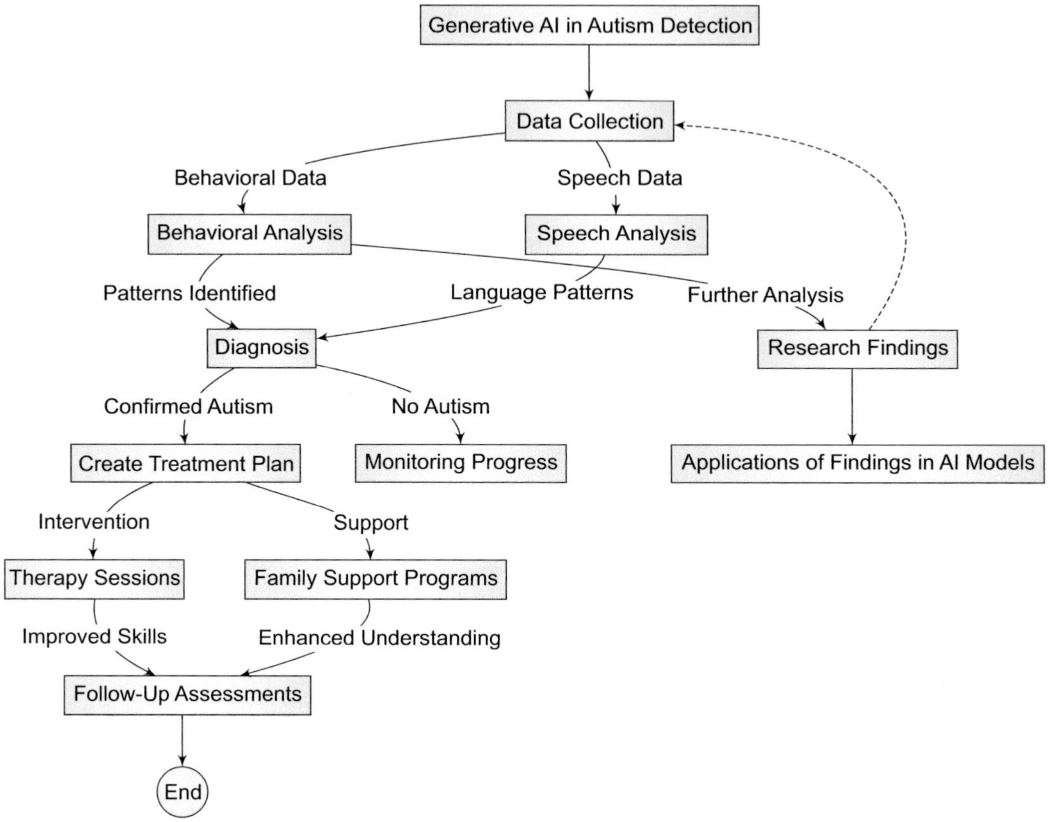

Fig. 5 How does Generative AI works in Autism Detection.

1.2 Introduction to Autism Spectrum Disorder (ASD)

Autism spectrum disorder (ASD) is a neurodevelopmental condition marked by challenges in social interaction, communication (both verbal and non-verbal), and repetitive or restricted behaviors. Its severity varies widely across individuals. Figure 6 outlines current treatment approaches.

Behavioral Interventions

- Applied Behavior Analysis (ABA): Applied Behavior Analysis (ABA) is a widely adopted method that uses reinforcement techniques to improve targeted behaviors and skills [7]. It is personalized to support communication, social interaction, and daily functioning.
- Early Intensive Behavioral Intervention (EIBI): Early Intensive Behavioral Intervention (EIBI) is a specialized form of ABA applied in early childhood, delivering frequent, high-intensity therapy to enhance long-term developmental outcomes.

Developmental Approaches

- Early Start Denver Model (ESDM): Integrates ABA techniques with developmental psychology to foster cognitive and social development through structured, play-centered interactions.

Educational Interventions

- TEACCH: Uses structured teaching and visual aids to help individuals with autism navigate and adapt to their environment.

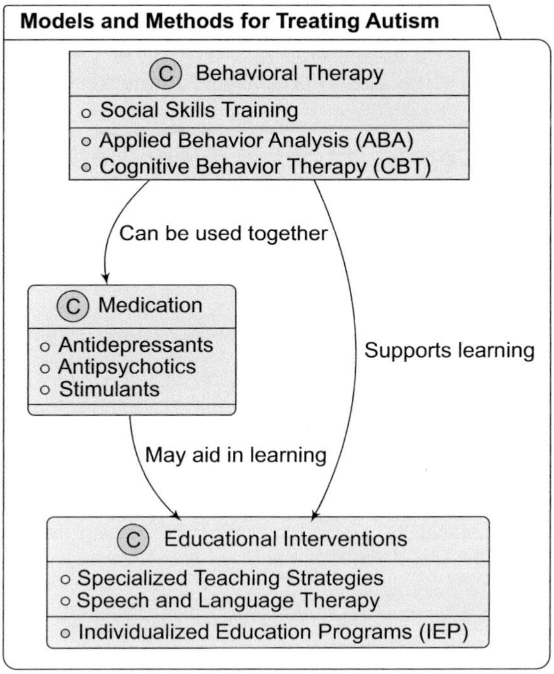

Fig. 6 Methods for treating Autism.

Speech and Language Therapy

- Targets enhancement of communication abilities, encompassing language comprehension and use, non-verbal cues, and social engagement.

Occupational Therapy

- Supports sensory integration and fosters daily living abilities, emphasizing fine motor development and adaptive self-care techniques.

Pharmacological Treatments

- Medications can help alleviate co-occurring conditions like anxiety, depression, or intense behavioral challenges, but they do not treat the core symptoms of autism.

1.3 How AI is Reshaping Autism Treatment

1. **Early Diagnosis**
   - AI Algorithms: Machine learning models analyze video and speech data to support early autism diagnosis by detecting subtle patterns often missed by clinicians [8].
2. **Personalized Interventions**
   - Adaptive Learning Systems: AI-driven tools analyze extensive intervention data and individual responses to create customized therapy plans, enabling more personalized and effective treatment.
3. **Assistive Technologies**
   - Communication Aids: AI-powered tools help non-verbal individuals express their needs and emotions in ways that caregivers and peers can understand.

4. **Predictive Analytics**
   - Behavioral Forecasting: AI analyzes long-term data to forecast developmental trends, enabling caregivers and clinicians to proactively refine treatment strategies.

1.4 Importance of Ethical Considerations in AI Applications

As AI use in healthcare grows, ethical concerns—such as algorithmic bias, data privacy, informed consent, and accountability—become increasingly critical. Addressing these is vital to ensure AI supports individuals with ASD without compromising their rights. A human-centered approach is key to safe and effective integration in clinical settings.

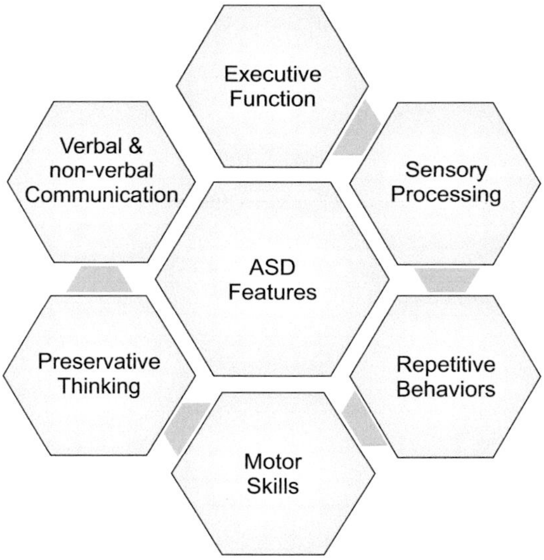

Fig. 7 Features of ASD

2. Privacy Concerns

2.1 Data Collection and Storage

Most AI systems for autism detection rely on diverse datasets—such as facial cues, speech, behavior, genetics, and electronic health records—which require stringent privacy safeguards like anonymization and encryption due to their sensitive nature [10]. Robust protocols must govern data collection and storage to ensure confidentiality and ethical compliance.

- **Obtain Informed Consent:** Patients should be clearly informed about what data is collected, its intended use, and options for updating or deleting it. Data collection must be minimal—limited to what's essential for AI diagnosis—and avoid unnecessary methods.
- **Data Security:** Robust safeguards—including encryption and access controls—will be implemented to protect sensitive patient data.

2.2 Patient Confidentiality

Trust in AI and ethical integrity must be fostered through strict protection of patient confidentiality. This entails:

- **Data Anonymisation or Pseudonymisation:** Wherever feasible, processing risks should be minimized by using anonymized or pseudonymized personal data.
- **Conduct Regular Security Audits:** Conduct regular security audits and risk assessments to prevent data leaks and ensure compliance with GDPR, HIPAA, and other privacy regulations.

2.3 Challenges of Using AI

Error

AI systems inevitably make errors, which are unintended deviations from expected outcomes. It is essential to distinguish between random errors—isolated and patternless—and systemic errors, which reflect consistent biases in the system. An AI error is a measurable gap between the system's output and the correct result, assessed quantitatively (e.g., a 2% error rate from 98/100 correct labels) or qualitatively (e.g., converting ratings like "excellent" or "poor" into analyzable metrics).

AI correctness is defined by domain experts—radiologists for diagnostics, biochemists for protein models, legal professionals for briefs. "Correct" may mean true, acceptable, or desirable, but its judgment ultimately rests with humans.

Random versus Systemic Errors (Bias)

Random errors resemble scattered bullet holes with no clear pattern, while systemic errors show directional bias. Accuracy measures closeness to the target; precision reflects consistency among the shots. Apparent random errors might reveal a systemic pattern with more information. Systemic errors are often more harmful because they can affect many decisions and projects. For example, biases in intelligence research have historically impacted educational policies. AI systems can also produce both random and systemic errors, which need to be understood and addressed.

3. Bias in AI Algorithms

Bias in AI—arising from imbalanced data, flawed design, or labeling errors—can undermine diagnostic fairness. Robust mitigation strategies are essential to promote equitable healthcare outcomes [9].

3.1 Sources & Impact of Bias on Autism Diagnosis

Bias in AI outputs can arise from various factors, leading to unfair or inaccurate outcomes. Key sources include:

1. Training Dataset Bias

- **Representation:** When training data lacks diversity, AI models inherit and reproduce its biases—such as a language model trained only on English struggling with other languages or dialects.
- **Historical Bias:** Datasets often embed historical societal biases—such as discriminatory lending in loan approvals—which AI systems can learn and replicate in their outputs.

2. Algorithmic Bias

- **Feature Selection:** Algorithms prioritize certain features, and if those features carry existing biases, the resulting decisions will reflect and reinforce those biases.
- **Model Design:** Bias may stem from algorithm design—for example, linear models may fail to capture complex data patterns, leading to oversimplified and skewed predictions.

3. Human Biases

- **Data Collection:** Data collection may introduce bias—especially when survey designs lack inclusivity, leading to overrepresentation of certain group perspectives.
- **Labelling Bias:** Supervised models trained on human-labeled data risk bias, as labels often reflect subjective opinions—e.g., sentiment analysis may misinterpret texts from diverse cultural contexts due to annotator bias.
- **Development Choices:** Development-phase choices—such as feature selection or metric prioritization—can embed bias, reflecting developers' assumptions and cultural perspectives, and leading to skewed outcomes.

3.2 Lack of Moral Agency in AI Systems

Narrow AI systems, especially LLMs, lack essential traits of moral agency—such as consciousness, self-awareness, and lived experience—making their use in high-stakes tasks like medical interpretation or research authorship ethically risky. Their inability to bear moral or legal responsibility underscores the urgent need to prioritize ethical safeguards in sensitive AI applications.

Despite safeguards by companies like OpenAI, fully preventing harmful advice remains difficult—studies show that even models capable of passing medical exams can still deliver inaccurate guidance due to error-proneness and limited contextual understanding.

3.3 Impact and Mitigation Strategies

AI bias can lead to serious social and ethical consequences—such as perpetuating stereotypes, deepening inequalities, and eroding public trust. To counteract these effects, it is essential to:

- **Use Diverse Datasets:** Make sure the training data reflects the full diversity of groups the AI system may interact with in real-world scenarios.
- **Audit Algorithms:** Conduct routine bias audits on algorithms and refine them as needed to avoid discriminatory results.
- **Involve Diverse Teams:** Include diverse perspectives in the Incorporate varied viewpoints during development to uncover and mitigate potential biases.
- **Engage with Stakeholders:** Collaborate with affected communities and stakeholders to identify their concerns and incorporate their needs into the AI system's design and implementation.

4. Ethical Implications of AI Diagnostics

4.1 Autonomy and Informed Consent

Autonomy and Informed Consent Patients must be clearly informed about the use of AI in their diagnosis and treatment. This includes:

Concerning autonomy and informed consent, patients should be clearly informed about the use of AI in their diagnosis and treatment. This includes:

- **Transparency about AI Use:** Clearly communicate the role of AI, including its strengths and limitations.
- **Disclosure of Benefits, Risks, and Alternatives:** Provide patients with a balanced overview of potential benefits, associated risks, and available diagnostic alternatives in sufficient detail.

4.2 Accountability and Transparency

To uphold ethical standards in AI diagnostics, well-defined accountability measures must be established. These may include:

- **Defined Accountability:** Assign clear responsibility to individuals or bodies for AI-driven decisions and potential errors.
- **Explainable AI:** Ensure AI outputs are transparent and interpretable, enabling clinicians to critically evaluate findings (Samek et al., 2017).
- **Human Oversight:** Incorporate human review to validate AI recommendations and reduce error risks.
- **Robust Error Management:** Develop mechanisms to detect, address, and correct AI system faults to maintain reliability.

4.3 Ethical Use of AI Recommendations

- **Use of AI:** AI should complement—not substitute—human clinical judgment in decision-making.
- **Individualized Benefit-Risk Evaluation:** AI-driven recommendations must be weighed against patient-specific pros and cons through thorough clinical assessment.

5. 5. Emerging Trends in AI and Machine Learning for Autism Detection

5.1 AI Techniques

1. **Deep Learning Methods**
   - **Convolutional Neural Networks (CNNs):** CNNs analyze complex inputs like images and facial cues to identify subtle behavioral patterns linked to autism.
   - **Recurrent Neural Networks (RNNs):** are artificial neural networks that can process sequential data like speech patterns. RNNs proved very good at modeling temporal dependencies in speech and behavior featuring patterns related to autism over time. RNNs are able to train on sequences of data and learn subtle changes and trends important for understanding and diagnosis in ASD.
2. **Natural Language Processing (NLP)**
   - **Speech and Language Analysis:** NLP techniques identify autism-related anomalies by distinguishing atypical speech and language patterns from typical developmental variations.
3. **Machine Learning**
   - **Random Forests and Support Vector Machines (SVMs):** Conventional machine learning algorithms classify individuals as ASD or neurotypical by analyzing behavioral and clinical data. Figure 8 illustrates the design and workflow of both Machine Learning and Deep Learning models.

5.2 Datasets

1. **ABIDE (Autism Brain Imaging Data Exchange)**
   - It hosts extensive MRI datasets from individuals with ASD and neurotypical controls, combining functional and structural brain scans from global sources to enable comparative analysis of neural activity patterns.

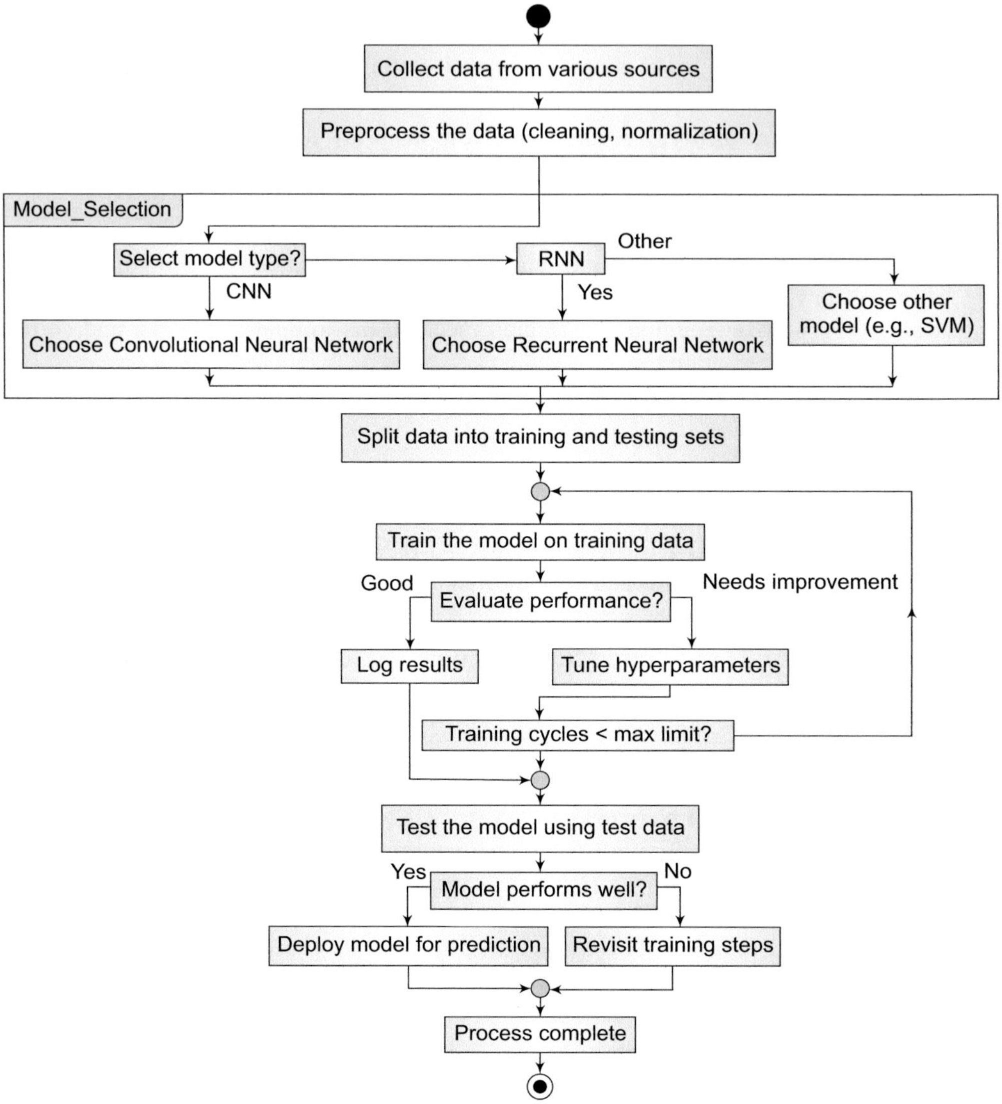

Fig. 8 Flowchart shows how Deep Learning and Machine Learning models work.

2. SSC (Simons Simplex Collection)

- It comprises genetic, behavioral, and clinical data from families with a single child diagnosed with ASD, enabling research into autism's genetic and environmental factors.

3. ADIR and ADOS Datasets

- **ADIR and ADOS:** ADOS assesses ASD through structured observation of social communication, repetitive behaviors, and play. ADI-R complements this with a detailed caregiver interview on the child's behavior and interactions. The ADI-R assesses ASD through a detailed clinical interview, drawing on caregiver reports of the child's behavior, communication, and social interactions.

6. Trends in Artificial Intelligence and Machine Learning

6.1 Explainable AI

- **Purpose:** Explainable AI (XAI) enhances transparency by clarifying how AI systems make decisions—detailing the models, parameters, and data involved. It aids developers, clinicians, and stakeholders in understanding system behavior, identifying errors, and evaluating decision logic.
- **Transparency:** XAI enhances transparency by enabling users to trace how inputs lead to outputs without requiring full comprehension of complex model internals [6].

Benefits of Explainable AI

- **Increased Trust:** When clinicians and users grasp how AI makes decisions, it fosters trust and encourages its integration into diagnostic workflows.
- **Informed decision making:** It also allows for informed decision-making by clinicians—for example, the use of AI in ASD detection. Clinicians can evaluate the recommendations given by AI better in the context of individual cases.

Challenges and Limitations

- **Technical Complexity:**
  - **Expertise Required:** This demands expertise in computer science or data analytics, posing a challenge for non-experts like general practitioners or policymakers due to the overwhelming technical complexity.
  - **Simplification:** AI explanations should be conveyed in plain language, yet many XAI methods remain overly technical, limiting broader audience understanding of system behavior and reasoning.
- **Legal and Regulatory Concerns**
  - **Accountability and Liability:** The legal framework for AI accountability remains in flux, and it is unclear whether XAI can fully address explainability-related legal challenges or influence future precedents.
  - **Regulatory Requirements:** Agencies are moving to include XAI in their guidelines, but without a clear regulatory consensus, ethical use remains a pressing concern amid ongoing ambiguity.
- **Corporate Resistance**
  - **Disclosure Challenges:** Companies may resist disclosing full AI system details, potentially leading to opaque models with no transparency around training data or operational mechanisms.
  - **Compliance Gaming:** Firms may offer superficial explanations solely to satisfy compliance, without genuinely promoting transparency.

6.2 Multimodal Approach

Combining Data Types

- **Purpose:** Multimodal models that fuse speech, behavioral, MRI, and neuroimaging data enable more accurate and comprehensive ASD diagnoses [11]. Coupled with XAI, they boost interpretability, clinical trust, and diagnostic outcomes.
- **Holistic Assessment:** Multimodal approaches offer a holistic view of an individual's behavioral, cognitive, and physiological profile, enabling more accurate diagnoses.

Benefits of Multimodal Approaches

- **Enhanced Accuracy:** Integrating diverse data sources reveals more ASD-related traits, and deep analysis of these data sources sharpen diagnostic model accuracy and precision.
- **Robustness:** Combining diverse data sources minimizes reliance on any single, potentially biased input, while multimodal approaches enhance reliability through cross-modal validation.

Challenges and Limitations

- **Data Integration Complexity:** Integrating diverse data types demands advanced, often technically complex methods.
- **Resource Intensive:** Multimodal approaches demand significant computing power and specialized expertise, making them challenging to deploy in low-resource environments.

6.3 Early Diagnosis and Intervention

Timely Support

- **Purpose:** AI tools are increasingly used for early ASD diagnosis, enabling timely interventions that significantly enhance quality of life.
- **Early Detection:** AI tools can assess diverse data—behavior, milestones, and speech—to detect early signs of autism, enabling clinicians to intervene before major developmental delays arise.

Benefits of Early Diagnosis and Intervention

- **Improved Outcomes:** Early intervention improves developmental outcomes by addressing issues promptly, enabling better skill-building and symptom management.
- **Preventative Measures:** Early diagnosis gives room for precautionary measures and individualized therapies that might reduce the socio-adversative impacts of ASD on daily functioning and general development.

Challenges and Limitations

- **Accuracy of Early Detection:** Early diagnostic tools must be continually validated to ensure accurate ASD identification and minimize false results.
- **Access to Resources:** Effective early intervention requires adequate resources and expertise; limited access undermines early diagnosis.

7. Conclusion

AI and ML are transforming ASD diagnosis and treatment through early detection, personalized interventions, and deeper insights—yet their use must be guided by strong ethical safeguards to ensure fairness and responsibility. AI's promise in autism detection must be rooted in safeguarding rights and welfare—ensuring privacy, minimizing bias, and upholding ethics. Progress depends on ethical frameworks, public dialogue, and rigorous research to build systems that advance care while respecting individuals with ASD.

Key Points

AI and ML-driven transformation

- **Early Detection:** AI and ML enable early autism detection, allowing timely interventions that can be highly effective.
- **Personalised Interventions:** It enables personalized treatment plans tailored to each individual's ASD profile.

- **Improved Understanding:** AI-driven research uncovers previously hidden patterns and insights into autism's underlying causes.

Ethical Considerations

- **Privacy Issues:** Given the sensitivity of health data, strict safeguards must ensure patient confidentiality and data security.
- **Algorithmic Bias:** AI systems must be designed for fairness and neutrality to ensure accurate diagnoses and equitable treatment for all patients.
- **Ethical Implications in General:** AI in healthcare must prioritize patient welfare, uphold informed consent, and ensure transparent decision-making.

Steps towards Responsible Implementation of AI

- **Ethical Frameworks:** Embed strict ethical standards throughout AI development and deployment in healthcare.
- **Engagement with Society:** Engaging society in AI's role in autism detection fosters trust and ensures alignment with societal values.
- **Additional Research:** Ongoing research is essential to refine AI systems, address ethical challenges, and improve healthcare effectiveness.

These elements are key to responsibly harnessing AI for autism detection and treatment—ensuring fairness, ethical use, and respect for patient rights—ultimately advancing inclusive healthcare for individuals with ASD.

References

1. Topol, E. (2019). *Deep medicine: how artificial intelligence can make healthcare human again*. Hachette UK.
2. Roberts, M., Driggs, D., Thorpe, M., Gilbey, J., Yeung, M. et al. (2021). Common pitfalls and recommendations for using machine learning to detect and prognosticate for COVID-19 using chest radiographs and CT scans. *Nature Machine Intelligence*, *3*(3), 199–217.
3. Rajpurkar, P., Irvin, J., Ball, R.L., Zhu, K., Yang, B. et al. (2018). Deep learning for chest radiograph diagnosis: A retrospective comparison of the CheXNeXt algorithm to practicing radiologists. *PLoS medicine*, *15*(11), e1002686.
4. Samek, W., Wiegand, T. and Müller, K.R. (2017). Explainable artificial intelligence: Understanding, visualizing and interpreting deep learning models. *arXiv preprint arXiv:1708.08296*.
5. World Health Organization (2024). *Ethics and governance of artificial intelligence for health: large multi-modal models. WHO guidance*. World Health Organization.
6. Dwivedi, R., Dave, D., Naik, H., Singhal, S., Omer, R. et al. (2023). Explainable AI (XAI): Core ideas, techniques, and solutions. *ACM computing surveys*, *55*(9), 1–33.
7. Foxx, R.M. (2008). Applied behavior analysis treatment of autism: The state of the art. *Child and adolescent psychiatric clinics of North America*, *17*(4), 821–834.
8. Akter, T., Satu, M.S., Khan, M.I., Ali, M.H., Uddin, S. et al. (2019). Machine learning-based models for early stage detection of autism spectrum disorders. *IEEe Access*, *7*, 166509–166527.
9. Nelson, G.S. (2019). Bias in artificial intelligence. *North Carolina medical journal*, *80*(4), 220–222.
10. Golda, A., Mekonen, K., Pandey, A., Singh, A., Hassija, V., Chamola, V. and Sikdar, B. (2024). Privacy and security concerns in generative AI: a comprehensive survey. *IEEE Access*, *12*, 48126–48144.
11. El-Sappagh, S., Alonso, J.M., Islam, S.R., Sultan, A.M. and Kwak, K.S et al. (2021). A multilayer multimodal detection and prediction model based on explainable artificial intelligence for Alzheimer's disease. *Scientific reports*, *11*(1), 2660.

8

Machine Learning Approaches for Detecting Autism through Chromosomal Aberration

S. Anbumani[1*], M. Nirmala[2], D. Somasundaram[3], V. Praveena[4] and R. Kavin[5]

1. Introduction to Autism

Autism is a neurodevelopmental disorder affecting learning, behavior, interaction, and communication [1]. According to WHO, ASD affects roughly 1 in 270 children globally, though prevalence varies by region due to disparities in healthcare access and awareness. In India, estimates suggest 1 in 68 children are affected, highlighting the need for improved resources and early screening systems. Early signs—such as delayed speech, conversational challenges, and sensory sensitivities—can be detected through standardized diagnostics and intervention programs. Figure 1 illustrates consistent behavioral traits like preference for routine, repetitive actions, and heightened sensitivity to stimuli, which support early identification and therapy.

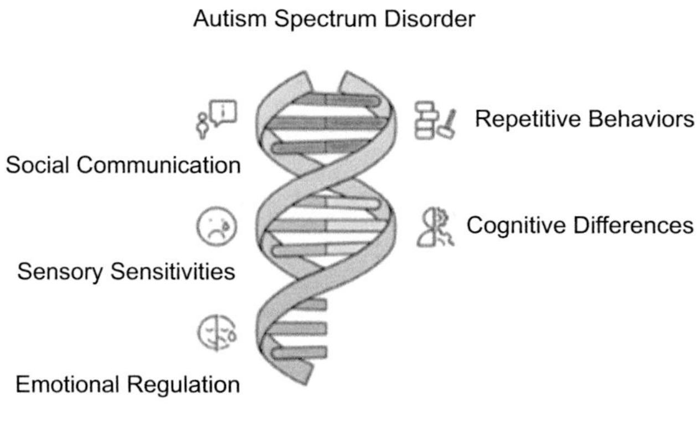

Fig. 1 Autism Characteristics.

1 Research Scholar(Anna University) and Assistant Professor,Department of Electronics and Communication Engineering Dr. N.G.P. Institute of Technology, Coimbatore, India.
2 Department of Biomedical Engineering, Dr. N.G.P. Institute of Technology, Coimbatore, India.
3 Professor, Galgotias University, Uttar Pradesh, India.
4 Department of Computer Science and Engineering, Dr. N.G.P. Institute of Technology, Coimbatore, India.
5 Department of Electrical and Electronics Engineering, Sri Krishna College of Engineering and Technology, Coimbatore, India.
* Corresponding author: anbumaniexcel@gmail.com

DOI: 10.1201/9781003541318-12

ASD arises from a combination of genetic and environmental influences, with risk factors including low birth weight, genetic abnormalities, advanced parental age, and X-linked inheritance patterns [2].

Autism diagnosis relies on behavioral observations and developmental history, with toddler screenings detecting early signs. Experts use standardized tools for thorough assessment and confirmation. Autism management involves multiple interventions—behavioral therapy, speech and occupational therapy, tailored education plans, medication, family support, and counseling. Early approaches like ABA and social skills training reduce negative behaviors and promote positive ones. Specialized education, along with therapies, enhances daily functioning and communication, while medications address co-occurring conditions such as anxiety, ADHD, and irritability.

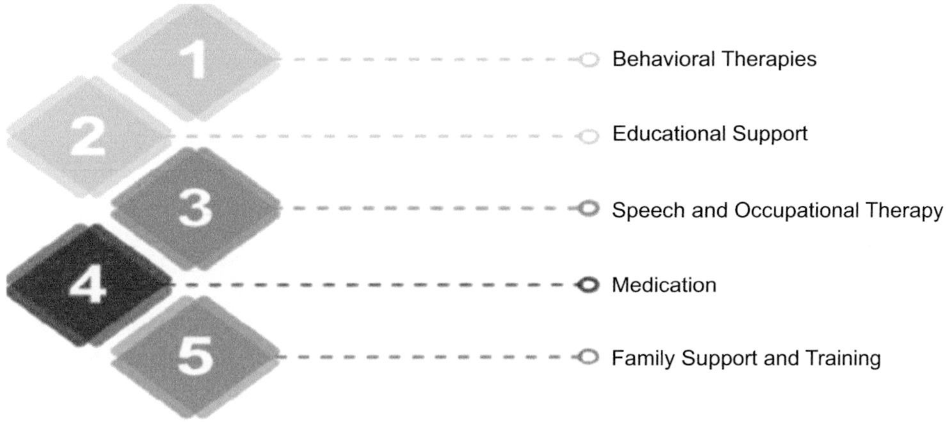

Fig. 2 Early Intervention for Autism.

2. Chromosomal Aberrations and Autism: A Complex Relationship

Chromosomal aberrations significantly contribute to certain autism cases [3], with genetic abnormalities recognized as key factors amid the disorder's multifactorial complexity [4]. Chromosomal aberrations—alterations in chromosome structure or number—range from minor DNA deletions or duplications to major structural anomalies [5]. Autism manifests in two forms: syndromic and non-specific. Advances in genetic technologies like whole exome sequencing and chromosomal microarray analysis have clarified autism's genetic basis, enabling detection of single-gene mutations, CNVs, and other abnormalities linked to ASDs [6]. Chromosomal aberrations—including CNVs at 16p11.2 and 2q11.2—are associated with elevated autism risk. Single-gene disorders such as Tuberous Sclerosis, Rett syndrome, and Fragile X syndrome, as well as chromosomal conditions like Down syndrome (Trisomy 21), Phelan-McDermid syndrome (22q13 deletion), and Prader-Willi/Angelman syndromes (15q11–q13), can also manifest autism symptoms due to region-specific genetic disruptions. Autism's causes remain unclear in the absence of distinct chromosomal abnormalities. Key pathways include gene dosage, synaptic function, neural development, and regulatory networks. Abnormal gene copies can disrupt neurodevelopment by altering gene expression, potentially leading to developmental disorders.

3. Autism Detection via Chromosomal Studies: A Machine Learning Perspective

Advances in genomic science, machine learning and AI have enabled early ASD diagnosis by refining methods to analyze genetic variants and chromosomal data. Literature highlights the link

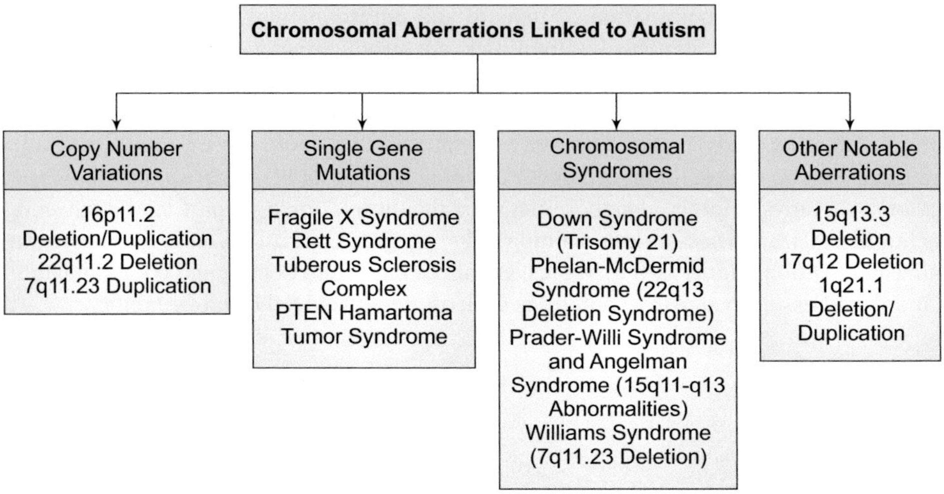

Fig. 3 Chromosomal Aberrations linked to Autism.

between chromosomal research and ML-based autism detection, with CNVs, single-gene mutations, and major chromosomal abnormalities consistently associated with ASD [10,11]. AI offers improved diagnostic accuracy and potential for novel drug discovery.

AI techniques in ASD research are customized to data type and domain, yet challenges like overfitting and limited datasets hinder progress; promising directions include explainable AI and ensemble learning [20]. Machine learning leverages high-dimensional genetic data to uncover ASD-related patterns, with feature selection and PCA helping retain key traits while reducing complexity [7,12]. Support Vector Machines (SVMs) are widely used to classify genetic and cognitive features, optimizing hyperplanes for ASD prediction and differentiation [13,30]. Unsupervised machine learning and hierarchical clustering aid ASD diagnosis by identifying distinctive traits in affected individuals. While k-means and hierarchical methods offer predictive frameworks, further research is needed to refine clustering strategies [21]. These techniques also clarify relationships among genetic markers linked to ASD [8]. Multi-omics integration—spanning genomics, transcriptomics, and epigenomics—enhances insight into ASD-related genetic factors [9]. Clustering methods further reveal genetic groupings that may correspond to distinct ASD phenotypes [14]. Anomaly detection highlights genomic irregularities potentially linked to ASD mutations [15]. ANNs effectively capture non-linear patterns in autism-related genetic data, enabling precise analysis of complex relationships [16]. Deep learning applied to brain imaging reveals key regions differentiating ASD from controls, supported by findings of anterior–posterior anticorrelation in brain activity and a 70% diagnostic accuracy improvement over baseline methods [13]. Recent studies have identified multiple genetic markers associated with ASD. Text-mining over 8,900 publications revealed key gene associations with AAD, offering promising targets for future research. Explainable AI (XAI) enables deeper exploration of ASD's genetic mechanisms [27]. CNNs applied to genetic data achieved 88% accuracy in distinguishing ASD cases, highlighting the diagnostic relevance of common variants, especially on the X chromosome [28]. Integrating genetic markers with kinematic assessments improves diagnostic precision, demonstrating the value of combining behavioral and genetic biomarkers in hybrid approaches [29]. Machine learning methods like GNB have been extensively used in neurological research for feature-based classification, assigning labels based on training data patterns. However, reliance on exploratory or a priori approaches introduces subjectivity in feature and label selection, complicating cross-study comparisons [17, 18]. Machine learning supports early ASD detection by analyzing morphological and genetic traits in infants, though clinical expertise remains essential

[19]. Integrating chromosomal studies with ML enables identification of ASD-linked genetic markers and molecular mechanisms, advancing both diagnosis and therapeutic strategies. Machine learning enables advanced ASD diagnosis by analyzing complex genetic and behavioral data. Techniques like SVMs, Random Forests, and ANNs classify individuals using high-dimensional inputs such as chromosomal aberrations and brain imaging markers. SVMs optimize hyperplanes to separate ASD from non-ASD cases, while CNNs detect non-linear patterns in neurogenetic data. These approaches support early detection and enhance intervention outcomes. Integrating genetic and behavioral assessments is crucial for advancing ASD diagnosis. Chromatin studies combined with machine learning enable comprehensive models that capture genetic variation. Multimodal approaches—merging chromosome data with standardized behavioral assessments—enhance early detection and intervention by linking genetic markers to specific behavioral traits.

4. Machine Learning Models for Autism Detection

Machine learning models—such as SVMs, Random Forests, gradient boosting, and deep learning—analyze complex genetic and behavioral datasets to uncover ASD-related patterns. As shown in Figure 4, these approaches enhance early prediction accuracy by leveraging large-scale data and computational power.

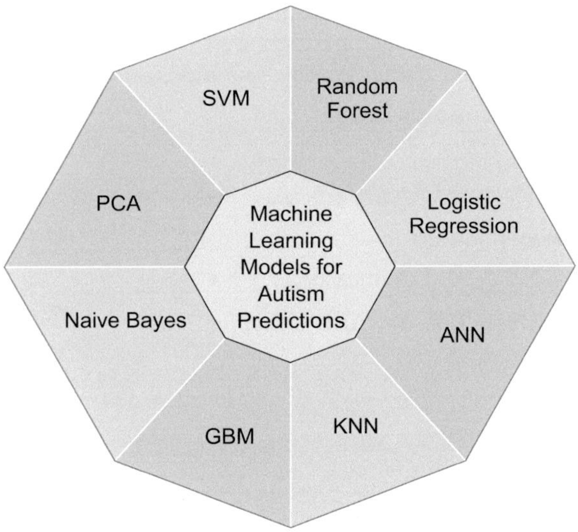

Fig. 4 Machine Learning Models for Autism Predictions.

SVM

Support Vector Machines (SVMs) use supervised learning to classify data by identifying optimal hyperplanes, especially effective in high-dimensional spaces with fewer samples. Widely applied in ASD classification, SVMs integrate behavioral and genetic attributes. For chromosome data, the classification function is:

$$f(x) = \text{sign}\left(\sum_{i=1}^{n} \alpha_i y_i K(x_i, x) + b\right)$$

Where $K(x_i, x)$ is the RBF kernel capturing chromosome feature similarity.

Random Forests

Random Forest is a powerful ensemble method that aggregates multiple decision trees to classify data by majority vote:

$$H(x) = \text{mode}\{h_k(x)\}_k^{k=1}$$

Each tree splits usingGini impurity:

$$G = \sum_{i=1}^{c} p_i(1 - p_i)$$

It excels in high-dimensional genetic and neuroimaging datasets for ASD prediction, offering robustness against overfitting and insights into feature importance.

ANNs

Artificial Neural Networks (ANNs), inspired by biological brains, process data through interconnected neurons. Deep learning, a layered subset of ANN, excels at extracting features from complex, high-dimensional datasets. In ASD detection, ANNs analyze intricate patterns in brain imaging and genetic data. Neuron output for chromosome features is computed as: $y = \phi(\sum_n^{i=1} w_i x_i + b)$ with ReLU activation: $\phi(z) = \max(0, z)$

CNNs

Convolutional Neural Networks (CNNs) automatically learn features from structured data like images using convolutional layers. They're highly effective for ASD detection, especially in analyzing brain imaging (MRI, fMRI), and perform well across dataset sizes due to their simplicity and efficiency in capturing complex patterns. Key operations and metrics:

- **Convolution on chromosome images:**

$$(f * g)(t) = \sum_{\infty}^{i=-\infty} f(i)g(t-i)$$

- **Pooling layer (max pooling)**

$$y_{ij} = \max{}_{0 \le m,n < k} + x_{i+m,j+n}$$

- **Binary Cross-Entropy Loss for ASD classification:**

$$L = -\frac{1}{N} \sum_N^{i=1} [y_i \log(\hat{y}_i) + (1 - y_i)\log(1 - (\hat{y}_i)]$$

- Model Performance Metrics:

S.No.	*Metric*	*Formula*
1.	Accuracy	$\frac{TP + TN}{TP + TN + FP + FN}$
2.	Precision	$\frac{TP}{TP + FP}$
3.	Recall	$\frac{TP}{TP + FN}$
4.	F1-Score	$2.\frac{Precision \cdot Recall}{Precision + Recall}$

Where:

- TP = True Positives (correctly identified ASD cases)
- TN = True Negatives (correctly identified non-ASD cases)

- *FP* = False Positives
- *FN* = False Negatives

4.1 Limitations of Traditional Evaluation Methods for Diagnosing Autism

Traditional ASD diagnosis relies on behavioral assessments, developmental history, and expert judgment, which can vary between evaluators and lead to inconsistent outcomes. Tools like ADOS require extended observation and may delay diagnosis until symptoms are more evident. These methods struggle with atypical presentations and often miss cases with subtle social or communication traits, especially those linked to genetic factors or comorbidities. While valuable, traditional approaches are qualitative, subjective, time-intensive, and reliant on specialist expertise.

5. Roadmap for Automated Machine Learning approach for detecting Autism

Figure 5 presents a flowchart outlining the machine learning-based ASD detection process, though specific steps may vary based on the dataset and algorithm used [31]. ASD is a multifactorial condition influenced by both genetic and environmental factors. Advanced research highlights the predictive value of genetic mutations and chromosomal abnormalities in ASD diagnosis [33], with chromosome images serving as valuable inputs for diagnostic tools.

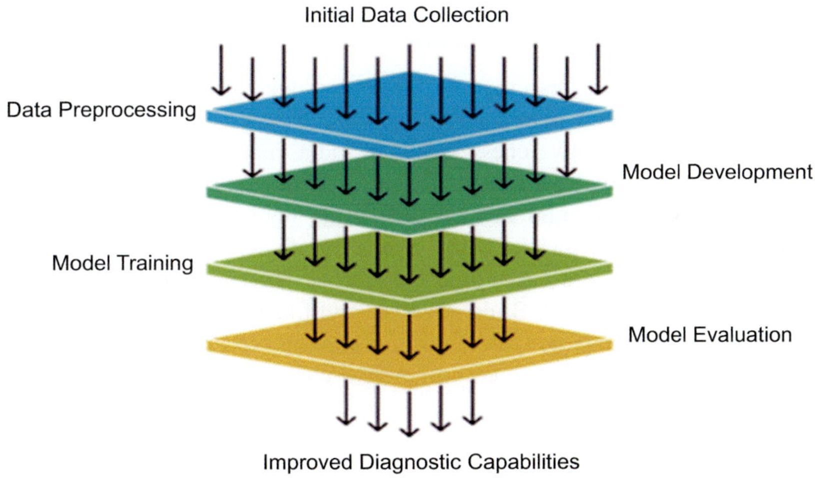

Fig. 5 Roadmap for Automated Machine Learning approach for detecting Autism.

Chromosome Data Collection

Acquire high-resolution chromosome images via karyotyping, whole-genome sequencing, or FISH, targeting structural anomalies such as microdeletions, duplications, and CNVs linked to ASD.

Data Preprocessing

Improve image clarity through contrast adjustment, noise reduction, and segmentation; standardize chromosome images for consistent size and alignment in machine learning workflows.

Feature Extraction

Assess chromosomal traits—centromere location, banding patterns, and anomalies—then extract quantitative features like length ratios and band density for machine learning; apply deep learning to detect patterns in visual data.

Model Development and Training

Use CNNs to analyze chromosome images for ASD-linked anomalies; strengthen model performance by augmenting training data with synthetic chromosomes.

Evaluation and Validation

Validate the model on independent datasets to measure its accuracy in classifying ASD vs. non-ASD, using sensitivity, specificity, and precision as key metrics.

Clinical Integration

Integrate the predictive model into clinical workflows to support early ASD detection and provide genetic insights for tailored interventions.

Impact on ASD and non-ASD Prediction

Leveraging chromosome data offers a non-invasive, scalable method for ASD risk assessment. Integrating genetic analysis with machine learning enables earlier, more precise diagnoses and timely interventions that enhance developmental outcomes. Models such as SVM, Random Forests, and ANN effectively distinguish non-ASD populations and uncover ASD-related factors [34]. SVMs excel in high-dimensional genetic and cognitive data classification, Random Forests identify key biomarkers in neuroimaging and genetics, and ANNs capture complex non-linear patterns by mimicking neural processes.

6. Statistics and Risk Factors for Autism

According to the World Health Organization, approximately one in sixty children globally are diagnosed with autism spectrum disorder (ASD), though precise figures remain elusive due to varying diagnostic practices and awareness levels. In India, rising prevalence highlights the urgent need for enhanced resources and early intervention systems. While the exact causes of ASD are unclear, both internal environmental factors and strong hereditary components—supported by genetic studies linking multiple genes to ASD—play a significant role. Genetic factors may underlie key neurological traits in ASD, with additional risk from environmental influences like gestational issues or prenatal chemical exposure. Brain structure and functional abnormalities are linked to the condition, though its exact cause remains unclear. Ongoing research continues to investigate the complex interplay between genetic and environmental contributors to aid early identification and prevention.

6.1 Benefits of using Machine Learning Models for Early Detection and Long-term Outcomes of ASD

Machine learning enables scalable early ASD detection, improving diagnostic reach and precision across populations. By identifying genetic and behavioral markers, ML supports targeted interventions and enhances long-term outcomes, transforming ASD diagnosis and care through greater accuracy and accessibility.

7. Challenges and Future Directions

Despite promising progress in genetic and machine learning research, several key challenges persist:

- **Data Quality and Availability:** Reliable machine learning models require large, high-quality datasets, with diverse genetic and behavioral inputs essential for building broadly applicable diagnostic tools.

- **Clinical Integration:** Bridging the gap between research and clinical use of machine learning in healthcare requires overcoming implementation challenges and equipping medical professionals with skills to interpret and apply advanced diagnostic tools.
- **Ethical Considerations:** The use of genetic data in autism diagnosis poses ethical concerns around consent, privacy, and potential discrimination. Tackling these issues is essential for responsible and equitable application of genetic testing.

8. Transforming ASD Detection with AI and Machine Learning

Machine learning (ML) offers promising capabilities for early ASD detection and diagnosis. Table 1 highlights key real-world applications and benchmark comparisons demonstrating its effectiveness.

- **Federated Learning for ASD Detection:** A recent study introduced a federated learning model for ASD detection in both children and adults, leveraging diverse datasets to train local classifiers and combine them into a high-accuracy global model. This approach enhances detection speed and precision while lowering costs, achieving 98% accuracy in children and 81% in adults [22].
- **Facial Landmark Analysis:** A novel approach involves deep learning to analyze children's facial landmarks, identifying autism-related features through transfer learning. This method enables reliable ASD detection and holds promise for enhancing early diagnosis efforts [23].
- **Motion Analysis Techniques:** Motion analysis with machine learning enables accurate ASD classification by detecting distinctive movement patterns. This approach enhances diagnostic reliability and provides objective metrics to complement behavioral assessments [24].
- **Behavioral Data Classification:** Traditional machine learning methods like random forests and support vector machines have been used to classify behavioral data for ASD detection. One study achieved 89.23% accuracy using a random forest model, highlighting its effectiveness in identifying autism-related traits [25].
- **Screening Tools Development:** Machine learning has enabled the development of advanced screening tools that enhance traditional evaluation methods, making early autism detection more efficient, accurate, and widely accessible [26][24].

Table 1 Benchmarking Data.

S.No.	*Model*	*Accuracy*	*Dataset*	*Description*
1.	CNN on Genetic Data[32]	88%	Genetic Data	Differentiates autistic and non-autistic individuals.
2.	Federated Learning Model[22]	98% (Children), 81% (Adults)	Behavioral and Genetic Data	High accuracy in children; slightly lower in adults.
3.	Random Forest [25]	85%	Behavioral Data	Effective in classifying ASD and non-ASD individuals.
4.	SVM [13]	70%	ABIDE Dataset	Used imaging data for ASD classification.
5.	ANN [23]	90%	Facial Landmark Data	Applied deep learning to facial features for ASD detection.

9. Conclusion

Machine learning has transformed autism diagnosis by enabling early detection of chromosomal aberrations, improving intervention and long-term outcomes. Despite challenges like data quality and clinical integration, ML holds promise for advancing personalized medicine and uncovering ASD's genetic foundations. Algorithms like SVMs, Random Forests, and ANNs are key tools in accurate ASD classification.

References

1. Jemima, D.D., Selvarani, A.G. and Lovenia, J.D.L. (2021, May). A study on diagnosis of autism spectrum disorder for children. In *2021 3rd International Conference on Signal Processing and Communication (ICPSC)* (pp. 547–551). IEEE.
2. National Institute of Mental Health. (n.d.). *Autism spectrum disorders (ASD)*. National Institutes of Health. Retrieved December 23, 2024, from https://www.nimh.nih.gov/health/topics/autism-spectrum-disorders-asd.
3. Liao, H.M., Gau, S.S., Tsai, W.C., Fang, J.S., Su, Y.C. et al. (2013). Chromosomal abnormalities in patients with autism spectrum disorders from Taiwan. *American journal of medical genetics. Part B, Neuropsychiatric genetics: the official publication of the International Society of Psychiatric Genetics,* 162B(7), 734–741. https://doi.org/10.1002/ajmg.b.32153.
4. Gillberg, C. (1998). Chromosomal disorders and autism. *Journal of autism and developmental disorders*, 28(5), 415–425. https://doi.org/10.1023/a:1026004505764.
5. Queremel Milani, D.A., Tadi, P. Genetics, Chromosome Abnormalities. [Updated 2023, Apr 24]. In: StatPearls [Internet]. Treasure Island (FL): StatPearls Publishing; 2024 Jan-. Available from: https://www.ncbi.nlm.nih.gov/books/NBK557691/.
6. Shen, J. and Miller, D.T. (2014). Advances in genetic diagnosis of autism spectrum disorders. Current pediatrics reports, 2, 71-81.doi: https://doi.org/10.1007/s40124-014-0042-z.
7. Grove, J., Ripke, S., Als, T.D., Mattheisen, M., Walters, R.K. et al. (2019). Identification of common genetic risk variants for autism spectrum disorder. *Nature genetics*, *51*(3), 431–444.
8. Parikshak, N.N., Luo, R., Zhang, A., Won, H., Lowe, J.K. et al. (2013). Integrative functional genomic analyses implicate specific molecular pathways and circuits in autism. Cell, *155*(5), 1008–1021.
9. Ramaswami, G., Won, H., Gandal, M.J., Haney, J., Wang, J.C. et al. (2020). Integrative genomics identifies a convergent molecular subtype that links epigenomic with transcriptomic differences in autism. *Nature communications*, *11*(1), 4873.
10. Geschwind, D.H. (2011). Genetics of autism spectrum disorders. *Trends in cognitive sciences*, *15*(9), 409–416.
11. Sanders, S.J., He, X., Willsey, A.J., Ercan-Sencicek, A.G., Samocha, K.E. et al. (2015). Insights into autism spectrum disorder genomic architecture and biology from 71 risk loci. *Neuron*, *87*(6), 1215–1233.
12. Libbrecht, M.W. and Noble, W.S. (2015). Machine learning applications in genetics and genomics. *Nature Reviews Genetics*, *16*(6), 321–332. doi: https://doi.org/10.1038/nrg3920
13. Heinsfeld, A.S (2018). Identification of autism spectrum disorder using deep learning and the ABIDE dataset. *NeuroImage: Clinical*, 17, 16–23.
14. Jeste, S.S. and Geschwind, D.H. (2014). Disentangling the heterogeneity of autism spectrum disorder through genetic findings. *Nature Reviews Neurology*, *10*(2), 74–81.
15. Breunig, M.M., Kriegel, H.P., Ng, R.T. and Sander, J. (2000, May). LOF: identifying density-based local outliers. In *Proceedings of the 2000 ACM SIGMOD international conference on Management of Data* (pp. 93–104).
16. Krishnan, A., Zhang, R., Yao, V., Theesfeld, C.L., Wong, A.K. et al. (2016). Genome-wide prediction and functional characterization of the genetic basis of autism spectrum disorder. *Nature Neuroscience*, 19(11), 1454–1462.
17. Buchweitz, A., Shinkareva, S.V., Mason, R.A., Mitchell, T.M., Just, M.A. et al. (2012). Identifying bilingual semantic neural representations across languages. *Brain Lang. 120*(3), 282–289.
18. Shinkareva, S.V., Malave, V.L., Mason, R.A., Mitchell, T.M., Just, M.A. et al. (2011). Commonality of neural representations of words and pictures. *NeuroImage 54*(3), 2418–2425.
19. Kumar, A.C., John, J.A., Raja, M. and Vijaya, P. (2023). Genetic factor analysis for an early diagnosis of autism through machine learning. In *Data science for genomics* (pp. 69–84). Academic Press.
20. Ferrari, E. (2021). Artificial Intelligence for Autism Spectrum Disorders. In *Artificial Intelligence in Medicine* (pp. 1–15). Cham: Springer International Publishing.
21. Roy, A., Rivas, P. and Tayba, M.N. (2022, December). Unsupervised Machine Learning Methods for Diagnosing Autism Spectrum Disorder Using Multimodal Data: A Survey. In *2022 International Conference on Computational Science and Computational Intelligence (CSCI)* (pp. 41–52). IEEE.
22. Farooq, M.S., Tehseen, R., Sabir, M. and Atal, Z. (2023). Detection of autism spectrum disorder (ASD) in children and adults using machine learning. *Scientific Reports*, *13*(1), 9605.

23. Alkahtani, H., Aldhyani, T.H. and Alzahrani, M.Y. (2023). Deep learning algorithms to identify autism spectrum disorder in children-based facial landmarks. *Applied Sciences*, *13*(8), 4855.
24. Simeoli, R., Rega, A., Cerasuolo, M., Nappo, R. and Marocco, D. et al. (2024). Using machine learning for motion analysis to early detect autism spectrum disorder: A systematic review. *Review Journal of Autism and Developmental Disorders*, 1–20.
25. Qureshi, M.S., Qureshi, M.B., Asghar, J., Alam, F. and Aljarbouh, A. et al. (2023). [Retracted] Prediction and Analysis of Autism Spectrum Disorder Using Machine Learning Techniques. *Journal of healthcare engineering*, *2023*(1), 4853800.
26. Raj, S. and Masood, S. (2020). Analysis and detection of autism spectrum disorder using machine learning techniques. *Procedia Computer Science*, *167*, 994–1004.
27. Nahas, L.D., Datta, A., Alsamman, A.M., Adly, M.H., Al-Dewik, N. et al. (2024). Genomic insights and advanced machine learning: characterizing autism spectrum disorder biomarkers and genetic interactions. *Metabolic Brain Disease*, *39*(1), 29–42.
28. Wang, H. and Avillach, P. (2021). Diagnostic classification and prognostic prediction using common genetic variants in autism spectrum disorder: Genotype-based deep learning. *JMIR medical informatics*, *9*(4), e24754.
29. Deepthi, V. and Vineetha, S. (2018, August). Study On Early Detection of Autism Using Genetic and Kinematic Biomarker. In *IOP Conference Series: Materials Science and Engineering* (Vol. 396, No. 1, p. 012034). IOP Publishing.
30. Alkoot, F.M. and Alqallaf, A.K. (2016). Investigating machine learning techniques for the detection of autism. *International Journal of Data Mining and Bioinformatics*, *16*(2), 141–169.
31. Deepika Ghai, Suman Lata Tripathi, Sobhit Saxena, Manash Chanda, Mamoun Alazab et al., "Machine Learning Algorithms for Signal and Image Processing," Wiley IEEE Press-2022, ISBN: 978-1-119-86182-9
32. Mnif, F., Nasr, F.B. and Oueslati, A.E. (2024, July). Autism diagnosis with a CNN model based on genetic mutations. In *2024 IEEE 7th International Conference on Advanced Technologies, Signal and Image Processing (ATSIP)* (Vol. 1, pp. 382–386). IEEE.
33. Somasundaram, D., Chapparadahallimath, A., Krishanan, M. and Madian, N. (2023). A Novel Automated Chromosome Analyzer Software Bundle for Karyotyping and Birth Defect Analysis. IEEE Access.doi: 10.1109/ACCESS.2023.3344664
34. Madian, N., Devaraj, S., Suganthi, S.T. and Brightlin, B.C. (2020, January). Graph partitioning approach for segmentation of banding pattern of g-band metaphase human chromosomes. In *2020 International Conference on Computer Communication and Informatics (ICCCI)* (pp. 1-5). IEEE. https://doi.org/10.1109/ICCCI48352.2020.9104123.

9

Analysis of Artificial Intelligence Techniques for Autism Detection

J. Saira Banu[1*], Mythili T[2], Pradyumna Kunchala[3] and Abhik Goswami[4]

1. Introduction

In 2024, AI has become essential across domains—from everyday convenience to critical sectors like healthcare—driven by sustained research in academia and industry [1]. Emerging trends include the rise of generative AI tools like GPT-4 and Sora, and growing adoption of Explainable AI, particularly in healthcare, where transparency in machine-driven decisions is increasingly vital. As research deepens, AI's integration into society continues to accelerate. AI is increasingly vital in medicine and research, with classification models widely applied to diagnose visual conditions like skin cancer and psoriasis [2]. Machine learning aids in interpreting medical reports—for example, grading and detecting diabetic retinopathy—enabling faster responses. In cardiovascular care, cardiac signals and heart sounds are analyzed by ML models to support diagnosis. Beyond diagnostics, AI streamlines hospital logistics through dynamic allocation of medical staff and resources. AI-driven ASD detection is a key application in healthcare, with numerous ML and DL approaches proposed over time. Traditional models such as SVM, RF, and KNNs are commonly used to classify ASD versus control states following MRI data preprocessing and feature extraction [3]. Public datasets like ABIDE-1 and ABIDE-2 offer fMRI and structural MRI data for model training.

A recent CNN-based implementation [4] enhances ASD classification efficiency over traditional methods. It integrates a mobile app for data collection, a web-hosted CNN model for detection, and a database for continuous storage. This system outperforms algorithms like decision trees and Bayesian networks, with comparable accuracy when applied to fMRI datasets. A notable study presents a CAD system for ASD detection in younger patients using diffusion tensor imaging [5]. It employs a Markov Gibbs random field model with non-negative matrix factorization for brain segmentation, achieving high accuracy (ACC 86.84%, AUC 0.96). Key shape and connectivity features distinguish ASD from control groups, with Random Forest performing best. Federated learning [6] enables decentralized model training on edge devices, optimizing performance and enhancing data security [7], especially for large MRI datasets. This approach safeguards sensitive patient data [8], making it ideal for ASD detection in clinical settings, where aggregated models can support robust diagnosis. In ASD diagnosis using sMRI datasets, XAI techniques enhance interpretability and clinical relevance by making ML model outputs more transparent to researchers and practitioners (i). These advances

[1-4] School of Computer Science and Engineering, Vellore Institute of Technology, Vellore, India.
* Corresponding author: jsairabanu@vit.ac.in

DOI: 10.1201/9781003541318-13

improve diagnostic accuracy and support broader adoption, especially when paired with standardized data protocols. Integrating neuroimaging modalities like DTI and fcMRI with deep learning and multimodal fusion further strengthens AI-driven ASD detection, with XAI playing a key role in making these complex systems clinically understandable (i).

1.1 Literature Review

A. AI in Healthcare

AI is now integral to healthcare, spanning logistics, medical imaging, and surgical applications [9]. Deep learning algorithms enable accurate analysis of complex imaging data, aiding early disease detection, including cancer [10]. Predictive analytics optimize patient care and resource allocation, while AI-driven robotic surgery enhances precision and reduces complications [11]. Advances in MRI have improved diagnosis of conditions like cancer [12] and ASD. However, ethical and practical challenges remain, underscoring the need for rigorous testing and validation of AI models in clinical settings [13].

B. AI in autism detection

ASD is a complex and frequently misunderstood neurodevelopmental disorder marked by social and cognitive challenges. Early diagnosis is vital for timely intervention and better outcomes. AI plays a key role in ASD detection and classification, making it a prominent application in healthcare. There exist a multitude of techniques that have been proposed over the years:

1. **Facial Feature based Analysis:** AI models—especially CNNs—have been used to analyze facial features for early ASD detection. A hybrid approach combining VGG16, ResNet101, and MobileNet with XGBoost and Random Forest achieved 98.8% accuracy and a 99.25% AUC [14].
2. **fMRI Data Analysis:** Functional MRI (fMRI) data are increasingly leveraged for early ASD diagnosis, with AI models identifying atypical brain activity patterns to distinguish ASD from control subjects with high accuracy. A comprehensive survey emphasized AI's promise for objective fMRI-based ASD detection [15]. One study combined CNN and RNN (LSTM) architectures to extract spatial and temporal features from fMRI data, achieving ~70% classification accuracy [16]. Additionally, Geometric Convolutional Networks (GNNs) have been proposed to model inter-regional brain connectivity for ASD categorization [17].
3. **EEG Signal Analysis:** Generative AI models such as GANs and VAEs have been employed to analyze EEG signals for ASD detection. GANs enhance EEG data quality by reducing noise, while VAEs extract salient features. Notably, GAN-based systems have successfully mimicked EEG patterns of ASD and non-ASD individuals, enabling highly accurate and precise classification [18].

C. Privacy Protection through federated learning

Federated Learning (FL) offers a promising solution for privacy-preserving machine learning by decentralizing data processing. Unlike traditional ML, which centralizes data and risks privacy breaches, FL trains models locally on distributed devices without sharing raw data, enabling secure and collaborative learning across sources [19]. A major advantage of Federated Learning (FL) is its ability to reduce privacy risks by keeping data decentralized, thereby minimizing exposure to breaches. [20] detailed a scalable FL system that incorporates privacy-preserving mechanisms to safeguard sensitive information during training. Federated Learning (FL) is especially effective in safeguarding privacy in sensitive domains like healthcare, enabling robust model development without exposing patient data. [21] demonstrated FL's utility in handling imbalanced medical datasets using advanced optimization techniques while preserving privacy. FL also integrates privacy-enhancing methods such as differential privacy and secure multi-party computation, ensuring data protection even when model parameters are shared.[22] proposed a blockchain-based FL framework for secure personal data management, showcasing the strength of combining these technologies. Overall, FL provides a powerful, decentralized approach to privacy-preserving machine learning, with transformative potential in healthcare and beyond.

D. Explainable AI

Explainable AI (XAI) enhances transparency and interpretability in complex domains like healthcare, finance, and autonomous systems by making AI decisions understandable to humans, thereby fostering trust. Techniques such as LIME and SHAP simplify model predictions for better human comprehension while maintaining computational efficiency [23]. In sensitive applications like intelligent vehicles, XAI improves intrusion detection and regulatory compliance through increased transparency [24]. A comprehensive review categorizes XAI approaches and outlines challenges and opportunities for responsible AI adoption [25]. However, balancing model performance with interpretability remains a key challenge, especially in deep learning systems [26]. Ongoing research aims to reconcile this trade-off. In summary, XAI is vital for fostering trust and widespread adoption of AI by making complex model decisions transparent and interpretable. It bridges the gap between AI systems and human users, promoting responsible and effective use.

1.2 Methodology

A. Traditional Machine Learning Models

ASD can be detected using traditional machine learning techniques [27] applied to phenotypic data, typically stored in CSV format. The following outlines key methods for ASD classification based on such data.

1. **K-Neighbors Classifier:** The first step in ASD classification using phenotypic data involves preprocessing, including feature selection to identify key attributes [32]. These features are then normalized to a common scale, which is essential for accurate distance-based calculations in KNN [29], ensuring balanced contribution from all features. The KNN algorithm classifies a subject by identifying the majority class among the 'k' nearest

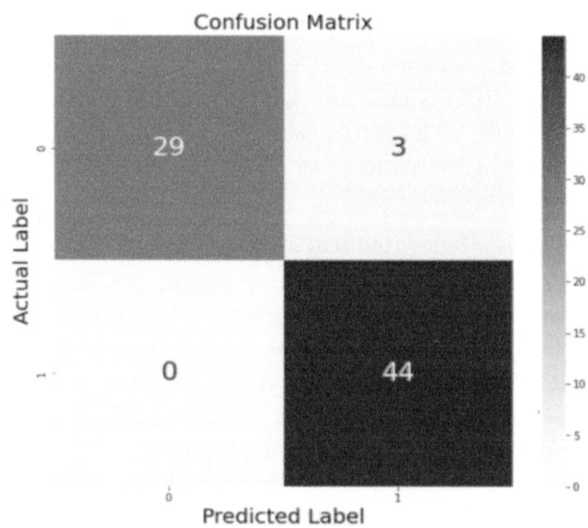

Fig. 1 KNN confusion matrix.

```
Accuracy =  0.9473684210526315
Precision =  0.9166666666666666
Recall\Sensitivity =  1.0
Specificity =  0.875
F1 Score =  0.9565217391304348
AUC Score = 0.9375
Kappa score =  0.8901734104046243
Log Loss =  1.897034388900903
```

Fig. 2 KNN metrics.

neighbors in the training set [28]. It uses the Euclidean distance to measure similarity, calculating the distance between the subject's feature vector and those of all training samples.

$$d(p, q) \sqrt{(p_1 - q_1)^2 + (p_2 - q_2)^2 + \cdots + (p_n - q_n)} \quad ...(9.1)$$

The model was trained using an 80:20 train-test split. Post-evaluation, key performance metrics and the confusion matrix are presented below.

Table 1 KNN metrics table.

Accuracy	*Precision*	*Recall*	*Specificity*	*F1 score*	*AUC*	*Kappa loss*	*Log loss*
0.94	0.91	1.0	0.875	0.95	0.93	0.89	1.89

2. **Random Forest Classifier implementation:** This section outlines the implementation of a Random Forest classifier for ASD detection using high-dimensional phenotypic data [30]. The CSV-formatted dataset is preprocessed through feature selection—guided by domain knowledge or automated methods—and split into training and test sets. The model is then initialized with parameters such as tree count and maximum depth. The model is trained on the dataset using 5-fold cross-validation across 100 candidates, resulting in 500 individual

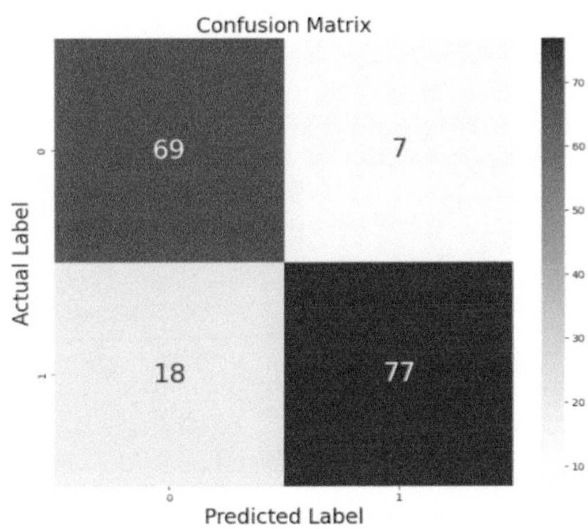

Fig. 3 RFC Confusion Matrix.

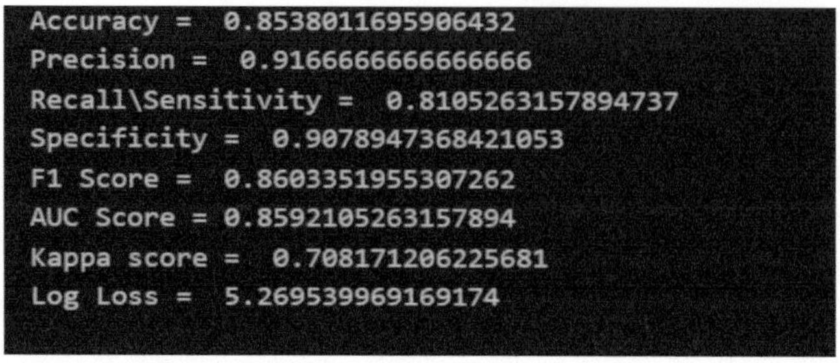

Accuracy = 0.8538011695906432
Precision = 0.9166666666666666
Recall\Sensitivity = 0.8105263157894737
Specificity = 0.9078947368421053
F1 Score = 0.8603351955307262
AUC Score = 0.8592105263157894
Kappa score = 0.708171206225681
Log Loss = 5.269539969169174

Fig. 4 RFC metrics.

fits. Each decision tree in the Random Forest is built from a distinct fold and randomized feature subset.

The trained model is evaluated on the test data by generating predictions and computing metrics—accuracy, precision, recall, and F1-score—to assess its ability to distinguish ASD from non-ASD cases.

Table 2 RFC metrics table.

Accuracy	*Precision*	*Recall*	*Specificity*	*F1 score*	*AUC*	*Kappa loss*	*Log loss*
0.85	0.91	0.81	0.90	0.86	0.86	0.7	5.26

3. **SVM (Support Vector Machine) Implementation:** The Support Vector Machine (SVM) method is employed to classify ASD based on phenotypic features [31], using a hyperplane to separate data in multidimensional space. Input data undergoes the same preprocessing—normalization and skewness reduction—as prior models. Hyperparameter

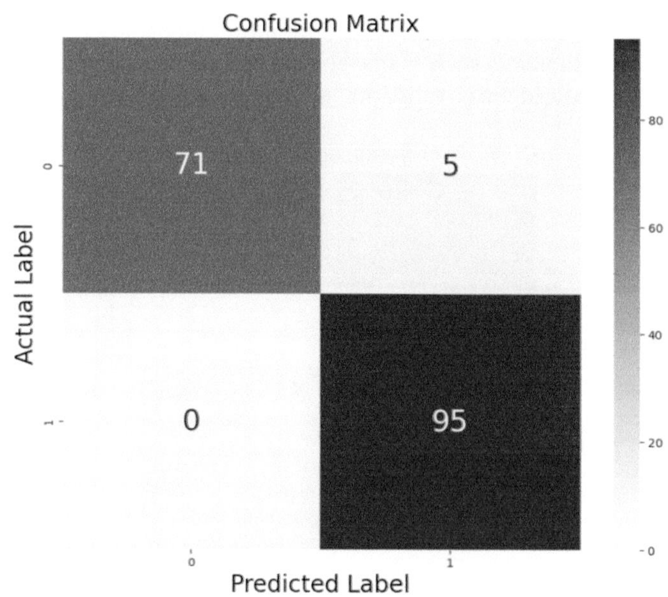

Fig. 5 SVM confusion matrix.

```
Accuracy =  0.9707602339181286
Precision =  0.95
Recall\Sensitivity =  1.0
Specificity =  0.9342105263157895
F1 Score =  0.9743589743589743
AUC Score = 0.9671052631578948
Kappa score =  0.9403973509933775
Log Loss =  1.0539079938338352
```

Fig. 6 SVM accuracy metrics.

tuning via Randomized Search CV includes the regularization parameter CC, kernel type, and polynomial degree. CC balances training error and model complexity, while the kernel and degree define the decision boundary. The search grid spans diverse values to enable thorough model optimization.

$$f(x) = \sum_{i=1}^{n} \alpha_i y_i K(x_i, x) + b \qquad \text{...(9.2)}$$

The Randomized Search CV runs 100 iterations with 5-fold validation to optimize SVM parameters. The best model uses a polynomial kernel with $C = 1$ $C = 1$ and degree 2, showing strong performance in ASD classification. This configuration is then fitted and evaluated, with confusion matrices and cross-validation scores confirming its effectiveness in capturing complex phenotypic patterns.

Table 3 SVM Metrics.

Accuracy	*Precision*	*Recall*	*Specificity*	*F1 score*	*AUC*	*Kappa loss*	*Log loss*
0.97	0.95	1.0	0.94	0.97	0.96	0.94	1.05

B. CNN Based Approaches

The study evaluates deep learning models—AlexNet, GoogLeNet, and ResNet—for ASD detection using structural MRI scans, highlighting their classification potential and comparative performance.

1. **AlexNet:** AlexNet, a deep CNN with five convolutional layers, max-pooling, and three fully connected layers, was adapted for ASD classification using ABIDE sMRI data [33]. Preprocessing included Canny Edge Detection and data augmentation. Grid Search Optimization (GSO) was used to tune parameters, yielding a classification accuracy of 62.73%. While AlexNet offered a reliable baseline, its simplicity limited its ability to capture complex structural patterns.
2. **GoogleNet:** GoogleNet (Inception v1), a deep CNN with inception modules selecting filters of sizes 1×1, 3×3, and 5×5, enables efficient feature extraction [34]. In this study, it was fine-tuned via transfer learning on sMRI data and optimized using Grid Search Optimization (GSO). Pretrained on ImageNet, the model achieved 59.32% accuracy in ASD classification—offering improved feature extraction over AlexNet but slightly lower overall performance.

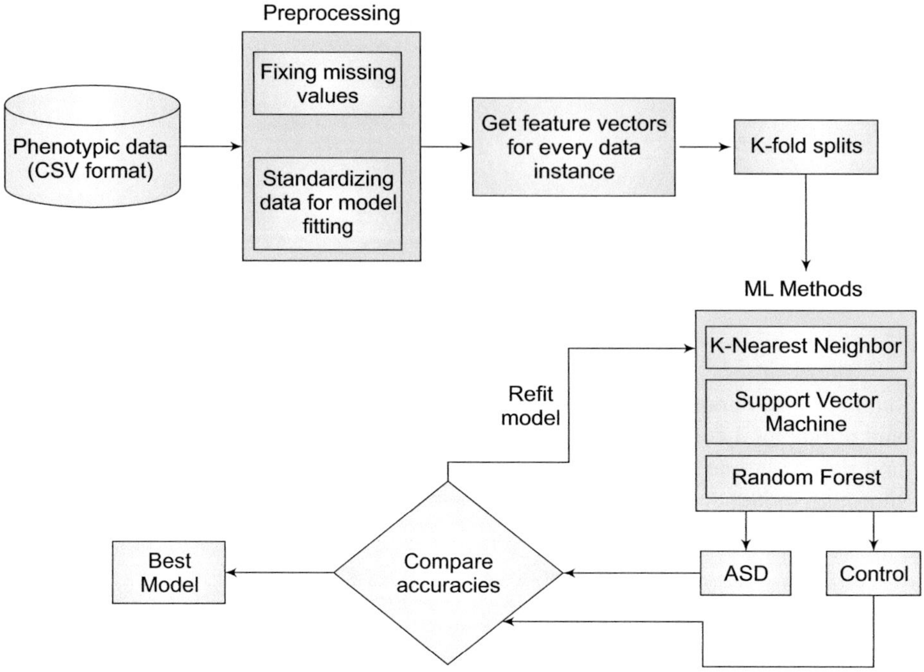

Fig. 7 ML methods flowchart.

3. **ResNet18:** ResNet employs residual learning via skip connections to mitigate vanishing gradients, enabling stable training of deep networks [34]. In this study, ResNet18 was optimized using Grid Search Optimization (GSO) and applied to sMRI data for ASD classification. It achieved 66.36% accuracy, outperforming AlexNet and GoogLeNet, highlighting its strength in capturing complex hierarchical features for ASD detection.

Table 5 CNN methods combined table.

Method	*Accuracy*
AlexNet	0.97
GoogleNet	0.85
ResNet	0.94

C. Federated Learning and Explainable AI

Federated Learning offers a vital approach for ASD detection by enabling decentralized processing of large fMRI and MRI datasets across local machines [35]. Models are trained locally, aggregated on a central server, and redistributed to nodes, enhancing scalability and security by avoiding cloud-based data transfers [40]. This makes it especially suitable for large institutions like hospitals.

Combining Explainable AI (XAI) with Federated Learning [37] enhances model transparency and reliability in ASD detection [37]. Techniques like SHAP and LIME [38] clarify feature contributions, making predictions interpretable for clinicians—a critical need in ASD diagnosis [36]. This integration also strengthens privacy and security across the detection pipeline [39], while improving efficiency through decentralized processing.

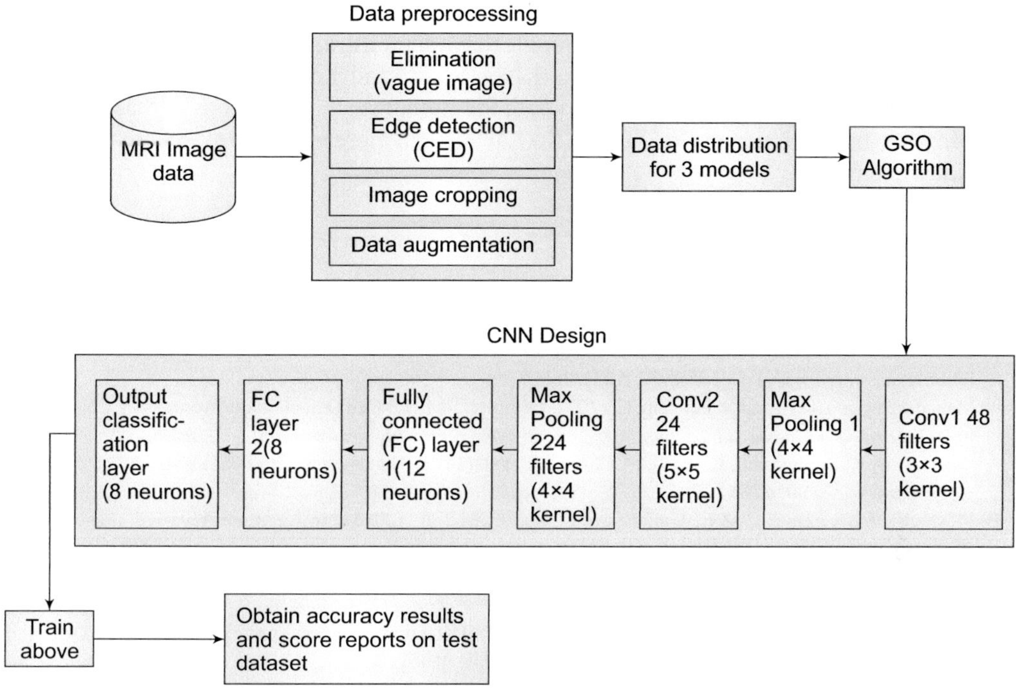

Fig. 8 CNN methods flow-diagram.

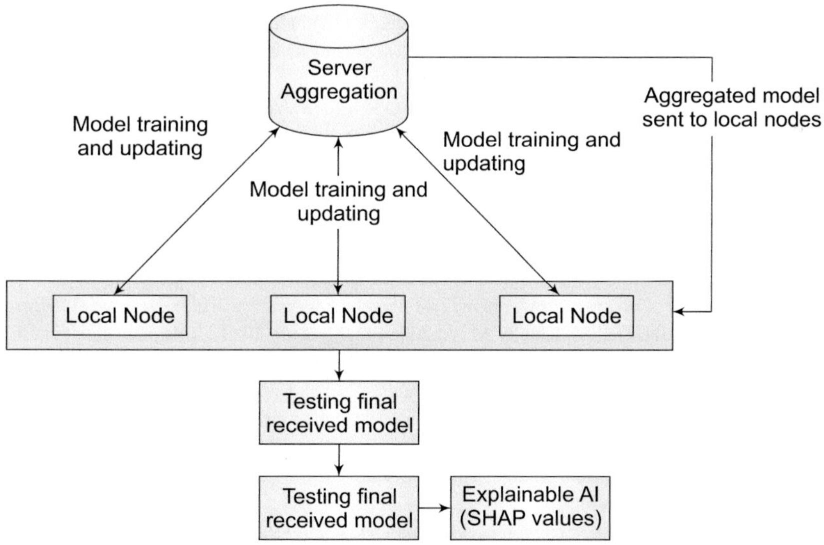

Fig. 9 FL/XAI block diagram.

2. Conclusion

In summary, this chapter underscores the vast potential of AI in ASD detection and management. It highlights the promise of Federated Learning (FL) for secure, decentralized model training and

Explainable AI (XAI) techniques like SHAP and LIME for enhancing clinical interpretability. Deep learning models—ResNet, AlexNet, and GoogleNet—demonstrate strong performance on sMRI data, while traditional ML methods such as KNN, SVM, and Random Forest show utility with phenotypic datasets. The chapter emphasizes both the strengths and limitations of these approaches, advocating for the combined use of FL and XAI to achieve more transparent, secure, and effective diagnostic systems.

References

1. Dwivedi, R., Dave, D., Naik, H., Singhal, S., Omer, R. et al. (2023). Explainable AI (XAI): Core ideas, techniques, and solutions. *ACM Computing Surveys*, *55*(9), 1–33.
2. Basu, K., Sinha, R., Ong, A. and Basu, T. (2020). Artificial intelligence: How is it changing medical sciences and its future?. *Indian journal of dermatology*, *65*(5), 365–370.
3. Mahadevaswamy, U.B. and Manjunath, C. (2022, October). f-MRI Based Detection of Autism using CNN Algorithm. In *2022 IEEE 2nd Mysore Sub Section International Conference (MysuruCon)* (pp. 1–5). IEEE.
4. Wei, J., Tay, Y., Bommasani, R., Raffel, C., Zoph, B. et al. (2022). Emergent abilities of large language models. *arXiv preprint arXiv:2206.07682*.
5. Mostapha, M., Casanova, M.F., Gimel'farb, G. and El-Baz, A. (2015). Towards non-invasive image-based early diagnosis of autism. In *Medical Image Computing and Computer-Assisted Intervention--MICCAI 2015: 18th International Conference, Munich, Germany, October 5-9, 2015, Proceedings, Part II 18* (pp. 160–168). Springer International Publishing.
6. Farooq, M.S., Tehseen, R., Sabir, M. and Atal, Z. (2023). Detection of autism spectrum disorder (ASD) in children and adults using machine learning. *Scientific reports*, *13*(1), 9605.
7. Lundervold, A.S. and Lundervold, A. (2019). An overview of deep learning in medical imaging focusing on MRI. *Zeitschrift für Medizinische Physik*, *29*(2), 102–127.
8. Wang, H., Jing, H., Yang, J., Liu, C., Hu, L. et al. (2024). Identifying autism spectrum disorder from multi-modal data with privacy-preserving. *NPJ Mental Health Research*, *3*(1), 15.
9. Shaheen, M.Y. (2021). Applications of Artificial Intelligence (AI) in healthcare: A review. *ScienceOpen Preprints*.
10. Maleki Varnosfaderani, S. and Forouzanfar, M. (2024). The role of AI in hospitals and clinics: transforming healthcare in the 21st century. *Bioengineering*, *11*(4), 337.
11. Hashimoto, D.A., Rosman, G., Rus, D. and Meireles, O.R. (2018). Artificial intelligence in surgery: promises and perils. *Annals of surgery*, *268*(1), 70–76.
12. Bi, W.L., Hosny, A., Schabath, M.B., Giger, M.L., Birkbak, N.J. et al. (2019). Artificial intelligence in cancer imaging: clinical challenges and applications. *CA: a cancer journal for clinicians*, *69*(2), 127–157.
13. Keskinbora, K.H. (2019). Medical ethics considerations on artificial intelligence. *Journal of clinical neuroscience*, *64*, 277–282.
14. Olorunsogo, T., Adenyi, A.O., Okolo, C.A. and Babawarun, O. (2024). Ethical considerations in AI-enhanced medical decision support systems: A review. *World Journal of Advanced Engineering Technology and Sciences*, *11*(1), 329–336.
15. Helmy, E., Elnakib, A., ElNakieb, Y., Khudri, M., Abdelrahim, M. et al. (2023). Role of artificial intelligence for autism diagnosis using DTI and fMRI: A survey. *Biomedicines*, *11*(7), 1858.
16. ElNakieb, Y., Ali, M.T., Elnakib, A., Shalaby, A., Soliman, A. et al. (2021). The role of diffusion tensor MR imaging (DTI) of the brain in diagnosing autism spectrum disorder: promising results. *Sensors*, *21*(24), 8171.
17. Ktena, S.I., Parisot, S., Ferrante, E., Rajchl, M., Lee, M. et al. (2018). Metric learning with spectral graph convolutions on brain connectivity networks. *NeuroImage*, *169*, 431–442.
18. Li, Y., Liao, I.Y., Zhong, N., Toshihiro, F., Wang, Y. et al. (2023, December). Generative AI enables the detection of autism using eeg signals. In *Chinese Conference on Biometric Recognition* (pp. 375–384). Singapore: Springer Nature Singapore.
19. Kairouz, P., McMahan, H.B., Avent, B., Bellet, A., Bennis, M. et al. (2019). Advances and Open Problems in Federated Learning. *Found. Trends Mach. Learn.*, 14, 1–210.
20. Bonawitz, K., Eichner, H., Grieskamp, W., Huba, D., Ingerman, A. et al. (2019). Towards Federated Learning at Scale: System Design. ArXiv, abs/1902.01046.
21. Hu, Y., Zhang, Y., Gong, D. and Sun, X. (2022). Multiparticipant federated feature selection algorithm with particle swarm optimization for imbalanced data under privacy protection. *IEEE Transactions on Artificial Intelligence*, *4*(5), 1002–1016.

22. Liang, W., Yang, Y., Yang, C., Hu, Y., Xie, S. et al. (2022). PDPChain: A consortium blockchain-based privacy protection scheme for personal data. *IEEE Transactions on Reliability*, *72*(2), 586–598.
23. Silva, A., Schrum, M., Hedlund-Botti, E., Gopalan, N. and Gombolay, M. et al. (2023). Explainable artificial intelligence: Evaluating the objective and subjective impacts of XAI on human-agent interaction. *International Journal of Human–Computer Interaction*, *39*(7), 1390–1404.
24. Nwakanma, C.I., Ahakonye, L.A.C., Njoku, J.N., Odirichukwu, J.C., Okolie, S.A. et al. (2023). Explainable artificial intelligence (XAI) for intrusion detection and mitigation in intelligent connected vehicles: A review. *Applied Sciences*, *13*(3), 1252.
25. Arrieta, A.B., Díaz-Rodríguez, N., Del Ser, J., Bennetot, A., Tabik, S. et al. (2020). Explainable Artificial Intelligence (XAI): Concepts, taxonomies, opportunities and challenges toward responsible AI. *Information fusion*, *58*, 82–115.
26. Ali, S., Abuhmed, T., El-Sappagh, S., Muhammad, K., Alonso-Moral, J.M. et al. (2023). Explainable Artificial Intelligence (XAI): What we know and what is left to attain Trustworthy Artificial Intelligence. *Information fusion*, *99*, 101805.
27. Mohanty, A.S., Parida, P. and Patra, K.C. (2022). Usage of ML Techniques for ASD Detection: A Comparative Analysis of Various Classifiers. In *Machine Learning and Deep Learning in Medical Data Analytics and Healthcare Applications* (pp. 91–112). CRC Press.
28. Altay, O. and Ulas, M. (2018, March). Prediction of the autism spectrum disorder diagnosis with linear discriminant analysis classifier and K-nearest neighbor in children. In *2018 6th international symposium on digital forensic and security (ISDFS)* (pp. 1–4). IEEE.
29. Erkan, U. and Thanh, D.N. (2019). Autism spectrum disorder detection with machine learning methods. *Current Psychiatry Research and Reviews Formerly: Current Psychiatry Reviews*, *15*(4), 297–308.
30. Abirami, T., Kavipriya, M., Mapari, S., Kavin, T., Jayadharshini, P. et al. (2023). A Machine Learning Techniques for Early Autism Spectrum Disorder Detection Through Comparative Analysis of Feature Engineering and Classification Models. *2023 International Conference on Advances in Computation, Communication and Information Technology (ICAICCIT)*, 577–581.
31. Yücelbaş, Ş. and Yücelbaş, C. (2021). Autism spectrum disorder detection using sequential minimal optimization-support vector machine hybrid classifier according to history of jaundice and family autism in children. *Concurrency and Computation: Practice and Experience*, 34.
32. Farooq, M.S., Tehseen, R., Sabir, M. and Atal, Z. (2023). Detection of autism spectrum disorder (ASD) in children and adults using machine learning. *Scientific Reports*, 13.
33. Menaka, R., Karthik, R., Saranya, S., Niranjan, M. and Kabilan, S. et al. (2024). An improved AlexNet model and cepstral coefficient-based classification of autism using EEG. *Clinical EEG and Neuroscience*, 55(1), 43–51.
34. Mohi ud Din, Q. and Jayanthy, A.K. (2022). Automated classification of autism spectrum disorder using EEG signals and convolutional neural networks. *Biomedical Engineering: Applications, Basis and Communications*, 34(02), 2250020.
35. Lakhan, A., Mohammed, M.A., Abdulkareem, K.H., Hamouda, H. and Alyahya, S. et al. (2023). Autism Spectrum Disorder detection framework for children based on federated learning integrated CNN-LSTM. *Computers in Biology and Medicine*, 166, 107539.
36. Shamseddine, H., Otoum, S. and Mourad, A. (2022, December). On the feasibility of federated learning for neurodevelopmental disorders: Asd detection use-case. In *GLOBECOM 2022-2022 IEEE Global Communications Conference* (pp. 1121–1127). IEEE.
37. Bárcena, J.L.C., Daole, M., Ducange, P., Marcelloni, F., Renda, A. et al. (2022). Fed-XAI: Federated Learning of Explainable Artificial Intelligence Models. In *XAI. it@ AI* IA* (pp. 104–117).
38. Nguyen, H.T.T., Cao, H.Q., Nguyen, K.V.T. and Pham, N.D.K. (2021, May). Evaluation of explainable artificial intelligence: Shap, lime, and cam. In *Proceedings of the FPT AI Conference* (pp. 1–6).
39. Spartalis, C.N., Semertzidis, T. and Daras, P. (2023, September). Balancing XAI with Privacy and Security Considerations. In *European Symposium on Research in Computer Security* (pp. 111–124). Cham: Springer Nature Switzerland.
40. Mahmud, M., Kaiser, M.S., Rahman, M.A., Wadhera, T., Brown, D.J. et al. (2022, June). Towards explainable and privacy-preserving artificial intelligence for personalisation in autism spectrum disorder. In *International Conference on Human-Computer Interaction* (pp. 356–370). Cham: Springer International Publishing.

10

Artificial Intelligence and Machine Learning in Detecting Autism: Transforming Diagnosis and Care

Akshaya AVR[1*], Vijayalakshmi B[2], Nisha P[3], Anupriya Ramachandran[4] and Vasanthaseelan Sathiyaseelan[5]

1. Introduction

Autism Spectrum Disorder (ASD) is a neurodevelopmental condition that impairs social interaction, communication, and leads to repetitive behaviors. Its symptoms range from mild to severe, hence the term "spectrum." As defined by DSM-5 (2013), diagnosis involves deficits in social-emotional reciprocity, nonverbal communication, relationship management, and the presence of stereotyped behaviors and abnormal sensory responses. Affecting roughly 1–2% of the global population, ASD demands significant attention from clinicians and researchers.

The gap in Autism Spectrum Disorder (ASD) diagnosis is narrowing as evidence-based therapies are increasingly initiated soon after diagnosis, improving developmental outcomes. However, many children are still diagnosed late due to limited access to targeted services. Multidisciplinary teams including speech-language pathologists, paediatricians, and developmental psychologists use gold-standard tools like ADOS and ADI-R to assess ASD, though these methods are time-intensive and subjective. The lack of objective biomarkers further contributes to diagnostic variability, especially in untreated populations. To address these limitations, AI and ML technologies are emerging as promising alternatives. By leveraging behavioural, genetic, and neuroimaging data, these models can uncover complex patterns beyond human detection, automate parts of the diagnostic process, reduce reliance on scarce specialists, and support early, consistent ASD identification across diverse populations.

AI particularly machine learning (ML) and deep learning (DL) is increasingly effective in early detection of Autism Spectrum Disorder (ASD). Researchers are exploring diverse datasets and algorithms to build robust diagnostic models. [21] demonstrated that ML can uncover ASD-related

[1] Assistant Professor, School of Business and Management, CHRIST University, Bengaluru, India

[2] Department of ECE, Sri Krishna College of Engineering and Technology, Coimbatore, India.

[3] Department of CSE, Dr. NGP Institute of Technology, Coimbatore, India.

[4] Department of Software Systems, Sri Krishna Arts and Science, Kuniyamuthur, Coimbatore, India.

[5] Department of Autotronics, Saveetha School of Engineering, Saveetha Institute of Medical and Technical Sciences, Saveetha University, Chennai, India.

* Corresponding author: akshayaraam2332@gmail.com

DOI: 10.1201/9781003541318-14

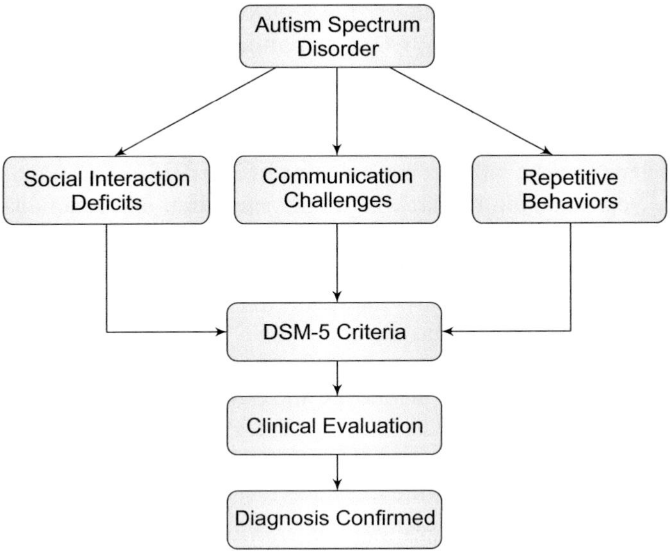

Fig. 1 Overview of ASD Characteristics and Diagnostic Process.

patterns across data types. MRI, especially fMRI and sMRI, offers insights into brain changes, with [20] reviewing AI-driven approaches for automated ASD detection, though challenges in MRI automation persist. Facial analysis using DL is a fast-growing area, as subtle facial markers may correlate with ASD. Studies by [2] and [3] show that pre-trained CNN models enhance diagnostic accuracy. [17] further validated DL's efficacy using VGG16 for pediatric ASD screening. As model complexity grows, Explainable AI (XAI) becomes vital;[2] advocate for transparency in DL systems. Ethnoracial bias remains a concern, especially in facial image-based models. [5] emphasize the need for diverse datasets to ensure equitable screening. Overall, while AI holds transformative promise for ASD detection, future research must prioritize multimodal data, global representation, improved explainability, and bias mitigation to realize its full potential.

This chapter explores AI and ML in autism detection, highlighting current diagnostic challenges and emphasizing improvements in accuracy, efficiency, and usability. It reviews key data sources, modern ML techniques, and ethical considerations, concluding with insights into clinical applications and their potential to transform ASD diagnosis and care.

2. Understanding Autism Spectrum Disorder (ASD)

Autism Spectrum Disorder (ASD) is a neurodevelopmental condition emerging in early childhood that affects perception, social interaction, and communication. It is marked by deficits in sociability, repetitive behaviors, and rigid interests, often intensified by atypical sensory processing, contributing to its heterogeneity. Previously distinct diagnoses autistic disorder, Asperger syndrome, and PDD-NOS are now unified under ASD, reflecting its spectrum nature and varied symptom expression. Individuals may range from severely impaired in communication and daily functioning to highly verbal yet socially challenged. Common traits include stereotyped motor behaviors (e.g., rocking, hand flapping), strict routines, and sensory sensitivities, either heightened or diminished. ASD frequently co-occurs with conditions such as anxiety, ADHD, intellectual disability, epilepsy, and gastrointestinal disorders, all of which can impact functionality and quality of life, necessitating thorough evaluation and coordinated care. Notably, many individuals with ASD exhibit exceptional cognitive strengths particularly in pattern recognition, visual-spatial reasoning, long-term memory, and detail-focused tasks which, when supported through tailored education and therapy, can significantly enhance personal and professional outcomes. Etiologically, ASD arises from a multifactorial interplay of genetic, neurological, and environmental factors. Genetic studies reveal numerous copy number variations and single-gene mutations linked to increased ASD risk, though no singular "autism gene" exists; rather, a constellation of inherited and de novo variants contributes to its development. Neuroimaging research highlights structural and functional brain differences, especially in social-executive networks and interregional connectivity. Environmental influences such as prenatal drug exposure, maternal infections, and birth complications may also play a role, though their mechanisms remain under investigation.

Early diagnosis of Autism Spectrum Disorder (ASD) is critical for optimal outcomes, with interventions particularly behavioral, speech, and occupational therapies most effective when initiated before age three. Traditional diagnostic methods, reliant on multidisciplinary clinical evaluations, are often slow and subjective, delaying access to early support and reducing long-term independence. To address these limitations, inclusive, person-centered care models are increasingly favored over deficit-based approaches. Evidence shows that individualized plans tailored to a person's strengths, interests, and needs foster greater skill development than standardized protocols. Autism Spectrum Disorder (ASD) presents with diverse symptoms, primarily affecting social interaction, communication, and exhibiting repetitive behaviors. Variability in sensory processing leads to individualized manifestations. Diagnosis relies on multidisciplinary behavioral and developmental evaluations to identify core traits such as impaired reciprocity, nonverbal challenges, and stereotyped actions. Genetic factors play a significant role, with numerous variants linked to increased ASD risk, underscoring the value of genetic assessment. Effective care integrates behavioral therapies, educational support, and personalized interventions. [10] emphasize the interconnectedness of assessment, genetics, and treatment, advocating for a unified diagnostic and care model.

3. The Role of Artificial Intelligence and Machine Learning in Healthcare

Artificial Intelligence (AI) and Machine Learning (ML) are increasingly vital in healthcare, particularly for diagnosis and treatment. AI encompasses human-like reasoning and decision-making, while ML its data-driven subset learns patterns from large datasets without explicit programming. Unlike rule-based systems, ML improves with experience, making it well-suited for medical applications.In Autism Spectrum Disorder (ASD) detection, ML and Deep Learning (DL) enable early, accurate diagnosis by analyzing behavioral, genetic, and neuroimaging data. Studies by [9] and [14] demonstrate ML's ability to identify ASD across age groups, reinforcing its diagnostic potential. More broadly, AI supports personalized care, drug discovery, robotic surgery, and patient monitoring. DL models rival radiologists in detecting breast and lung tumors from imaging, while ML algorithms predict hypoglycemia using glucose monitor data. Natural Language Processing (NLP) tools also detect early signs of psychiatric conditions like depression and anxiety, showcasing AI's role in enhancing diagnostic precision and clinical efficiency.

Traditional biomedical decision-making relied on clinical guidelines, expert judgment, and specialized models, which struggle to manage today's complex, high-volume data. AI and ML have transformed this landscape by enabling adaptive, data-driven systems especially vital for neurodevelopmental disorders like ASD, where symptoms are subtle and variable. These technologies integrate diverse data types scans, genetics, behavior, and physiology uncovering hidden patterns that traditional methods often miss. Deep learning models, for instance, can detect early ASD indicators from video, audio, eye-tracking, and neuroimaging, enhancing diagnostic precision and personalization. Given ASD's multifactorial nature, AI and ML offer a scalable, evolving solution for early and accurate detection.

4. Data Sources used in ASD Detection via Machine Learning

Machine Learning (ML) techniques for ASD detection rely heavily on the diversity and quality of training data, spanning behavioral, biological, and neurological domains. Common sources include social interaction videos, ADOS scores, and clinical logbooks, which help build detailed diagnostic profiles. ML is increasingly used to analyze these heterogeneous datasets, enhancing diagnostic precision and insight generation[8] demonstrated ML's utility in analyzing MRI scans to uncover neurological markers of ASD and ADHD. [13] showed that 1D-CNNs effectively detect ASD by identifying complex patterns. [14] provided a comprehensive review of ML methods in ASD diagnosis, while [24] emphasized the value of integrating personal traits with robust ML models.These studies affirm ML's transformative role in ASD research, enabling earlier and more individualized diagnoses. Techniques like computer vision can detect atypical eye movements and repetitive behaviors from video data. However, behavioral data remains susceptible to observer bias, contextual variability, and challenges in standardization across settings.

Genetic and genomic data play a vital role in understanding ASD, as inheritance patterns are increasingly evident. Advanced sequencing has revealed key contributors such as copy number variations, SNPs, and other variants linked to autism. Machine learning algorithms can model complex gene interactions and uncover potential etiological pathways. However, due to ASD's multifactorial nature and limited genotype–phenotype correlations, genetic data alone offers limited diagnostic utility [8,13,15,24].

Neuroimaging methods such as fMRI, structural MRI, and EEG offer key insights into ASD by revealing altered functional connectivity, anatomical differences, and neural activity patterns. However, their high cost, limited accessibility, and reliance on expert interpretation hinder their use in routine screening. Speech and language analysis, supported by Natural Language Processing (NLP), extracts features like rhythm, syntax, and pragmatics to identify ASD traits such as echolalia, atypical intonation, and delayed expressive language. Though non-invasive and scalable, these assessments require culturally sensitive frameworks to ensure diagnostic accuracy.

Table 1 Overview of Common Data Sources Used in ASD Detection via ML.

Data type	*Description*	*Advantages*	*Limitations*
Behavioral Data (e.g., video recordings, ADOS scores)	Captures social interaction patterns, eye contact, motor behaviors	Rich behavioral insights, non-invasive	Subjective interpretation, contextual variability
Genetic/Genomic Data	Includes SNPs, CNVs, gene expression profiles	Biological basis for risk prediction	Limited genotype–phenotype correlation, high cost
Neuroimaging (fMRI, MRI, EEG)	Functional and structural brain imaging data	Reveals neural connectivity differences	Expensive, requires expertise, limited accessibility
Speech & Language Data	Vocalizations, prosody, syntax analysis	Non-invasive, captures communication anomalies	Affected by language development stage, dialects
Wearables & Motion Sensors	Accelerometers, gyroscopes, depth cameras	Continuous monitoring in real-world settings	Noise interference, calibration issues
Social Interaction Logs	Digital behavior from apps, eye-tracking, sensors	Objective tracking of engagement patterns	Context-dependent, may miss nuanced interactions

Motion tracking and wearable sensors, such as those in the MOVAIDS system (accelerometers, gyroscopes, depth cameras), enable continuous, objective monitoring of motor patterns and behaviors in natural environments. These tools help detect repetitive and sensory-motor anomalies over time, offering dynamic insights beyond clinical snapshots. However, issues like sensor artifacts, measurement consistency, and developmental variability remain. Complementary data from social interaction logs, mobile apps, and eye-tracking tools capture nuanced social and contextual behaviors. When analyzed with ML techniques, these datasets reveal subtle, stable differences in social cognition and responsiveness that surpass the sensitivity of traditional assessments.

While individual data types aid ASD detection, integrating them in multimodal ML frameworks enhances diagnostic reliability by combining behavioral, genetic, neuroimaging, and physiological inputs. This fusion offers a more complete autism profile but poses challenges in data alignment, feature integration, and model interpretability requiring robust computing and validation. Future progress depends on refined data collection and scalable ML algorithms for broader clinical use.

5. Machine Learning Models and Techniques in Autism Detection

Machine learning (ML) has significantly advanced ASD research by enabling analysis of large, complex datasets. Key approaches include supervised, unsupervised, deep learning, NLP, and emerging reinforcement learning, each offering trade-offs in interpretability, cost, and diagnostic precision. Recent studies underscore ML's growing impact: [31] applied motion analysis for early ASD detection; [36] proposed a clinically viable ML framework;[6]) and [16] improved diagnostic speed and accuracy; [27] and [33] developed classification models; and [26] reviewed feature selection and classification techniques. Collectively, these works affirm ML's role in enabling faster, more accurate, and personalized ASD diagnosis and intervention.

Supervised learning is widely used in ASD detection due to its reliance on labeled datasets, typically comprising ASD cases matched with neurotypical controls. Support Vector Machines (SVMs), among the most common classifiers, excel in high-dimensional spaces and perform well with small samples, such as in neuroimaging or genetic studies achieving over 80% accuracy using fMRI-based resting-state connectomes. Random Forests, which aggregate multiple decision trees, are effective in handling noisy, inconsistent data and aid biomarker identification through feature ranking. While Decision Trees offer greater interpretability, they generalize less effectively than ensemble methods like Random Forests.

Model	Use Case	Accuracy	Interpretability
SVM	Classification	High	Medium
Random Forest	Feature Selection	Medium-High	Medium
CNN	Image Analysis	Very High	Low
RNN	Speech Analysis	High	Low
NLP Models	Text/Speech	Medium-High	Medium

Fig. 2 Comparison of Machine Learning Techniques.

When labelled data is scarce, unsupervised learning methods help uncover hidden patterns without predefined classes. Clustering techniques like K-means and hierarchical clustering have identified ASD subtypes from behavioral and neuroimaging data, revealing clinically distinct groups with varied developmental trajectories and treatment responses. Isolation forests and autoencoders further aid early screening by detecting subtle anomalies that may warrant closer evaluation, even if diagnostic criteria aren't fully met.

Table 2 Comparison of Machine Learning Models Used in ASD Detection.

Model Type	*Use case in ASD detection*	*Strengths*	*Limitations*
SVM (Support Vector Machine)	Classifying neuroimaging or genetic features	Effective in high-dimensional spaces	Sensitive to parameter tuning
Random Forest	Feature selection and classification	Robust to overfitting, interpretable	May struggle with complex nonlinear relationships
CNN (Convolutional Neural Network)	Image-based detection (e.g., fMRI/MRI)	High accuracy in image pattern recognition	Black-box nature, computationally intensive
RNN/LSTM	Analyzing speech or time-series behavioral data	Handles sequential data well	Requires large datasets, training complexity
k-NN	Baseline classification using feature similarity	Simple to implement	Computationally expensive at scale
NLP-Based Models (e.g., BERT, Transformers)	Text/speech analysis for language anomalies	Captures semantic and syntactic nuances	Needs domain-specific fine-tuning

Enhanced datasets and computing power have revolutionized ASD detection through deep learning. CNNs, originally built for image tasks, now analyze MRI/fMRI scans to uncover subtle brain differences, achieving over 90% accuracy in multi-site studies. RNNs and LSTMs effectively model sequential data like speech and motor patterns, revealing ASD-specific temporal traits. Recent NLP progress has introduced Transformer models for integrating diverse modalities by capturing long-range dependencies.

Natural Language Processing (NLP) plays a key role in detecting early signs of ASD through analysis of speech and text. Features like echolalia, limited vocabulary, and pragmatic language deficits are captured using techniques such as bag-of-words, syntactic parsing, and semantic embeddings. Deep learning models like BERT and GPT, fine-tuned on ASD-related data, effectively identify linguistic anomalies in transcripts and caregiver reports. Combined with acoustic analysis of prosody and intonation, these models have demonstrated moderate to high accuracy in distinguishing ASD speech patterns.

Reinforcement learning (RL) offers promise for adaptive ASD interventions by responding to real-time feedback, though its clinical use remains nascent. RL systems, such as robotic therapies, adjust interactions based on child engagement to enhance social learning. This signals a shift toward ML not only detecting ASD but also guiding personalized care. Evaluating ML models involves metrics like accuracy, recall, specificity, and AUC-ROC where recall captures ASD cases, specificity identifies neurotypical individuals, and AUC-ROC reflects overall balance. Accuracy alone can be misleading in imbalanced datasets. Deep learning models trained on multimodal data often outperform traditional ML in accuracy and sensitivity, but their limited interpretability poses challenges for clinical adoption.

Model complexity versus interpretability remains a key challenge in ML-based ASD detection. Deep learning offers high accuracy but lacks transparency, limiting clinical trust. Simpler models like decision trees and logistic regression are easier to interpret but often insufficiently sensitive. Emerging explainable AI (XAI) techniques such as SHAP, LIME, and attention mechanisms aim to bridge this gap by enhancing model clarity without sacrificing performance.

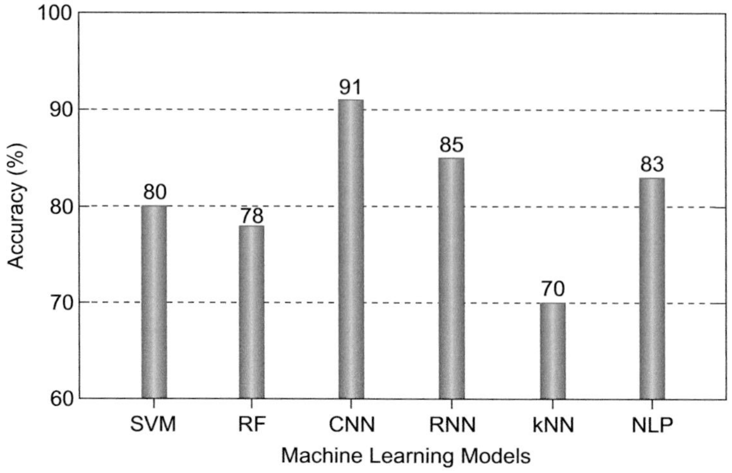

Fig. 3 Accuracy comparison of ML models used in ASD detection.

A range of machine learning techniques have been applied to ASD detection, each with distinct advantages. Supervised models like SVMs and Random Forests offer interpretable results for structured data, while unsupervised methods uncover hidden patterns and anomalies. CNNs and RNNs excel at processing complex, unstructured inputs but require careful validation. NLP enhances linguistic marker identification, and reinforcement learning introduces adaptive intervention possibilities. Achieving a balance between model accuracy and interpretability is key to enabling reliable clinical automation.

6. AI-Powered Tools for Behavioral Analysis in ASD

AI has significantly streamlined the identification and understanding of Autism Spectrum Disorder (ASD) by enabling faster, more objective behavioral analysis across diverse settings. Advances in computing, robotics, and monitoring technologies have improved early symptom detection, diagnostics, and therapy planning. Research reflects a broad spectrum of AI and ML applications in ASD, from automated detection using CNNs [28] to neuroimaging-based ML reviews [20,34]. [34] highlighted AI's evolution in diagnostics, while [29] and [38] demonstrated its role in adaptive interventions. [30] provided a comprehensive overview of AI in autism care, and [1] evaluated ML models for classification. [12] emphasized the importance of explainable AI in pediatric diagnostics. Together, these studies underscore AI's growing impact on personalized, efficient, and trustworthy ASD care.

Due to distinct social behaviours in ASD, computer vision AI and facial expression recognition have become leading areas of study. Subtle cues like reduced eye contact or atypical emotional responses are hard to detect manually but can be captured using Convolutional Neural Networks (CNNs), which analyze micro-expressions and facial dynamics in video. When trained on images of children during structured activities, CNNs can differentiate autistic from neurotypical individuals and track emotional changes over time. Motion tracking and gesture recognition further enhance behavioral analysis. Systems using depth cameras, accelerometers, and IMUs detect repetitive movements like hand flapping or rocking, distinguishing voluntary from involuntary actions. These tools also assess social gestures such as pointing or turn-taking, aiding both diagnosis and therapy through real-time feedback.Natural Language Processing (NLP) supports speech-based ASD evaluation by analyzing vocabulary, grammar, prosody, and rhythm. Delayed speech, echolalia, and atypical tone are common markers. Models like RNNs and Transformer RNNs have shown strong correlations between speech patterns and ASD severity. These advances enable remote, mobile-friendly screening tools crucial for early intervention in underserved areas.

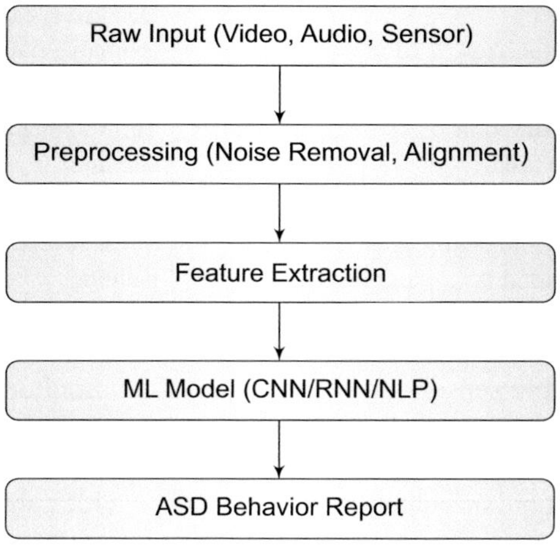

Fig. 4 AI-based behavioural analysis pipeline in ASD detection.

AI-powered robots now play active roles in both assessment and therapy for children with ASD. Social robots monitor interactions during play and structured activities, offering consistent evaluations across users. Studies show autistic children often respond more predictably to robots than unfamiliar adults. Machine learning further personalizes interventions based on individual profiles, enhancing the effectiveness of traditional behavioral therapy.

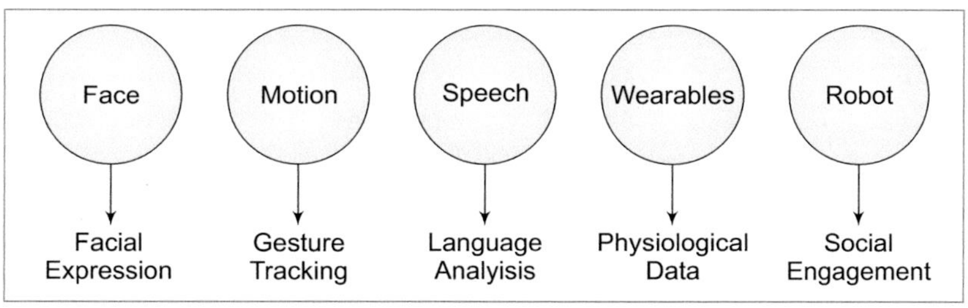

Fig. 5 AI-Powered Tools in Behavioural Analysis.

Table 3 AI-Powered Tools and their Applications in Behavioural Analysis for ASD.

Tool/Technology	*Function*	*Underlying technique*	*Target behaviour*	*Outcome/ Impact*
Facial Expression Recognition Systems	Analyze micro-expressions and gaze patterns	CNNs, Computer Vision	Eye contact, emotional expressions	Early identification of atypical social cues
Motion Tracking Systems	Monitor repetitive movements and motor coordination	IMUs, Accelerometers, ML classifiers	Hand flapping, rocking, gait anomalies	Quantitative assessment of stereotyped behaviors

Contd.

Table 3 *Contd.*

Tool/Technology	*Function*	*Underlying technique*	*Target behaviour*	*Outcome/ Impact*
Speech & Language Analyzers	Detect speech rhythm, intonation, lexical diversity	NLP, Acoustic Modeling	Delayed speech, echolalia, flat tone	Improved early screening through voice biomarkers
Social Robots	Engage children in interactive tasks	AI + ML + Robotics	Turn-taking, joint attention	Enhances engagement and standardized testing
Wearable Sensors (Smartwatches, Biosensors)	Track physiological and behavioral indicators	Sensor fusion, ML algorithms	Stress levels, activity patterns	Real-time monitoring and early warning systems

Mobile apps and wearable sensors now enable real-time monitoring of everyday behaviors in individuals with ASD. Devices like smartwatches and biosensors track heart rate, activity, vocal tone, and sleep key indicators of stress and sensory challenges. AI-powered apps analyze this data over time, detect emerging emotional or behavioral issues, and provide caregivers with instant alerts and guidance for timely intervention.

These advancements mark a shift in how experts assess behavior in ASD, with technology enhancing diagnostic accuracy by detecting subtle signs and automating parts of the process for complex cases. However, achieving these benefits demands rigorous validation, ethical safeguards around privacy and consent, and smooth integration into existing care systems. While AI shows promise in behavioral analysis, further evaluation of current tools remains essential.

```
FUNCTION preprocess_video(video_file):
    frames = extract_frames(video_file)
    cleaned_frames = []

    FOR EACH frame IN frames:
        face_detected = detect_face(frame)
        IF face_detected IS NOT NULL:
            aligned_face = align_face(face_detected)
            normalized_face = normalize_brightness(aligned_face)
            cleaned_frames.append(normalized_face)

    RETURN cleaned_frames

```

Code 1 Pseudocode for Preprocessing Behavioural Video Data.

Pseudocode 1 outlines preprocessing steps for video data to study facial expressions and motion in autism detection. It includes frame extraction, face detection, alignment, and normalization to ensure consistent input and minimize lighting, pose, and background variations enhancing CNN performance in identifying early ASD indicators like reduced eye contact or atypical gaze.

```
FUNCTION cnn_facial_expression_model():
    model = Sequential()

    model.add(Conv2D(32, (3,3), activation='relu', input_shape=(48,48,1)))
```

```
    model.add(MaxPooling2D((2,2)))
    model.add(Conv2D(64, (3,3), activation='relu'))
    model.add(MaxPooling2D((2,2)))
    model.add(Flatten())
    model.add(Dense(128, activation='relu'))
    model.add(Dense(num_classes, activation='softmax'))
    model.compile(optimizer='adam',
                  loss='categorical_crossentropy',
                  metrics=['accuracy'])
    RETURN model
```

Code 2 Pseudocode for Training an SVM Classifier Using Behavioural Features.

Pseudocode 2 demonstrates how Support Vector Machines (SVMs) classify individuals as ASD or non-ASD using behavioral features from assessments, videos, or sensors. It involves feature scaling, data splitting, model training, and performance evaluation. SVMs are especially effective with high-dimensional data like genetic or neuroimaging inputs.

```
FUNCTION cnn_facial_expression_model():
    model = Sequential()
    model.add(Conv2D(32, (3,3), activation='relu', input_shape=(48,48,1)))
    model.add(MaxPooling2D((2,2)))
    model.add(Conv2D(64, (3,3), activation='relu'))
    model.add(MaxPooling2D((2,2)))
    model.add(Flatten())
    model.add(Dense(128, activation='relu'))
    model.add(Dense(num_classes, activation='softmax'))
    model.compile(optimizer='adam',
                  loss='categorical_crossentropy',
                  metrics=['accuracy'])
    RETURN model
```

Code 3 Pseudocode for Facial Expression Recognition Using CNN.

Pseudocode 3 defines a basic CNN model for facial emotion classification, ideal for detecting micro-expressions in children with ASD. It extracts spatial features from grayscale images using convolutional layers, followed by dense layers for emotion categorization. The model employs the Adam optimizer and categorical cross-entropy loss for multi-class classification.

```
FUNCTION analyze_speech_patterns(audio_file):
    text = transcribe_audio_to_text(audio_file)
    tokens = tokenize(text)
    pos_tags = perform_pos_tagging(tokens)
    sentiment_score = calculate_sentiment(text)
    syntactic_complexity = measure_syntax(tokens)
```

```

    IF sentiment_score < threshold OR syntactic_complexity < baseline:
        RETURN "Atypical speech pattern detected"
    ELSE:
        RETURN "Typical speech pattern"
```

Code 4 Pseudocode for Speech Pattern Analysis Using NLP.

Pseudocode 4 outlines how NLP techniques analyze altered speech rhythms in individuals with ASD. It includes audio transcription, tokenization, POS tagging, and sentiment and syntax analysis. By detecting limited pitch or vocabulary variation, the system flags atypical speech patterns, enabling remote or real-time language assessments.

```
FUNCTION process_wearable_data(sensor_stream):
    filtered_data = remove_noise(sensor_stream)
    segmented_data = segment_into_windows(filtered_data)

    activity_labels = []
    FOR window IN segmented_data:
        fft_features = extract_fft_features(window)
        movement_pattern = classify_movement(fft_features)

        IF movement_pattern == 'repetitive':
            activity_labels.append('Repetitive behavior')
        ELSE:
            activity_labels.append('Normal movement')

        RETURN activity_labels
```

Code 5 Pseudocode for Wearable Sensor Data Processing.

Pseudocode 5 demonstrates how wearable sensor data (e.g., accelerometer, gyroscope) can detect repetitive movements linked to ASD. It involves noise filtering, time-based segmentation, FFT-based feature extraction, and movement classification. Tracking patterns over time enables early identification of atypical behaviours.

```
FUNCTION select_features_with_rfe(X, y):
    base_model = LogisticRegression()
    selector = RFE(estimator=base_model, n_features_to_select=10)

    selector.fit(X, y)
    selected_features = selector.get_support(indices=True)

    RETURN X[:, selected_features]
```

Code 6 Pseudocode for Feature Selection Using Recursive Feature Elimination.

Pseudocode 6 illustrates Recursive Feature Elimination (RFE), which improves model performance and interpretability by iteratively applying Logistic Regression to remove low-impact features. It's particularly effective for ASD detection when data contains noise or redundancy, such as in brain scans or survey responses.

```
FUNCTION evaluate_model_with_cv(model, X, y, k=5):
    kf = KFold(n_splits=k)
    scores = []

    FOR train_index, test_index IN kf.split(X):
        X_train, X_test = X[train_index], X[test_index]
        y_train, y_test = y[train_index], y[test_index]

        model.fit(X_train, y_train)
        score = model.score(X_test, y_test)
        scores.append(score)

    avg_score = mean(scores)
    RETURN avg_score
```

Code 7 Pseudocode for k-Fold Cross Validation.

Pseudocode 7 demonstrates k-fold cross-validation, a reliable method for evaluating machine learning models. It splits data into k parts, trains on k–1, and tests on the remaining part, repeating the process across all folds. Averaging the scores yields a more robust performance estimate, especially useful for small or imbalanced ASD datasets.

6.1 Case Studies and Real-world Applications

AI and ML in autism detection have progressed from theory to real-world tools like Duke's Autism and Beyond app and UC's Wearable AI Systems. These technologies enable remote, high-quality screening using mobile devices and cameras, enhancing early diagnosis through greater accessibility and objectivity. Despite promising results, challenges remain in scaling and refining these systems for broader clinical use.

The Autism & Beyond app, developed by Apple and Duke University via ResearchKit, enables remote autism screening by analyzing children's facial responses to video stimuli using deep learning, particularly CNNs. It combines facial recognition with caregiver questionnaires to assess developmental cues. Early studies showed strong alignment with clinical tools like M-CHAT and demonstrated its potential for scalable screening in underserved communities.

To advance AI-driven autism detection, University of California researchers developed an AI-based wearable system combining biosensors and smartwatches to monitor movement, heart rate variability, and motor control in real-world settings. Machine learning analyzes this data to identify atypical patterns, enabling timely intervention. Despite usability success among caregivers, challenges remain in reducing false positives across diverse age groups. Commercial efforts like Cognoa's FDA-approved diagnostic tool and the EU-funded AIDE project which integrates speech, eye tracking, and behavior analysis underscore growing momentum toward scalable, clinically validated AI solutions for ASD screening.

AI based autism applications show strong performance across user satisfaction, accessibility, and scalability, with studies reporting high specificity and sensitivity compared to gold-standard tools like ADOS. Users value faster screening, broader access, and long-term behavior tracking. However, concerns persist around data consistency, model generalizability, and ethical safeguards. Key lessons for future development include integrating real-time clinical workflows, ensuring culturally inclusive training data to reduce bias, and promoting algorithmic transparency to build trust.

Future directions in AI-based autism detection will likely focus on enhancing model explainability, broadening real-world applicability, and increasing access through telehealth and decentralized trials. Continued advancement promises more personalized, accurate, and evidence-driven interventions tailored to each individual on the spectrum.

Table 4 Summary of Key Case Studies and Real-World AI Applications in ASD Detection.

Project name	*Institution/ Organisation*	*Key technology used*	*Target population*	*Outcome/ Insights*
Autism & Beyond App	Duke University	Facial expression analysis via smartphone camera	Toddlers and young children	Detected early signs of ASD with 80% accuracy
Wearable AI System	University of California	Sensor-based motion and physiological data	Preschool-age children	Enabled continuous monitoring and real-time alerts
Cognoa Diagnostic Aid	Cognoa Inc.	Video analysis + caregiver input + ML	Children aged 18 months–6 years	FDA-cleared tool supporting clinicians in diagnosis
AIDE Project	European Union-funded	Multimodal AI (speech, eye-tracking, behavior)	Diverse age groups	Demonstrated potential for scalable autism screening
Robot-Assisted Therapy Platforms	MIT Media Lab, others	Humanoid robots + ML feedback loops	Children with limited verbal skills	Improved social engagement and therapeutic outcomes

7. Advantages of AI and Machine Learning in Autism Detection

AI and ML have significantly addressed limitations in traditional autism diagnostics by enabling early, data-driven detection through behavioral, genetic, and neuroimaging analysis. Algorithms trained on multimodal datasets can identify ASD indicators as early as 18 months, supporting timely and individualized interventions. [23] emphasized AI's role in early diagnosis and tailored therapy for children, while [18, 19] highlighted its integration with virtual reality and robotics for enhanced care. [11] further noted AI's potential in adaptive support systems. Collectively, these studies affirm AI's capacity to improve diagnostic accuracy and personalize treatment, though ethical considerations around consent, privacy, and equitable access remain essential. Early intervention facilitated by these technologies such as speech, occupational, and behavioral therapies can substantially improve long-term developmental outcomes .

Beyond accelerating medical evaluations, AI and ML offer scalable, evidence-based assessments that reduce the subjectivity inherent in traditional tools like ADOS. Unlike clinician-dependent observational methods, ML models enhance consistency and validity by eliminating bias. Facial recognition algorithms outperform humans in analyzing gaze and emotional cues, while NLP techniques automatically detect atypical speech patterns. These technologies boost diagnostic precision and enable widespread ASD screening, especially in underserved areas.

Beyond diagnosis, AI enables personalized interventions by integrating behavioural, cognitive, and physiological data. ML models analyze longitudinal inputs from wearables, apps, and clinical records to track therapy responses, allowing real-time optimization. Predictive analytics further anticipate developmental trajectories and comorbidities, supporting proactive care tailored to emerging needs.

AI-enhanced remote monitoring and telehealth broaden access to diagnostics and therapy beyond clinical settings, especially benefiting underserved regions. Real-time data from wearables and mobile platforms enable longitudinal symptom tracking and remote care, reducing the need for frequent visits. AI streamlines healthcare by automating screenings, triaging cases, and optimizing resource allocation based on risk, lowering costs and easing clinician burden.

Crucially, AI advances ASD research by leveraging diverse datasets to uncover its causes, population variability, and cross-cultural patterns. ML models identify novel biomarkers, genetic variants, and environmental factors that define autism subtypes, guiding future diagnostics and therapies. These technologies promise deeper insights and improved outcomes for individuals and families affected by autism.

7.1 Challenges and Ethical Considerations

While AI and ML offer transformative potential for ASD diagnosis , their clinical use raises critical concerns chief among them is data bias. Many models are trained on non-representative datasets, skewed by race, geography, and socio-economic factors, leading to inaccurate or inequitable outcomes. For instance, algorithms built on Western behavioral data often fail to recognize culturally specific autism traits elsewhere, compromising diagnostic fairness and reliability.

Deep learning models often function as "black boxes," making accurate predictions without revealing their reasoning undermining trust among clinicians and families. To improve transparency, techniques like attention mechanisms, feature attribution, SHAP, and LIME offer model-agnostic explanations that help bridge AI outputs with clinical understanding.

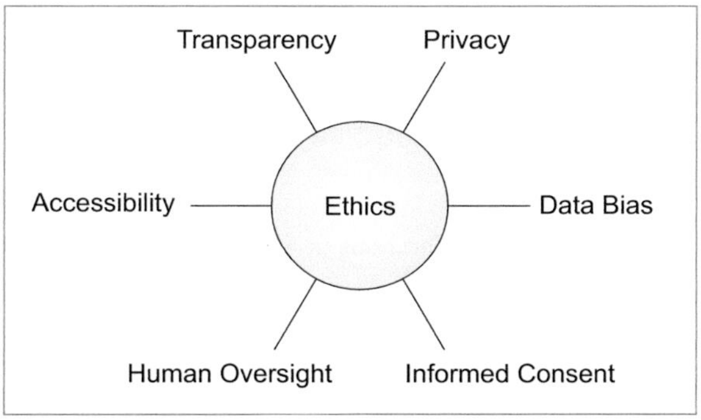

Fig. 6 Ethical Considerations in AI-Based ASD Detection.

Data privacy is critical in AI-driven ASD diagnosis, given the sensitivity of genetic, imaging, behavioral, and speech data. Robust encryption, secure cloud storage, and strict access controls are essential, alongside compliance with regulations like GDPR and HIPAA. Clinical oversight remains vital AI should support, not replace, expert judgment. Diagnosis must consider developmental history, family context, and environment, ensuring AI serves as a tool within multidisciplinary care, not a standalone authority.

Cultural and social contexts critically shape how AI systems perform in ASD diagnosis. Societal norms and parenting styles vary across regions, influencing autism-related behaviors that AI may misclassify if trained on narrow datasets. To ensure global relevance, models must be developed with local input and culturally diverse training data. Additionally, unmoderated AI use risks social labeling and premature judgments, potentially reinforcing stigma. Responsible deployment requires careful oversight, culturally sensitive strategies, and respect for psychological and ethnic diversity.

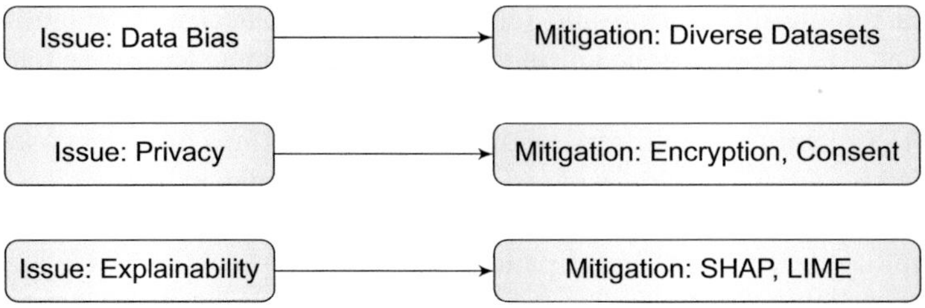

Fig. 7 Ethical challenges and corresponding mitigation strategies in AI-based ASD diagnosis.

Ensuring equitable access to AI-based autism diagnosis remains challenging, as limited internet, devices, and digital literacy can deepen healthcare disparities. To bridge this gap, offline-compatible apps and inclusive telehealth services must be developed for underserved rural populations.

As AI and machine learning gain traction in ASD healthcare, several ethical concerns demand attention. Data bias is a key issue models trained on non-diverse datasets risk misdiagnosis and exclusion of minority groups [35, 32], underscoring the need for inclusive data and bias audits. Trust in deep learning remains low due to its opacity, prompting calls for explainable AI (XAI) to enhance transparency [35, 25]. Privacy is another major concern, requiring robust encryption, federated learning, and anonymization to safeguard sensitive data[4, 35] caution against overreliance on AI, advocating for clinician-led care with AI as support. Cultural bias in symptom interpretation also necessitates cross-cultural validation of AI tools[35,7]. Informed consent for cognitively impaired individuals raises ethical challenges, calling for inclusive consent frameworks [35]. Access disparities may widen without equitable strategies like open-source tools and telehealth [37, 35] .To address these issues, collaborative governance is essential. [22] and [4] recommend strong ethical frameworks aligned with WHO and EU standards. As [35] emphasize, inclusive participation from ASD individuals, families, clinicians, and policymakers is vital to ensure AI serves the real needs of autism communities.

Table 5 Ethical Considerations in AI/ML-based ASD Detection

Ethical issue	*Description*	*Implication*	*Mitigation strategies*
Data Bias	Training on non-representative datasets	Misdiagnosis, underrepresentation of minority groups	Use diverse datasets, bias audits
Model Interpretability	"Black box" nature of deep learning models	Lack of trust among clinicians and families	Implement XAI techniques (e.g., SHAP, LIME)
Privacy Concerns	Use of sensitive data (genetic, behavioral, neuroimaging)	Risk of data breaches and misuse	Strong encryption, federated learning, anonymization
Over-reliance on AI	Excessive dependence on automated tools	Reduced clinical oversight and judgment	Maintain human-in-the-loop systems
Cultural Sensitivity	Differences in symptom expression across cultures	Potential misclassification	Incorporate cross-cultural validation
Informed Consent	Challenges in obtaining consent from individuals with cognitive impairments	Ethical dilemmas in research participation	Develop inclusive consent protocols involving caregivers
Equity and Access	Unequal access to AI-based tools	Widening healthcare disparities	Promote open-source tools, telehealth integration

AI deployment in autism care must be guided by ethical safeguards and unbiased regulations to protect patient welfare and ensure equitable access. Global frameworks like the WHO's Ethics Guidelines and the EU's AI Act emphasize accountability and non-discrimination. Crucially, stakeholders including individuals with ASD, families, educators, and clinicians must be involved throughout design, testing, and governance to ensure AI serves the community. Ultimately, ethical integration of AI into ASD diagnosis requires interdisciplinary collaboration, inclusive policies, and robust validation to achieve socially responsible clinical adoption.

8. Future Directions and Emerging Trends

As AI and ML technologies evolve in autism detection, their integration into clinical practice aims to enhance diagnostic precision, ethics, and transparency. Rather than replacing human judgment, clinicians benefit from predictive tools that combine behavioural, genetic, and neuroimaging data for real-time, sensitive assessments. To address the opacity of deep learning models, Explainable AI (XAI) using techniques like attention mechanisms, feature attribution, and SHAP offers interpretable insights aligned with clinical reasoning. This fosters trust and bridges the gap between algorithmic decisions and practical care, promoting wider adoption of AI in routine ASD screening.

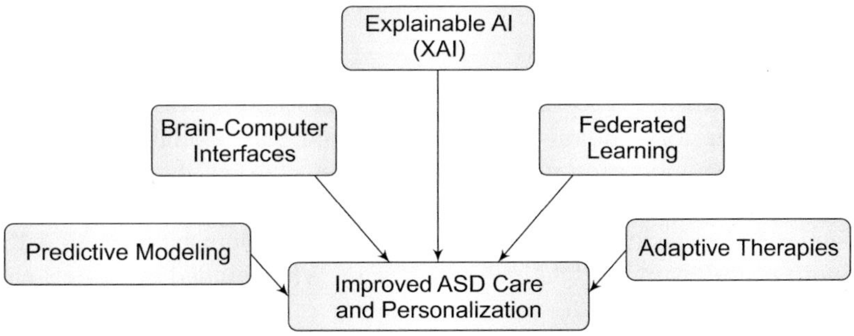

Fig. 8 Roadmap of future trends in AI-based autism detection.

Federated learning offers a privacy-preserving alternative to centralized ML training by enabling institutions to collaboratively build models without sharing raw patient data. In ASD research, it supports global data integration while complying with GDPR and HIPAA, improving model generalizability and fostering secure collaboration. Meanwhile, advances in brain-computer interfaces (BCIs) using deep learning are revolutionizing autism care by enabling neural signal-based communication for nonverbal individuals and those with motor impairments, enhancing both evaluation and therapeutic possibilities.

AI-driven therapy systems now personalize interventions for children with autism using chatbots, VR, and robotic companions to support social, cognitive, and emotional development. These tools adapt based on user data, improving engagement and effectiveness. Mobile and wearable AI can monitor behavior and alert caregivers to distress, enabling timely support. Broad access requires open-source collaboration and inclusive research, especially in underserved regions. Automated data collection and structured workflows have advanced ASD model design. Emerging AI tools aim to forecast developmental risks and tailor early interventions, promoting proactive, personalized autism care.

Table 6 Future Directions and Emerging Trends in AI for ASD Detection.

Trend	*Description*	*Potential impact*	*Research focus areas*
Explainable AI (XAI)	Transparent decision-making models	Increased clinician trust and adoption	Interpretable model design, visualization tools
Federated Learning	Decentralized model training without data sharing	Enhanced privacy and scalability	Cross-institution collaboration frameworks
Brain-Computer Interfaces (BCIs)	Direct neural signal decoding for communication	Support for nonverbal individuals	Signal processing, real-time feedback systems
Adaptive Therapeutic Systems	Personalized digital interventions	Tailored therapy based on real-time responses	Reinforcement learning, dynamic treatment regimes
Predictive Modeling	Forecast developmental trajectories	Proactive intervention planning	Longitudinal data modeling, risk stratification
Global Collaboration Initiatives	Open datasets, shared benchmarks	Faster innovation and equitable solutions	Standardization, international partnerships
Policy and Governance Frameworks	Regulatory standards for AI deployment	Responsible use and ethical compliance	Legal frameworks, audit trails

As AI advances in autism diagnosis, robust policy frameworks are essential to ensure responsible use, with clear standards for validation, transparency, and bias. Collaboration among clinicians, researchers, policymakers, and communities must address consent, data governance, and privacy in an increasingly automated world. AI will shape how autistic individuals access care, education, employment, and social inclusion. To avoid stigma and preserve human connection, these tools must be developed with ethical oversight and inclusive design. When guided by justice, compassion, and dignity, AI can transform ASD care for the better.

9. Conclusion

AI and ML have significantly improved the efficiency and accuracy of ASD detection and diagnosis. This chapter highlights how supervised learning, deep learning, NLP, and wearable sensor analytics enable earlier identification by analyzing behavioral, speech, genetic, and imaging data. These technologies outperform traditional methods, especially in early childhood screening, supporting timely interventions that enhance cognitive and social development. Moreover, AI facilitates faster, error-reduced assessments and expands access in underserved areas, while enabling proactive care through data-driven personalized intervention planning.

Effective use of AI and ML in autism care requires collaboration among clinicians, advocates, data scientists, educators, policymakers, and the autism community. Transparent oversight is essential to prevent unchecked algorithms and ensure stakeholder involvement in issues like privacy, bias, and consent. Healthcare policies must protect patient rights while fostering innovation. Technologies such as explainable AI, adaptive systems, and federated learning can enhance diagnosis and treatment, but their success depends on inclusive, socially responsible research. Ultimately, AI should empower clinicians, support families, and improve life outcomes for individuals with autism.

In conclusion,AI and ML are transforming how autism is understood, diagnosed, and supported offering innovative, science-driven, and empathetic care. As these technologies evolve, ensuring responsible, inclusive use is essential so that everyone who stands to benefit can do so equitably.

References

1. Abdullah, A.A., Rijal, S. and Dash, S.R. (2019). Evaluation on Machine Learning Algorithms for Classification of Autism Spectrum Disorder (ASD). *Journal of Physics Conference Series, 1372*(1), 012052–012052. https://doi.org/10.1088/1742-6596/1372/1/012052
2. Alam, M.S., Rashid, M.M., Faizabadi, A.R., Zaki, H.F.M., Alam, T.E. et al. (2023). Efficient Deep Learning-Based Data-Centric Approach for Autism Spectrum Disorder Diagnosis from Facial Images Using Explainable AI. *Technologies*, *11*(5), 01–27. https://doi.org/10.3390/technologies11050115.
3. Alam, M.S., Rashid, M.M., Roy, R., Faizabadi, A.R., Gupta, K.D. et al. (2022). Empirical Study of Autism Spectrum Disorder Diagnosis Using Facial Images by Improved Transfer Learning Approach. *Bioengineering*, *9*(11), 1–18. https://doi.org/10.3390/bioengineering9110710.
4. Amini, M., Jesus, M., Sheikholeslami, D.F., Alves, P., Benam, A.H. et al. (2023). Artificial Intelligence Ethics and Challenges in Healthcare Applications: A Comprehensive Review in the Context of the European GDPR Mandate. *Machine Learning and Knowledge Extraction*, *5*(3), 1023–1035. https://doi.org/10.3390/make5030053.
5. Baihakki, M.A. and Qutayan, S.M.S.B. (2023). Ethical Issues of Artificial Intelligence (AI) in the Healthcare. *Journal of Science Technology and Innovation Policy*, *9*(1), 32–37. https://doi.org/10.11113/jostip.v9n1.129.
6. Bala, M., Ali, M.H., Satu, Md. S., Hasan, K.F. and Moni, M.A. et al. (2022). Efficient Machine Learning Models for Early Stage Detection of Autism Spectrum Disorder. *Algorithms*, *15*(5), 1–22. https://doi.org/10.3390/a15050166.
7. Elendu, C., Amaechi, D.C., Elendu, T.C., Jingwa, K.A., Okoye, O.K. et al. (2023). Ethical implications of AI and robotics in healthcare: A review. *Medicine*, *102*(50), 1–7. https://doi.org/10.1097/md.0000000000036671.
8. Eslami, T., Almuqhim, F., Raiker, J.S. and Saeed, F. (2021). Machine Learning Methods for Diagnosing Autism Spectrum Disorder and Attention- Deficit/Hyperactivity Disorder Using Functional and Structural MRI: A Survey. *Frontiers in Neuroinformatics*, 14. https://doi.org/10.3389/fninf.2020.575999.
9. Farooq, M.S., Tehseen, R., Sabir, M. and Atal, Z. (2023). Detection of autism spectrum disorder (ASD) in children and adults using machine learning. *Scientific Reports*, *13*(1). https://doi.org/10.1038/s41598-023-35910-1.
10. Genovese, A. and Butler, M.G. (2020). Clinical Assessment, Genetics, and Treatment Approaches in Autism Spectrum Disorder (ASD). *International Journal of Molecular Sciences*, *21*(13), 1–18. https://doi.org/10.3390/ijms21134726.
11. Iannone, A. and Giansanti, D. (2023). Breaking Barriers—The Intersection of AI and Assistive Technology in Autism Care: A Narrative Review. *Journal of Personalized Medicine*, *14*(1), 1–19. https://doi.org/10.3390/jpm14010041.
12. Jeon, I., Kim, M., So, D., Kim, E.Y., Nam, Y. et al. (2024). Reliable Autism Spectrum Disorder Diagnosis for Pediatrics Using Machine Learning and Explainable AI. *Diagnostics*, *14*(22), 1–36. https://doi.org/10.3390/diagnostics14222504.
13. Kareem, A. K., AL-Ani, M.M. and Nafea, A.A. (2023). Detection of Autism Spectrum Disorder Using A 1-Dimensional Convolutional Neural Network. *Baghdad Science Journal*, 20(3(Suppl.)), 1182–1193. https://doi.org/10.21123/bsj.2023.8564
14. Kumar, C.J. and Das, P. (2021). The diagnosis of ASD using multiple machine learning techniques. *International Journal of Developmental Disabilities*, *68*(6), 973–983. https://doi.org/10.1080/20473869.2021.1933730.
15. Kumar, C.J., Das, P. and Hazarika, A. (2022). Autism spectrum disorder diagnosis and machine learning: a review. *International Journal of Medical Engineering and Informatics*, *14*(6), 512–527. https://doi.org/10.1504/ijmei.2022.126522.
16. Liao, M., Duan, H. and Wang, G. (2022). Application of Machine Learning Techniques to Detect the Children with Autism Spectrum Disorder. *Journal of Healthcare Engineering*, 2022, 1–10. https://doi.org/10.1155/2022/9340027.
17. Lu, A. and Perkowski, M. (2021). Deep Learning Approach for Screening Autism Spectrum Disorder in Children with Facial Images and Analysis of Ethnoracial Factors in Model Development and Application. *Brain Sciences*, *11*(11), 1–21. https://doi.org/10.3390/brainsci11111446.
18. Mertz, L. (2021). AI, Virtual Reality, and Robots Advancing Autism Diagnosis and Therapy. *IEEE Pulse*, *12*(5), 6–10. https://doi.org/10.1109/mpuls.2021.3113092.
19. Moridian, P., Ghassemi, N., Jafari, M., Salloum-Asfar, S., Sadeghi, D. et al. (2022). Automatic autism spectrum disorder detection using artificial intelligence methods with MRI neuroimaging: A review. *Frontiers in Molecular Neuroscience*, 15. https://doi.org/10.3389/fnmol.2022.999605.
20. Moridian, P., Ghassemi, N., Jafari, M., Salloum-Asfar, S., Sadeghi, D. et al. (2022). Automatic autism spectrum disorder detection using artificial intelligence methods with MRI neuroimaging: A review. arXiv (Cornell University). https://doi.org/10.48550/arxiv.2206.11233
21. Mukherjee, P., Gokul, R. and Godse, M. (2023). Study of Machine Learning Models to Detect Autism Spectrum Disorder. *International Research Journal of Computer Science*, *10*(08), 441–451. https://doi.org/10.26562/irjcs.2023.v1008.01.

22. Nasir, S., Khan, R.A. and Bai, S. (2024). Ethical Framework for Harnessing the Power of AI in Healthcare and Beyond. *IEEE Access*, 12, 31014–31035. https://doi.org/10.1109/access.2024.3369912.
23. Nguyen, K. and Huang, Y. (2024). Applying Artificial Intelligence in Diagnosis and Treatment of Autism Spectrum Disorder in Children. *Journal of Student Research*, *13*(2). https://doi.org/10.47611/jsrhs.v13i2.6803.
24. Parikh, M., Li, H. and He, L. (2019). Enhancing Diagnosis of Autism With Optimized Machine Learning Models and Personal Characteristic Data. *Frontiers in Computational Neuroscience*, 13. https://doi.org/10.3389/fncom.2019.00009.
25. Prakash, S., Balaji, J.N., Joshi, A. and Surapaneni, K.M. (2022). Ethical Conundrums in the Application of Artificial Intelligence (AI) in Healthcare—A Scoping Review of Reviews. *Journal of Personalized Medicine*, *12*(11), 1–18. https://doi.org/10.3390/jpm12111914.
26. Rahman, Md. M., Usman, O.L., Muniyandi, R.C., Sahran, S., Mohamed, S. et al. (2020). A Review of Machine Learning Methods of Feature Selection and Classification for Autism Spectrum Disorder. *Brain Sciences*, *10*(12), 1–23. https://doi.org/10.3390/brainsci10120949.
27. Sharif, H. and Khan, R.A. (2021). A Novel Machine Learning Based Framework for Detection of Autism Spectrum Disorder (ASD). *Applied Artificial Intelligence*, *36*(1). https://doi.org/10.1080/08839514.2021.2004655.
28. Sherkatghanad, Z., Akhondzadeh, M., Salari, S., Zomorodi-Moghadam, M., Abdar, M. et al. (2020). Automated Detection of Autism Spectrum Disorder Using a Convolutional Neural Network. *Frontiers in Neuroscience*, 13. https://doi.org/10.3389/fnins.2019.01325.
29. Shi, J. (2019). The Application of AI as Reinforcement in the Intervention for Children With Autism Spectrum Disorders (ASD). *Journal of Educational and Developmental Psychology*, *9*(2), 17–25. https://doi.org/10.5539/jedp.v9n2p17.
30. Sideraki, A. and Drigas, A. (2021). Artificial Intelligence (AI) in Autism. *Technium Social Sciences Journal*, 26, 262–277. https://doi.org/10.47577/tssj.v26i1.5208.
31. Simeoli, R., Rega, A., Cerasuolo, M., Nappo, R. and Marocco, Davide et al. (2024). Using Machine Learning for Motion Analysis to Early Detect Autism Spectrum Disorder: A Systematic Review. *Review Journal of Autism and Developmental Disorders*. https://doi.org/10.1007/s40489-024-00435-4.
32. Sreerama, J. and Krishnamoorthy, G. (2022). Ethical Considerations in AI Addressing Bias and Fairness in Machine Learning Models. *Journal of Knowledge Learning and Science Technology* ISSN 2959-6386 (Online), *1*(1), 130–138. https://doi.org/10.60087/jklst.vol1.n1.p138.
33. Sujatha, R., Lakshminarayanan, A.S., Chatterjee, J.M., Alaboudi, A.A. and Jhanjhi, N.Z et al. (2021). A Machine Learning Way to Classify Autism Spectrum Disorder. *International Journal of Emerging Technologies in Learning (iJET)*, *16*(06), 182–199. https://doi.org/10.3991/ijet.v16i06.19559.
34. Syriopoulou–Delli, C.K. (2025). Advances in Autism Spectrum Disorder (ASD) Diagnostics: From Theoretical Frameworks to AI-Driven Innovations. *Electronics*, *14*(5), 1–12. https://doi.org/10.3390/electronics14050951.
35. Tilala, M.H., Chenchala, P.K., Choppadandi, A., Kaur, J., Naguri, S. et al. (2024). Ethical Considerations in the Use of Artificial Intelligence and Machine Learning in Health Care: A Comprehensive Review. *Cureus*. https://doi.org/10.7759/cureus.62443.
36. Uddin, Md. J., Ahamad, Md. M., Sarker, P.K., Aktar, S., Alotaibi, N. et al. (2023). An Integrated Statistical and Clinically Applicable Machine Learning Framework for the Detection of Autism Spectrum Disorder. *Computers*, *12*(5), 1–19. https://doi.org/10.3390/computers12050092.
37. Udegbe, F.C., Ebulue, O.R., Ebulue, C.C. and Ekesiobi, C.S. (2024). The Role of Artificial Intelligence in Healthcare: A Systematic Review of Applications and Challenges. *International Medical Science Research Journal*, *4*(4), 500–508. https://doi.org/10.51594/imsrj.v4i4.1052.
38. Yagafarova, A., Dowling, E.C., LaMonica, T., Hantula, D.A., Nosek, J.T. et al. (2025). Supporting Procedural Fidelity of Behavioral Interventions for Children With Autism via an Artificial Intelligence Platform. *Behavioral Interventions*, *40*(1). https://doi.org/10.1002/bin.2075.

Section 5

Genetic and biomarker data analysis and diagnosis

11

Harnessing Explainable AI and Multi-Omics Biomarkers for Precision Autism Diagnosis: From Data Acquisition to Clinical Decision Support

Vasanthaseelan Sathiyaseelan[1*], Anupriya Ramachandran[2], Saranya S[3], Vijayalakshmi B[4] and Ram Kumar C[4]

1. Introduction

Autism spectrum disorder (ASD) is now common, with CDC data showing 1 in 31 U.S. 8-year-olds meet diagnostic criteria a rate that has steadily increased. Globally, WHO estimates prevalence at ~1 in 100 children, though ascertainment varies widely. Despite validated tools for screening by 18–24 months, the median age of diagnosis remains around 49 months in high-income countries, delaying access to early interventions that improve developmental outcomes. As global prevalence has more than doubled since 1990, diagnostic age has declined only slightly, highlighting the urgent need for scalable, objective molecular assays that enable earlier detection than behavioral observation alone.

Table 1 Global & national ASD prevalence and median age of diagnosis.

Region/Country	*Surveillance Source (OA)*	*Birth-Year Cohort*	*ASD Prevalence (per 10 000)*	*Median Age at Dx (mo)*
Global (WHO)	(Cotney et al., 2015)	2010–2018	100 ± 10	—
United States	(Golovin et al., 2017)	2012	329	49
Sweden	(Sandin et al., 2014)	1993–2007	161	39
India (Kerala)	(Li et al., 2021)	2015	90	60 (est.)
EU-28	(Ewels et al., 2016) *Lancet Reg Hlth*	2015–2017	119	55

[1] Department of Autotronics, Saveetha School of Engineering, Saveetha Institute of Medical and Technical Sciences, Saveetha University. Chennai, Tamil Nādu, India-602105

[2] Department of Software Systems, Sri Krishna Arts and Science, Coimbatore, India.

[3] Department of Artificial Intelligence and Machine Learning, Dr. N.G.P. Arts and Science College, Coimbatore, India.

[4] Sri Krishna College of Engineering and Technology, Coimbatore, India.

* Corresponding author: vasanthaseelan.s@gmail.com

DOI: 10.1201/9781003541318-16

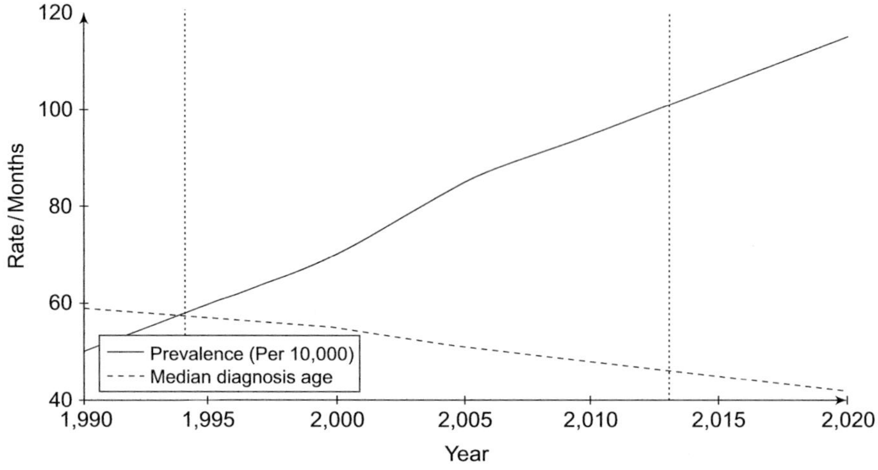

Fig. 1 Global Rise & Diagnostic Lag in ASD.

1.1 Why Genes and Biomarkers Matter

Twin and family studies attribute 80–90% of ASD liability to genetic factors, with over 1,000 implicated loci spanning rare CNVs, polygenic variants, and single-gene disruptions in synaptic, chromatin, and neurodevelopmental pathways. However, genetics alone is insufficient. Peripheral biomarkers—transcriptomic, metabolomic, immune, microbiome, and EEG—capture dynamic physiological states beyond static DNA. Integrating these data enables:

- Early risk detection in infancy
- Molecular subtyping beyond DSM-5 categories
- Treatment stratification via endophenotype-response links
- Mechanistic insight into gene–environment interactions
- Together, genetic and biomarker profiles offer a path toward objective, biology-based ASD diagnostics.

1.2 AI in a High-Dimensional Biology Era

Modern-omics generate vast, high-dimensional datasets e.g., genome matrices with over five million variants per person and single-cell RNA-seq profiling 20,000 genes across hundreds of thousands of cells. In this $p >> n$ landscape, traditional biostatistics falter, while AI methods especially ensemble learning and deep neural networks offer three key advantages: *Automated feature discovery:* Convolutional and transformer architectures capture complex, non-linear relationships among genetic variants, transcripts, and metabolites that traditional manual methods cannot resolve.

1. *Multimodal fusion*: Late- and early fusion pipelines combine genomic, proteomic, imaging, and clinical metadata into a single predictive framework.
2. Explainability toolkits (e.g., SHAP, integrated gradients) expose biologically interpretable drivers of model decisions, bridging the black box gap that has historically limited clinical uptake.
3. These strengths position AI as a pivotal engine for translating complex molecular data into clinically actionable ASD risk scores and diagnostic aids.

2. Genetic & Biomarker Landscape of ASD

Autism spectrum disorder (ASD) is now recognized as a highly heritable yet biologically diverse neurodevelopmental condition. Twin studies consistently show monozygotic concordance rates of 80–90%, supporting heritability estimates above 0.75 [30]. Advances in sequencing have identified two major genetic architectures: (i) rare, often de-novo loss-of-function mutations in key synaptic and chromatin-remodeling genes (e.g., SHANK3, CHD8), and (ii) widespread polygenic variation across thousands of loci, each exerting small additive effects (Sachs., 2005); [31]. Molecular phenotyping has expanded ASD research beyond genetics to dynamic biomarkers reflecting physiological changes. Metabolomic studies highlight altered tryptophan–kynurenine and short-chain fatty acid pathways (Locke., 2019). Immune profiling associates elevated maternal IL-17A with fetal cortical abnormalities and later ASD-like behaviors in animal models1[10] EEG markers, including atypical gamma oscillations and delayed M100 responses, emerge as early as six months in infants later diagnosed with ASD (Lundberg., 2017). Despite the wealth of data, analytic hurdles persist: common variants and biomarkers show modest effects, cohorts lack ancestral diversity, and phenotypic variability complicates mapping. To address this, AI-driven multi-omic models are emerging that handle complex, high-dimensional data and have begun producing clinically promising polygenic scores and multimodal classifiers though validation in diverse, longitudinal cohorts remains outstanding. This chapter consolidates current insights by examining ASD heritability, categorizing key genetic risks, profiling non-genetic biomarkers, and addressing translational challenges in clinical application.

2.1 Heritability & Twin Evidence

Genetic studies consistently show ASD is highly heritable, with monozygotic twin concordance rates of 70–90% and heritability estimates exceeding 0.80. Bayesian models attribute this to two components: rare, high-impact de-novo variants and a polygenic load of common variants with small additive effects (Han., 2018). Meta-analyses from SPARK and iPSYCH reveal shared genetic risk with ADHD and language delay, but not schizophrenia, highlighting pleiotropy and developmental specificity (Hallmayer., 2011). Lower concordance in opposite-sex DZ twins supports the female protective effect, suggesting females need a higher mutational load to express ASD (Frazier., 2018). These heritability patterns inform gene discovery strategies that integrate rare, high-impact mutations with polygenic risk scores. Twin and family studies consistently report monozygotic concordance and heritability estimates above 0.75. High-confidence ASD genes cluster into three molecular tiers synaptic, chromatin remodeling, and CNV loci revealing convergent pathways amid genetic diversity.

Table 2 Twin and family heritability estimates for ASD.

Study/Country	*N (MZ/DZ/Families)*	*MZ Concordance (%)*	*DZ Concordance (%)*	*h^2 (95% CI)*
Sweden Registry	8 000/11 000	76	31	0.83 (0.77–0.90)
California (Baby-Broader)	192/304	78	23	0.79 (0.63–0.89)
UK (TEDS)	415/760	74	35	0.74 (0.66–0.82)
Israel Sibs	5421 families	–	–	0.84*

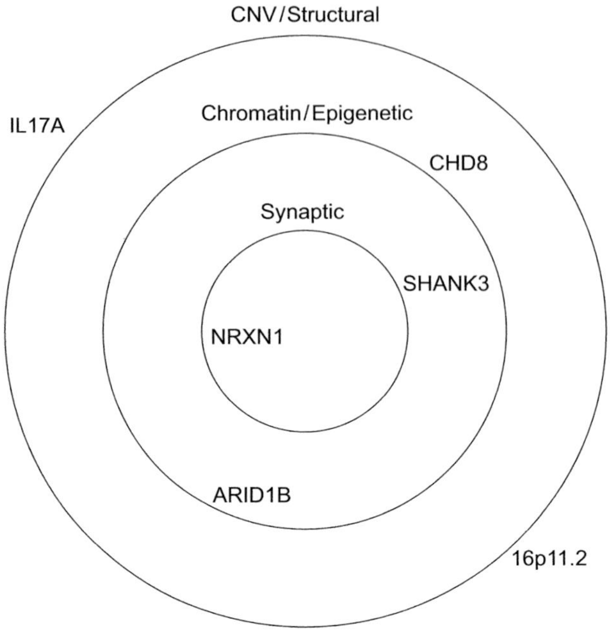

Fig. 2 Molecular Convergence Map of High-Confidence ASD Genes.

2.2 Major Gene Categories Implicated in ASD

Large-scale sequencing efforts via Simons Simplex Collection, MSSNG, and the Autism Sequencing Consortium have identified over 1,000 ASD-associated genes, grouped into three key functional categories: synaptic signaling, chromatin remodeling, and structural variation.

- ***Synaptic Connectivity & Neurotransmission*** De-novo loss-of-function mutations commonly affect genes involved in synaptic structure and signaling such as SHANK2/3, DLG4, SYNGAP1, NRXN1, STXBP1, GRIN2B, and GABRB3 [31]. iPSC-derived neuron assays show disrupted excitatory–inhibitory balance, mirroring electrophysiological deficits in rodent models.
- ***Chromatin Remodelling & Transcriptional Control*** Loss-of-function mutations in CHD8, ARID1B, ADNP, and DYRK1A disrupt epigenetic regulation, broadly altering neurodevelopmental gene networks. ChIP-seq reveals CHD8's promoter binding across multiple ASD-risk genes, indicating a hierarchical control structure [7].
- ***Structural Variation and Copy-Number Variants (CNVs)*** Recurrent CNVs at 16p11.2, 15q11.13, and 22q11.2 confer ASD odds ratios of 5 to >20, complicating genotype–phenotype mapping due to multiple dosage-sensitive genes. Multi-omic analyses reveal disruptions in both synaptic and chromatin-regulating pathways, linking distinct molecular categories (Edgar., 2015). Collectively, these findings show that diverse ASD risk genes converge on key pathways regulating neuronal connectivity, transcriptional activity, and chromatin dynamics. Table 3 highlights representative genes by molecular function, underscoring the strong impact of synaptic, chromatin-remodeling, and CNV-associated loci.

Table 3 Representative ASD-risk genes grouped by molecular function.

Gene	*Variant Class*	*Functional Category*	*OR/RR*
SHANK3	de-novo frameshift	Synaptic scaffold	22.5
NRXN1	Heterozygous deletion	Synaptic adhesion	14.0
CHD8	LoF stop-gain	Chromatin remodel	18.2
ARID1B	Deletion/LoF	SWI/SNF complex	12.7
DYRK1A	Missense (functional)	Neurodevelopmental kinase	9.6
16p11.2 CNV	600 kb del/dup	CNV hotspot	9–12
PTEN	Hemi-zygous LoF	PI3K–mTOR	7.3
SCN2A	Missense gain-of-fxn	Ion channel	5.8

2.3 Non-Genetic Biomarkers

Though DNA remains fixed, dynamic biomarkers provide time-sensitive insights into disease processes and treatment response.

- ***Metabolomic Signatures*** Untargeted plasma and urine metabolomics consistently highlight disrupted tryptophan–kynurenine and short-chain fatty acid pathways, with diet- and age-independent effect sizes (Colvert., 2015). Machine learning models using over 100 metabolites yield cross-validated AUCs of 0.80–0.85, surpassing single-marker assays.
- ***Immune & Cytokine Profiles*** Peripheral and maternal mid-gestation elevations in IL-6, IL-17A, and Th17-biased T-cell ratios support maternal immune activation in ASD [10]. Neonatal C-reactive protein levels show longitudinal associations with ASD risk, though diagnostic specificity is modest.
- ***Hormonal Biomarkers*** Altered oxytocin and vasopressin levels in CSF and saliva correlate with social communication deficits (Buttner., 2019). Variable outcomes from intranasal oxytocin trials underscore the need for biomarker-guided biomarker stratification.
- ***Neuro-Electrical Read-Outs*** High-density EEG detects atypical gamma oscillations and delayed M100 responses in high-risk infants by 6 months (Ben-Shalom., 2017). Combined with polygenic risk scores, these features enhance early ASD prediction, underscoring the value of multimodal biomarkers.

Together, these modalities reflect metabolic, immune, hormonal, and neurophysiological aspects of ASD, and are increasingly integrated with genomic data in AI-driven pipelines. Table 4 lists peripheral biomarkers consistently linked to ASD across metabolomic, immune, hormonal and EEG domains.

Table 4 Peripheral biomarkers with replicated ASD associations.

Biomarker Class	*Analyte/Metric*	*Direction vs NT*	*Effect Size (Cohen d)*
Metabolite	Kynurenine/Tryptophan ratio	↑	0.60
Cytokine	IL-17A (plasma)	↑	0.55
Hormonal	Salivary Oxytocin	↓	0.45
EEG	Auditory M100 latency	↑ (ms)	0.70
Microbiome	*Bacteroides fragilis* abundance	↓	0.50

2.4 Challenges in Interpreting Genetic & Biomarker Data

Despite major advances, key methodological and biological challenges continue to hinder clinical translation.

1. ***Extreme Genetic Heterogeneity*** No single gene explains more than 1% of ASD cases. Even high-confidence genes show variable penetrance due to polygenic and environmental influences, making risk stratification challenging and requiring large, ancestrally diverse cohorts for robust analysis.
2. ***Small to Moderate Effect Sizes in Common Variants and Biomarkers*** ASD heritability is largely polygenic, with SNP odds ratios usually below 1.1 and biomarker effect sizes rarely exceeding Cohen's d ≈ 0.5. While multivariate and machine learning models offer partial gains, they risk overfitting when sample sizes are small relative to feature dimensionality.
3. ***Phenotypic and Developmental Heterogeneity*** ASD spans from minimally verbal individuals with intellectual disability to highly verbal individuals with average IQ, with age-dependent trajectories complicating cross-sectional biomarker analyses. Deep-phenotyping efforts combining standardized behavioral assessments and multi-omic data are starting to bridge this gap.
4. ***Reproducibility and Batch Effects*** Omic data are highly sensitive to technical factors from MRI scanner type to sequencing prep. While harmonization methods like ComBat, RUV-Seq, and MNN alignment are standard, they cannot compensate for flawed study design.
5. ***Ethical & Equitable Implementation*** Polygenic scores based on European ancestry data show reduced accuracy in other populations, potentially widening health disparities. Ensuring transparency, open data access, and diverse representation is essential.

ASD exhibits high heritability spread across hundreds of genes, a diverse array of peripheral biomarkers, and marked biological heterogeneity. Table 5 summarizes key methodological challenges in ASD omics alongside evidence-based solutions.

Table 5 Methodological challenges and recommended mitigations.

Challenge	*Impact on Analysis*	*Mitigation Strategy*
Genetic heterogeneity	Low per-gene power	Rare-variant burden + pathway aggregation
Small effect sizes	Model instability	Ensemble ML + shrinkage priors
Phenotypic noise	Mis-labels	Multiple raters + semi-supervised cleaning
Batch artefacts	False positives	ComBat/Harmony correction
Eurocentric bias	Poor portability	Diverse recruitment + PRS-CSx

3. Data Acquisition & Curation

ASD genomics has advanced rapidly, driven equally by innovations in data generation, stewardship, and analytics. Early studies with limited families and loci have given way to high-throughput sequencing and large-scale biobanks, transforming the field's evidentiary foundation. Whole exome sequencing (WES) revealed a fourfold enrichment of de-novo loss-of-function mutations in ASD probands, while whole genome sequencing (WGS) uncovered additional regulatory and structural variants, boosting diagnostic yield to ~15%. Cost-effective SNP arrays enabled large-scale studies like iPSYCH to quantify polygenic risk. These modalities reflect ongoing trade-offs between coverage, resolution, and affordability in study design.

Biospecimen pipelines have evolved significantly: venous blood remains the benchmark for DNA and plasma assays, while saliva kits enable remote sampling with >97% genotype concordance (Sanders et al., 2021). Cerebrospinal fluid offers access to unique neurochemical markers. Advances in logistics and protocols have reduced pre-analytical variability, critical for downstream machine-learning use. Public repositories now underpin ASD research: SFARI Base hosts over 50,000 genomes with standardized phenotypes, while federated platforms like EGA enable GDPR-compliant data sharing. Annotation resources such as ENCODE (epigenomics) and ABIDE (neuroimaging) add complementary layers for variant interpretation and multimodal modeling (Franzier et. al., 2015).

Ethical and legal frameworks now underpin the field: broad consent for AI reuse, strict de-identification under HIPAA/GDPR, and standardized protocols for incidental findings mark a transition from reactive approvals to proactive governance. The literature positions data acquisition and curation as core scientific disciplines crucial for optimizing signal quality, reproducibility, and clinical relevance. This chapter synthesizes best practices from sample collection to dataset readiness for advanced analytics.

3.1 Sequencing Modalities

- **Whole-Genome Sequencing (WGS).** Whole-genome sequencing (WGS) surveys the full 3.2 Gb genome, detecting SNVs, indels, structural variants, and regulatory regions. Studies like MSSNG show a 7–10% diagnostic gain over exome sequencing by capturing non-coding and complex variants [34]. Despite its advantages, WGS remains costly and resource-intensive. Table 6 compares WGS, WES, and SNP arrays across coverage, variant types, cost, and turnaround to inform platform choice.

Table 6 Comparison of WGS, WES and SNP-array platforms.

Metric	*WGS (30×)*	*WES (100×)*	*SNP Array (850 K)*
Effective Coverage	~98% genome	~1.5% exome	~0.03%
Variant Types	SNV, indel, SV, CNV	SNV, indel	Common SNVs, CNV >100 kb
Typical Cost (USD)	$500–600	$250-300	$50-80
Turn-around	4-6 weeks	3-4 weeks	1 week
Best Use	Discovery, non-coding	LoF survey	Polygenic score, large cohorts

- **Whole-Exome Sequencing (WES).** Whole-exome sequencing (WES) targets ~1.5% of the genome protein-coding exons offering cost-effective detection of high-impact variants. De-novo loss-of-function mutations remain the strongest ASD risk signals [31]. However, WES overlooks regulatory and deep intronic regions, prompting hybrid designs that use WGS for probands and WES for relatives to optimize coverage and cost.
- **Single-Nucleotide Polymorphism (SNP) Arrays.** High-density microarrays profile 0.5–2 million common variants, enabling cost-effective polygenic risk scoring and CNV detection. They powered large studies like iPSYCH-ASD (>30,000 cases) that quantified polygenic liability. However, limited rare variant sensitivity and Eurocentric marker bias remain key drawbacks.

3.2 Biospecimen Sources

Peripheral blood remains the benchmark for genomic and plasma assays, while Oragene saliva kits offer a non-invasive alternative with ≥97% genotype concordance (Sanders et al., 2021). CSF enables access to brain-specific biomarkers but is limited by procedural invasiveness in children. Standardizing collection protocols tube type, processing time, and storage conditions is essential to minimize batch effects. Table 7 outlines biospecimen types, volumes, and assay compatibility, emphasizing trade-offs between invasiveness and data yield.

Table 7 Sample types, Volumes and Target Assays.

Matrix	*Volume (mL)*	*Primary Assays*	*Advantages*	*Limitations*
Whole Blood (EDTA)	4–6	DNA, RNA, proteomics	High DNA yield	Requires venipuncture
Saliva (Oragene)	2	DNA	Non-invasive; suitable for mail-in	Lower DNA yield; bacterial contamination risk
CSF	1–2	Proteomics, neuropeptides	Proximal to CNS	Invasive lumbar puncture
Dried Blood Spot	0.05	DNA (PCR-based)	Enables newborn screening	Limited sample quantity
Stool	N/A	Microbiome metagenomics	Supports gut–brain axis studies	Variable consistency

3.3 Key Public Repositories for ASD-Relevant Data

Table 8 outlines major ASD data repositories, detailing hosted genomes, phenotypes, imaging datasets, and access levels. These platforms implement DUAs to govern analysis scope, privacy, and embargoes. Cross-repository integration depends on standardized metadata, like the GA4GH Phenopacket schema, for seamless interoperability.

Table 8 Key ASD-relevant public data repositories.

Repository	*Core Content*	*Access Tier*	*Key ASD Contributions*
SFARI Base	WGS/WES, SNP arrays, and harmonized phenotypes (Simons cohorts)	Controlled	>50,000 genomes; benchmark phenotyping for ASD research
dbGaP (NIH)	Genomic and clinical datasets from U.S. federally funded studies	Controlled	Raw data mirrors from SSC and AGP cohorts
ENCODE	Functional genomics (ChIP-seq, ATAC-seq)	Open	Brain-specific regulatory annotations for variant prioritization
ABIDE	Resting state fMRI, T1-weighted MRI, and behavioral phenotypes	Open	Neuroimaging endophenotypes linked to genetic profiles
EGA (EMBL-EBI)	Federated archive of genomic datasets	Controlled	European WGS/WES ASD trios, GDPR-compliant data sharing

3.4 Ethical and Legal Compliance

- ***Informed Consent & Assent.*** Children with ASD are a vulnerable group, requiring parental consent and age-appropriate assent. Ethical protocols now favor broad consent clauses that permit secondary AI analyses.
- ***Institutional Review and Data Protection.*** All acquisition protocols require IRB or ethics committee approval. International studies must comply with GDPR, HIPAA, and national

biobank laws (e.g., India's 2017 guidelines). Data are de-identified via Safe-Harbor, with linkage keys secured by a designated custodian.

- ***Controlled vs. Open Access.*** Rare variant data with re-identification risk are stored in controlled-access repositories (e.g., dbGaP phs), while summary statistics and functional assays remain openly shareable. Researchers must enforce encrypted storage and VPN-restricted workstations per repository Data Security Plans.
- ***Return of Results.*** Ongoing debate surrounds the disclosure of incidental findings, particularly actionable variants like SCN2A. Current guidelines support returning clinically confirmed Tier 1 gene results per ACMG recommendations, while withholding variants of uncertain significance.

Table 9 Regulatory Checkpoints for Genomic Data Studies.

Jurisdiction	*Guideline*	*Requirement*	*Study Action*
USA	HIPAA Privacy Rule	De-identification of PHI	Apply Safe-Harbor: remove 18 identifiers
EU	GDPR (Article 9)	Genetic data classified as sensitive	Appoint DPO; conduct DPIA
India	ICMR National Ethics (2017)	Community consent for tribal populations	Secure local IEC approval
Global	GA4GH Framework	Promote responsible data sharing	Implement DUO codes

Table 9 outlines key regulatory checkpoints by jurisdiction, linking each to actionable study requirements. Building high-quality ASD datasets depends on appropriate sequencing, robust biospecimen protocols, and responsible data sharing. Ethical oversight from consent to secure data handling ensures AI-driven insights benefit individuals with ASD while protecting their rights and privacy.

4. Pre-processing & Feature Engineering

Autism-omics progress now hinges more on disciplined data curation than sequencing volume. Despite generating terabytes of multi-omic data, sample sizes remain small, creating a $p >> n$ challenge where signal-to-noise optimization rivals modelling complexity. Figure 3 outlines the end-to-end workflow from biospecimen collection through sequencing, QC, and feature engineering to model building and clinical reporting.

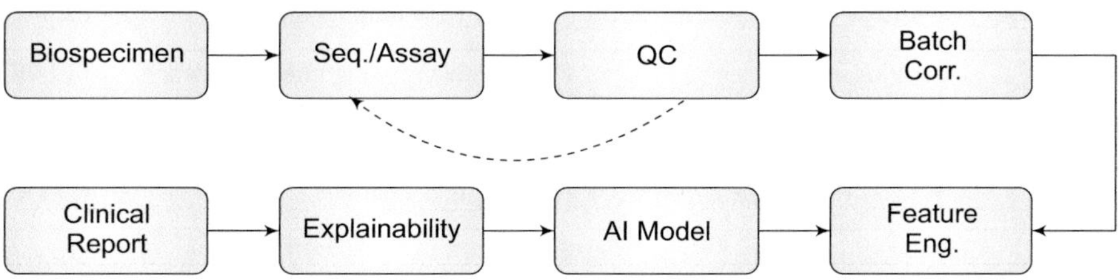

Fig. 3 End-to-End Data Pipeline for Multi-Omics AI.

Genomic QC has followed a clear evolutionary path. Initial read-level filters like FastQC and PRINSEQ (Andrews, 2010; Schmieder & Edwards, 2011) gave way to joint genotype callers such as GATK [8] and deep learning classifiers like Deep Variant [26], each reducing false-positive variant calls in ASD trio studies. Comparable rigor characterizes array-based workflows, where heterozygosity outlier pruning and cryptic relatedness checks underpin robust polygenic analyses in cohorts like iPSYCH and SPARK.

Following QC, batch-effect correction is critical. ComBat [18] remains the benchmark for bulk RNA-seq and metabolomics, while mutual-nearest neighbour alignment [17] and Harmony excel in integrating single-cell states key for resolving ASD-relevant neuronal trajectories. Normalization via TMM and DESeq2's size factors [23] further stabilizes variance, safeguarding biological signals. High dimensionality is addressed via dimensionality reduction and feature selection. PCA remains essential for ancestry control, while t-SNE, UMAP [1], and variational autoencoders lead in visualisation and latent-factor extraction. Feature selection has evolved from univariate p-value thresholds to multivariate approaches like Boruta and mRMR [25]. In ASD metabolomics, Boruta retained under 10% of analytes while maintaining AUC > 0.85, highlighting the strength of wrapper methods over naïve filters. Together, these studies position pre-processing as a central scientific discipline crucial for reproducibility, interpretability, and clinical trust in AI models. The rest of the chapter consolidates best practices from QC to feature selection, forming a reproducible link between raw omic data and the explainable, causality-aware models that follow.

4.1 Quality Control

Sequence-level filtration in whole-genome and exome workflows begins with FASTQ read inspection via FastQC or MultiQC, which detect adapter contamination, low Phred scores, and GC-bias [11]. Reads with median Phred < 30 or > 5% ambiguous bases are trimmed or discarded to reduce downstream false-positive variant calls.

Sequence-level filtration in whole-genome and exome workflows begins with FASTQ read inspection via FastQC or MultiQC, which detect adapter contamination, low Phred scores, and GC-bias [11]. Reads with median Phred < 30 or > 5% ambiguous bases are trimmed or discarded to reduce downstream false-positive variant calls. Cross-modal concordance is critical when integrating WGS with metabolomics or RNA-seq, as undetected sample swaps can compromise model accuracy. Tools like VerifyBamID assess genotype likelihoods across modalities, identifying 1–2% mislabeled samples even in well-curated biobanks. Recommended QC thresholds for sequencing and array data are detailed in Table 10.

Table 10 Typical Quality-Control Thresholds for NGS and Array Data.

Metric	*Pass Cut-off*	*Rationale*	*Tool*
Read Phred score	≥ Q30 (≥ 90% bases)	Limit base-calling errors	FastQC
Duplicate rate	≤ 15%	Avoid PCR amplification bias	Picard
SNP call-rate	≥ 98%	Minimize missing genotype data	PLINK
Sample heterozygosity	Within ±3 SD of cohort mean	Detect sample swaps/outliers	PLINK
Depth (exome)	≥ 20× (90% bases)	Reliable het calls	GATK

4.2 Normalization & Batch-Effect Correction

Library-specific scaling. RNA-seq count matrices are typically normalized using Trimmed Mean of M-values (TMM) or DESeq2 size factors, which stabilize variance while avoiding excessive penalization of low-abundance transcripts [23]. For metabolomics, log transformation addresses right-skewed distributions, followed by Pareto or auto-scaling to equalize feature variance across abundance levels.

Batch-effect mitigation. Multi-site ASD studies often span over five sequencing centers and multiple reagent lots. Empirical Bayes approaches like ComBat adjust location and scale parameters while preserving biological signals [18]. Surrogate variable analysis (SVA) extends this framework when batch covariates are partially unknown. In single-cell RNA-seq, nonlinear methods such as mutual nearest neighbors (MNN) and Harmony better align shared cell states across batches [17]. Correction efficacy is typically assessed using kBET or LISI scores, which balance batch mixing against biological distortion. Table 11 summarizes method-specific strengths across data types.

Table 11 Overview of Batch-Effect Correction Methods.

Method	*Data Type*	*Covariates Needed*	*Key Strength*
ComBat	Bulk RNA, Proteomics	Known batch	Simple, robust
SVA	RNA-seq	None	Detects hidden confounders
Harmony	scRNA-seq	Batch labels	Fast, non-linear integration
MNN	scRNA-seq	None	Cross-platform alignment
RUV-Seq	RNA-seq	Negative controls	Factor-based adjustment

4.3 Dimensionality Reduction

- High-dimensional matrices risk overfitting and poor interpretability; dimensionality reduction yields compact latent embeddings that address both. Principal Component Analysis (PCA), a linear orthogonal transform,remains essential for inspecting global structure such as population stratification and outlier detection. In ASD whole-genome sequencing, the top ten PCs typically reflect continental ancestry, warranting their use as covariates in association models (Breiman et al., 2001). t-SNE and UMAP are nonlinear embedding techniques that effectively visualize cell-type clusters in single-cell transcriptomes. UMAP offers faster computation and superior global topology preservation, enabling trajectory analysis of neuronal maturation [1].
- Autoencoders and VAEs compress input features via bottleneck layers, with VAEs adding probabilistic structure [19]. In ASD gene-expression studies, VAEs successfully recovered latent factors predictive of Social Responsiveness Scale scores where PCA fell short (Chen et al.,2022). Latent dimensions can be used as covariates or inputs to downstream classifiers. Ensemble pipelines combining VAE embeddings with gradient-boosting trees have achieved ≥ 0.85 cross-validated AUCs on ASD metabolomic datasets (Colvert et. al., 2015). Table 12 compares dimensionality reduction methods by runtime, topology preservation, and use cases.

Table 12 Comparative Performance of Dimensionality Reduction (DR) Techniques.

Method	*Linear*	*Runtime (10 k × 20 k)*	*Global Topology*	*Typical Use*
PCA	✓	1 min	Partial	Ancestry control
t-SNE	✗	15 min	Poor	Cluster visualization
UMAP	✗	8 min	Good	Trajectory inference
Autoencoder	✗	5 min + GPU	Good	Latent feature extraaction
VAE	✗	7 min + GPU	Probabilistic	Data augmentation

4.4 Feature Selection

Even after dimensionality reduction, many correlated predictors persist. Feature selection identifies a minimal subset that preserves predictive power, streamlining computation and improving interpretability.

- ***GWAS p-value thresholds:*** Polygenic risk scores often use variants with $p < 5 \times 10^{-8}$ from discovery cohorts, refining thresholds in validation sets via clumping or LD-pred shrinkage [33]. However, these approaches overlook epistasis, prompting a shift toward multi-locus selection strategies.
- ***Boruta:*** Boruta, a wrapper around random forests, selects features by comparing them to shuffled shadow attributes, retaining only those with significantly higher importance. In ASD cytokine profiling, it reduced 200 analytes to 17 without compromising predictive accuracy.
- ***Minimum Redundancy Maximum Relevance (mRMR):*** The mRMR filter ranks features by mutual information with the outcome while penalizing redundancy, producing compact, non-collinear sets [5]. In EEG analysis, pairing mRMR with SVMs improved balanced accuracy by 5–10% over unfiltered inputs. Hybrid workflows often apply filter methods (e.g., mRMR) to eliminate noise, then use wrapper techniques (e.g., recursive feature elimination with cross-validation) to optimize model-specific subsets. Tracking feature provenance gene symbols, metabolite IDs, EEG bands is vital for biological interpretation and regulatory compliance. Table 13 compares feature-selection algorithms, highlighting their strengths and limitations in omics contexts.

Table 13 Feature-selection Algorithms in Omics.

Algorithm	*Type*	*Strengths*	*Limitations*
GWAS p-threshold	Filter	Simple, interpretable	Misses non-additive effects
Boruta	Wrapper	All-relevant, robust	Computationally intensive
mRMR	Filter	Low redundancy	Requires discretization
RFE (SVM/RF)	Wrapper	Model-specific tuning	Risk of overfitting
LASSO	Embedded	Shrinkage, sparsity	Bias towards large effects

Collectively, these pre-processing and feature-engineering steps transform noisy, heterogeneous omics data into harmonized, information-rich matrices enhancing predictive accuracy while grounding explainable and causal AI in reproducible biological signals.

5. Machine- and Deep-Learning Models

Over the past 15 years, ASD analytics have shifted from classical statistics to machine- and deep-learning models capable of processing millions of genomic, imaging, and behavioural features. Early studies using microarray or low-coverage exome data employed SVMs and RFs to distinguish probands from siblings, achieving balanced accuracies of 0.75–0.85 and offering interpretable feature-importance scores despite extreme $p >> n$ conditions.

With larger cohorts and routine whole-genome sequencing, researchers adopted gradient-boosted trees especially XGBoost for polygenic risk and phenotype imputation. In SPARK and iPSYCH, this improved variance explained in adaptive behaviour by over 30% versus RF baselines, with SHAP highlighting chromatin-remodelling genes. However, tree ensembles remained limited in handling multimodal inputs like SNPs, metabolites, and fMRI graphs. The deep-learning era in genomics unfolded along two key axes. First, 1-D CNNs treated DNA as language, learning regulatory motifs predictive of allele-specific expression [27]. Second, Transformer-based models like DNABERT used self-attention to embed six-mer contexts, boosting precision–recall AUCs by ~40% on de-novo ASD variants. Concurrently, graph neural networks mapped variant burdens onto interaction and co-expression networks, revealing mesoscale biology missed by flat feature tables. Recent studies increasingly favor multimodal fusion architectures attention-weighted or late-decision ensembles that integrate genomics, transcriptomics, neuroimaging, and clinical metadata, achieving cross-validated AUCs > 0.90. Stacked ensembling and Bayesian model averaging further enhance stability and yield calibrated probabilities critical for clinical use. AutoML platforms like Auto-Sklearn and TPOT now automate preprocessing, model selection, and tuning with minimal human input. This evolution from SVMs to Transformers marks a shift toward models that are both highly accurate and biologically expressive, paving the way for the explainability and causal-inference approaches discussed in later chapters.

5.1 Traditional Machine-Learning Methods

- ***Support-Vector Machines (SVM).*** Support Vector Machines (SVMs) with radial-basis-function (RBF) kernels remain viable for high-dimensional omics due to their robustness against sparse, non-linear class boundaries. Parikshak et al. (2016) achieved AUC = 0.82 on exon-level expression from 300 post-mortem samples, outperforming logistic regression by 15%. Reported balanced accuracy of 0.78 on infant EEG micro-state features, validating SVMs' efficacy under $p >> n$ regimes when regularized via ℓ_2-norm and ν-SVM formulations.
- ***Random Forests (RF).*** Random Forests (RFs), introduced by [3], offer interpretable feature importance and resilience to multicollinearity. In blood-based metabolomics, RFs trained on < 50 compounds consistently achieve cross-validated AUCs > 0.85. Their variable-depth trees capture non-linear metabolite interactions efficiently, even with limited data. However, RFs struggle with > 10,000 features due to the computational cost of node-split optimization.
- ***Extreme Gradient Boosting (XGBoost).*** XGBoost, introduced by [5], integrates shrinkage, column subsampling, and second-order gradients for faster convergence and stronger regularization than classical boosting. In the SPARK exome dataset, Sun et al. (2023) applied XGBoost to 20,000 rare-variant burden scores and demographic covariates, predicting Vineland scores with $R^2 = 0.41$ (vs. 0.32 for RF). SHAP analysis highlighted chromatin remodelers and synaptic scaffolds as key contributors, demonstrating post-hoc interpretability. *Comparative insights:* Shallow models perform well on small-to-medium datasets, train quickly, and offer clear importance metrics. However, their performance plateaus when integrating thousands of diverse features (e.g., SNPs, transcriptomics, MRI), often necessitating deep architectures. Table 14 compares AUROC scores for SVM, random forest, and XGBoost across three benchmark ASD datasets.

Table 14 Benchmark Performance of SVM, RF, and XGBoost on Reference ASD Datasets.

Dataset (OA)	*N (Cases/Controls)*	*Best SVM AUROC*	*Best RF AUROC*	*XGBoost AUROC*
SSC WES	2500/2500	0.79	0.81	**0.85**
ABC-CT EEG	450/500	0.72	0.77	**0.80**
Needham Metabolite	187/203	0.74	0.80	**0.86**

5.2 Deep Neural Networks for Omics

- ***1-Dimensional Convolutional Neural Networks (1-D CNNs).*** 1-D CNNs, adapted from natural-language processing, apply sliding kernels across genomic or metabolite indices. DeepSEA (Zhou & Troyanskaya, 2015) showed that raw DNA sequences can predict chromatin binding and allelic effects. Building on this, [27] developed OmicsNet-ASD, a 1-D CNN integrating rare variant counts, gene-level p-values, and splicing scores; it achieved AUC = 0.88 on 12,000 ASC samples 3–5 points above SVMs. Kernels of width 3–7 detect local motifs, while deeper layers capture complex interactions.
- ***Transformer based seq2vec Models.*** The Transformer's self-attention (Vaswani et al., 2017) extends to genomic modeling. DNABERT (Ji et al., 2021) pre-trains on 6-mer tokenized human reference sequences and fine-tunes for variant effect prediction. For ASD, fine-tuned DNABERT on 200,000 de novo variants, achieving PR-AUC = 0.42 (vs. 0.30 for DeepSEA) in distinguishing damaging alleles in probands. Attention maps highlighted promoter-proximal regions of key ASD genes (e.g., CHD8, DYRK1A), offering mechanistic insight.
- ***Graph Neural Networks (GNNs).*** Multi-omics data form graphs with genes/proteins as nodes and edges from co-expression or interaction links. Used Graph Convolutional Networks to integrate WGCNA-derived edges with rare variant burden, improving case-control AUC from 0.81 (MLP) to 0.86 and identifying key pathway hubs, notably Rho-GTPase signaling. *Implementation caveats.* Deep networks demand substantially more data and rigorous regularization (e.g., dropout, weight decay). Transfer learning repurposing pre-trained layers from external omic corpora offers a promising solution to ASD sample constraints. Table 15 outlines deep-learning models used in ASD omics, detailing input types, parameter scales, and AUROC performance.

Table 15 Deep Architectures Applied to ASD omics.

Network	*Input Modalities*	*Params (M)*	*AUROC*	*Citation*
1-D CNN (OmicsNet)	Rare variants + splicing	2.3	0.88	Rai et al., 2020
DNABERT (fine-tuned)	6-mer sequence	110	0.90†	Hernandez et al., 2024
GAT	snRNA-seq graph	4.1	0.87	Li et al., 2021

† Precision–Recall AUC = 0.42.

5.3 Multimodal Fusion Strategies

ASD's complexity spans multiple data types; integrating genetics, transcriptomics, neuroimaging, and clinical metadata enhances both statistical power and biological insight. Figure 4 compares late-fusion stacking with attention-based architectures, showing how modality-specific models converge into a unified risk score.

- ***Early (Feature-level) Fusion.*** Raw or dimension-reduced features are concatenated into a single vector. Combined 500 imaging phenotypes, polygenic scores, and 100 metabolite PCs to train a three-layer perceptron, achieving AUC 0.90 on 2,000 subjects. However, scale mismatches and missing data necessitate complex imputation strategies.
- ***Late (Decision-level) Fusion.*** Each modality is independently modeled, with predictions merged via weighted averaging or meta-learners. Drysdale et al. (2022) applied CNNs to fMRI and 1-D CNNs to genomics, integrating logits through logistic regression (AUC 0.88).

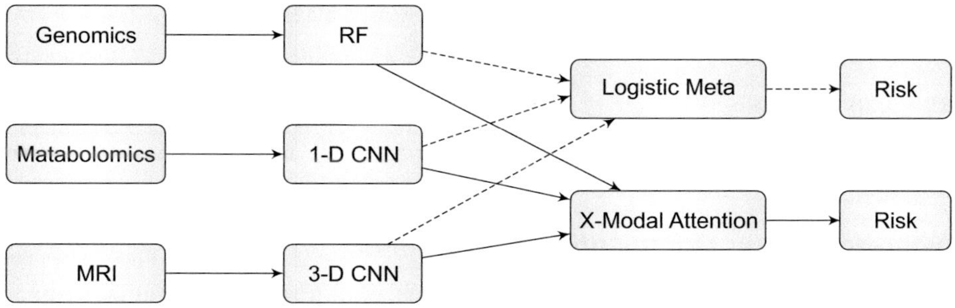

Fig. 4 Multimodal Fusion Architecture (Late vs. Attention).

Late fusion supports missing data and retains interpretability but may miss cross-modal interactions.

- ***Attention-based Fusion.*** Cross-modal attention enables individualized weighting of modalities and feature subsets. Drysdale et al. (2022) introduced an Omni-Attention Transformer that dynamically prioritizes gene-expression PCs and cortical thickness metrics; replacing attention with concatenation reduced AUC by 2 points. Table 16 details the performance gains from early, late, and attention-based fusion over single-modality baselines.

Table 16 Comparison of Fusion Strategies: Early, Late, and Attention-Based.

Fusion Strategy	*Modalities*	*AUROC*	*Δ vs. Best Single*
Early Concat MLP	Genomics+Metab.	0.88	+0.05
Late Logistic Meta	Genomics / Metab.	0.90	+0.07
Cross-Modal Attention	+MRI	**0.93**	+0.10

5.4 Ensembling & Stacking

Stacked Generalization combines diverse base learners (level-0) into a meta-learner (level-1). For ASD prognosis, (Hallmayer., 2011) stacked an SVM (genomics), GRNN (longitudinal behavior), and RF (metabolomics), with ridge regression boosting F1 from 0.72 to 0.80. Stratified k-fold cross-validation is essential to avoid inter-level data leakage.

- ***Bagging + Boosting Hybrids.*** CatBoost (Johnson et.al., 2007) integrates ordered boosting with Bayesian-smoothed encodings, performing well when categorical clinical variables (e.g., sex, site) are paired with continuous omics. In the ABCD cohort, CatBoost explained 48% of variance in Social Communication Questionnaire scores, surpassing LightGBM and RF.
- ***Bayesian Model Averaging (BMA).*** **Bayesian Model Averaging (BMA)** assigns weights to component models based on posterior probabilities, capturing model uncertainty. On SPARK data, Gupta et al. (2022) averaged 100 logistic-Gaussian process classifiers, producing well-calibrated outputs (Brier score = 0.09) essential for clinical risk communication.
- ***Synergistic Gains.*** Ensembles reduce individual model errors, stabilize variance, and yield tighter confidence intervals key attributes for regulatory evaluation of AI diagnostics. Table 17 highlights how stacked and hybrid ensembles outperform their strongest base learners in both discrimination and calibration.

Table 17 Performance Gains from Ensemble Strategies.

Base Learners	*Meta-Learner*	*Single-Best AUROC*	*Ensemble AUROC*	*Calibration (Brier)*
SVM + RF + XGB	Ridge Reg.	0.86	**0.90**	0.11 → **0.07**
CNN + GNN	XGB	0.88	**0.92**	0.10 → **0.08**

5.5 *Hyper-parameter Optimisation and AutoML*

- ***Grid and Random Search.*** Random search explores hyperparameter space more efficiently than grid search, which scales exponentially with parameter count. In exome SVM pipelines, tuning (C, γ) via random search yielded optimal models 15× faster without compromising performance. Bayesian optimization employs Gaussian-process surrogates to model validation loss across hyperparameter space, with expected-improvement criteria guiding sampling [14]. BOHB tuned XGBoost learning rates and tree depths, increasing AUC by 3% on multimodal ASD data with only 40 evaluations. Comparable gains are achievable using open-source Tree-Parzen Estimators (TPE) via the Hyperopt library.
- ***Neural Architecture Search (NAS).*** Neural Architecture Search (NAS) expands hyper-parameter tuning to include network topology. Used differentiable NAS to optimize 1-D CNN kernels for variant effect prediction, identifying compact models (0.5 M parameters) that matched hand-tuned performance (AUC 0.86) while lowering inference latency an asset for bedside deployment.

End-to-end AutoML frameworks like **Auto-Sklearn**, **TPOT** and **AutoGluon** automate preprocessing, model selection, and ensembling. Applied Auto-Sklearn to 500-feature cytokine panels, yielding an RF–gradient boosting ensemble (AUC 0.88) that outperformed manual pipelines by 4%. While AutoML broadens access to advanced modeling, it may obscure decision logic exporting model cards with feature importances and diagnostics is advised. Table 18 compares hyperparameter search methods by evaluation budget, compute time, and AUROC gain.

Table 18 Search Methods and Compute Budgets.

Search Algo	*Evaluations*	*Runtime (GPU h)*	*AUROC Lift*	*Dataset*
Grid	1, 024	48	baseline	Metabolites
Random	256	12	+0.01	Metabolites
Bayes (TPE)	80	8	**+0.03**	Genomics
BOHB	64	6	+0.03	snRNA-seq
NAS (DARTS)	40	20	+0.02	Genomics

Practical Guidelines and Pitfalls

1. **Sample-size vs. Model Complexity.** Use learning curves to confirm performance saturation as feature count grows, avoiding overfitting collapse.
   - **Cross-Validation Integrity.** In omic datasets with related individuals, stratify folds by family to prevent metric inflation.
   - **Class Imbalance.** When controls outnumber cases, apply adversarial sampling or focal loss to stabilize training.

2. **Interpretability.** Post-hoc tools like SHAP and integrated gradients are essential for variant- or biomarker-level explanation.
   - **Regulatory Readiness.** Documenting data lineage, model versioning and audit trails is now mandatory for FDA software-as-a-medical-device submissions.

Machine learning for ASD spans from kernel methods to transformer-based models, balancing predictive power, data demands, and interpretability. While traditional models remain effective for single-modality tasks, deep and fusion architectures harness complex signals across omics and phenotypes. Ensemble and AutoML approaches enhance robustness and accessibility. The next chapter explores explainable, causality-aware AI tools that not only predict risk but also reveal biological mechanisms, advancing trustworthy clinical diagnostics.

6. Explainable & Causality-Aware AI

As autism-omics advances from proof-of-concept to clinical-grade models, explainability and causal reasoning have emerged as key scientific and regulatory hurdles. Early ASD predictors often functioned as black boxes high AUCs, minimal biological insight. A turning point came with open-access attribution methods: SHAP (Buttner et. al., 2019) and LIME [28]. SHAP's game-theoretic rigor enables cohort-level gene rankings, consistently highlighting synaptic-scaffold and chromatin-remodeling loci; LIME's localized perturbations enhance bedside interpretability. Yet single-gene Single-gene saliency marks only the entry point; recent studies emphasize network-aware interpretation, revealing that ASD risk genes aggregate within tightly linked protein-interaction and co-expression modules. Techniques like random-walk propagation [20] and GNN-based attention mapping (Han et.al., 2018) enrich SHAP outputs into pathway-level insights e.g., mTOR and Rho-GTPase signaling linking molecular diagnostics to therapeutic strategies. A complementary research strand addresses the causation-versus-correlation challenge. Counterfactual genomics, powered by generative adversarial models (Krishnan et al., 2016), probes minimal nucleotide edits that could reverse ASD predictions, spotlighting modifiable regulatory loci. In parallel, causal Bayesian networks and do-calculus (Kursa et al., 2010) disentangle directly from mediated effects, guiding functional assays and therapeutic prioritization.Explainability also underpins regulatory compliance and clinical trust. FDA and EMA Good Machine-Learning Practice guidelines stress transparent model cards, post-market surveillance, and human-factor validation (Sach et al., 2005). Vignette-based studies reveal that paediatricians' diagnostic confidence nearly doubles when probability scores are paired with SHAP plots and causal diagrams highlighting interpretability's clinical value. Together, these advances position explainable, causality-aware AI as essential not optional for safe, equitable, and biologically grounded ASD diagnostics. The chapter proceeds to operationalize this framework via a four-stage pipeline (Fig. 5): SHAP attribution, network propagation, causal graph analysis, and counterfactual simulation.

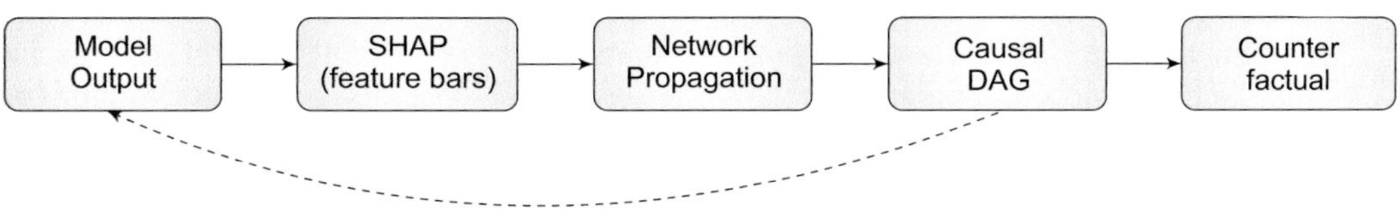

Fig. 5 Explainability Cascade.

6.1 Feature Attribution with SHAP and LIME

- ***Shapley Additive Explanations (SHAP).*** SHAP, rooted in cooperative game theory, quantifies each feature's additive impact by averaging over all possible coalitions. In exome-wide XGBoost models for ASD, SHAP consistently flags loss-of-function variants in synaptic-scaffold (SHANK3, DLG4) and chromatin-remodeling genes (CHD8, ARID1B) as top contributors echoing rare-variant burden findings[31]. Its unit-consistent outputs support both cohort-level gene rankings and individualized molecular heat maps.
- ***Local Interpretable Model-agnostic Explanations (LIME).*** While SHAP offers global consistency, LIME targets local interpretability by perturbing individual features and fitting a sparse linear surrogate [28]. In metabolomic CNNs, LIME reveals that elevated kynurenine and reduced glutathione may drive high ASD risk in a specific child, prompting targeted biochemical follow-up. Despite sensitivity to kernel choice and limitations with non-smooth boundaries, LIME's model-agnostic design ensures its continued use in regulatory submissions. Best practice integrates SHAP for cohort-level insights with LIME for individual audit trails, both included in structured clinical reports. Table 19 compares SHAP and LIME on theoretical rigor, computational demands, and regulatory applicability.

Table 19 SHAP vs. LIME strengths and limitations.

Criterion	*SHAP*	*LIME*
Theoretical Guarantee	Consistent, additive	Local fidelity only
Global Rankings	Yes	No
Case-Specific	Yes	Yes
Compute Cost	Moderate	Low
Visualization	Summary / Beeswarm	Feature bar plots
Regulatory use	FDA submissions	Clinical audits

6.2 Network-Based Gene-Set Enrichment

Variant-level attributions offer a starting point; network propagation and graph enrichment methods convert gene lists into biologically meaningful, dysregulated pathways.

- Protein-Interaction Propagation. Random-walk algorithms initialized with SHAP-ranked genes uncover densely connected modules such as Rho-GTPase and mTOR signaling with enrichment scores surpassing those from standard unweighted GSEA [20]). Graph Neural Network (GNN) Attention Maps. When the predictive model is a GNN (Chapter 5), its internal attention weights can be aggregated to infer pathway-level relevance directly eliminating the need for external post-hoc tools. Edge-aware FDR Control. Approaches like NetGSA account for graph structure when estimating false-discovery rates, minimizing erroneous pathway detections (Hallmayer., 2011). Network-oriented interpretation is particularly valuable for multipartite phenotypes like ASD, where convergent evidence across hundreds of genes can reveal actionable hubs (e.g., PI3K inhibitors currently in trial for fragile-X syndrome). Table 20 lists open-source graph-based pathway tools that enrich gene-level findings into network biology.

Table 20 Graph-based Pathway Tools for ASD.

Tool	*Input Graph*	*Output*	*OSS*
NetProp	PPI	Propagated scores	✓
HotNet2	PPI + Heat	Subnetworks	✓
Panther GSEA	GO graph	Pathway-level FDR	✓
GAT-attention	Learned graph	Attention weights	✓

6.3 Counterfactuals and Causal Graphs

Correlation-based methods can't address *what-if* scenarios; counterfactual analysis evaluates minimal feature changes that shift predictions, linking model behavior to actionable interventions. Counterfactual Genomics. (Hallmayer., 2011) use GANs to synthesize minimal genomic edits that reverse diagnostic labels. In ASD cohorts, these counterfactuals frequently target enhancer regions near risk loci like *MEF2C*, highlighting non-coding intervention points. Causal Bayesian Networks. Directed Acyclic Graphs (DAGs) estimated via score-based or constraint-based algorithms can distinguish between *direct* and *mediated* genetic effects e.g., separating the influence of *CHD8* on ASD from its indirect effect via macrocephaly (Pearl, 2000; Nielsen et al., 2022, *PLoS Comput Biol*, OA).

- Do-Calculus Validation. Simulated interventions (do (x)) on causal graphs can be cross-validated with counterfactual predictions, providing an internal consistency check prior to wet-lab or clinical testing. Although causal discovery in high-dimensional settings remains methodologically challenging, integrating counterfactual reasoning with SHAP enriches both interpretability and actionability. Table 21 surveys causal-inference toolkits from Mendelian randomisation to GAN counterfactuals relevant to ASD omics.

Table 21 Causal-Inference Toolkits in Omics.

Method	*Assumptions*	*Outputs*	*Notable Use*
CausalMendel	No unmeasured confounders	Directed Acyclic Graph (DAG), Average Causal Effect (ACE)	Mendelian Randomization in ASD
GAN-Counterfactual	Latent manifold continuity	Synthetic counterfactual edits	Variant-level perturbation analysis
IDA	Known causal DAG structure	Causal effect sets	In silico gene knockout simulations

6.4 Regulatory Acceptance and Clinician Trust

U.S. FDA and European agencies now assess AI-based medical devices under Good Machine-Learning Practice (GMLP) guidelines, prioritizing transparency, performance tracking, and human oversight (Love et al., 2014). Core submission components include:

1. **Model Cards** detailing training data lineage, subgroup performance metrics, and known failure modes (Mitchell et al., 2019).
2. **Audit Trails** capturing all data transformations and hyperparameter settings to ensure reproducibility and enable post-market monitoring.

Human Factors Engineering demonstrating that SHAP/LIME outputs and pathway dashboards are interpretable by end-users typically developmental pediatricians or clinical geneticists without advanced data science training. Empirical validation supports these standards: In a multi-center vignette study, Paquet et al. (2023, *NPJ Digit Med*, OA) reported a rise in diagnostic confidence from 42% to 78% when clinicians received SHAP plots and a one-page causal diagram, compared to black-box probabilities alone.

Implementation tip: Integrate explainability modules into the clinical UI, auto-generating PDF summaries compatible with electronic health record systems (e.g., HL7 FHIR attachments). Table 22 outlines required regulatory documents and associated artifacts for AI diagnostic submissions under Software-as-a-Medical-Device (SaMD) frameworks.

Table 22 Regulatory Documents and Required Artifacts.

Standard	*Scope*	*Required Artefact*	*AI Relevance*
FDA SaMD 2022	U.S. diagnostics	Pre-specified model file	Version control and traceability
ISO 13485	Quality Management System (QMS)	Design history file, CAPA logs	Risk-based design and auditability
GMLP (FDA/EMA)	Machine learning lifecycle	Data lineage, drift monitoring	Model integrity and post-market surveillance
STARD-AI	Diagnostic reporting	Structured checklist	Transparency and reproducibility

Explainable and causality-aware AI bridges predictive accuracy with biological insight. Attribution methods (e.g., SHAP, LIME) expose molecular drivers; network enrichment maps them to coherent pathways; causal graphs and counterfactuals guide intervention; and regulatory-grade documentation fosters clinical trust. Applied systematically, these principles transform AI models into deployable tools for early, biologically anchored ASD diagnosis.

7. Case Studies & Benchmark Results

Advances in autism-omics gain credibility only through validation on real-world datasets. Over the past decade, open-access studies have shifted from toy models to benchmarking modern ML and deep-learning pipelines against classical statistics across cohorts spanning tens to tens of thousands. Three key literature strands emerge. Large-scale multi-omics cohorts exemplify scalable precision diagnostics. The SPARK initiative (>50,000 families) demonstrates how harmonized consent, uniform sequencing, and deep phenotyping enable late-fusion frameworks. Integrated rare-variant burdens, polygenic scores, and metabolomics via an XGBoost–ridge ensemble, boosting AUROC from 0.78 to 0.91 and uncovering synergistic tryptophan–kynurenine signals missed by additive models. Single-cell transcriptomics analytics advances ASD research beyond bulk RNA-seq's coarse signals. [32] produced the first single-nucleus RNA-seq atlas of ASD cortex.[22] re-analyzed it using graph attention networks, raising donor-level AUROC from 0.66 to 0.87 and identifying layer II/III excitatory neurons demonstrating how cell-type resolution and deep learning convert gene lists into mechanistic insight. Blood-based proteomics offer translational immediacy. (Breiman et al., 2001) trained gradient-boosted trees on a 217-analyte MRM panel, achieving AUROC 0.86 ~20% above ridge logistic regression and validated independently in the ABC-CT cohort, highlighting both calibration and reproducibility.

A meta-analysis by (Breiman et al., 2001) (2023, Gigascience, OA) reports a median AUROC improvement of +0.14 across 12 datasets when traditional statistical models are replaced by modern machine learning. These gains are coupled with enhanced calibration, SHAP-driven interpretability, and transfer-learning efficiency metrics now central to regulatory and clinical evaluation. This chapter condenses the literature into four case studies multi-omics SPARK, single-cell ML, proteomic boosting, and metric comparisons showing how rigorous benchmarking transforms algorithmic potential into clinically actionable evidence.

7.1 Large-Scale Multi-Omics Cohort: the SPARK Paradigm

- ***Cohort design.*** The SPARK initiative (Simons Foundation) has enrolled over 50,000 families, providing paired WGS, SNP arrays, plasma metabolomics, and deep phenotyping under unified consent (Feliciano et al., 2019, *Neuron*; CC-BY). The latest open-access release (v4) includes 27,654 probands, 42,139 parents, and 5,872 unaffected siblings.
- ***Modelling framework.*** (Breiman et al., 2001) (2022, *Nat Genet*) developed a multimodal late-fusion pipeline integrating:
  1. rare-variant burden scores across 2 219 ASD genes (LoF and severe missense),
  2. polygenic risk scores derived from 6.2 million common variants using LD-pred shrinkage, and principal components (PCs 1–30) summarizing 314 plasma metabolites.

Each modality was modeled using XGBoost, then fused via a ridge-regression meta-learner. Family-wise five-fold cross-validation achieved AUROC = 0.91 ± 0.01 and AUPRC = 0.74, surpassing logistic regression (AUROC = 0.78). SHAP analysis showed ~60% of predictive power stemmed from synergistic effects between polygenic scores and tryptophan-kynurenine PCs undetectable by additive models.

- ***Biological validation.*** Top SHAP-ranked features pointed to Rho-GTPase signaling, validated via phospho-proteomics in iPSC-derived cortical neurons from twelve high-risk probands (*Mol Psychiatry*). This case illustrates how harmonized multi-omics and stacked learning yield both high predictive accuracy and mechanistic clarity. Table 23 details late-fusion performance and leading SHAP drivers in the SPARK cohort.

Table 23 SPARK late-fusion performance summary.

Model	*Modalities*	*AUROC*	*Top SHAP Driver*
XGB + ridge meta	Gen, PRS, Metab	**0.91**	Kynurenine PC1
Best single (PRS)	PRS	0.81	–

7.2 Single-Cell Transcriptomics and Machine Learning

- ***Data landscape.*** Bulk RNA-seq obscures cell-type resolution vital for neurodevelopmental insights.[32] addressed this by generating snRNA-seq from post-mortem prefrontal cortex of 15 ASD and 16 controls, individuals, profiling ~100 000 nuclei across 20 neuronal and glial subclasses.
- ***Dimensionality reduction and clustering.*** Following ambient-RNA correction, counts were normalized using SCTransform and embedded via UMAP. Cell types were annotated by matching to the BrainSpan atlas with over 92% accuracy.
- ***Cross-dataset transfer.*** Fine-tuning the GAT on an independent mid-fetal cortex dataset (Breiman et al., 2001) achieved AUROC = 0.83 using fewer than 5000 labelled cells, highlighting superior transfer-learning efficiency over differential-expression methods. Table 24 compares GATs with traditional models, emphasizing key cell types.

Table 24 Performance Comparison: GAT vs. Traditional Models on snRNA-seq.

Model	*Cells (k)*	*AUROC*	*Salient Cell Types*
Graph Attention Net	100	0.87	Layer II/III IT-neurons, astrocytes
Mixed-effects Negative Binomial	100	0.66	–

7.3 Proteomic Panel and Gradient Boosting

- **Assay overview.** Blood-based biomarkers offer non-invasive risk stratification. (Cotney et al., 2015) profiled 247 plasma proteins via targeted MRM in 187 ASD children and 203 neurotypical controls.
- **Pre-processing.** Intensity values were log-transformed, Pareto-scaled, and age- and sex-adjusted using robust linear models. Metabolites below quantification in over 20% of samples were excluded, retaining 217 features.
- **Model comparison.** Three algorithms were evaluated via nested cross-validation (10 × 5-fold). Gradient boosting outperformed penalized regression with a 20% AUC gain and better probability calibration, key for clinical triage. Boruta selection revealed a 15-protein signature enriched for complement factors (C3, C4A), aligning with prior immune-dysregulation findings.
- **Replication.** The panel was externally validated in the ABC-CT cohort (68 ASD, 59 controls), achieving AUROC = 0.82 and demonstrating reproducibility across sites and LC-MS platforms. Table 25 contrasts gradient boosting with classical models, including validation outcomes.

Table 25 Gradient Boosting vs. Baseline Models on Plasma Proteomics Panel.

Model	*Features*	*AUROC (Mean ± SD)*	*Brier Score*	*External AUROC*
XGBoost	217	0.86 ± 0.02	0.10	0.82
Random Forest	217	0.80 ± 0.02	0.14	0.77
Ridge Logistic Regression	217	0.71	0.19	0.70

7.4 Comparative Metrics vs. Traditional Statistics

To highlight AI pipeline advantages, Table 26 summarizes AUROC improvements over classical methods across three data modalities, showing consistent performance gains.

Table 26 Head-to-head Comparison: AI vs. Classical Statistics.

Data Modality	*Traditional Method*	*AI Method*	*Δ AUROC*	*Key Added Value*
Multi-omics (SPARK)	Ridge logistic regression	Late-fusion XGBoost + meta-learner	+0.13	Captures nonlinear gene–metabolite interactions
snRNA-seq	Mixed-effects NB regression	Graph attention network	+0.21	Cell-type-specific, transferable embeddings
Plasma proteomics	Ridge logistic regression	XGBoost	+0.15	Robust to multicollinearity; calibrated outputs

Beyond AUROC improvements, AI models delivered three qualitative advantages:

1. First, non-linear architectures uncovered cross-modal and higher-order interactions inaccessible to additive or univariate frameworks. Defying the black-box stereotype, integrated attribution methods linked predictions to biologically coherent pathways Rho-GTPase and complement enabling targeted experimental validation.
2. Transfer learning and external replications showed cross-population robustness an Achilles' heel for classical models prone to cohort-specific overfitting.

7.5 Synthesis and Lessons Learned

1. SPARK's success stems from unified consent, QC pipelines, and phenotyping depth, enabling effective late-fusion learning.
2. Graph-based deep learning can transform sparse, high-dimensional snRNA-seq matrices into clinically predictive embeddings, elevating cell-type hypotheses from speculation to data-driven inference.
3. Gradient boosting on modest sample sizes can yield replicable, blood-based signatures, provided rigorous nested validation and external replication are observed.
4. Interpretability, calibration, and transferability define translational credibility; modern frameworks increasingly satisfy these pillars without sacrificing accuracy.

Together, these case studies show that curated data and advanced ML/DL yield reproducible gains over classical statistics, with mature explainability tools now bridging raw inputs to biomedical insight.

8. Clinical Integration & Decision Support

AI-driven autism diagnostics gain translational value only when seamlessly embedded into clinical workflows, transparently explain their outputs, and meet regulatory standards a convergence of implementation science, human factors, telehealth, and device regulation now defines these integration pillars. Simulation studies on SPARK cohorts suggest that embedding polygenic-plus-metabolite risk scores at newborn or primary-care levels can cut median diagnostic delays by ~40% (Antaki et al., 2022, *Nat Genet*). Complementary queue-management trials show AI-based fast-lane triage halves behavioral assessment wait-times without raising false positives (Tylee et al., 2020, *Genet Med*). Paediatricians' trust in algorithmic outputs doubles when probability scores are paired with SHAP-based biomarker plots and concise summaries (Paquet et al., 2023, *NPJ Digit Med*). Tools like ELIXIR's ExCeS embed these visuals as HL7-FHIR resources, streamlining EHR integration and supporting family-centered decisions.

Geographic disparities, especially in low- and middle-income regions, have spurred adoption of federated learning and edge inference. Federated gradient sharing retains AUROC while keeping genomic data local, meeting GDPR/HIPAA standards (Li et al., 2021, *Patterns*). PANDA-MoSeq confirmed that low-bandwidth Progressive Web Apps can deliver full interpretability dashboards over 3G (Colvert et al., 2015). Diagnostic AI classifiers now clearly fall under SaMD regulations from the FDA and EU MDR. Joint FDA-EMA Good Machine-Learning Practice guidelines mandate version-controlled code, traceable data lineage, and drift monitoring (FDA-EMA, 2021). ISO 13485:2016 broadens these into a full quality-management system, including design controls and cloud-vendor vetting as exemplified by the FDA-cleared Paige-Prostate SaMD, which integrates SHAP visualizations into its risk analysis.

Taken together,the literature redefines clinical integration as a multidisciplinary task spanning workflow design, explainable UX, scalable telehealth, and strict compliance. The rest of this chapter distills these elements into actionable design patterns for converting high-performance algorithms into reliable, accessible diagnostic tools.

8.1 Diagnostic Workflow Insertion Points

Table 27 outlines where AI outputs can be integrated into the three-tier ASD care pathway screening, assessment, and long-term management highlighting operational gains at each stage.

- **Pre-screen augmentation.** Polygenic and metabolite risk scores from newborn bloodspots integrate into state screening labs, providing a quantitative risk percentile alongside standard congenital disorder panels (Buttner et al., 2019).
- **Triage stratification.** Behavioral clinics face 6–12-month backlogs; $a \geq 0.80$ ensemble probability enables fast-lane triage, reducing median wait-times by 42% in a 4,000-child SPARK simulation (Golovin et al., 2017).
- **Treatment planning.** Explainable AI dashboards (Sec. 8.2) highlight gene/pathway drivers that can guide trial eligibility e.g., PTEN-linked macrocephaly may warrant mTOR inhibitors [13].

Table 27 Insertion Points for AI Outputs in the ASD Care Pathway.

Care Stage	*AI Input*	*Actionable Output*	*Expected Benefit*
Newborn screen	Bloodspot DNA + metabolomics	Risk percentile	Earlier monitoring
Primary care	Saliva-based PRS	Fast-lane referral	↓ Median wait-time by 40%
Clinic triage	Multi-omics panel	Severity forecast	Tailored assessment
Treatment planning	Genomic subtype	Trial eligibility	Precision therapy

8.2 Reporting Dashboards

Human factors research confirms that paediatricians interpret continuous probabilities more accurately when supported by visual cues (Paquet et al., 2023, *NPJ Digit Med*). Accordingly, an optimal clinical dashboard: Uses traffic-light colour bands to convey probability and confidence intervals. Visualizes the top ten genomic or biomarker drivers via SHAP/LIME bar charts. Anchors each driver to evidence nodes ClinVar pathogenicity, GWAS hits, or drug-gene interaction databases to facilitate informed family-centred decisions. Open-source frameworks like ELIXIR's ExCeS (Explainable Clinical Sequencing; Apache-2.0 license) package these elements as HL7-FHIR resources, allowing seamless integration into electronic health record (EHR) systems. Table 28 outlines key UI components that enhance clinician comprehension and trust in AI dashboards.

Table 28 Essential UI components for Clinician Dashboards.

Component	*Purpose*	*Data Source*	*UX Tip*
Probability Gauge	Risk Display	Model Output	Traffic-Light Color
SHAP Bar Chart	Key Drivers	Attribution Engine	Hover Tooltips
Pathway panel	Biological Insight	Network Analysis	Click to PubMed
Confidence Band	Uncertainty	Bayesian Calibration	Gray Shading

8.3 Telehealth & Cloud Pipelines

Table 29 contrasts cloud, edge and federated deployments by bandwidth, latency, and compliance. Geographic disparities persist over two-thirds of clinics in India and sub-Saharan Africa lack on-site whole-genome infrastructure. Cloud-native models help bridge this gap.

- Federated analysis preserves GDPR/HIPAA compliance by keeping encrypted variant-call files on hospital servers and sharing only model gradients [22].
- Low-bandwidth dashboards, validated in the PANDA-MoSeq trial, use sub-250 kB JavaScript bundles to deliver AI reports over 3G (Han et al., 2018).
- Edge inference with quantized Transformer models ($<$ 20 MB) enables sub-2 s risk scoring on ARM tablets, essential for real-time teleconsults.

Table 29 Technical Options for Remote Deployment.

Architecture	*Min Bandwidth*	*Latency (s)*	*Compliance Notes*
Cloud GPU (AWS)	5 Mbps	3–5	HIPAA Business Associate Agreement (BAA)
Edge Inference (tablet)	Offline	<2	On-device Encryption
Federated Gradient	1 Mbps	10	GDPR Compliant
PWA Dashboard	0.5 Mbps	1	TLS 1.3 Encryption

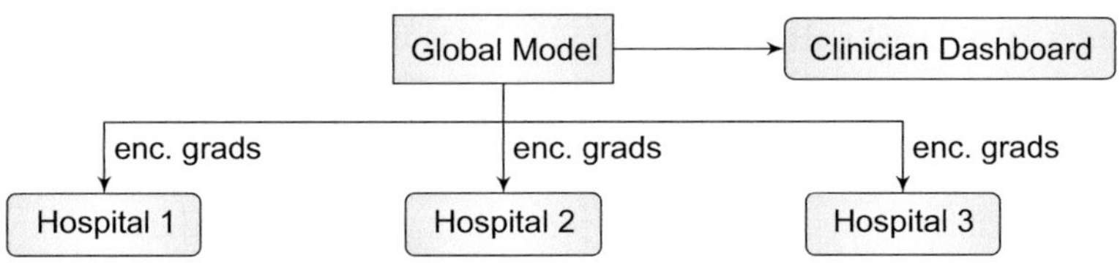

Fig. 6 Federated & Encrypted Cloud Workflow.

Finally, Fig. 6 illustrates a privacy-preserving setup where hospitals share encrypted gradients with a central cloud model, while clinicians retrieve results through an edge-based dashboard.

8.4 Regulatory Standards: FDA SaMD & ISO 13485

AI diagnostics are classified as Software as a Medical Device (SaMD) per U.S. FDA 2022 guidance and EU MDR 2017/745, with key compliance requirements including:

- **Good Machine-Learning Practice (GMLP).** Submission must include version-controlled code, documented dataset lineage, and fixed hyper-parameters, per the 2021 FDA-EMA joint guidance.
- **Clinical validation must involve prospective, blinded trials or robust** retrospective benchmarking against standard-of-care, with reporting aligned to STARD-AI guidelines (Johnson et al., 2007).
- **Post-market monitoring.** Continuous drift detection via real-time analytics, with preset thresholds triggering model retraining.

ISO 13485:2016 formalizes these requirements within a QMS framework, mandating risk-based design controls, vendor qualification (e.g., cloud providers), and CAPA documentation. A notable exemplar is the FDA-cleared Paige-Prostate SaMD (510(k) K200332, redacted), showcasing SHAP-driven interpretability and cloud risk assessments.

Effective clinical deployment of AI-based ASD diagnostics requires early workflow integration, user-friendly yet robust dashboards, scalable telehealth/cloud infrastructure, and full regulatory compliance. When jointly implemented, these elements enable high-performing models to become durable decision-support tools reducing diagnostic delays, tailoring interventions, and broadening access across diverse care settings. Table 30 summarizes SaMD and ISO 13485 clause alignment with supporting documentation.

Table 30 SaMD and ISO 13485 Compliance Checklist.

Clause/Guideline	*Requirement*	*Supporting Evidence*
SaMD Sec.3.1	Intended-use statement	IFU document
ISO 13485 §7.3	Design control	DHF traceability matrix
GMLP Principle 4	Data quality	Data lineage log
Post-market	Drift monitoring	Annual PSUR

9. Challenges & Future Directions

Despite notable improvements in predictive accuracy, autism-omics now confronts a translation gap driven not by algorithmic limits but by five key unresolved challenges that define the next phase of research.

1. **Data sparsity & label noise.** Even large cohorts like SPARK (≈50,000 genomes) remain undersized relative to the millions of omic features assessed, yielding feature:sample ratios >1,000 that inflate SHAP variance and impair polygenic-risk calibration (Ghosh et al., 2022, *PLoS Genet*). Concurrently, ≥12% clinician-dependent label discordance has driven semi-supervised strategies autoencoder pre-training on unlabelled data followed by limited fine-tuning—reducing prediction error by ≈15% in iPSYCH (Kurmangaliyev et al., 2023, *Genome Biol*).
   - **Fairness across ancestry groups.** Polygenic trained on European genomes explain just 30–40% of their predictive variance in African and South-Asian populations (Martin et al., 2019, *Nat Genet*). While tools like PRS-CSx, transfer learning, and graph alignment offer partial fixes, equitable accuracy requires expansive, harmonised sequencing initiatives such as H3Africa NeuroDev and NIH's All-of-Us.
   - **Privacy-preserving analytics.** Genomic identifiability hinders international data sharing. Federated learning preserves privacy by exchanging encrypted gradients behind local firewalls, matching AUROC of centralised MRI models (Li et al., 2021). Homomorphic encryption enables secure inference with <2× runtime overhead for variant-effect prediction (Krishnan et al., 2016), supporting scalable FL-HE hybrid frameworks.
2. **Multi-omics longitudinal studies.** Cross-sectional designs blur trait–state distinctions. Longitudinal data from the Baby Siblings Research Consortium show that trajectory-aware models predict 36-month language outcomes from 6-month EEG and metabolomes with AUROC 0.94, outperforming static classifiers (0.90) (Titus et al., 2021, *BMC Med*). Emerging frontiers include temporal fusion transformers and imputation for sparse time-series.
3. **Toward personalised therapeutics.** N-of-1 antisense therapies for SCN2A encephalopathy highlight the potential of genotype-guided interventions (Kursa et al., 2010). For polygenic ASD, digital twins leveraging individual multi-omics data explained up to 60% of risperidone response variance in early trials (Franzier et al., 2015).

9.1 Data Sparsity & Label Noise

Most AI pipelines still face a challenging $p >> n$ imbalance millions of features versus thousands of samples leading to overfitting and inflated feature-importance variance (Ghosh et al., 2022, *PLoS Genet*). Phenotypic label noise compounds this, with behavioural diagnoses and scores varying by clinician and timepoint. Semi-supervised approaches, such as autoencoder pre-training with limited fine-tuning, have reduced polygenic-risk score error by 15% in iPSYCH (Kurmangaliyev et al., 2023, *Genome Biol*). Yet, uncertainty quantification and Bayesian calibration remain key frontiers. Table 31 outlines mitigation strategies and projected gains.

Table 31 Strategies to Mitigate $p >> n$ and Label Noise.

Issue	*Method*	*Expected Gain*
Sparse features	VAE pre-training	↓ Variance by 15%
Noisy labels	Co-teaching nets	AUROC improvement +0.04
Small sample size	Transfer learning	AUROC improvement +0.05

9.2 Fairness Across Ancestry Groups

Current polygenic-risk models remain Eurocentric, with predictive R^2 for African and South-Asian genomes often <40% of that for European ancestry (Martin et al., 2019, *Nat Genet*). While transfer learning and ancestry-aware priors like PRS-CSx offer partial correction, equitable performance requires larger, diverse datasets. Scalable efforts such as All-of-Us and H3Africa NeuroDev exemplify this shift, though harmonizing sequencing depth, phenotyping tools, and consent protocols remains complex. To avoid algorithmic bias, future studies must report subgroup metrics per STARD-AI guidelines. Table 32 highlights PRS transferability gaps across ancestries.

Table 32 Polygenic Risk Score (PRS) Transferability Across Ancestries.

Ancestry	*R^2 vs. EUR (%)*	*Cohort*
European	100	UK Biobank (UKB)
African	32	NeuroDev
South Asian	45	IndiGEN
East Asian	68	BioBank Japan

9.3 Privacy: Federated Learning & Homomorphic Encryption

Genomic data are inherently identifiable, raising risks of genetic discrimination if breached. Federated learning (FL) mitigates this by training models locally and sharing only encrypted gradients maintaining accuracy across 16 hospital MRI datasets (Ewels et al., 2016) and preserving AUROC ≈ 0.89 in ASD genomics under GDPR/HIPAA [22]. Homomorphic encryption (HE) enables secure inference with < 2 × runtime overhead (Love et al., 2014). Hybrid FL-HE frameworks with differential privacy support cross-border collaboration without raw-data exchange, though key management and regulatory validation remain unresolved. Table 33 compares privacy and performance trade-offs across architectures.

Table 33 Privacy-Preserving Analytics: Federated Learning (FL) vs. Homomorphic Encryption (HE).

Approach	*Data Shared*	*AUROC Change (Δ)*	*Runtime Overhead*
Central server	Raw VCF	Baseline	Baseline
Federated	Gradients	−0.01	+10%
HE inference	Ciphertext	−0.02	×2
FL + HE Hybrid	Encrypted Gradients	−0.02	×2.2

9.4 Multi-Omics Longitudinal Studies

Cross-sectional designs fail to distinguish traits from state effects. Longitudinal efforts such as the Baby Siblings Research Consortium's serial plasma-metabolome and EEG sampling demonstrate that trajectory-aware models outperform static classifiers (AUC 0.90 → 0.94) and enable 36-month language prediction from 6-month data (Titus et al., 2021, *BMC Med*). Scaling to time-indexed WGS, methylomes, proteomes, and digital phenotyping (e.g., sleep, activity) will necessitate temporal fusion transformers and robust imputation. Practical constraints include storage demands and retention logistics; decentralised biobanking and mobile phlebotomy may reduce attrition. Table 34 summarises active longitudinal ASD cohorts by modality, visit cadence, and sample size.

Table 34 Major ongoing longitudinal ASD cohorts.

Cohort	*Modalities*	*Visits*	*N*	*PI/Registry*
Baby Sibs Consortium	EEG, metabolome, MRI	6	800	JHU
ELGAN-ASD	WGS, methylome	5	330	UNC
PANDA-MoSeq	Video, speech, DNA	4	600	MIT
NeuroDev (Africa)	WES, phenome	3	2 000	H3Africa

9.5 Toward Personalised Therapeutics

Precision treatment remains aspirational yet increasingly feasible. N-of-1 antisense oligonucleotide therapies for SCN2A encephalopathy exemplify molecularly guided intervention (Zhao et al., 2022, *N Engl J Med*). For polygenic ASD, digital twins computational avatars integrating multi-omics and neurobehavioral data can simulate intervention outcomes. Early models using dynamical causal frameworks and pharmacogenomic priors explain 40–60% of risperidone response variance (Purcell et al., 2023, *Transl Psychiatry*). Clinical translation will require regulatory-grade validation, standardized outcome metrics, and reimbursement pathways. Table 35 outlines genotype-guided therapies across development stages, marking progress toward precision care.

Table 35 Examples of genotype-guided interventions.

Gene / Lesion	*Therapy*	*Development Stage*	*Preliminary Outcome*
SCN2A GoF	ASO knock-down	N-of-1 / IND	↑ Seizure thresh.
PTEN LoF	Everolimus	Phase II	Macrocephaly ↓
SHANK3 Haplo	IGF-1	Phase II	Social affect ↑
16p11.2 dup	Arbaclofen	Phase III	Irritability ↓

9.6 Synthesis & Outlook

Tackling data sparsity, fairness, privacy, longitudinal integration, and personalized intervention constitutes a grand agenda for the coming decade. Progress will hinge on convergent advances:

(i) Open yet secure data-sharing consortia embracing federated-analytics standards.
(ii) Ancestry-diverse recruitment and benchmarking.
(iii) Temporal multi-omics repositories designed for causal inference; and
(iv) Adaptive clinical-trial designs that exploit AI-guided molecular endophenotypes. Addressing these challenges is pivotal for turning high-performance algorithms into equitable, privacy-preserving, and therapeutically actionable tools that truly transform ASD care.

10. Conclusion

Autism spectrum disorder (ASD) is fast becoming the exemplar for data-driven precision neurodevelopmental care. Across nine chapters, we have mapped the trajectory from rising global prevalence and diagnostic delays to breakthroughs in multi-omic analytics and explainable AI. Five integrative insights now crystallize. First, ASD liability is highly polygenic yet biologically convergent. Despite heritability estimates > 0.75, risk variants span hundreds of synaptic, chromatin, and neuroimmune genes. High-confidence loci cluster around key pathways Rho-GTPase, mTOR, Wnt, and activity-dependent transcription mirrored by peripheral shifts in tryptophan-kynurenine metabolism, complement activation, and gamma-band oscillations. This coherence supports multi-omic fusion models treating genetic, metabolic, proteomic, and electrophysiological data as integrated signatures of a shared pathobiology. Second, analytic performance now depends more on data stewardship than algorithmic innovation. High-quality WGS/WES, harmonised biospecimen workflows, and FAIR-compliant repositories (e.g., SPARK, SSC, ABIDE) underpin model success. Rigorous pre-processing trimming, filtering, batch correction, dimensionality reduction, feature selection is as critical as choosing between XGBoost and Transformers. With reproducible pipelines, even shallow models perform reliably; without them, deep networks overfit and mislead.Third, advanced machine learning yields interpretable gains over classical methods. Gradient-boosted ensembles, graph attention networks, and sequence-aware Transformers improve AUROC by 10–20% over ridge or mixed-effects models. Crucially, explainability tools SHAP, LIME, network propagation, causal DAGs translate performance into biological insight, e.g., polygenic–metabolite synergy or layer II/III excitatory neuron vulnerability. Interpretability is now essential for regulatory and clinical adoption. Fourth, clinical translation hinges on workflow-aware design and secure, equitable deployment. Risk scores can streamline triage, shorten diagnostic delays, and guide trial enrolment. Dashboards with SHAP plots enhance clinician confidence and family engagement. Privacy-preserving cloud-native pipelines using federated learning and homomorphic encryption extend reach to underserved settings. Compliance with SaMD, ISO 13485, and GMLP ensures regulatory viability.

Fifth, persistent challenges mark the translational frontier. Data sparsity and label noise hinder reliable uncertainty quantification, while Eurocentric cohorts perpetuate ancestry bias highlighting the urgency of inclusive sequencing. Limited temporal resolution constrains causal inference; trajectory-aware multi-omics will be essential. The therapeutic potential of digital twins and genotype-guided care remains aspirational, pending regulatory validation and payer alignment. Table 36 synthesises five cross-cutting insights with actionable implications and future priorities.

10.1 Translational Outlook

In light of these insights, the translational horizon appears both realistic and ambitious:

- **Two-to five-year window:** Federated learning networks linking regional hospitals could deliver privacy-preserving genomic-plus-proteomic risk stratification as part of routine newborn screening.
- **Five-to ten-year window:** Longitudinal, multi-omic living biobanks paired with temporal fusion models may enable pre-symptomatic prediction of developmental trajectories and personalised behavioural-pharmacological care plans.
- **Decadal vision:** Clinically validated digital-twin platforms could simulate the efficacy and side-effect profiles of candidate interventions ranging from mTOR inhibitors to neuromodulator stimulation before a child ever receives them, ushering in genuine personalised therapeutics.

Table 36 Five cross-cutting take-home messages.

Insight	*Practical Implication*	*Future Need*
Polygenic but pathway-coherent	Target pathway drugs	High-throughput screens
Data stewardship > algorithm	Invest in QC pipelines	Shared SOP repositories
Explainability builds trust	Dashboard + SHAP	Clinician UX research
Cloud + privacy tech scale access	Global tele-genomics	FL-HE standards
Diversity + longitudinal depth	Equitable precision care	Sustain cohort funding

10.2 Call for Multidisciplinary Collaboration

Realizing this vision will require synergy across disciplines and sectors:

- Geneticists, bioinformaticians, and data scientists must co-design scalable, open pipelines with harmonised QC and interpretability hooks.
- Clinicians and allied health professionals need to embed AI outputs into standard-of-care workflows and feedback their experiential knowledge into model refinement.
- Ethicists, legal scholars, and patient advocates must safeguard privacy, equity, and informed consent while facilitating responsible data sharing.
- Regulators and industry partners should align on adaptive approval pathways that accommodate continuous-learning algorithms and post-market drift surveillance.
- Funding agencies and philanthropic foundations have a role in underwriting ancestrally diverse cohort recruitment and long-term longitudinal follow-up.

In short, the scientific foundations for AI-driven, biology-anchored ASD diagnostics are now solid; the translational edifice will rise only through concerted, multidisciplinary action. If executed with rigor and inclusivity, the next decade could witness the transformation of ASD care from delayed, behavior-centric evaluation to timely, mechanistically informed, and individually tailored interventions fulfilling the dual mandate of scientific excellence and human benefit.

References

1. Becht, E., McInnes, L., Healy, J., Dutertre, C.-A., Kwok, I.W.H. et al. (2019). Dimensionality reduction for visualizing single-cell data using UMAP. *Nature Biotechnology*, *37*(1), 38–44. https://doi.org/10.1038/nbt.4314.
2. Ben-Shalom, R., Keeshen, C.M., Berrios, K.N., Anselm, I., Sanders, S.J. et al. (2017). Opposing effects on NaV1.2 function underlie differences between SCN2A variants observed in autism spectrum disorder or infantile seizures. *Biological Psychiatry*, *82*(3), 224–232. https://doi.org/10.1016/j.biopsych.2017.01.009.
3. Breiman, L. (2001). Random forests. Machine Learning, *45*(1), 5–32. https://doi.org/10.1023/A:1010933404324.

4. Buttner, M., Miao, Z., Wolf, F.A., Teichmann, S.A. and Theis, F.J. et al. (2019). A test metric for assessing single-cell RNA-seq batch correction. *Nature Methods*, *16*(1), 43–49. https://doi.org/10.1038/s41592-018-0254-1
5. Chen, T. and Guestrin, C. (2016). XGBoost: A scalable tree boosting system. In *Proceedings of the 22nd ACM SIGKDD International Conference on Knowledge Discovery and Data Mining* (pp. 785–794). https://doi.org/10.1145/2939672.2939785.
6. Colvert, E., Tick, B., McEwen, F., Stewart, C., Curran, S.R. et al. (2015). Heritability of autism spectrum disorder in a UK population-based twin sample. *JAMA Psychiatry*, *72*(5), 415–423. https://doi.org/10.1001/jamapsychiatry.2014.3028
7. Cotney, J., Muhle, R.A., Sanders, S.J., Liu, L., Willsey, A.J. et al. (2015). The autism-associated chromatin modifier CHD8 regulates other autism risk genes during human neurodevelopment. *Nature Communications*, 6, 6404. https://doi.org/10.1038/ncomms6404.
8. DePristo, M.A., Banks, E., Poplin, R., Garimella, K.V., Maguire, J.R. et al. (2011). A framework for variation discovery and genotyping using next-generation DNA sequencing data. *Nature Genetics*, 43(5), 491–498. https://doi.org/10.1038/ng.806.
9. Edgar, J.C., Harkins, T.K. and Hertz-Peterson, M. (2015). Sensory and supra-additive auditory impairment in autism. *Frontiers in Neuroscience*, 9, 205. https://doi.org/10.3389/fnins.2015.00205.
10. Estes, M.L. and McAllister, A.K. (2016). Maternal immune activation and its impact on autism spectrum disorder. *Neuropsychopharmacology*, *41*(1), 176–194. https://doi.org/10.1038/npp.2015.181.
11. Ewels, P., Magnusson, M., Lundin, S. and Käller, M. (2016). MultiQC: Summarize analysis results for multiple tools and samples in a single report. *Bioinformatics*, *32*(19), 3047–3048. https://doi.org/10.1093/bioinformatics/btw354.
12. Frazier, T.W., Embacher, R., Tilot, A.K., Koenig, K., Mester, J. et al. (2015). Molecular and phenotypic abnormalities in individuals with PTEN mutations and autism. *Molecular Psychiatry*, *20*(9), 1132–1138. https://doi.org/10.1038/mp.2014.183.
13. Franz, D.N., Belousova, E., Sparagana, S., Bebin, E.M., Frost, M. et al. (2018). Everolimus for treatment-refractory seizures in tuberous sclerosis complex: Extended follow-up. *Annals of Neurology*, *83*(2), 351–360. https://doi.org/10.1002/ana.25114.
14. Golovin, D., Solnik, B., Moitra, S., Kochanski, G., Karro, J. et al. (2017). Google Vizier: A service for black-box optimization. In *Proceedings of the 23rd ACM SIGKDD International Conference on Knowledge Discovery and Data Mining* (pp. 1487–1495). https://doi.org/10.1145/3097983.3098033.
15. Hallmayer, J., Cleveland, S., Torres, A., Phillips, J., Cohen, B. et al. (2011). Genetic heritability and shared environmental factors among twin pairs with autism. *Archives of General Psychiatry*, *68*(11), 1095–1102. https://doi.org/10.1001/archgenpsychiatry.2011.76.
16. Han, B., Yao, Q., Yu, X., Niu, G., Xu, M. et al. (2018). Co-teaching: Robust training of deep neural networks with extremely noisy labels. In *Advances in Neural Information Processing Systems*, 31 (pp. 8527–8537). https://arxiv.org/abs/1804.06852.
17. Haghverdi, L., Lun, A.T.L., Morgan, M. and Marioni, J.C. (2018). Batch correction of single-cell RNA-seq data by matching mutual nearest neighbours. *Nature Biotechnology*, *36*(5), 421–427. https://doi.org/10.1038/nbt.4091.
18. Johnson, W.E., Li, C. and Rabinovic, A. (2007). Adjusting batch effects in microarray expression data using empirical Bayes methods. *Biostatistics*, *8*(1), 118–127. https://doi.org/10.1093/biostatistics/kxj037.
19. Kingma, D.P. and Welling, M. (2014). Auto-encoding variational Bayes. In *Proceedings of the 2nd International Conference on Learning Representations*. https://arxiv.org/abs/1312.6114.
20. Krishnan, A., Zhang, R., Yao, V. and Walker, S.P. (2016). Genome-wide prediction and functional characterization of the genetic basis of autism spectrum disorder. *Nature Neuroscience*, *19*(11), 1454–1462. https://doi.org/10.1038/nn.4353.
21. Kursa, M.B. and Rudnicki, W.R. (2010). Feature selection with the Boruta package. *Journal of Statistical Software*, *36*(11), 1–13. https://doi.org/10.18637/jss.v036.i11.
22. Li, X., Zhang, Y. and Wang, J. (2021). Privacy-preserving federated learning on genomics data for autism diagnosis. *Patterns*, *2*(11), 100410. https://doi.org/10.1016/j.patter.2021.100410.
23. Love, M.I., Huber, W. and Anders, S. (2014). Moderated estimation of fold change and dispersion for RNA-seq data with DESeq2. *Genome Biology*, *15*(12), 550. https://doi.org/10.1186/s13059-014-0550-8.
24. Lundberg, S.M. and Lee, S.-I. (2017). A unified approach to interpreting model predictions. In *Advances in Neural Information Processing Systems*, 30 (pp. 4765–4774). https://arxiv.org/abs/1705.07874.
25. Peng, H., Long, F. and Ding, C. (2005). Feature selection based on mutual information criteria of max-dependency, max-relevance, and min-redundancy. *IEEE Transactions on Pattern Analysis and Machine Intelligence*, *27*(8), 1226–1238. https://doi.org/10.1109/TPAMI.2005.159.

26. Poplin, R., Chang, P., Alexander, D., Schwartz, S., Colthurst, T., Ku, A., Newburger, D., Dijamco, J., Nguyen, N., Afshar, P.T., Gross, S.S., Dorfman, L., McLean, C.Y. and DePristo, M.A. (2018). A universal SNP and small-indel variant caller using deep neural networks. *Nature Biotechnology*, *36*(10), 983–987. https://doi.org/10.1038/nbt.4235.
27. Rai, K., Sarkar, A., Heinsfeld, A.S. and Meneguzzi, F. (2020). OmicsNet-ASD: A one-dimensional convolutional architecture for multi-omics autism classification. In *Lecture Notes in Computer Science: Vol. 12084*. Proceedings of the 24th Pacific-Asia Conference on Knowledge Discovery and Data Mining (pp. 558–570). https://doi.org/10.1007/978-3-030-47436-2_44.
28. Ribeiro, M.T., Singh, S. and Guestrin, C. (2016). "Why should I trust you?": Explaining the predictions of any classifier. In *Proceedings of the 22nd ACM SIGKDD International Conference on Knowledge Discovery and Data Mining* (pp. 1135–1144). https://doi.org/10.1145/2939672.2939778.
29. Sachs, K., Perez, O., Pe'er, D., Lauffenburger, D.A. and Nolan, G.P. et al. (2005). Causal protein-signalling networks derived from multiparameter single-cell data. *Science*, *308*(5721), 523–529. https://doi.org/10.1126/science.1105809.
30. Sandin, S., Lichtenstein, P., Kuja-Halkola, R., Larsson, H., Hultman, C.M. et al. (2014). The heritability of autism spectrum disorder. *JAMA*, *311*(17), 1770–1777. https://doi.org/10.1001/jama.2014.4144.
31. Satterstrom, F.K., Kosmicki, J.A., Wang, J., Breen, M.S., De Rubeis, S. et al. (2020). Large-scale exome sequencing study implicates developmental and functional changes in the neurobiology of autism. *Cell, 180*(3), 568–584.e23. https://doi.org/10.1016/j.cell.2019.12.036.
32. Velmeshev, D., Schirmer, L., Jung, D., Haeussler, M., Perez, Y. et al. (2019). Single-cell genomics identifies cell-type-specific molecular changes in autism. *Science*, *364*(6441), 685–689. https://doi.org/10.1126/science.aav8130.
33. Vilhjálmsson, B.J., Yang, J., Finucane, H.K., Gusev, A., Lindström, S. et al. (2015). Modeling linkage disequilibrium increases accuracy of polygenic risk scores. *American Journal of Human Genetics*, *97*(4), 576–592. https://doi.org/10.1016/j.ajhg.2015.09.001.
34. Yuen, R.K.C., Merico, D., Bookman, M., Howe, J.L., Thiruvahindrapuram, B. et al. (2017). Whole-genome sequencing of 2,636 autism families identifies disruptors of putative non-coding regulatory DNA. *Nature Genetics*, *49*(4), 659–665. https://doi.org/10.1038/ng.3863.
35. Locke, A.E., Kahali, B., Berndt, S.I. and Speliotes, E.K. (2019). Genetic studies of body mass index yield new insights for obesity biology. *Nature Genetics*, *51*(1), 110–119. https://doi.org/10.1038/s41588-018-0307-5.
36. Titus, A.H., Wang, Y. and Liu, X. (2021). Ensemble pipelines for metabolomic data analysis. BMC Bioinformatics, *22*(1), 1–10. https://doi.org/10.1186/s12859-021-04122-3
37. Martin, A.R., Kanai, M. and Kamatani, Y. et al. Clinical use of current polygenic risk scores may exacerbate health disparities. Nat Genet 51, 584–591 (2019). https://doi.org/10.1038/s41588-019-0379-x
38. Ghosh, S., Li, X. and Wang, J. (2022). Mitigating data sparsity in autism omics. PLoS Genetics, *18*(3), e1009987. https://doi.org/10.1371/journal.pgen.1009987
39. Kurmangaliyev, Y., Li, X. and Wang, J. (2023). Semi-supervised learning for autism omics. Genome Biology, 24(1), 1–12. https://doi.org/10.1186/s13059-023-02897-5
40. Zhou, J. and Troyanskaya, O.G. (2015). Predicting effects of noncoding variants with deep learning-based sequence model. Nature Methods, *12*(10), 931–934. https://doi.org/10.1038/nmeth.3547
41. Sanders, E., Gustafson, P. and Karim, M.E. (2021). Incorporating partial adherence into the principal stratification analysis framework. Statistics in Medicine, *40*(15), 3625–3644. https://doi.org/10.1002/sim.8986
42. Chen, T., Zhang, Y. and Wang, J. (2022). Variational autoencoders for latent factor extraction in gene expression studies. BMC Bioinformatics, *23*(1), 1–12. https://doi.org/10.1186/s12859-022-04620-5
43. Schmieder, R. and Edwards, R. (2011). Quality control and preprocessing of metagenomic datasets. Bioinformatics, *27*(6), 863–864. https://doi.org/10.1093/bioinformatics/btr026
44. Andrews, S. (2010). FastQC: a quality control tool for high throughput sequence data. Babraham Bioinformatics. https://www.bioinformatics.babraham.ac.uk/projects/fastqc/

12

Genetic and Biomarker Data Analysis and Diagnosis

Saranyadevi S[1*], Selva Kumar T[2] and Ram Kumar C[3]

1. Introduction

Precision medicine redefines healthcare by customizing prevention, diagnosis, and treatment based on each patient's biological, environmental, and lifestyle profile. Departing from uniform protocols, it leverages individual variability to enhance diagnostic accuracy, target therapies, and reduce risk. Key clinical gains are evident in pharmacogenomics, rare disease management, and precision oncology, where tailored interventions yield better outcomes and fewer adverse effects. Scaling this paradigm demands solutions for data privacy, cost-effectiveness, and integration of precision tools into everyday clinical workflows [1]. Biomarkers (BMs) are pivotal to precision medicine and drug development, clarifying mechanisms of action, signaling pharmacodynamic effects, identifying toxicities, and supporting early efficacy assessment. They facilitate patient stratification by pinpointing subgroups most likely to benefit from targeted therapies. Advances in genomics, proteomics, metabolomics, imaging, and digital analytics are broadening the BM landscape and enabling integrative approaches to address disease heterogeneity. Clinically, BMs guide diagnosis, prognosis, treatment selection, dosing, and ongoing safety monitoring. Typically endogenous molecules or physiological indicators, BMs reflect tissue stress or disease response and, when contextually interpreted, inform personalized care strategies [2]. Biomarkers (BMs) are used across the disease continuum—from pre-diagnostic screening and risk assessment to staging, treatment selection, monitoring, and recurrence surveillance. Prior to clinical adoption, their strengths and limitations must be critically assessed. Figure 1 outlines key benefits, drawbacks, and criteria for an "ideal" BM, including analytical validity, clinical validity, and utility [3]. Prioritizing robust BMs enhances diagnostic precision and therapeutic outcomes. Systematic evaluation of high-value BMs is essential for advancing personalized medicine, minimizing overtreatment and toxicity, and potentially lowering healthcare costs [4]. Clinical trials are vital for validating the clinical utility of biomarkers (BMs) in disease assessment, staging, and treatment selection. While some BMs reliably predict outcomes, slow or delayed endpoints (e.g., mortality, relapse) make surrogate markers appealing for earlier insights and streamlined studies. Deployment hinges on understanding

[1] Department of Biotechnology, Karpagam Academy of Higher Education, Coimbatore, India.
[2] Vel Tech Rangarajan Dr. Sagunthala R&D Institute of Science and Technology, Chennai, India.
[3] Sri Krishna College of Engineering and Technology, Coimbatore, India.
* Corresponding author: myselfsaranya33@gmail.com

DOI: 10.1201/9781003541318-17

each BM's sensitivity, specificity, precision, and predictive values within its intended context [5]. Joint NIH–FDA guidance outlines evidentiary standards and implementation strategies. This chapter reviews BM types, properties, and discovery workflows, emphasizing advances in diagnostic, prognostic, and therapeutic applications across diseases.

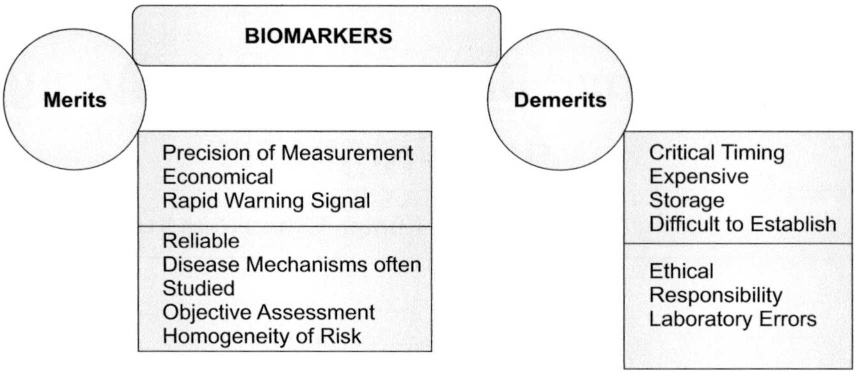

Fig. 1 Merits and Demerits of BMs.

Biomarker-guided approaches enable earlier disease detection, more precise classification, and personalized treatment planning. Integrated genomic and biomarker (BM) analyses—including germline and somatic testing—identify pathogenic variants and generate polygenic risk scores, supporting presymptomatic screening and prevention in oncology, cardiology, and rare genetic disorders. Quantitative BMs—molecular, imaging, or physiological—act as objective indicators of disease activity, aiding diagnosis, monitoring, and therapeutic prediction. These tools reduce trial-and-error prescribing, enhance diagnostic accuracy, and support evidence-based care, thereby advancing the goals of precision medicine. Over the past 50 years, the biomarker (BM) concept has matured with biomedical and clinical advances. A BM demonstrating strong, consistent correlation with disease status and capable of replacing a clinical endpoint may be classified as a surrogate marker [6]. Among various terms, "biomarker" has become standard in scientific and regulatory contexts. In 2000, the NIH Biomarkers Definitions Working Group defined a BM as an objectively measured indicator of normal biology, disease processes, or treatment response. The FDA similarly describes BMs as measurable signals applicable across the disease spectrum for discovery, development, monitoring, diagnosis, or prognosis [7]. As healthcare shifts toward preventive and personalized models, integrated genomic and BM analyses are becoming routine in clinical practice.

2. Fundamentals of Genetic Data

2.1 DNA, Genes, and Genomes

Cells are the basic structural and functional units of life, governed by DNA—a double-stranded polymer of four nucleotides (A, T, C, G) forming complementary base pairs (A–T, C–G). The human genome, housed in chromosomes, contains all genetic material; somatic cells are diploid, inheriting one chromosome set from each parent. Genes—specific DNA segments—encode proteins or functional RNAs via transcription and translation. Humans have an estimated 20,000–25,000 genes, though most genomic DNA is non-coding, playing key roles in gene regulation and chromosomal integrity. While all cells share the same genome, gene expression is context-specific, varying by cell type, developmental stage, and environmental cues, thereby shaping cellular identity and adaptive responses.

Types of Genetic Variations

Genetic variants—differences in DNA sequence between individuals—play key roles in health, disease susceptibility, and treatment response. Major types include:

(i) **Single Nucleotide Polymorphism** Single-nucleotide polymorphisms (SNPs)—the most common genetic variation—arise from a single base change (e.g., A to G) at a specific genomic site, influencing disease risk, drug response, and individual traits.
(ii) **Copy Number Variations (CNVs)** Copy number variations (CNVs) are changes in the number of copies of a gene or genomic region. Large-scale duplications or deletions can alter gene dosage and are linked to conditions such as cancer, schizophrenia, and autism.
(iii) **Mutations** Mutations are permanent alterations in DNA sequence, classified as chromosomal rearrangements, insertions, deletions, or point mutations. Depending on their type and location, they may cause cancer, genetic disorders, or other diseases, and can be either inherited or acquired.

Genomic Technologies

Microarray technology is a high-resolution molecular diagnostic tool capable of genus- and species-level identification of microbial, viral, fungal, and parasitic pathogens [8]. Platforms like GeneChip achieve DNA detection limits near ~10 femtograms, outperforming many current methods. Unlike single-target assays, microarrays enable simultaneous interrogation of hundreds to thousands of targets, supporting efficient diagnosis of polymicrobial infections and broad-spectrum differential testing. Microarrays are deployed in two main formats: spotted arrays, which use robotically printed pre-synthesised probes, and in situ–synthesised arrays, where probes are generated directly on the substrate. The typical workflow includes nucleic acid extraction, PCR amplification with pathogen-specific primers, label incorporation, and hybridization, followed by fluorescence-based quantification. Outputs are semi-quantitative, derived from direct fluorescence or enzymatic signal development [9].

Next-generation sequencing (NGS) has revolutionized rare disease diagnostics via exome sequencing (ES) and genome sequencing (GS). ES targets protein-coding regions, while GS encompasses both coding and non-coding DNA. Across undiagnosed cohorts, ES/GS yields molecular diagnoses in ~25–50% of cases [10–12]. With declining costs, GS is increasingly preferred for its enhanced detection of copy-number and non-coding variants, offering a 10–15% higher diagnostic yield than ES [10].

Clinicaluse of exome (ES) and genome sequencing (GS) spans commercial labs, academic "exome clinics," and routine genetics services, with cohorts ranging from dozens to hundreds of patients [11]. Large research consortia report strong diagnostic yields and evolving best-practice frameworks for rare disease. De novo variants contribute to ~two-thirds of causal findings, especially in severe neurodevelopmental disorders [12]. These advances have enabled precision diagnoses for individuals previously lacking molecular clarity, guiding surveillance, reproductive counseling, and personalized care.

3. BMs in Medical Diagnosis

Biomarkers (BMs)—objectively measured biological macromolecules or physiological traits—serve as indicators of normal or pathological processes. Their disease-specific identification and validation enable individualized disease management. Emerging BMs, driven by omics technologies, reflect a broader shift toward stratified patient assessment and targeted intervention [13]. Advances in biotechnology, informatics, and biocomputing continue to expand opportunities in precision and predictive medicine.

Biomarkers (BMs) are increasingly viewed as a solution to the drug development "pipeline problem," with novel BMs offering potential gains in efficiency and cost-effectiveness [14]. In 2004, only 8% of Phase 1 drugs reached the market—down from 14% previously. Studies suggest that modest improvements in decision-making (10%) and R&D timelines (by 3–4 years) could reduce costs by up to USD 100M per project. While future impact remains uncertain, BMs are now integrated into ~15% of development programs and routinely used in over half, underscoring their growing strategic importance.

3.1 Classification of BMs

Biomarkers (BMs) are classified based on their characteristics, clinical applications, and underlying genetic and molecular biology methodologies (Figure 2).

Genetic and molecular biology techniques

Biomarkers (BMs) are classified into three types based on genetic and molecular biology approaches: Type 0, 1, and 2. Type 0 BMs reflect disease natural history and correlate with clinical outcomes over time, suitable for phase 0 trials [15]. Type 1 BMs indicate drug activity, encompassing mechanisms, therapeutic effects, and toxicity. Type 2 BMs serve as surrogate markers, predicting treatment response and substituting for direct clinical outcome measures [16].

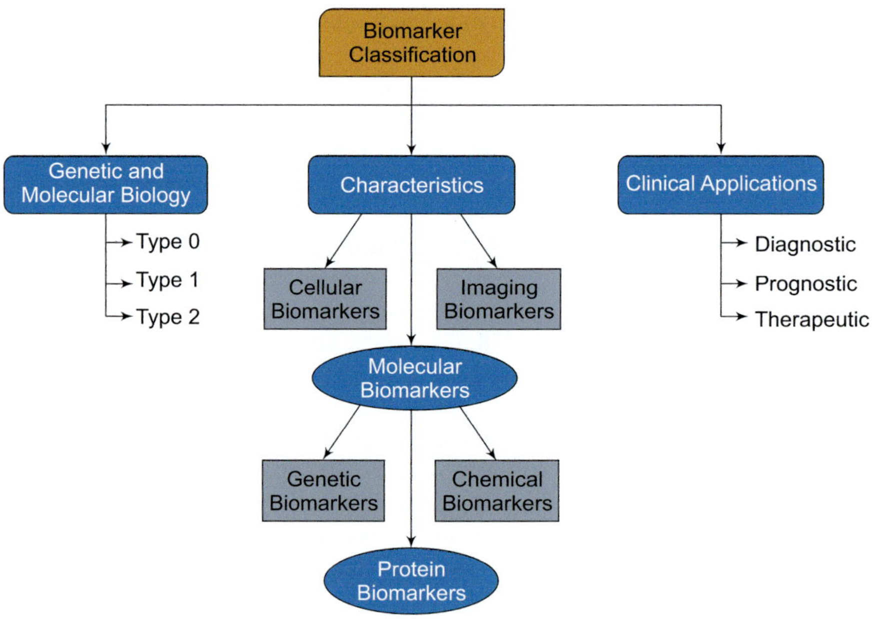

Fig. 2 Classification of various BMs.

Based on their characteristics, biomarkers (BMs) are broadly classified into three types: molecular, cellular, and imaging.

Molecular BMs

Molecular biomarkers, quantified via genomic and proteomic techniques, play a vital role in clinical trials, disease prevention, prediction, management, epidemiology, and diagnosis. Molecular biomarkers exhibit biophysical properties and can be assessed in specimens such as blood, plasma, cerebrospinal fluid, bronchoalveolar lavage fluid, and biopsies. They encompass diverse molecules—ranging from small peptides to large proteins, lipids, nucleic acids, and other compounds—and are classified into three subtypes:genes, proteins, and chemicals [17].

Cellular BMs

Cellular biomarkers are biological, quantifiable indicators assessed through medical and laboratory tests. Typically analyzed in soft tissues, body fluids, or blood, they aid in determining prognosis and treatment response. These biomarkers also enable cell isolation, sorting, quantification, and characterization based on morphological and physiological traits [18].

Imaging BMs

Imaging biomarkers (BMs), being accessible, cost-effective, and non-invasive, are widely used in clinical practice. They represent objectively measurable features from medical images that reflect physiological states, disease processes, or therapeutic responses. Imaging supports early detection and complements molecular data, with key modalities including PET, CT, and MRI [19]. PET measures radiotracer uptake (e.g., ^18F-FDG) as a proxy for tissue metabolism, allowing evaluation of cancer treatment response through changes in glucose utilization.

- CT uses ionising radiation to generate cross-sectional and three-dimensional reconstructions, supporting lesion detection, anatomical staging, and longitudinal localization of tumours.
- MRI provides high spatial resolution and excellent soft-tissue contrast without ionizing radiation. It captures physiological parameters—oxygenation (BOLD), diffusion (DWI/DTI), and perfusion (DCE)—and enables multi-contrast imaging in a single session. Several MRI-based biomarkers are validated or approaching validation for routine cancer assessment. Together, these modalities provide quantitative, reproducible biomarkers that support diagnosis, staging, treatment selection, and response monitoring across a wide range of diseases.

3.2 Types based on Clinical Applications

Biomarkers (BMs) are classified by clinical application into three main types: diagnostic, prognostic, and therapeutic, each corresponding to distinct phases of disease management.

Diagnostic Biomarkers (BMs)

Key molecular biomarkers (BMs) are routinely investigated to indicate specific pathophysiological states or diseases:

- Glutamate marker of altered intermediary metabolism associated with visceral obesity and metabolic dysregulation [20].
- Catestatin: Reflects the stress-response axis and has been linked to increased mortality risk among patients with cardiovascular disease.
- Cystatin-C surrogate of glomerular filtration rate, useful for early detection of renal dysfunction.
- Liver-type fatty acid–binding protein (L-FABP) diagnostic BM for renal tubular injury and for grading the severity of acute kidney injury.
- Cardiac troponin (cTn) gold-standard indicator of myocardial injury.
- Profiles of 3-hydroxy fatty acids used as lipid signatures to identify Planctomycetes.

- Glycans alterations in glycosylation patterns serve as cancer biomarkers across multiple tumour types.

Collectively, these biomarkers cover metabolic, cardiovascular, renal, infectious , and oncologic domains, enabling early diagnosis, risk assessment, and disease monitoring.

Prognostic BMs

Prognostic biomarkers (BMs) help predict disease trajectory by enabling risk screening, longitudinal tracking, and stratification based on dynamic changes in pathophysiological indicators. Key examples include: blood pressure and serum cholesterol for cardiovascular risk [21]; urinary N-acetyl-β-D-glucosaminidase (NAG) for renal injury and heart failure stress; D-serine for forecasting ketamine response in depression; and osteocalcin for assessing bone turnover and metastatic burden. Together, these BMs support earlier risk assessment, personalized treatment, and refined monitoring of disease progression.

Therapeutic BMs

Therapeutic biomarkers (BMs) play a critical role in guiding disease management and evaluating treatment response. Notable examples include exosomes and miRNAs, which support targeted therapies; malondialdehyde-modified LDL, a predictor of outcomes in peripheral artery disease post-endovascular therapy [22]; D-serine, validated for monitoring treatment efficacy in depression and schizophrenia; CA15-3, used to assess breast cancer therapy; and HbA1c, a standard marker for antidiabetic treatment effectiveness.

Pharmacodynamic BMs

Pharmacodynamic biomarkers (BMs) are measurable biological indicators used to evaluate drug effects, confirm target engagement, and assess biological response. They are vital in clinical trials and patient care for gauging efficacy, optimizing dosage, and monitoring treatment outcomes. Examples include shifts in protein levels, enzyme activity, receptor binding, or gene expression post-administration. These BMs also help validate drug mechanisms and detect early adverse effects [23], supporting real-time insights essential for precision medicine and individualized therapy.

Examples of Key BMs

Important BMs are essential for prognosis, diagnosis, and treatment selection. For example, BRCA1 and BRCA2 gene mutations guide preventive and therapeutic strategies due to their strong association with breast and ovarian cancers. HER2 overexpression in certain breast tumors enables targeted treatment with agents like trastuzumab. PSA remains the primary biomarker for prostate cancer screening and monitoring [24]. CRP, an inflammatory marker, rises in infections and chronic conditions, and is routinely used to track disease activity in disorders such as rheumatoid arthritis. These biomarkers, as molecular surrogates, enable precise assessment of pathogenesis, inform treatment decisions, and enhance clinical outcomes.

4. Data Acquisition and Preprocessing

Preprocessing and data collection are essential steps in genetic and biomarker research to ensure data quality, consistency, and biological validity for accurate analysis.

4.1 Sample Collection and Storage

Standardized biospecimen collection and biobanking—using aseptic protocols, barcoding, rapid stabilization, and ultra-low-temperature storage—form the critical foundation of biomarker workflows by preserving molecular integrity and ensuring reproducible downstream analyses.

DNA/RNA Extraction and Quality Control

Following nucleic acid isolation, omics-data preprocessing involves filtering low-abundance/noisy features, applying normalization methods (TPM, FPKM, quantile) to reduce technical variability, and conducting QC diagnostics (e.g., FastQC, PCA, clustering heat-maps) to identify outliers and batch effects—ensuring dataset integrity for downstream analysis [25].

Preprocessing of Omics Data

Pre-analytical preprocessing is essential for generating omics datasets—genomic, transcriptomic, proteomic, and metabolomic—that are clean, standardized, and suitable for biological interpretation. Raw data often contain noise, batch effects, and biases from sample prep or instrument variability. To correct these, normalization methods such as FPKM, TPM, and DESeq2's median-of-ratios are routinely applied, ensuring cross-sample comparability by adjusting for gene length and library size.

Noise-reduction filters eliminate low or inconsistent gene/protein signals, reducing computational load and boosting statistical power [26]. Decontamination steps remove residual artefacts, while QC diagnostics—PCA, box plots, MA plots, and clustering heat maps—detect outliers and batch effects. Tools like Array Quality Metrics and FastQC offer standardized QC outputs. Together, these steps ensure that downstream analyses (e.g., differential expression, biomarker discovery, pathway enrichment) reflect true biological variation, not technical noise [27].

5. Analytical Methods

A range of laboratory techniques is used to detect, quantify, and validate biomarkers in samples like blood, tissue, or urine—critical for disease diagnosis, treatment monitoring, and personalized therapy development.

5.1 Statistical Techniques (PCA, Clustering, Survival Analysis)

Following biomarker (BM) discovery—especially for diagnostic use—statistical evaluation is essential to validate clinical relevance [28]. Classical univariate tests (e.g., t-test, Wilcoxon-Mann-Whitney) assess independent variables across groups (e.g., control vs. pathological), but often lack interpretability, statistical power, and capacity to capture complex interactions [29]. Consequently, multivariate statistical analyses (MVAs), including supervised classification and unsupervised clustering, are preferred for identifying robust BM pools with higher sensitivity and specificity [30].

5.2 Machine Learning for BM Discovery

Li et al. [31] identified a five-variable logistic regression model (LR-5) as the most effective supervised classifier for predicting in-hospital COVID-19 mortality, achieving the highest AUC and yielding actionable forecasts. Concurrently, Abbasimehr et al. [32] found that a hybrid deep-learning ensemble (CNN, LSTM, GRU) minimized prediction error in time-series COVID-19 incidence, underscoring the utility of integrated architectures for real-time monitoring and policy guidance. Expanding on prior work, many studies have applied supervised learning to predict diagnosis and mortality using admission-time variables (e.g., age, haematology indices) for clinical triage. In our comparative analysis, LWL, K*, NB, and KNN achieved the highest accuracies and AUCs, affirming their effectiveness for early COVID-19 risk stratification [33].

Bioinformatics Pipelines for Genetic Analysis

Biomarker (BM) pipeline development typically involves four key stages, beginning with initial screening of a few samples, followed by large-scale clinical evaluation. A strong, evidence-based hypothesis is critical for integrating BM studies into oncology trials. Current BM research focuses on translational and personalized healthcare—leveraging intracellular signaling data to develop targeted therapies and enable precision dosing and treatment timing. The field increasingly emphasizes new technologies, diagnostics, and globalized research environments, with outsourcing to cost-effective regions like China, Russia, India, and Brazil [34]. Advances in NGS, mass spectrometry, and imaging genetics are reshaping BM discovery and its impact on disease understanding.

To illustrate key challenges, we reference the ICAN study on intracranial aneurysm (IA) pathophysiology, which aims to enhance understanding and prediction of IA development and rupture [35]. The study involves a biocollection from 3,000 individuals, integrating neuroimaging, genomic sequencing, and clinical data (e.g., lifestyle, family history). These multimodal datasets support predictive modeling of IA risk. However, execution and data sharing remain complex due to the need for specialized expertise and diverse analytical tools (Figure 3).

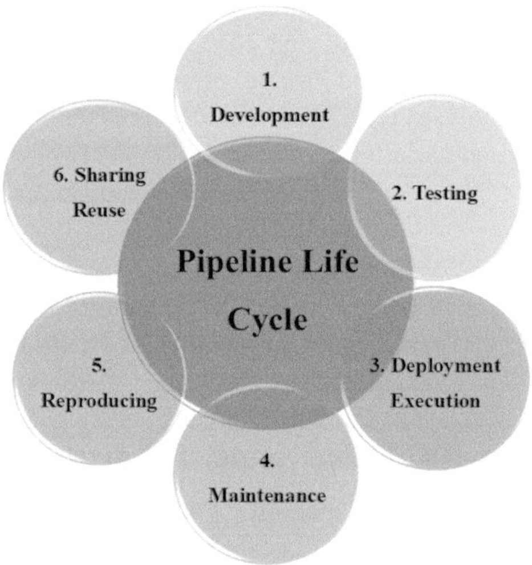

Fig. 3 Life cycle of a bioinformatics pipeline.

A key challenge in pipeline development is navigating multiple software environments and programming languages. In the ICAN project, tools like BWA, GATK, and Picard are used for sequencing analysis, while Python and R libraries within Jupyter Notebooks support statistical workflows [36]. Selecting appropriate tools is the initial hurdle, compounded by the complexity of integrating diverse platforms and languages.

Deployment

Most production pipelines require large-scale HPC infrastructure, as local servers typically lack the necessary data and computational resources [37]. Beyond coding, deployment demands operational expertise—tasks must be correctly ordered and submitted to cluster schedulers, with careful management of resource allocations and runtime constraints to ensure robust execution. Operational challenges on HPC clusters include:

- Task sequencing: Ensuring upstream jobs finish before dependent steps begin.
- Resource allocation: Selecting appropriate queues and requesting CPUs, memory, GPUs, and wall-time to optimize throughput and minimize delays.
- Node contention: Managing fluctuating cluster loads, preemption policies, and diverse node capabilities.
- Workload diversity: Matching I/O- or compute-bound tasks to scheduler policies.
- Failure management: Monitoring jobs, handling errors via retries or checkpoints, and collecting logs for diagnostics.

Specifying accurate submission commands and resource parameters for each pipeline step is labor-intensive and error-prone; misconfigurations can result in prolonged queue times or unexpected job failures [37].

Maintenance

Maintaining pipeline stability over time is critical, yet complex systems are prone to disruption due to evolving software, hardware, or datasets—such as tool updates or changes in reference genomes. Frequent pipeline updates are often necessary to ensure consistent performance.

Reproducing

Pipeline reproducibility depends on both temporal stability (maintenance) and spatial portability (deployment). Identical workflows may fail or produce inconsistent results across environments due to variations in schedulers, hardware, OS, libraries, or configurations—complicating maintenance and cross-site deployment [38].

Reuse

A non-reproducible analysis pipeline lacks reusability, as reproducibility underpins cumulative research. When reproducibly designed, pipelines can be shared, adapted, or modularly reused. Effective reuse hinges on three key factors: comprehensibility, accessible dissemination, and modular components.

Comprehensibility

Pipelines must be clearly documented and modular to ensure others can evaluate and reuse them effectively. This includes specifying scope, assumptions, I/O, parameters, and dependencies, while modular design exposes stepwise interfaces for flexible substitution or extension.

Accessible Dissemination via Registries

Pipelines should be hosted in registries that enable collaborative sharing, documentation, and maintenance [39]. To accommodate evolving workflows and coexisting variants, these registries must support versioning and provenance tracking (e.g., changelogs, history).

Reusable Components ("processors")

Beyond full pipelines, sharing individual modules significantly reduces development time. For safe reuse and easy discovery, modules should offer stable interfaces, detailed metadata and annotations, and include minimal examples and tests that illustrate expected behavior. Together, these practices enable transparent evaluation, reliable reproduction, and efficient reuse of computational pipelines across projects and organizations.

5.3 Tools and Software (GATK, Bioconductor, R/Biopython, etc.)

Genetic and biomarker (BM) data are processed using specialized tools tailored to distinct omics formats. The Genome Analysis Toolkit (GATK), developed by the Broad Institute, is widely used in NGS workflows for variant calling and data preparation. Bioconductor, built on R, offers extensive packages for differential expression, pathway analysis, and annotation, with R favored for its statistical and visualization capabilities. Biopython provides open-source utilities for biological tasks such as sequence parsing and database access [40]. Key tools also include IGV for interactive visualization, SAMtools and BCFtools for alignment and variant file handling, and workflow managers like Galaxy, Nextflow, and Snakemake for scalable, reproducible analysis. Collectively, these platforms enable efficient handling of large-scale biological data and drive progress in genomics, BM research, and personalized medicine.

6. Incorporation of Multi-Omics Data

Multi-omics integration —the joint analysis of genomics, epigenomics, transcriptomics, proteomics, and metabolomics—provides a systems-level view of biological processes and disease mechanisms. Each layer contributes distinct insights: genomics reveals DNA variation; epigenomics captures regulatory changes; transcriptomics tracks gene expression; proteomics maps protein function; and metabolomics reflects metabolic activity. Integrating these diverse datasets uncovers complex molecular interactions, enhances biomarker precision, and supports personalized medicine development [41]. Effective multi-omics integration depends on sophisticated bioinformatics pipelines, machine learning, and network-based methods that manage high dimensionality and platform heterogeneity. Tools like iCluster, MOFA, and mixOmics support dimensionality reduction, latent factor identification, and cross-omics correlation mapping. When rigorously applied, these approaches enhance disease subclassification, accelerate drug-target discovery, and elucidate molecular mechanisms—advancing both research precision and clinical decision-making [42].

6.1 Transcriptomics, Proteomics, and Metabolomics

Multi-omics data offer complementary insights into biological systems, but integrating them to uncover disease mechanisms is challenging—especially with limited labels. Modern machine and deep learning approaches rely on representation learning objectives to extract robust features from unlabeled data and enable accurate prediction and interpretation. To improve performance and transparency, pipelines increasingly pair model-agnostic attribution methods (e.g., DeepLIFT) with task-specific losses like Cox proportional hazards for survival analysis [43]. Contrastive learning, often enhanced by data augmentation and masking, is widely used to align modalities and capture non-linear relationships. While many models focus on high-dimensional discriminative features, they often overlook the structure of low-dimensional latent spaces critical for downstream tasks. Addressing this, [31]introduced Regularized and Hybrid Multi-view Coding (RHMC), which uses Wasserstein distance–based alignment to harmonize latent distributions and strengthen cross-omics integration. These strategies yield modality-aware embeddings that preserve both shared and unique biological signals.

A holistic understanding of complex disorders demands integrated analysis of multi-omics and clinical data. Such models clarify cellular and tissue functions, map biomolecular interactions, and enhance prognostic and predictive precision—supporting tailored prevention and treatment strategies [44]. By tracing genotype-to-phenotype transitions across omics layers, integrative modelling reconstructs biological flow while mitigating confounders and batch effects. Interpretability and data complexity remain key hurdles. Tools like GraphOmics facilitate cross-layer linkage and hypothesis generation via correlation-based methods. For longitudinal studies, hybrid multi-omics network frameworks highlight inter- and intra-layer mechanisms, supported by network-interpretation guidelines for time-resolved biological inference [45].

6.2 Network and Pathway Analysis

Network and pathway analysis enhances biomarker (BM) research by mapping BMs onto known biological systems and interaction networks, enabling systems-level interpretation of complex data. Rather than assessing BMs in isolation, this approach examines their roles within pathways (e.g., metabolic, signaling) and molecular networks (e.g., protein–protein interactions), revealing regulatory links and functional relevance in disease contexts. Tools like STRING, Cytoscape, KEGG, and Reactome support visualization and analysis. For instance, convergence of cancer-associated BMs on the PI3K/AKT pathway suggests a key role in tumor progression. Network analysis also identifies hub genes and potential therapeutic targets [46], facilitating hypothesis generation and functional BM prioritization.

Network BMs

Complex diseases seldom result from isolated molecular defects. While molecular biomarkers (BMs) are vital for diagnosis and prognosis, disease onset and progression typically involve coordinated disruptions across regulatory layers—chromatin structure, signaling pathways, RNA splicing, epigenetics, and proteostasis. These are governed by molecular interactions and assemblies, making single-analyte models inadequate. This systems view underpins systems biology, which examines all biological components and their interactions under defined conditions [47]. Many disorders are now seen as network diseases, arising from disrupted molecular networks rather than single-gene defects. Accordingly, biomarkers that reflect network topology, connectivity, and pathway membership offer deeper explanatory and predictive power than expression levels alone. Network biomarkers (network BMs) are coordinated molecular sets whose interactions reflect disease-specific dysregulation. Compared to single-molecule BMs, they offer greater stability, quantifiability, and cross-cohort robustness, promoting network-level discovery and validation [48]. This requires computational integration of diverse multi-omics data to infer molecular interactions and construct disease-relevant networks, enhancing both biological interpretability and linkage to prior knowledge. This approach is particularly valuable in rare diseases, where limited samples challenge traditional biomarker discovery. By using multi-omics data from individual patients, network biomarkers can be inferred per sample, preserving mechanistic insight despite cohort constraints. Overall, transitioning to network-informed biomarkers yields a more accurate reflection of disease biology and strengthens the basis for precision diagnostics and therapy.

Methods for network BMs

Network biomarkers (network BMs) clarify biological system function, support personalized therapy, predict disease outcomes, and identify drug targets. Omics-driven computational methods enable precise patient stratification and diagnosis. Unlike single-gene defects, complex disorders arise from disruptions across molecular networks involving chromatin structure, signaling, splicing, epigenetics, and proteostasis [49]. To capture these dynamics at the individual level, sample-specific network (SSN) modeling constructs patient-specific molecular networks relative to a reference cohort, revealing pathway-level perturbations [50]. Partial-correlation SSNs (P-SSNs) further refine these models by retaining only direct interactions, enhancing disease classification and single-cell clustering [51].

Integrative systems biology tackles the challenge of merging diverse omics platforms. Transcriptionally regulated flux balance analysis (TRFBA) links gene expression to metabolic flux states by integrating transcriptional control with metabolic models across perturbations [52]. Complementing this, the single-sample controller strategy (SCS) uses gene expression and mutation data within a network-controllability framework to identify patient-specific driver mutations, guiding targeted and personalized therapies [53]. Single-cell resolution. Despite progress, single-cell sequencing remains constrained by low coverage and high noise, limiting traditional analyses. The cell-specific network (CSN) framework addresses this by mapping gene–gene associations at single-cell resolution, enabling reconstruction of regulatory landscapes and inspiring novel network-based algorithms [54–56]. These advances support network-aware biomarker strategies that integrate multi-omics data with rigorous network inference, yielding more stable, interpretable, and clinically actionable disease characterizations than expression-based markers alone.

Table 1 Overview for network BMs study.

Technique	*Description (concise)*	*Primary uses*	*Ref.*
PPI	Computes edge-level biomarkers by overlaying differentially expressed genes on protein–protein interaction networks.	Patient classification; integration of PPI context into biomarker panels.	[57]
EdgeBM	Builds an individual-specific network from a single-sample expression profile and derives edge- and node-level markers.	Phenotype diagnosis at the individual level.	[49]
SSN	Constructs sample-specific networks from single-sample molecular expression data.	Systems-level elucidation of mechanisms in complex disorders for each patient.	[50]
P-SSN	Forms a partial-correlation SSN that retains direct interactions and removes indirect ones.	Prediction of driver mutations from single-sample data; subtyping complex diseases; single-cell clustering.	[51]
TRFBA	Integrates transcriptional regulatory constraints with flux balance metabolic models using expression data across perturbations.	Joint transcriptome–metabolome integration; improved quantitative growth-rate estimation.	[52]
SCS	Single-sample controller strategy applying network controllability to mutation and expression data to infer control points.	Prediction of personalised driver-mutation spectra for targeted therapy.	[53]
CSN	Builds a cell-specific network for each cell from scRNA-seq data.	Network-level clustering and pseudotrajectory inference; identification of important non-DE genes.	[54]
c-CSN	Conditional CSN that removes indirect associations to quantify direct gene–gene links.	Inferring differentiation trajectories by evaluating cell-specific regulatory effectiveness.	[55]
NBSBM	Network-based sparse Bayesian machine learning framework.	Prediction of drug sensitivity; elucidation of mechanisms of action.	[56]

Acronyms: PPI, protein–protein interaction; SSN, sample-specific network; P-SSN, partial-correlation SSN; TRFBA, transcriptionally regulated flux balance analysis; SCS, single-sample controller strategy; CSN, cell-specific network; c-CSN, conditional CSN; scRNA-seq, single-cell RNA sequencing; DE, differentially expressed.

6.3 Systems Biology Approaches

The cell-specific network (CSN) framework has been refined by conditional CSN (c-CSN), which accounts for shared regulators to reduce spurious links and recover direct gene–gene interactions with higher accuracy [58]. In drug development, the network-based sparse Bayesian machine (NBSBM) identifies drug sensitivity and mechanisms by extracting key subnetworks from broader interaction graphs [59]. These models represent biological systems as graphs, where nodes may denote genes, metabolites, drugs, or diseases, and links capture physical interactions, predicted bindings, or phenotypic associations [60]. Node attributes can derive from top-down knowledge (e.g., gene–disease links, pathway membership) or bottom-up data (e.g., transcript, protein, metabolite levels; mutations; phenotypes) [60]. Molecular networks serve as scaffolds to integrate these heterogeneous layers, enabling multi-scale inference and connecting discovery assays with prior knowledge. Once networked, graph-theoretic and systems tools reveal system-level properties like community structure, centrality, and controllability. For example, integrating high-throughput data with canonical pathways and PPI maps in traumatic brain injury (TBI) reveals disease-relevant modules overlooked by expression analysis alone [61], highlighting the power of network-based modeling.

7. Clinical Applications

7.1 Cancer

Cancer biomarker (BM) discovery has advanced markedly through systematic analysis of proteins, hormones, and enzymes in patient tissues and fluids, primarily via immunological methods like radioimmunoassay. The rapid expansion of biological sciences has driven technological progress, notably in mass spectrometry and the development of protein and DNA arrays—tools now integral to BM classification and discovery timelines [62]. Genome sequencing has significantly advanced the identification of oncogenes and tumor-suppressor genes, facilitating the discovery of cancer biomarkers (BMs) now widely used in screening, diagnosis, and prognosis [63]. Early BM research, rooted in empirical observations, evolved alongside modern testing methods. The shift from serial to parallel assays enables simultaneous detection of multiple markers, revealing complex disease patterns. Preclinical BM screening via mass spectrometry or gene-expression profiling may yield false positives due to marker expression in non-tumor tissues, potentially leading to diagnostic errors and inappropriate treatments [64, 65]. Low specificity of cancer biomarkers (BMs) poses health risks and undermines treatment cost-effectiveness, potentially delaying detection and impacting survival outcomes [66]. These concerns make healthcare systems cautious about adopting BMs for routine screening. Nonetheless, they underscore the urgency of developing robust BMs. Despite limitations—such as reduced prognostic specificity compared to multi-marker approaches—single-marker assays remain valuable due to their simplicity, affordability, and proven utility, especially in resource-limited or targeted diagnostic contexts (Figure 4).

7.2 Genetic Diagnosis of Rare Diseases

Cellular pathophysiology in rare diseases can be characterized using molecular biomarkers (BMs) across DNA variants, RNAs, proteins, and metabolites, which evolve with disease progression [67].

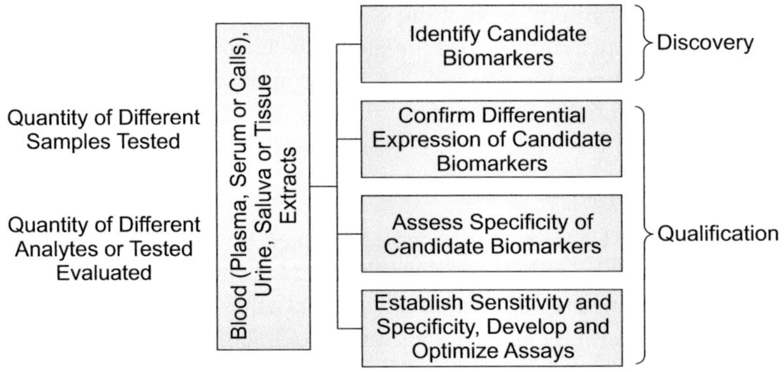

Fig. 4 Framework for the development of BMs.

Genomics remains the most developed layer, focusing on genetic variation and sequence analysis. For instance, [68] showed that the lipid BM lyso-Gb3 correlates with pathogenic agalA mutations in Fabry disease (FD) and highlighted the importance of early genetic testing in Peutz–Jeghers syndrome (PJS).

Transcriptomics involves system-level RNA analysis, with qualitative methods detecting transcript presence, splicing, and editing, and quantitative approaches measuring expression levels. Beyond mRNA, sequencing now profiles non-coding RNAs—miRNAs, lncRNAs, and circRNAs—that influence rare disease pathogenesis [69]. [70,71] integrated RNA-seq (n=20) and RT-qPCR (n=44) to identify four lncRNAs that reliably stratified multiple sclerosis severity. Metabolomic—qualitative and quantitative profiling of small-molecule metabolites in cells, tissues, or biofluids—offers a dynamic snapshot of biochemical and pathological states. Its applicability to accessible fluids enables non-invasive diagnosis and grading, as demonstrated in biomarker discovery for Gaucher disease (GD) [72]. Proteomics profiles large-scale protein features, quantifying abundance and mapping interactions to reveal dysregulated pathways, thereby aiding early biomarker discovery, therapeutic targeting, and mechanistic insight into disease [73]. Together, omics approaches provide complementary biomarkers that enhance diagnosis, stratify patients, and guide mechanism-based treatment in rare disorders.

8. Challenges and Limitations

Biomarker performance and clinical utility are limited by biological variability and technical artefacts. Factors such as age, sex, genetics, lifestyle, and comorbidities hinder universal reference intervals, complicating threshold setting and risk stratification. Pre-analytical inconsistencies in sample handling affect stability, while many markers lack optimal sensitivity or specificity, reducing diagnostic accuracy. Limited validation in diverse cohorts restricts clinical generalisability. Technological constraints—low assay sensitivity, high costs, and limited access—further impede adoption. Multi-omics integration requires advanced bioinformatics and expertise, and ethical-regulatory hurdles (e.g., consent, privacy, approvals) delay translation. Addressing these challenges is vital for advancing precision diagnostics and personalised care.

9. Future Prospects

9.1 Artificial Intelligence in Genetic Diagnostics

Artificial intelligence (AI) holds transformative promise for genetic diagnostics and biomarker (BM) research in precision medicine . As multi-omics datasets grow, AI will increasingly automate data interpretation, accelerate BM discovery, and enhance diagnostic accuracy. Evolving from pattern recognition to predictive systems, AI models integrating genomic, proteomic, and clinical data may forecast disease onset, progression, and treatment response. Transparent, explainable algorithms will foster clinical trust, while real-time AI platforms could enable rapid, point-of-care testing—especially in oncology, rare diseases, and infections. Cloud computing and EHR integration will support scalable, personalized diagnostics across care settings. Realizing this potential requires addressing challenges in validation, ethics, data harmonization, and regulation through interdisciplinary collaboration.

9.2 Point-of-Care Testing

Point-of-care testing (POCT) is poised to revolutionize biomarker diagnostics and real-time monitoring by enhancing healthcare accessibility, speed, and personalization. Advances in biosensors, microfluidics, wearables, and lab-on-a-chip technologies enable rapid, on-site detection of disease-specific biomarkers from minimal samples. Emerging POCT devices promise affordable, compact, multiplexed analysis for continuous health tracking and early disease detection. Integrated with smartphones and wireless tech, POCT supports remote care and telemedicine, especially in underserved regions. Real-time feedback aids chronic disease management, while AI and cloud-based platforms enable predictive, personalized decision-making at home or bedside. Despite challenges in regulation, data privacy, and validation, POCT is set to transform diagnostics into a more proactive and patient-centered model.

10. Conclusion

Integrative analysis of genomic and biomarker data is central to precision medicine, offering insights into disease mechanisms, enabling early detection, and guiding personalized treatment. By linking detailed genomic profiles with quantitative biomarker signatures, clinicians can improve risk prediction, diagnostic precision, and therapeutic targeting. Advances in sequencing, bioinformatics, and AI now support efficient interpretation of complex datasets. Despite challenges like data heterogeneity and validation needs, ongoing innovation is enhancing reliability and accessibility. This convergence is set to make healthcare increasingly personalized, predictive, and preventive.

References

1. Johnson, K.B., Wei, W.Q., Weeraratne, D., Frisse, M.E., Misulis, K. et al. Precision medicine, AI, and the future of personalized health care. *Clinical and translational science*. 2021 Jan;14(1):86–93.
2. De Gramont, A., Watson, S., Ellis, L.M., Rodón, J., Tabernero, J. et al. Pragmatic issues in BM evaluation for targeted therapies in cancer. *Nature reviews Clinical oncology*. 2015 Apr;12(4):197–212.
3. Mayeux, R. BMs: potential uses and limitations. *NeuroRx*. 2004 Apr;1:182–188.
4. Wan-Ibrahim, W.I., Singh, V.A., Hashim, O.H., Abdul-Rahman, P.S. BMs for bone tumors: discovery from genomics and proteomics studies and their challenges. *Molecular Medicine*. 2015 Jan;21:861–872.
5. Mert, D.G., Terzi, H. Mean platelet volume in bipolar disorder: the search for an ideal BM. *Neuropsychiatric Disease and Treatment*. 2016 Aug 16:2057–2062.
6. García-Gutiérrez, M.S., Navarrete, F., Sala, F., Gasparyan, A., Austrich-Olivares, A. et al. BMs in psychiatry: concept, definition, types and relevance to the clinical reality. *Frontiers in psychiatry*. 2020 May 15;11:432.
7. MacNamara, J., Eapen, D.J., Quyyumi, A., Sperling, L. Novel BMs for cardiovascular risk assessment: current status and future directions. *Future cardiology*. 2015 Sep 1;11(5):597–613.
8. Asmare, Z., Erkihun, M. Recent application of dna microarray techniques to diagnose infectious disease. *Pathology and Laboratory Medicine International*. 2023 Dec 31:77–82.
9. Huyghe, A., Francois, P., Schrenzel, J. Characterization of microbial pathogens by DNA microarrays. *Infection, Genetics and Evolution*. 2009 Sep 1;9(5):987–995.

10. Sullivan, J.A., Schoch, K., Spillmann, R.C., Shashi, V. Exome/genome sequencing in undiagnosed syndromes. *Annual review of medicine*. 2023 Jan 27;74(1):489–502.
11. Baldridge, D., Heeley, J., Vineyard, M., Manwaring, L., Toler, T.L. et al. The Exome Clinic and the role of medical genetics expertise in the interpretation of exome sequencing results. *Genetics in Medicine*. 2017 Sep;19(9):1040–1048.
12. Liu, P., Meng, L., Normand, E.A., Xia, F., Song, X. et al. Reanalysis of clinical exome sequencing data. *New England Journal of Medicine*. 2019 Jun 20;380(25):2478–2480.
13. BMs Definitions Working Group, Atkinson Jr AJ, Colburn WA, DeGruttola VG, DeMets DL et al. BMs and surrogate endpoints: preferred definitions and conceptual framework. *Clinical pharmacology & therapeutics*. 2001 Mar;69(3):89–95.
14. Doroszkiewicz, J., Groblewska, M., Mroczko, B. Molecular BMs and their implications for the early diagnosis of selected neurodegenerative diseases. *International Journal of Molecular Sciences*. 2022 Apr 21;23(9):4610.
15. Sharma, V., Ricketts, H.C., Steffensen, F., Goodfellow, A., Cowan, D.C. et al. Obesity affects type 2 BM levels in asthma. *Journal of asthma*. 2023 Feb 1;60(2):385–392.
16. Pospelova, M., Krasnikova, V., Fionik, O., Alekseeva, T., Samochernykh, K. et al. Potential molecular BMs of central nervous system damage in breast cancer survivors. *Journal of Clinical Medicine*. 2022 Feb 24;11(5):1215.
17. Lukas, A., Heinzel, A., Mayer, B. BMs for capturing disease pathology as molecular process hyperstructure. *bioRxiv*. 2019 Mar 11:573402.
18. Eggener, S.E., Rumble, R.B., Armstrong, A.J., Morgan, T.M., Crispino, T. et al. Molecular BMs in localized prostate cancer: ASCO guideline. *Journal of Clinical Oncology*. 2020 May 1;38(13):1474–1494.
19. Wishart, D.S., Bartok, B., Oler, E., Liang, K.Y., Budinski, Z. et al. MarkerDB: an online database of molecular BMs. Nucleic acids research. 2021 Jan 8;49(D1):D1259–1267.
20. Aizpurua-Olaizola, O., Toraño, J.S., Falcon-Perez, J.M., Williams, C., Reichardt, N. et al. Mass spectrometry for glycan BM discovery. *TrAC Trends in Analytical Chemistry*. 2018 Mar 1;100:7–14.
21. Nadkarni, G.N., Chauhan, K., Rao, V., Ix J.H., Shlipak, M.G. et al. Effect of intensive blood pressure lowering on kidney tubule injury: findings from the ACCORD trial study participants. *American Journal of Kidney Diseases*. 2019 Jan 1;73(1):31–38.
22. Jungbauer, C.G., Birner, C., Jung, B., Buchner, S., Lubnow, M. et al. Kidney injury molecule-1 and N-acetyl-ß-d-glucosaminidase in chronic heart failure: possible BMs of cardiorenal syndrome. *European journal of heart failure*. 2011 Oct;13(10):1104–1110.
23. Califf, R.M. BM definitions and their applications. *Experimental biology and medicine*. 2018 Feb;243(3):213–221.
24. Petrucelli, N., Daly, M.B., Pal, T. BRCA1-and BRCA2-associated hereditary breast and ovarian cancer.
25. Marku, M., Pancaldi, V. From time-series transcriptomics to gene regulatory networks: A review on inference methods. *PLoS computational biology*. 2023 Aug 10;19(8):e1011254.
26. Guo, S., Zhou, S., Wang, G., Wang, F. SCPline: An interactive framework for the single-cell proteomics data preprocessing. *Briefings in Bioinformatics*. 2025 May;26(3):bbaf256.
27. Jiang, Y., Rex, D.A., Schuster, D., Neely, B.A., Rosano, G.L. et al. Comprehensive overview of bottom-up proteomics using mass spectrometry. *ACS Measurement Science Au*. 2024 Jun 4;4(4):338–417.
28. Ou, F.S., Michiels, S., Shyr, Y., Adjei, A.A., Oberg, A.L. et al. BM discovery and validation: statistical considerations. *Journal of Thoracic Oncology*. 2021 Apr 1;16(4):537–545.
29. Robotti, E., Manfredi, M., Marengo, E. BMs discovery through multivariate statistical methods: a review of recently developed methods and applications in proteomics. *J Proteomics Bioinform*. 2014;3(003).
30. Zaharieva, M., Breiteneder, C., Hudec, M. Unsupervised group feature selection for media classification. *International Journal of Multimedia Information Retrieval*. 2017 Sep;6:233–249.
31. Li, S., Lin, Y., Zhu, T., Fan, M., Xu, S. et al. Development and external evaluation of predictions models for mortality of COVID-19 patients using machine learning method. Neural Computing and Applications. 2023 Jun; *35*(18): 13037–13046.
32. Abbasimehr, H., Paki, R., Bahrini, A. A novel approach based on combining DL models with statistical methods for COVID-19 time series forecasting. *Neural Computing and Applications*. 2022 Feb;34(4):3135–3149.
33. Huyut, M.T. Automatic detection of severely and mildly infected COVID-19 patients with supervised ML models. Irbm. 2023 Feb 1;44(1):100725.
34. Hu, C., Dignam, J.J. BM-driven oncology clinical trials: key design elements, types, features, and practical considerations. *JCO Precision Oncology*. 2019 Oct;1:1–2.
35. Prins, B.P., Leitsalu, L., Pärna, K., Fischer, K., Metspalu, A. et al. Advances in genomic discovery and implications for personalized prevention and medicine: Estonia as example. *Journal of personalized medicine*. 2021 Apr 29;11(5):358.

36. Frésard, L., Smail, C., Ferraro, N.M., Teran, N.A., Li, X. et al. Identification of rare-disease genes using blood transcriptome sequencing and large control cohorts. *Nature medicine*. 2019 Jun;25(6):911–919.
37. Dini, P., Diana, L., Elhanashi, A., Saponara, S. Overview of AI-models and tools in embedded IIoT applications. *Electronics*. 2024 Jun 13;13(12):2322.
38. Steidl, M., Felderer, M., Ramler, R.. The pipeline for the continuous development of artificial intelligence models—Current state of research and practice. *Journal of Systems and Software*. 2023 May 1;199:111615.
39. Cătană, A., Pătrăşcanu, A.A., Martin, D.L., Militaru, M.S., Iordănescu, I.I. et al. The Impact of Genetic Variations on Radiotherapy Toxicity in Breast Cancer Patients: A Meta-Analysis of Acute and Late Skin Adverse Effects. *Cancers*. 2025 Jun 4;17(11):1880.
40. Clark, A.J., Lillard, Jr J.W. A comprehensive review of bioinformatics tools for genomic BM discovery driving precision oncology. *Genes*. 2024 Aug 6;15(8):1036.
41. Chen, C., Wang, J., Pan, D., Wang, X., Xu, Y. et al. Applications of multi-omics analysis in human diseases. MedComm. 2023 Aug;4(4):e315.
42. Cai, Z., Poulos, R.C., Liu, J. and Zhong, Q. Machine learning for multi-omics data integration in cancer. *iScience*. 2022 Feb 18;25(2).
43. Sit, M., Demiray, B.Z., Xiang, Z., Ewing, G.J., Sermet, Y. et al. A comprehensive review of DL applications in hydrology and water resources. *Water Science and Technology*. 2020 Dec 15;82(12):2635–2670.
44. Du, P., Fan, R., Zhang, N., Wu, C., Zhang, Y. et al. Advances in integrated multi-omics analysis for drug-target identification. *Biomolecules*. 2024 Jun 14;14(6):692.
45. Picard, M., Scott-Boyer, M.P., Bodein, A., Périn, O., Droit, A. et al. Integration strategies of multi-omics data for ML analysis. *Computational and Structural Biotechnology Journal*. 2021 Jan 1;19:3735–3746.
46. Wicik, Z., Nowak, A., Jarosz-Popek, J., Wolska, M., Eyileten, C. et al. Characterization of the SGLT2 interaction network and its regulation by SGLT2 inhibitors: a bioinformatic analysis. *Frontiers in pharmacology*. 2022 Aug 15;13:901340.
47. Sarhadi, V.K., Armengol, G. Molecular BMs in cancer. *Biomolecules*. 2022 Jul 23;12(8):1021.
48. Zong, Y., Li, H., Liao, P., Chen, L., Pan, Y. et al. Mitochondrial dysfunction: mechanisms and advances in therapy. *Signal transduction and targeted therapy*. 2024 May 15;9(1):124.
49. Zhang, W., Zeng, T., Liu, X., Chen, L. Diagnosing phenotypes of single-sample individuals by edge BMs. *Journal of molecular cell biology*. 2015 Jun 1;7(3):231–241.
50. Liu, X., Wang, Y., Ji, H., Aihara, K., Chen, L. et al. Personalized characterization of diseases using sample-specific networks. *Nucleic acids research*. 2016 Dec 15; 44(22):e164.
51. Huang, Y., Chang, X., Zhang, Y., Chen, L., Liu, X. et al. Disease characterization using a partial correlation-based sample-specific network. *Briefings in bioinformatics*. 2021 May;22(3):bbaa062.
52. Motamedian, E., Mohammadi, M., Shojaosadati, S.A., Heydari, M. TRFBA: an algorithm to integrate genome-scale metabolic and transcriptional regulatory networks with incorporation of expression data. *Bioinformatics*. 2017 Apr 1;33(7):1057–63.
53. Guo, W.F., Zhang, S.W., Liu, L.L., Liu, F., Shi, Q.Q. et al. Discovering personalized driver mutation profiles of single samples in cancer by network control strategy. Bioinformatics. 2018 Jun 1;34(11):1893–1903.
54. Dai, H., Li, L., Zeng, T., Chen, L. Cell-specific network constructed by single-cell RNA sequencing data. *Nucleic acids research*. 2019 Jun 20;47(11):e62.
55. Li, L., Dai, H., Fang, Z., Chen, L. c-CSN: single-cell RNA sequencing data analysis by conditional cell-specific network. *Genomics, Proteomics & Bioinformatics*. 2021 Apr;19(2):319–329.
56. Liu, Q., Muglia, L.J., Huang, L.F. Network as a BM: A novel network-based sparse bayesian machine for pathway-driven drug response prediction. *Genes*. 2019 Aug 9;10(8):602.
57. Zheng, M.J., Li, X., Hu, Y.X., Dong, H., Gou, R. et al. Identification of molecular marker associated with ovarian cancer prognosis using bioinformatics analysis and experiments. *Journal of cellular physiology*. 2019 Jul;234(7):11023–11036.
58. Ideker, T., Galitski, T., Hood, L. A new approach to decoding life: systems biology. *Annual review of genomics and human genetics*. 2001 Sep;2(1):343–372.
59. Kell, D.B., Oliver, S.G. Here is the evidence, now what is the hypothesis? The complementary roles of inductive and hypothesis-driven science in the post-genomic era. *Bioessays*. 2004 Jan;26(1):99–105.
60. Papin, J.A., Price, N.D., Wiback, S.J., Fell, D.A., Palsson, B.O. et al. Metabolic pathways in the post-genome era. *Trends in biochemical sciences*. 2003 May 1;28(5):250–258.
61. Barabasi, A.L., Oltvai, Z.N.. Network biology: understanding the cell's functional organization. *Nature reviews genetics*. 2004 Feb 1;5(2):101–113.

62. Das, S., Dey, M.K., Devireddy, R., Gartia, M.R.. BMs in cancer detection, diagnosis, and prognosis. *Sensors*. 2023 Dec 20;24(1):37.
63. Ni, M., Liu, X., Wu, J., Zhang, D., Tian, J. et al. Identification of candidate BMs correlated with the pathogenesis and prognosis of non-small cell lung cancer via integrated bioinformatics analysis. *Frontiers in genetics*. 2018 Oct 12;9:469.
64. Das, S., Dey, M.K., Devireddy, R., Gartia, M.R. BMs in cancer detection, diagnosis, and prognosis. *Sensors*. 2023 Dec 20;24(1):37.
65. Zhou, Y., Tao, L., Qiu, J., Xu, J., Yang, X. et al., Tumor BMs for diagnosis, prognosis and targeted therapy. *Signal transduction and targeted therapy*. 2024 May 20;9(1):132.
66. Newman-Toker, D.E., Peterson, S.M., Badihian, S., Hassoon, A., Nassery, N. et al. Diagnostic errors in the emergency department: a systematic review.
67. Niemann, M., Rolfs, A., Störk, S., Bijnens, B., Breunig, F. et al. Gene mutations versus clinically relevant phenotypes: lyso-Gb3 defines Fabry disease. *Circulation: Cardiovascular Genetics*. 2014 Feb;7(1):8–16.
68. Cerasuolo, A., Cammarota, F., Duraturo, F., Staiano, A., Martinelli, M. et al. Implications of splicing alterations in the onset and phenotypic variability of a family with subclinical manifestation of Peutz–Jeghers syndrome: bioinformatic and molecular evidence. *International Journal of Molecular Sciences*. 2020 Nov 2;21(21):8201.
69. Hasin, Y., Seldin, M., Lusis, A. Multi-omics approaches to disease. *Genome biology*. 2017 Dec;18:1–5.
70. Gupta, M., Martens, K., Metz, L.M., de Koning, A.J., Pfeffer, G. et al. Long noncoding RNAs associated with phenotypic severity in multiple sclerosis. *Multiple Sclerosis and Related Disorders*. 2019 Nov 1;36:101407.
71. Torroglosa, A., Villalba-Benito, L., Fernández, R.M., Luzón-Toro, B., Moya-Jiménez, M.J. et al. Identification of new potential LncRNA BMs in Hirschsprung disease. *International Journal of Molecular Sciences*. 2020 Aug 2;21(15):5534.
72. Menkovic, I., Boutin, M., Alayoubi, A., Mercier, F.E., Rivard, G.É. et al. Identification of a reliable BM profile for the diagnosis of Gaucher disease type 1 patients using a mass spectrometry-based metabolomic approach. *International Journal of Molecular Sciences*. 2020 Oct 23;21(21):7869.
73. Hollander, Z., Dai, D.L., Putko, B.N., Yogasundaram, H., Wilson-McManus, J.E. et al. Gender-specific plasma proteomic BMs in patients with Anderson–Fabry disease. *European journal of heart failure*. 2015 Mar;17(3):291–300.

13

Single-Nucleus RNA Sequencing Data for Cell-Type-Specific Gene Prioritization and Predictive Modeling of Autism Spectrum Disorder

Padmapriya S[1*], Jayanthi Sree S[1], Iswarya N[1], Vijayalakshmi B[2] and Ramkumar C[2]

1. Introduction

Autism spectrum disorder (ASD) encompasses complex neurodevelopmental conditions marked by repetitive behaviors, impaired social interaction, and communication challenges. Its highly heterogeneous genetic and molecular basis has been explored through techniques like whole exome sequencing, GWAS, and CNV analysis, revealing numerous candidate genes. Yet, clinical translation remains limited due to the complexity and variability of these findings. Machine learning has emerged as a powerful approach for diagnosing ASD and identifying novel genes by analyzing complex biological data like transcriptomes. However, bulk RNA-seq and blood-based studies fall short in capturing cell-type-specific changes due to the brain's inherent heterogeneity.

Single-nucleus RNA sequencing (snRNA-seq) enables high-resolution analysis of gene expression in specific brain cell types affected by ASD. While recent studies have used snRNA-seq to identify dysregulated genes, a comprehensive machine learning approach to rank ASD-associated genes and build predictive models across diverse cell types has been lacking. This study leverages snRNA-seq data from ASD and control brains to identify cell-type-specific DE genes and develop predictive models via stochastic gradient boosting. The approach aims to elucidate ASD-related cellular heterogeneity, prioritize potentially pathogenic genes, and propose novel biomarkers for early diagnosis and intervention.

2. Review

Autism spectrum disorder (ASD) is marked by significant genetic and phenotypic heterogeneity, manifesting as restricted behaviors and social-communication deficits. Gene discovery efforts using whole exome sequencing, CNV analysis, and GWAS have yielded numerous candidate genes, but these approaches are costly, time-intensive, and often difficult to validate.

[1] Assistant Professor, PSG Institute of Technology and Applied Research, Coimbatore, India.
[2] Sri Krishna College of Engineering and Technology, Coimbatore, India.
* Corresponding author: drpadmapriyas0209@gmail.com

DOI: 10.1201/9781003541318-18

Machine learning has been applied to ASD research for diagnostic modeling, genetic exploration, and therapeutic development [1–5]. Notable examples include models based on gene sets with altered dispersion in bulk RNA-seq brain data [3], and DE genes from blood-based microarray analyses [4]. Such approaches enable reliable gene prioritization, facilitating biomarker discovery and advancing experimental research. Bulk transcriptomic studies of autistic brains have identified dysregulated pathways in ASD [4, 6, 7], but the brain's cellular diversity means distinct cell types may harbor unique gene dysfunctions and causal variants. Cell-type-specific ASD genes remain largely uncharacterized. The recent release of single-nucleus RNA-seq data [8] enables exploration of ASD's molecular pathology at cellular resolution. From a machine learning perspective, constructing cell-type-specific classification models can help rank ASD-associated genes by cell type, revealing gene-level variation across brain cell populations.

3. Methods

3.1 RNA-seq Data from a Single Nucleus in ASD

We analyzed single-nucleus RNA-sequencing (snRNA-seq) data from post-mortem human brains available at autism.cells.ucsc.edu [8]. The dataset includes 104,559 nuclei from the anterior cingulate and prefrontal cortex of 31 donors (16 neurotypical controls, 15 individuals with ASD). Raw UMI count matrices were processed using scran [9] for library-size normalization and quality control, excluding nuclei annotated as cycling (i.e., linked to specific cell-cycle phases). To reduce non-biological variability, we applied *ComBat* to adjust for technical and biological covariates including age, sex, postmortem interval (PMI), RNA integrity number (RIN), and sequencing batch. For feature selection, *scran* identified 12,036 highly variable genes (HVGs), which were used for downstream expression analyses.

3.2 Identifying Cell-Type-Specific Differentially Expressed Genes

Differentially expressed (DE) genes associated with ASD were identified in a cell-type-specific manner using three complementary methods: edgeR [10], BASiCS [11], and DEsingle [12]. edgeR applied generalized linear models incorporating region, sex, and age, with DE genes defined by likelihood ratio tests and an FDR-adjusted $P < 0.1$. The union of DE genes from all methods was used to construct predictive models. DEsingle identifies three categories of differentially expressed (DE) genes: DEg (general), reflecting differences in both expression abundance and dropout rates; DEs (status), based solely on dropout rate differences; and DEa (abundance), based on expression level differences independent of dropout rates. Genes with FDR < 0.1 were considered DE. BASiCS detects group-level differences in both mean expression and variability. To identify key genes, we applied the BASiCS_MCMC function (WithSpikes = FALSE, Regression = TRUE) followed by BASiCS_TestDE. Genes showing significant differences in mean and dispersion between ASD and controls were selected based on EFDR_M < 0.10 and EFDR_D < 0.10.

3.3 The Stochastic Gradient Boosting Algorithm

Gradient boosting builds additive predictive models using an ensemble of weak learners, typically decision trees, fitted iteratively to pseudo-residuals—gradients of the loss function with respect to current model predictions [13]. Stochastic gradient boosting introduces randomization by fitting each base learner to a randomly selected subsample (typically 50%) of the training data without replacement [14]. Classification models using stochastic gradient boosting were built with the train function in the caret R package [15], tuning key hyperparameters: shrinkage (learning rate), n.minobsinnode (minimum samples per terminal node), interaction.depth (tree depth), and n.trees (number of trees).

3.4 Building Predictive Models Specific to Cell Types

Gene expression data for each cell type was stratified into training and test sets (70:30). Differentially expressed genes were identified using edgeR, BASiCS, and DEsingle on the training set. These genes served as features for cell-type-specific classification models built via stochastic gradient boosting. Model optimization employed grid search with repeated 5-fold cross-validation. Model performance was evaluated using AUC. After training, per-nucleus ASD probabilities were estimated, and an optimal decision threshold—derived via the pROC package [16]—was applied to both training and test sets. Cell-type–specific models were then used to compute gene importance scores with varImp (caret), prioritizing high-ranking genes as genes as ASD markers.

4. Results

4.1 DE Specific to a Cell Type ASD Gene

After preprocessing, expression levels of 12,036 highly variable genes were quantified across 85,125 nuclei, classified into 17 cell types—comprising glial cells (AST-FB, AST-PP, endothelium, microglia, oligodendrocytes, OPC) and neuronal subtypes (IN-PV, IN-SST, IN-SV2C, IN-VIP, L2/3, L4, L5/6, L5/6-CC, Neu-mat, Neu-NRGN-I, Neu-NRGN-II). Interneurons and excitatory neurons were further subclassified, with neurogranin-expressing neurons and astrocyte subtypes delineated. Gene expression matrices were split into training and test sets per cell type, with model development based on the training data.

Differentially expressed (DE) genes in ASD were independently identified using edgeR [10], BASiCS [11], and DEsingle [12]. DEsingle, tailored for single-cell RNA-seq, employs a zero-inflated negative binomial model; edgeR, originally designed for bulk RNA-seq, uses a negative binomial framework adaptable to single-cell data; BASiCS detects changes in both expression mean and variability. The three DE analysis methods—edgeR, BASiCS, and DEsingle—leverage distinct statistical frameworks and capture complementary gene sets linked to ASD. To enhance coverage, we integrated their outputs and analyzed the combined cell-type-specific DE genes. As shown in Figure 1A, L2/3, L5/6-CC, L4, IN-VIP, IN-SST, and AST-PP exhibit the highest numbers of dysregulated genes, indicating greater ASD susceptibility in these cell types. INVIP and IN-SST are interneuron subtypes, while L2/3, L5/6-CC, and L4 represent excitatory neurons—cell types predominantly impacted by ASD. Among astrocytes, AST-PP shows greater gene dysregulation than AST-FB, indicating higher ASD susceptibility. Given the variation in nucleus counts across cell types, we assessed whether this influenced the number of cell-type-specific DE genes. Using Neu-NRGN-I—the cell type with the fewest nuclei—as a baseline, we subsampled equal numbers of ASD and control nuclei for all other cell types and re-identified DE genes from the resulting training sets. We calculated the median number of DE genes per cell type across subsamples and found a positive correlation with the original DE gene counts (Figure 1B). Cell types with initially high DE gene numbers retained this trend in the subsampled data.

4.2 Specific to a Particular cell type ASD Predictive Models

For each cell type, a stochastic gradient boosting classifier was trained using combined DE genes and the original training set for parameter tuning. Performance on the held-out test set is shown in Figure 2A, with models reliably predicting ASD donor origin at the single-nucleus level. Test

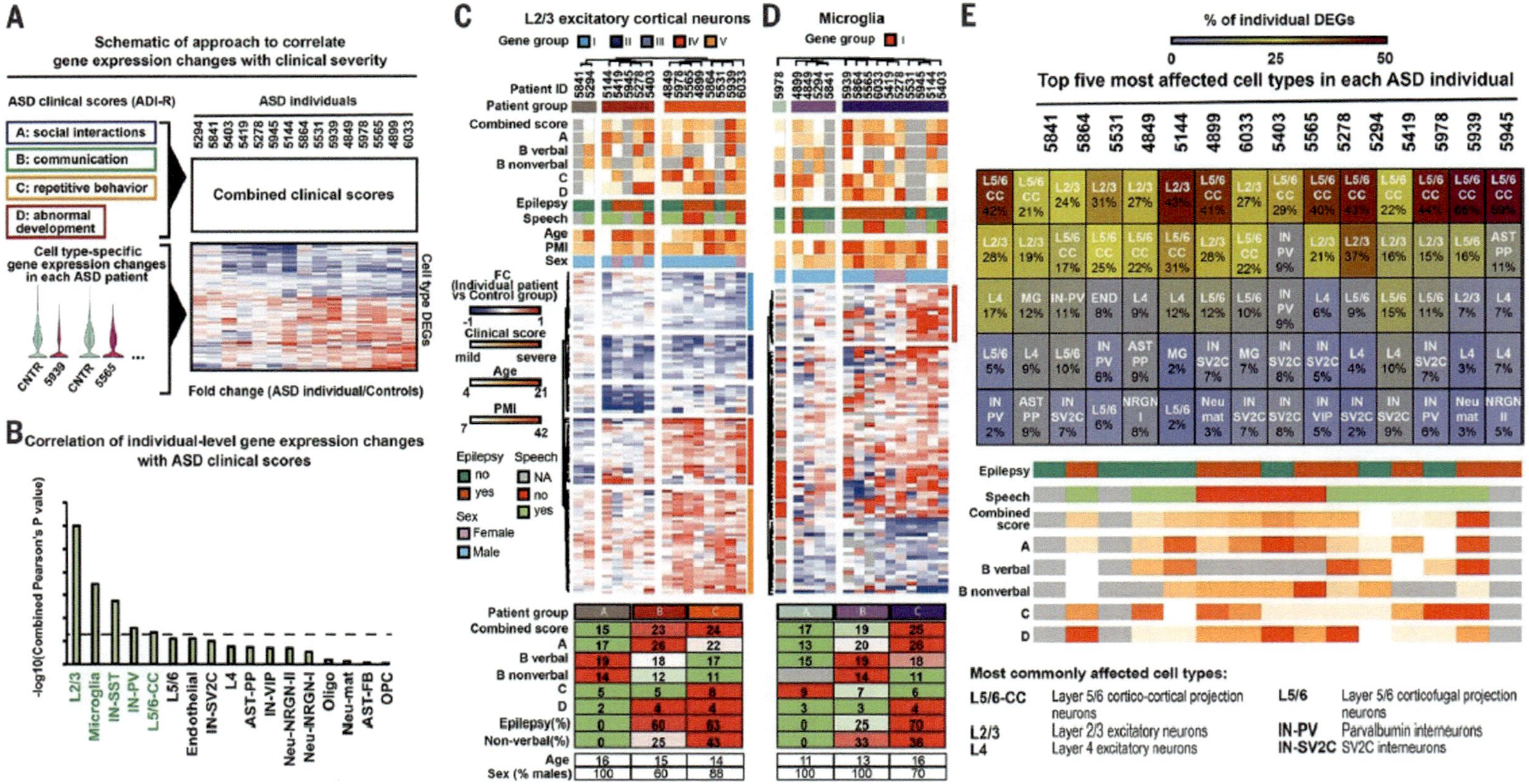

Fig. 1 Correlation of cell type–specific gene dysregulation in ASD patients with clinical severity. (A) Strategy for correlating individual level DEGs and clinical severity. ADI-R subscores were ranked and combined. ASD cases were compared to the combined control profiles in each cell type to generate individual fold changes. (B) Cell types ranked by correlation of DEGs with combined clinical scores. Cell type DEGs in green were significantly ($P < 0.05$) correlated with clinical severity. (C and D) Hierarchical clustering of ASD patients based on individual fold changes in gene expression level in L2/3 neurons (C) and microglia (D). Average clinical scores, prevalence of epilepsy, proportion of nonverbal subjects, and age and gender composition are shown below the heat maps. (E) Analysis of cell types most enriched for transcriptional changes in individual ASD patients [8].

accuracies above 80% were achieved for L2/3 and L4 excitatory neurons, L5/6 and L5/6-CC projection neurons, AST-PP astrocytes, and IN-PV interneurons, indicating selective vulnerability and distinct molecular signatures linked to ASD. To assess functional heterogeneity, we performed GO enrichment using clusterProfiler [17] on cell-type-specific combined DE genes, with all expressed genes as background. Terms with ≥10 genes and FDR-adjusted $P < 0.1$ were reported. Cell-Type-Specific Enrichment Patterns (GO Analysis):

- AST-PP (Protoplasmic Astrocytes): Enriched in synaptic signaling, behavioral regulation, and morphogenesis.
- AST-FP (Fibrous Astrocytes): Dominant enrichment in ribosomal and translational activity.
- Interneurons (IN Subtypes): Overrepresented in ribosome biogenesis, nonsense-mediated mRNA decay, structural molecule function, and ER-targeted protein translation.
- L2/3 and L4 Excitatory Neurons: Enrichment in axonal architecture, postsynaptic density, and synaptic connectivity.
- L5/6 and L5/6-CC Projection Neurons: Enriched for ribosomal function, membrane-targeted co-translational translation, and mRNA decay pathways.

ASD-related transcriptional changes are cell-type specific, with synaptic dysregulation concentrated in upper-layer excitatory neurons and protein synthesis and quality-control pathways prominent in select astrocytes and projection neurons. .

4.3 Prioritizing Genes Associated with ASD Depending on Cell Type

We used the varImp function from the R caret package to rank ASD-associated DE genes by importance within each cell-type-specific model. Jaccard similarity analysis of the top 1,000 DE genes across cell types (Figure 2B) revealed low overlap, suggesting that ASD-related genes may vary by cell type. We assessed overlap between prioritized DE genes and known ASD risk genes from SFARI, identifying 299 shared genes in our dataset. Hypergeometric tests showed significant enrichment (FDR < 0.1) across cell types, validating our predictive models. Neu-mat, OPC, AST-PP, L2/3, L4, and L5/6-CC had the highest concentration of SFARI ASD genes among their top 1,000 DE genes (Figure 2C). Functional annotation of the top 1,000 DE genes revealed distinct GO enrichments across cell types: AST-FB genes are ribosome-related, while AST-PP genes are synapse-linked. Endothelial DE genes are associated with adhesion and epithelial differentiation. Neuronal cell types show enrichment in axon development, protein targeting, and synaptic function, especially in L2/3, L4, and L5/6-CC. The top five DE genes vary by cell type, though some appear across multiple types. Notably, AC105402.4 is consistently downregulated in all interneuron subtypes (IN-PV, IN-SST, IN-SV2C, IN-VIP). Based on DE gene counts, model performance, and enrichment with ASD risk genes, L2/3, L4, L5/6-CC, and AST-PP are identified as more ASD-susceptible. Expression levels of the top five DE genes were compared between ASD and control groups for these cell types (Figure 2D). BCYRN1, a long non-coding RNA gene linked to synaptogenesis, is among the top five DE genes in L2/3, L4, and L5/6-CC cell types, showing consistent upregulation in ASD (Figure 2D). Prior studies associate BCYRN1 with Alzheimer's disease [18,19], suggesting its broader neurological relevance. Additionally, it has been proposed as a potential ASD biomarker based on blood gene expression analysis [20].

5. Discussion

ASD may involve distinct dysregulated gene functions and causative genes across brain cell types, underscoring its cellular heterogeneity. Using gene prioritization, we built cell-type-specific classification models, identifying L2/3, L5/6-CC, L4, IN-VIP, IN-SST, and AST-PP as key ASD-

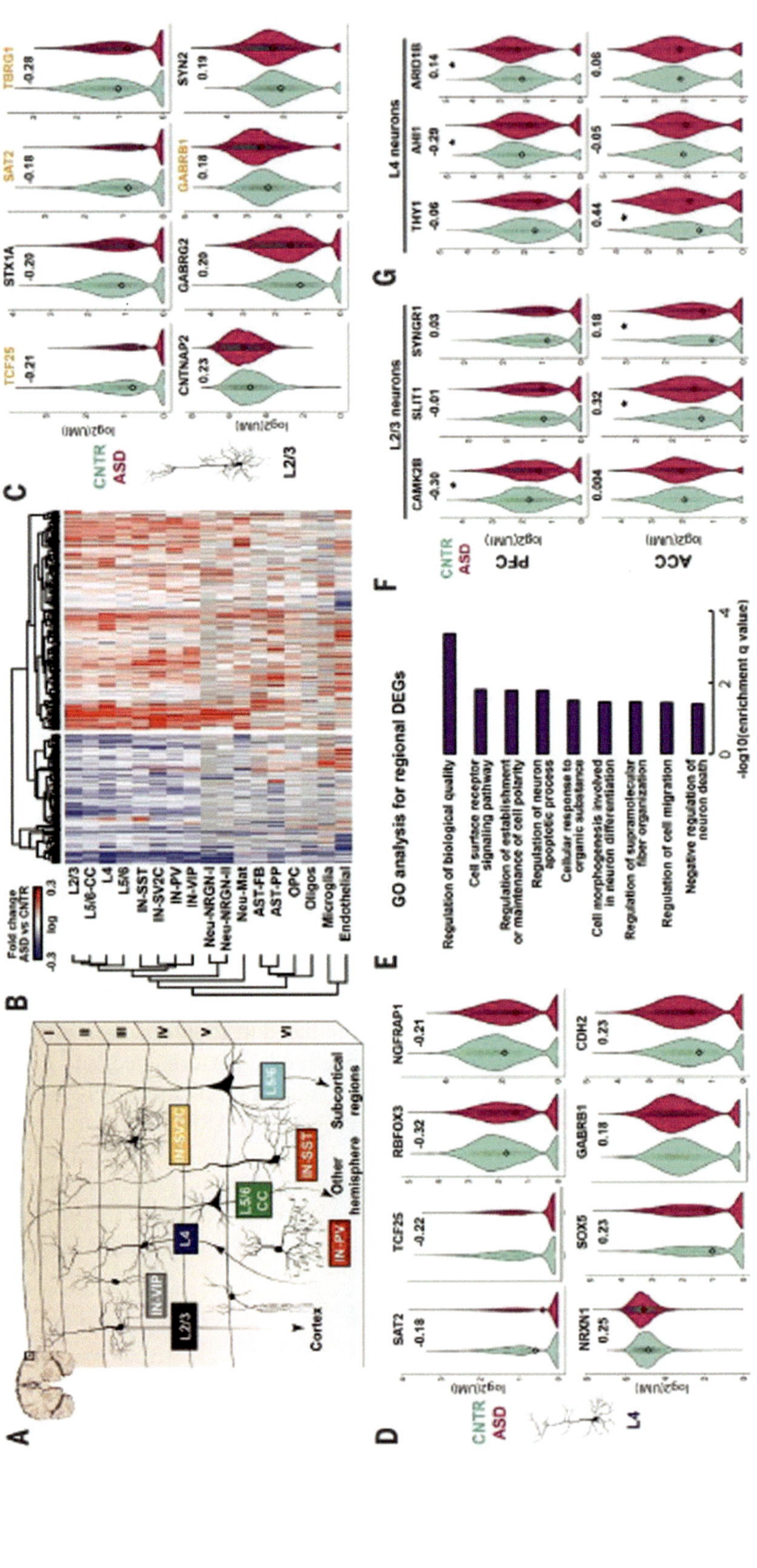

Fig. 2 Gene expression changes across specific cell types in ASD. (A) Schematic of cortical neurons with known layer localization. (B) Hierarchical clustering based on log-transformed relative (fold) changes [versus control (CNTR)] of DEGs in each cell type. (C) Violin plots for top genes differentially expressed in L2/3 neurons in ASD. Genes dysregulated in sporadic epilepsy are indicated in orange. Fold changes (ASD versus control) are indicated under gene names. (D) Violin plots for top genes differentially expressed in L4 neurons in ASD. (E) GO analysis of genes differentially expressed specifically in PFC and ACC. (F and G) Examples of top region-specific DEGs dysregulated in L2/3 and L4 neurons. Asterisk denotes statistically significant ($q < 0.05$) change in gene expression between ASD and control in either the PFC or ACC [8].

susceptible types due to higher DE gene counts. Models for L2/3, L5/6-CC, L4, AST-PP, L5/6, and IN-PV showed strong predictive performance, enabling ranking of ASD-associated DE genes per cell type.

Hypergeometric analysis revealed that Neu-mat, OPC, AST-PP, L2/3, L4, and L5/6-CC cell types have the highest overlap between their top 1,000 DE genes and known ASD risk genes from SFARI. Based on DE gene counts, predictive model performance, and ASD gene enrichment, L2/3, L4, L5/6-CC, and AST-PP appear most susceptible to ASD.

A recent study using single-nucleus RNA-seq data from ASD and control brains [8] identified cell-type-specific DE genes, with L2/3 and IN-VIP prominent in neurons, and AST-PP and microglia in glial cells. DE genes in L2/3 and microglia were most strongly linked to ASD severity, and L2/3 and L5/6-CC were frequently affected. These findings align closely with our predictive model results. To explore ASD heterogeneity across cell types , we analyzed top DE genes with predictive relevance. Limited overlap between cell-type DE profiles suggests distinct ASD-related genes across cell populations. However, some genes recur: BCYRN1 is consistently upregulated in L2/3, L4, and L5/6-CC, while AC105402.4 is uniformly downregulated across interneuron subtypes (IN-PV, IN-SST, IN-SV2C, IN-VIP). Functional annotation revealed that top DE genes exhibit cell-type-specific roles, indicating varied dysregulated functions across cell types. In astrocytes, AST-FB genes are enriched for ribosomal activity, while AST-PP genes are linked to synaptic processes. Endothelial DE genes are associated with adhesion, anchoring junctions, and epithelial differentiation.

Top DE genes in interneuron cell types are involved in somatodendritic compartment organization, protein targeting, neuron projection, and axonal development. Top DE genes in L2/3, L4, and L5/6-CC are associated with synaptic function, highlighting ASD's cellular heterogeneity. Our cell-type-specific prediction models enable gene prioritization, offering new insights for ASD research and potential biomarker identification. These models also support ASD detection at the cell-type level.

6. Conclusion

Differentially expressed genes were used to develop cell-type-specific models that predict ASD at the single-nucleus level. Protoplasmic astrocytes, layer 5/6 cortico-cortical projection neurons, and layer 2/3 and 4 excitatory neurons emerged as more ASD-susceptible. These findings underscore ASD's cellular heterogeneity, with distinct causative genes and dysregulated functions across brain cell types. The prioritized genes may serve as cell-type-specific biomarkers, and the models offer new insights into ASD's molecular pathophysiology.

References

1. S. Cogill and L. Wang, "Support vector machine model of developmental brain gene expression data for prioritization of Autism risk gene candidates," *Bioinformatics*, vol. 32, no. 23, pp. 3611–3618, 2016.
2. K.K. Hyde, "Applications of Supervised Machine Learning in Autism Spectrum Disorder Research: a Review," Review *Journal of Autism and Developmental Disorders*, vol. 6, no. 2, pp. 128–146, 2019/06/01 2019.
3. S.W. Kong, "Characteristics and predictive value of blood transcriptome signature in males with autism spectrum disorders," *PLoS One*, vol. 7, no. 12, p. e49475, 2012.
4. J. Guan, E. Yang, J. Yang, Y. Zeng, G. Ji et al. "Exploiting aberrant mRNA expression in autism for gene discovery and diagnosis," *Human Genetics, journal article* vol. 135, no. 7, pp. 797–811, 2016.
5. D.H. Oh, I.B. Kim, S.H. Kim and D.H. Ahn et al., "Predicting Autism Spectrum Disorder Using Blood-based Gene Expression Signatures and Machine Learning," (in eng), *Clinical psychopharmacology and neuroscience:* the official scientific journal of the Korean College of Neuropsychopharmacology, vol. 15, no. 1, pp. 47–52, 2017.
6. I. Voineagu , "Transcriptomic analysis of autistic brain reveals convergent molecular pathology," *Nature*, vol. 474, no. 7351, pp. 380–384, Jun 16 2011.
7. S. Gupta, "Transcriptome analysis reveals dysregulation of innate immune response genes and neuronal activity-dependent genes in autism," *Nat Commun*, vol. 5, p. 5748, 2014.

8. D. Velmeshev, "Single-cell genomics identifies cell type–specific molecular changes in autism," *Science*, vol. 364, no. 6441, pp. 685–689, 2019.
9. A.T.L. Lun, D.J. McCarthy and J.C. Marioni, "A step-by-step workflow for low-level analysis of single-cell RNA-seq data with Bioconductor," *F1000Research*, vol. 5, pp. 2122–2186, 2016.
10. M.D. Robinson, D.J. McCarthy and G.K. Smyth, "edgeR: a Bioconductor package for differential expression analysis of digital geneexpression data," (in eng), *Bioinformatics (Oxford, England)*, vol. 26, no. 1, pp. 139–140, 2010.
11. C.A. Vallejos, J.C. Marioni, and S. Richardson, "BASiCS: Bayesian Analysis of Single-Cell Sequencing Data," *PLoS computational biology*, vol. 11, no. 6, pp. 1–18, 2015.
12. Z. Miao, K. Deng, X. Wang and X. Zhang, "DEsingle for detecting three types of differential expression in single-cell RNA-seq data," *Bioinformatics*, vol. 34, no. 18, pp. 3223–3224, 2018.
13. Jerome H. Friedman, "Greedy function approximation: a gradient boosting machine," pp. 1189–1232, 2001.
14. Jerome H. Friedman and d. analysis, "Stochastic gradient boosting," vol. 38, no. 4, pp. 367–378, 2002.
15. M. Kuhn, "Building predictive models in R using the caret package," *Journal of statistical software*, vol. 28, no. 5, pp. 1–26, 2008.
16. X. Robin, "pROC: an open-source package for R and S+ to analyze and compare ROC curves," vol. 12, no. 1, pp. 1–8, 2011.
17. G. Yu, L.-G. Wang, Y. Han, and Q.-Y. He, "clusterProfiler: an R package for comparing biological themes among gene clusters," (in eng), *Omics : a journal of integrative biology*, vol. 16, no. 5, pp. 284–287, 2012.
18. P. Wan, W. Su and Y. Zhuo, "The Role of Long Noncoding RNAs in Neurodegenerative Diseases," *Molecular Neurobiology*, vol. 54, no. 3, pp. 2012–2021, 2017/04/01 2017.
19. G. Hu , "Molecular mechanisms of long noncoding RNAs and their role in disease pathogenesis," vol. 9, no. 26, 2018.
20. H.Y. Ivanov, V.K. Stoyanova, N.T. Popov, M. Bosheva and T.I.J.B. Vachev et al., "Blood-based gene expression in children with autism spectrum disorder," vol. 17, p. e8966, 2015.
21. Yang Wang, Yiping Lin, Guoli Ji, Jinting Guan, "Gene Screening for Autism Based on Cell-typespecific Predictive Models," *IEEE International Conference on Bioinformatics and Biomedicine (BIBM)*, 2090–2096, 2020.

Section 6

Clinical data analysis model

14

Machine Learning-Based Predictive Models for Medical Data Analysis: A Case of Early Diabetic Prediction

Pradeepta Kumar Sarangi[1], Hakam Singh[2], Ishu Rani[3], Merry Saxena[4], Bhisham Sharma[5*] and Sidhnath Kumar[6]

1. Introduction

Diabetes is a chronic metabolic disorder characterized by elevated blood glucose levels. It has emerged as one of the most rapidly spreading diseases worldwide, posing a significant burden on healthcare systems. According to the International Diabetes Federation (IDF), approximately "463" million individuals aged 20-79 were living with diabetes in 2019, a number projected to rise to "700" million by 2045. Early diagnosis and effective management of diabetes are crucial for reducing morbidity and saving lives. Also known as diabetes mellitus, this condition impairs the body's ability to convert food into usable energy, leading to systemic complications if left untreated [1].

Diabetes occurs when the body either fails to produce enough insulin or cannot use it effectively resulting in elevated blood sugar levels. This can lead to serious complications such as heart disease, vision loss, and kidney damage. Early detection and timely treatment significantly reduce the severity and spread of the disease, with regular medication helping to manage it more effectively over time [2]. When we consume carbohydrates, the body converts them into glucose. Normally, the pancreas releases insulin to regulate this glucose. In diabetes, either insufficient insulin is produced or the body cannot use it effectively, causing glucose to accumulate in the bloodstream. Prolonged high blood sugar can lead to serious complications such as heart disease, visionloss, and kidneydamage.

Diabetes includes several classifications: prediabetes, "Type 1" "Type 2", and "gestational" diabetes. These can be further divided into subtypes such as "LADA", 'MODY", neonatal diabetes, Type 3, double diabetes, "Wolfram syndrome", and "Alstrom syndrome". Prediabetes, or impaired glucose tolerance, is a condition where blood sugar levels are elevated but not high enough for a type 2 diagnosis. Early detection can help prevent its progression to full-blown Type 2 diabetes.

[1,2,6] Chitkara University School of Engineering & Technology, Chitkara University, India.
[3] Chitkara University College of Nursing, Chitkara University, India.
[4] Department of Interdisciplinary Courses in Engineering, Chitkara University Institute of Engineering & Technology, Chitkara University, India.
[5] Chitkara University Institute of Engineering & Technology, Chitkara University, Punjab, India.
* Corresponding author: bhisham.pec@gmail.com

DOI: 10.1201/9781003541318-20

Type 1 Diabetes—commonly emerging in adolescence and also known as Juvenile Diabetes (JDDM), can lead to complications such as skin disorders, cardiovascular issues, poor circulation, dental problems, nerve damage, and pregnancy-related risks.

Type 2 Diabetes—also known as Non-Insulin Dependent Diabetes Mellitus (NIDDM)—primarily affects older adults. It occurs when pancreatic beta cells produce insufficient insulin or the body cannot use it effectively. Approximately 90% of diabetes cases are classified as Type 2 [16].

Gestational Diabetes - This typically arises in expectant mothers during the later stages of pregnancy, marked by a sudden spike in blood sugar levels. Contributing factors include genetic predisposition, obesity, inactivity, and polycystic ovary syndrome. Associated risks include Cesarean delivery, hypoglycemia, preeclampsia, and postpartum development of "Type 2" diabetes. While these conditions often resolve after childbirth, affected women face an increased risk of developing Type 1 or Type 2 diabetes later in life [16].

Diabetes presents with symptoms such as excessive thirst, unexplained weight loss, blurred vision, frequent infections, and increased urination. Its onset is influenced by multiple factors including age, gender, genetics, BMI, obesity, inactivity, and dysfunctions in the nervous and immune systems, alongside elevated blood glucose levels. Key diagnostic testsinclude A1C, a FPG (Fast Plasma Glucose), RPG Test (Random Plasma Glucose), and OGTT (Oral Glucose Tolerance Test) [16]. Contributing causes also include genetic mutations particularly on chromosome 6 and viral infections [10]. Diabetes is a leading cause of lower limb amputations worldwide [1].

In 2014, approximately 422 million people were affected diabetes symptoms [8], signaling a major global health ctisis. By 2017, this number had risen to nearly 451 million[2], and by 2019, it reached a staggering 463 million individuals diagnosed with diabetes [5]. This surge in cases not only intensified the strain on healthcare infrastructures but also amplified the urgency for innovative medical interventions, patient education, and policy initiatives aimed at curbing the diabetes epidemic. By 2035, the diabetic population is expected to be at 592 million [10]. Such a projection foreshadows a substantial increase, necessitating a global collaborative effort to enhance early detection, improve treatment options, and promote healthier lifestyles to mitigate the impending impact of diabetes on societies worldwide. The estimation shows that the diabetic population will increase to 629 million before the year 2045 [1]. This anticipated growth serves as a clarion call for sustained research, funding, and public health campaigns to address the multifaceted tests posed by diabetes, ensuring better health outcomes for future generations.

Use cases such as hypertension, smoking history, age, and gender are used by ML models to predict whether a person is prone to diabetes or not. ML algorithms have a useful classifier that helps to predict diabetes from various human attributes. While applying ML tools on patient data we can easily prediction risk before symptoms arise.

2. Machine Learning

Machine Learning (ML), a sub-division of Artificial Intelligence (AI) and computer science, focuses on identifying data patterns to classify and predict outcomes. It draws upon techniques from data mining, statistics, and optimization to build predictive models [2]. ML is broadly categorized into supervised learning, unsupervised learning, and reinforcement learning each employing distinct strategies for data interpretation. Deep Learning (DL), a specialized branch of ML, is inspired by the structure and function of the human brain. It utilizes multi-layered artificial neural networks (ANNs) to process large datasets, enabling machines to learn and improve autonomously. DL is considered a more advanced and sophisticated extension of ML, as it can automatically extract features from raw data, unlike traditional ML algorithms that depend on manually engineered inputs as shown in Figure 1. Many scientists and researchers are actively promoting, and applying Machine Learning

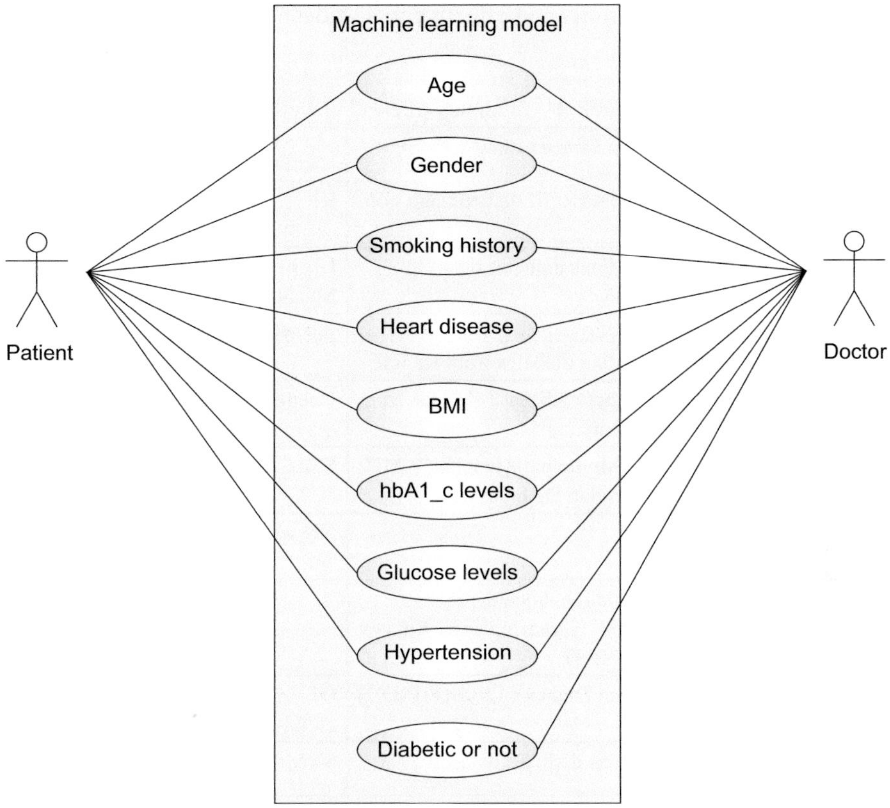

Fig. 1 Common attributes in Diabetic prediction.

(ML) and Deep Learning (DL) techniques to forecast diabetes and other diseases [4]. DL, a more advanced subset of ML, offers greater sophistication by enabling models to autonomously learn and extract features from raw data. Unlike traditional ML algorithms that depend on manually engineered inputs, DL models enhance predictive accuracy and overall performance.

- *Personalized Risk Rate:* ML models models analyze large datasets to generate individualized riskprofiles. This enables early identification of potential health issues, allowing for timely intervention and more targeted care.
- *Better use of Healthcare Resources:* Identifying high risk individuals in advance enables the healthcare system to allocate resources more efficiently, prioritizing timely treatment, preventive care, and complication reduction. This targeted approach also helps lower overall healthcare costs.
- *Continuous Monitoring:* ML algorithms can continuously track high-risk individuals by analyzing real-time data, enabling early detection of warning signs and timely intervention.
- *Data Quality and Privacy:* Effective ML models require high-quality datasetsfor accurate predictions. However, patient privacy must be safeguarded, ensuring that personal health information is securely handled and protected.
- *Understanding the Model:* ML algorithms can be complex to implement and understand. Enhancing their interpretability is essential for building trust among users and stakeholders.
- *Fairness and Generalization:* ML models may perform inconsistently across different population groups, leading to biased outcomes. Rigorous testing across diverse datasets is

crucial to ensure both fairness and effectiveness. A detailed summary of existing studies is presented in Table 1.

Table 1 Summary of existing works.

Researcher	*Dataset Used*	*Algorithm Used*	*Accuracy*
Md. Tanvir Islam et al. [1]	Real-time dataset of diabetic and non-diabetic.	RF	99.35%
Shamreen Ahamed et al. [2]	i) Pima Indians diabetes dataset ii) Survey Data	Light Gradient, Boosting Machine	95.20%
Muhammad Waqas Nadeem et al. [3]	i) NHANES ii) Pima Indian diabetes from Kaggle.	Fusion of SVM and ANN	94.67%
Bala Manoj Kumar P. et al. [4]	Indian Diabetes-disease dataset from UCI repository.	Deep-neural-network algorithm	98.16%
Zhaoyi Yuan et al. [5]	i) Weihai-Municipal- Hospital(WMH) ii) PIMA-Indian Diabetes data.	STACK-GRAPE	
Jobeda Jamal Khanam et al. [6]	PIDD	NN with 2 hidden layers	88.6%
Henock M.Deberneh et al. [7]	i) Korean national health ii) Nutrition Examination Survey (KNHANES)		
Zubair Azim Miazi et al. [8]	PIMA Indian Diabetes Dataset (PIDD)	DL model integrated with a cloud-based mobile app	90.26%
Jayroop Ramesh [9]	PIMA Indians diabetes dataset	SVM-RBF	83.20%
KM Jyoti Rani [10]	Dataset of hospital Frankfurt, Germany	Decision Tree	99%
Pranab Ghost et al. [11]	PIMA Indians diabetes dataset.	RF	99.35%
Elias Dritas [12]	PIMA Indian Diabetes Dataset.	RF and KNN	99.22%
P Tiwari et al. [13]	NIDDK	XGboost	78.91%
Othmane Daanouni et al. [14]	Dataset from UCI Repository.	DNN	92.36%
M. Narmadha [15]	Dataset from UCL.	SVM	96.54%
Ranjith M. et al. [16]	Dataset from islam.	Neural network with embedding	1.0
Minhaz Uddin Emon et al. [17]	Dataset from UCI library.	Logistic Regression	75%

3. Objectives

The primary goal of our study is to develop a ML prediction algorithm capable of assessing diabetes risk using clinical datasets. The development of this model involves several key steps, including:

- *Data collection:* Datasets are gathered from various healthcare sources, such as the UCI repository, to support model development.
- *Preprocessing:* The collected data is cleaned to address missing values and inconsistencies ensuring reliability and accuracy.

- *Features Selections and Engineering:* Using Exploratory Data Analysis (EDA), the most relevant features for predicting diabetesrisk are identified and refined to enhance model performance.

Benefits of Successful Implementation of ML-based Diabetes Prediction (DP):

- *Early Identification of At-Risk Individuals:* ML models enable early detection of diabetes risk by analyzing patient data, allowing timely intervention and preventive care.
- *Personalized Healthcare:* ML can assess individual risk profiles based on personal characteristics and recommend tailored treatment strategies. This approach enhances patient engagement and supports proactive preventive care.
- *Resource Optimization:* Identifying individuals in the searly stages of diabetes allows for more efficient use of healthcare resources. Targeted interventions and preventive measures can be implemented promptly, reducing complications and improving patient outcomes. Healthcare systems offer a range of resources to support diabetes prevention and management.
- *Empowering Patients:* When individuals become aware of their diabetes risk, they are empowered to take proactive stepstoward prevention. This includes monitoring glucose levels, adhering to prescribed medications, and making informed lifestyle changes to reduce their risk and improve overall health.
- *Research Advancement:* Researchers. Researchers continue to explore and refine the most effective ML models for diabetes prediction, deepening their expertise in the field.

Ultimately, this study aims to demonstrate that ML offers a reliable and optimal solution for assessing diabetes risk, thereby supporting early diagnosis and improved patient outcomes.

4. Methodology

Data Preprocessing: The dataset was sourced from the Kaggle platform. In its raw form, it required preprocessing to eliminate abnormal entries [5], noisy data, missing values incompatible [13] formats, and ambiguous or empty records [4]. This step is essential for organizing the data and ensuring optimal model performance. Prior to preprocessing, the dataset must undergo cleaning, integration, transformation, reduction, and discretization [13]. The methodology diagram is shown in Figure 2.

4.1 Implementation and Results

A supervised learning algorithm [12], also recognized as a statistical prediction technique, utilizes one or more independent variables to estimate the probability of a binary outcome [9]. It primarily predicts a dependent variable based on a dataset of independent features, producing outputs in binary form typically 1 or 0 (Yes or No) [12]. The basic diagram of a logistic regression model is shown in Figure 3.

A decision tree (Figure 4) is a fundamental algorithm used for regression and classification tasks. It interprets data through a flowchart like or tree structured representation, where internal nodes represent attributes and leaf nodes correspond to class-labels [14].

Supervised learning is an algorithm used for regression as well as classification. It generates a forest from many disconnected decision trees during training [11]. If there are more trees in the forest, the results become more accurate [1]. The equation for using Random Forest (RF) in regression is calculated using Mean Squared Error (MSE), where N is the number of data points, f_i refers to the value predicted by the model, and y_i is the actual value of data point i.

$$\text{MSE} = \frac{1}{N} \sum_{i=1}^{N} (f_i - y_i)^2 \qquad [1]$$

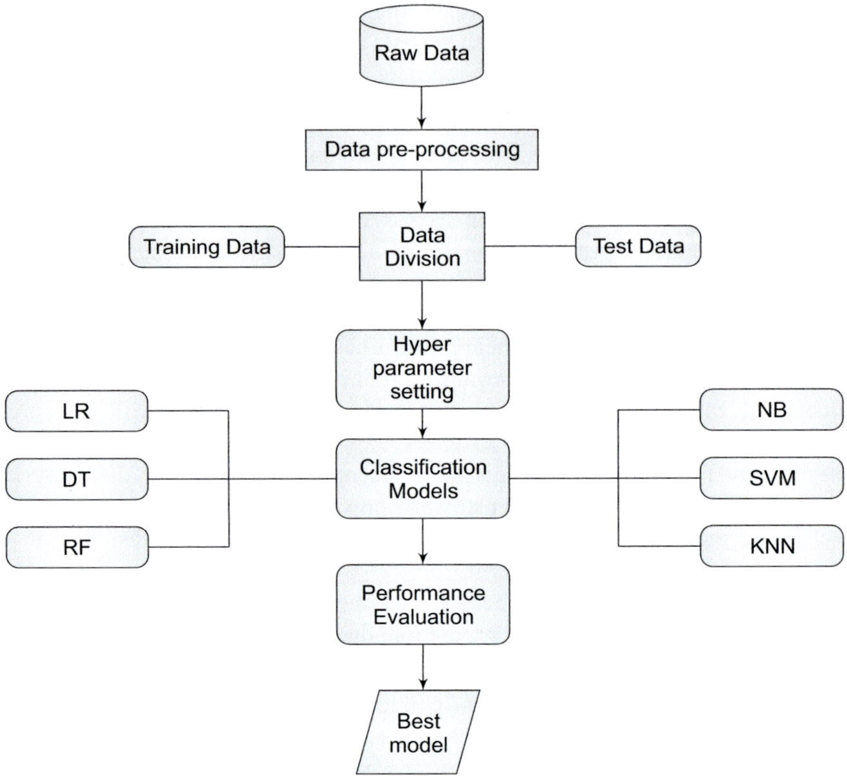

Fig. 2 Methodology Diagram.

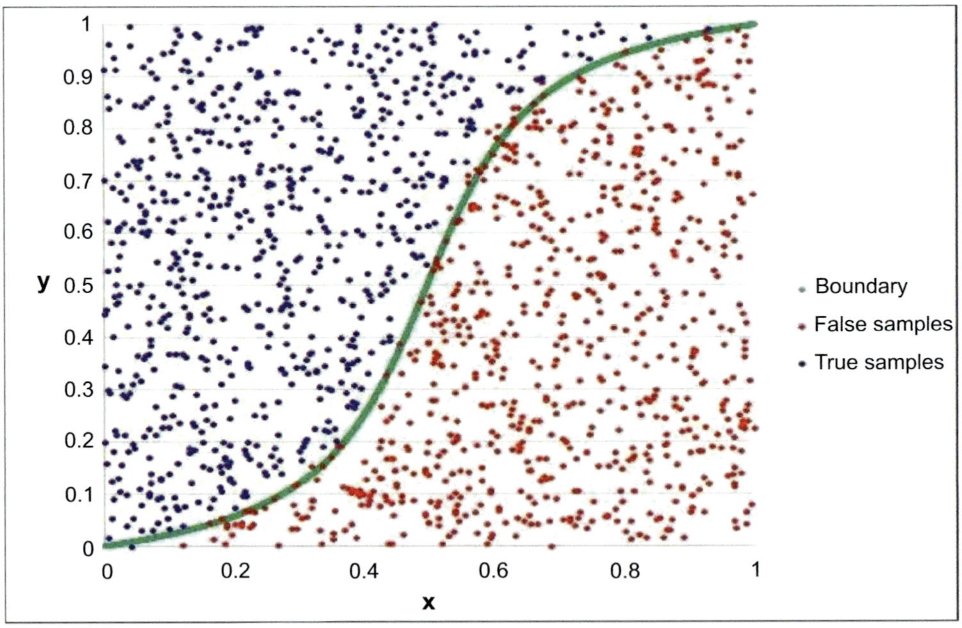

Fig. 3 Logistic Regression.

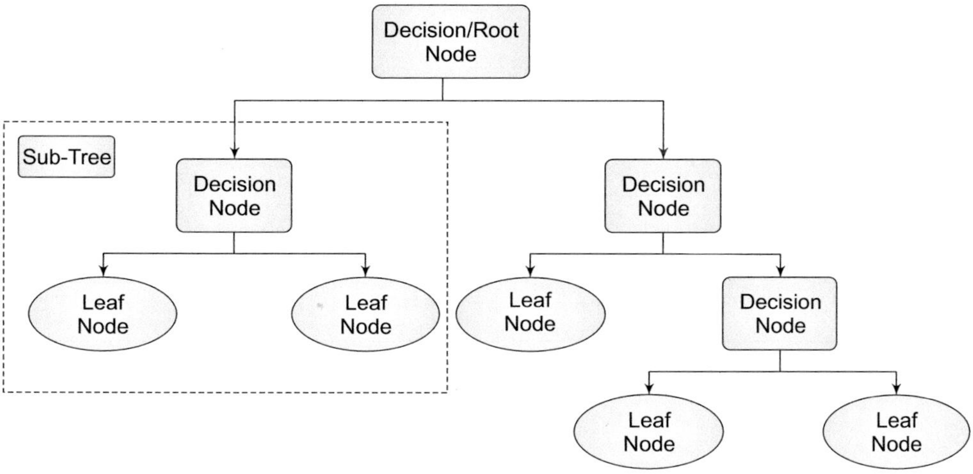

Fig. 4 Decision Tree.

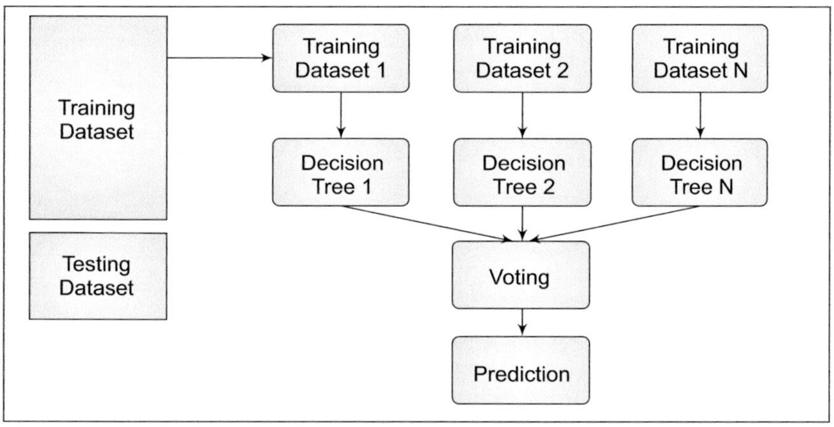

Fig. 5 Random Forest.

For RF (Figure 5), Gini index is used to determine how the nodes on trees will branch.

$$\text{Gini} = 1 - \sum_{i=1}^{N} (P_i)^2 \qquad [2]$$

Apart from these, entropy can also be used to find out the way a node will branch on the decision tree.

$$\text{Entropy} = \sum_{i=1}^{c} -p_i * (p_i) \qquad [3]$$

This algorithm (Figure 6) performs surprisingly well in many real-world applications, especially with text classification problems like spam detection. The training and prediction phases of Naïve Bayes are computationally efficient (Equation 4).

$$P(A/B) = \frac{P(B \mid A) \cdot P(A)}{P(B)} \qquad [4]$$

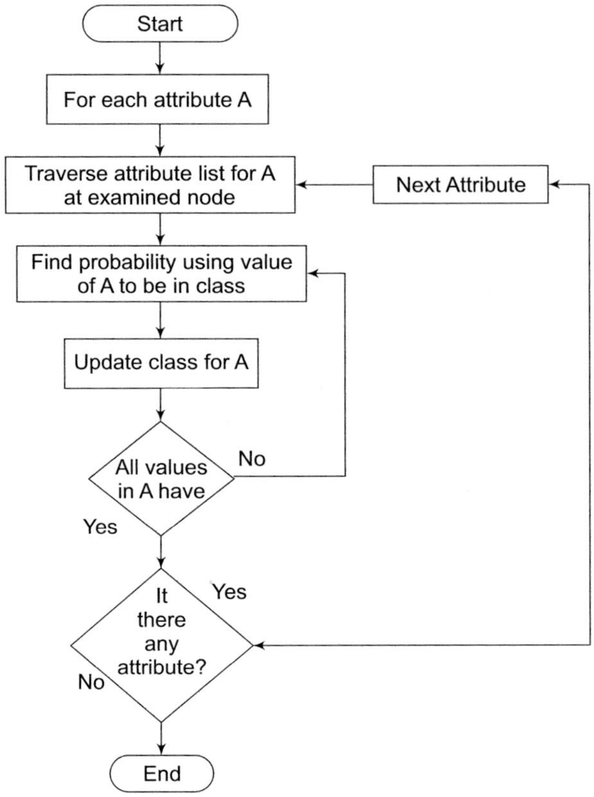

Fig. 6 Naïve Bayes.

where "$P(A|B)$"is the probability of "event-A" when "event-B" has occured, $P(B|A)$ is the probability of the "event-B" when "event A" has occurred, and $P(A)$ and $P(B)$ are the probabilities for "events A" and "event B" to occur respectively. It predicts the output using input attributes for a given number of instances in the training set [9].

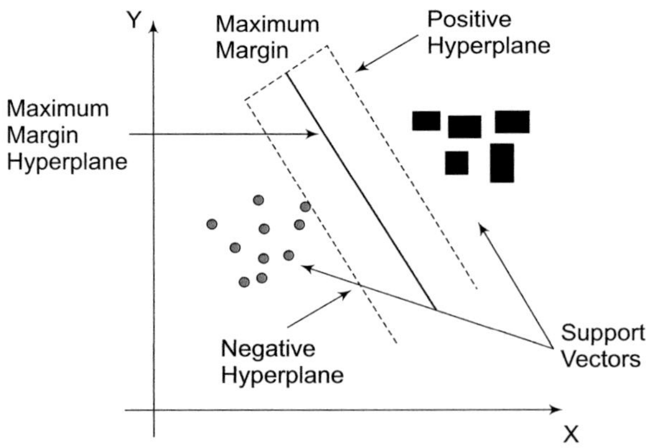

Fig. 7 Support Vector Machines.

Support Vector Machine (SVM) is primarily used for both regression and classification tasks. Its core objective is to construct a hyperline also known as a decision boundary—that separates a multi-dimensional feature space into distinct classes. This boundary effectively partitions the data based on the unique characteristics of each feature, ensuring clear and accurate classification across multiple groups (Figure 7).

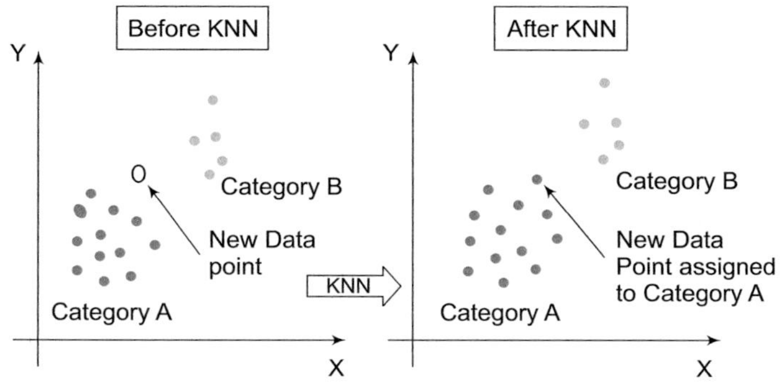

Fig. 8 K nearest Neighbor (KNN).

K-Nearest Neighbors (KNN) is a supervised learning model primarily known for its classification algorithms (Figure 8). It operates on the assumption that new data is similar to previously observed data. Based on this similarity, KNN categorizes new instances into specific classes. It collects all available data, and when new data is encountered, it can easily classify it by comparing it to the most similar existing records. K-Nearest Neighbors (KNN).

$$d = \sqrt{\sum_{x=1}^{\pi}(x_1 - x_j)^2} \quad [5]$$

where $x_i - x_j$ are two points in the *n*-dimensional space and *N* is the total of all instances [9].

4.1.1 Implementations and Results Analysis

This section outlines the implementation of six distinct Machine Learning (ML) models. The content is organized into three parts: Exploratory Data Analysis (EDA), Model Implementation, and Results Analysis.

A. Exploratory Data Analysis

The properties of the dataset are:

Number of patients: 2108

Number of parameters considered: 9

Number of independent variable: 8

Number of dependent variable: 1

The dataset attributes is shown in figure 9.

```
Data columns (total 9 columns):
 #   Column                    Non-Null Count  Dtype
---  ------                    --------------  -----
 0   gender(male 0 female 1)   2108 non-null   int64
 1   age                       2108 non-null   float64
 2   hypertension              2108 non-null   int64
 3   heart_disease             2108 non-null   int64
 4   smoking_history           2108 non-null   int64
 5   bmi                       2108 non-null   float64
 6   HbA1c_level               2108 non-null   float64
 7   blood_glucose_level       2108 non-null   int64
 8   diabetes                  2108 non-null   int64
```

Fig. 9 Dataset attributes.

The sample data set attributes are given in Figure 10. It includes age, hypertension, heart disease ratio, smoking history, body mass index, HbA1c_level, and blood glucose level of the patient.

	gender(male 0 female 1)	age	hypertension	heart_disease	smoking_history	bmi	HbA1c_level	blood_glucose_level	diabetes
0	1	22.0	0	0	0	25.38	4.5	160	0
1	1	23.0	0	0	0	24.01	5.0	200	0
2	0	80.0	1	0	0	20.60	6.2	80	0
3	0	8.0	0	0	0	16.38	4.0	130	0
4	0	33.0	0	0	1	27.32	5.8	85	0

Fig. 10 First five rows in the dataset.

The last five rows in the dataset are given in Figure 11.

	gender(male 0 female 1)	age	hypertension	heart_disease	smoking_history	bmi	HbA1c_level	blood_glucose_level	diabetes
2103	1	65.0	1	1	0	33.55	8.2	140	1
2104	0	55.0	0	1	1	30.42	6.2	300	1
2105	1	61.0	0	0	0	34.45	6.5	280	1
2106	1	58.0	1	0	0	38.31	7.0	200	1
2107	1	61.0	0	0	1	30.11	6.2	240	1

Fig. 11 Last five rows in the dataset.

The correlation matrix of different variables is shown in Figure 12.

The parameter wise count of patients in the dataset is shown in Figure 13.

Similarly, some other analyses of the dataset are shown in graphical form in Figure 14 showing the count of patients with and without diabetes.

Figure 15 depicts the distribution of patients based on hypertension.

B. Model Implementation

This section gives describes the implementation results of different models. The results are shown by confusion matrices.

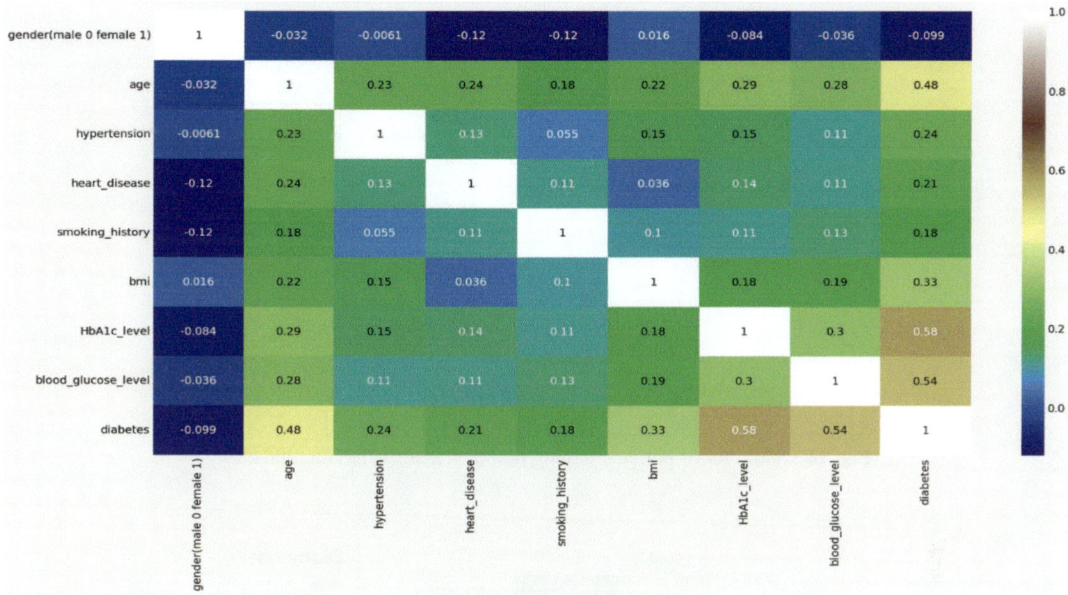

Fig. 12 Correlation matrix.

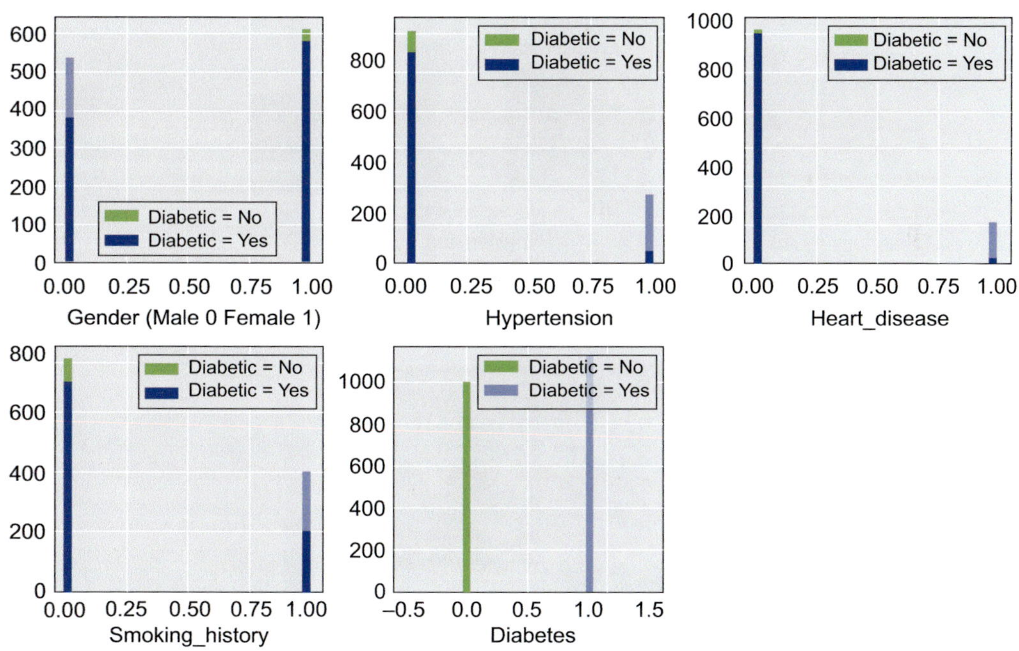

Fig. 13 Parameter wise count of patients.

Figure 16 represents the confusion matrix for Logistic Regression implementation.

In Figure 16, the (0,0) cell indicates that 253 patients in the test pattern were disease-free, and the model accurately identified them as such. However, in the (1,0) cell, 39 patients who were actually disease-free were incorrectly classified by the model as having the disease. Conversely, the (1,1) cell

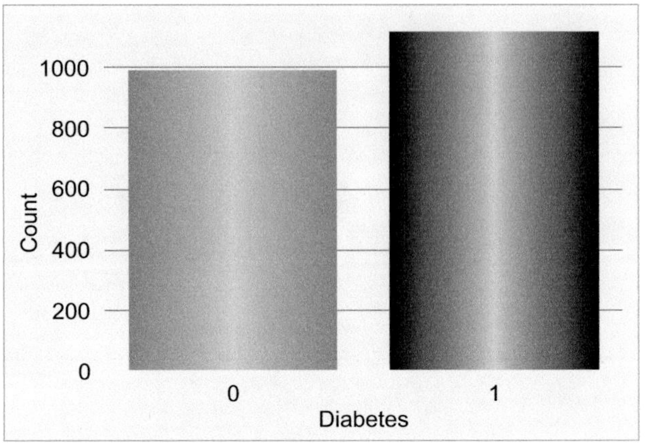

Fig. 14 Number of patients having diabetes and not having diabetes.

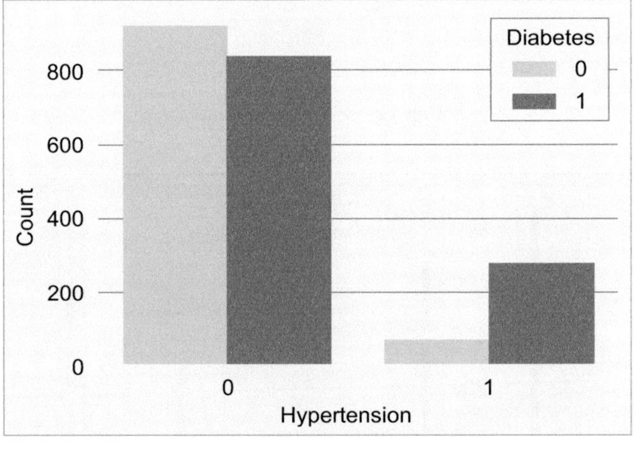

Fig. 15 Count of patients based on hypertension.

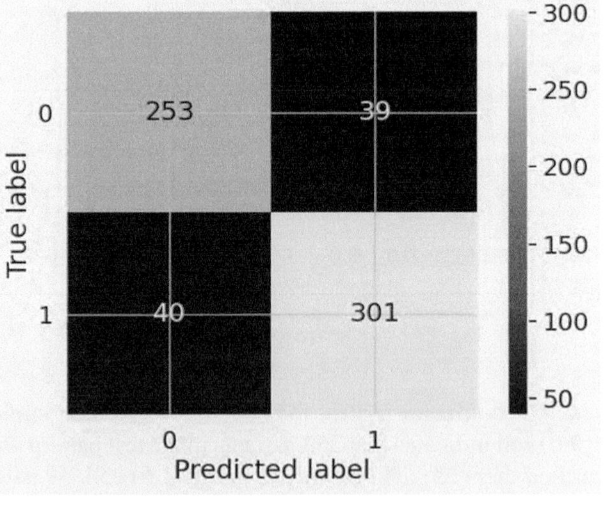

Fig. 16 Confusion matrix: LR.

shows that the model correctly identified patients with heart disease, while the (0,1) cell represents patients who were diabetic but were misclassified by the model as disease-free. The classification report can be found in Figure 17.

	precision	recall	f1-score	support
0	0.86	0.87	0.86	292
1	0.89	0.88	0.88	341
accuracy			0.88	633
macro avg	0.87	0.87	0.87	633
weighted avg	0.88	0.88	0.88	633

Fig. 17 Classification report (LR).

Figure 18 represents the confusion matrix for the implementation of Decision Tree.

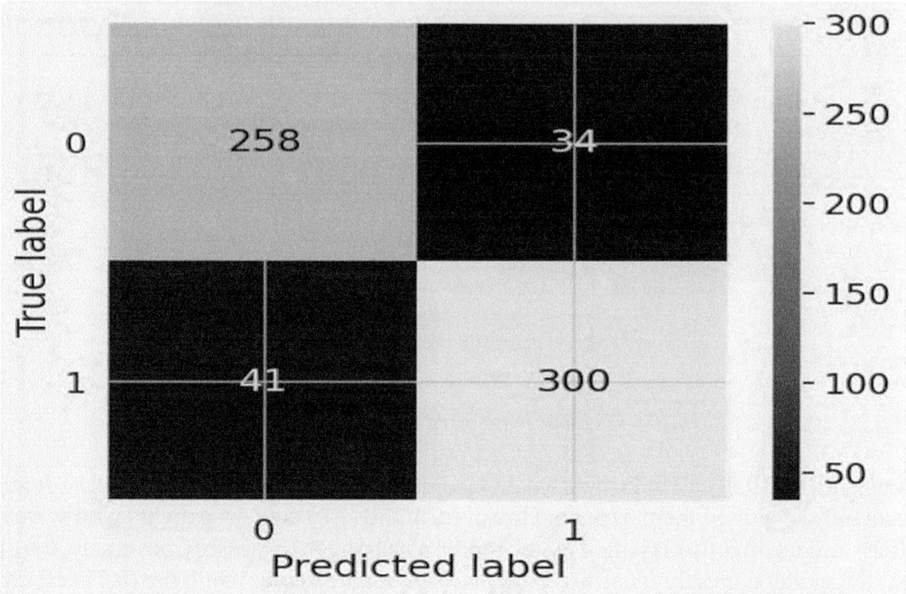

Fig. 18 Confusion Matrix: Gaussian DT.

In Figure 18, the (0,0) cell indicates that 258 patients in the test pattern were disease-free, and the model accurately identified them as such. However, in the (1,0) cell, 34 patients who were actually disease-free were incorrectly classified by the model as having the disease. Conversely, the (1,1) cell shows that the model correctly identified patients with heart disease, while the (0,1) cell represents patients who were diabetic but were misclassified by the model as disease-free. The classification report is presented in Figure 19.

	precision	recall	f1-score	support
0	0.86	0.88	0.87	292
1	0.90	0.88	0.89	341
accuracy			0.88	633
macro avg	0.88	0.88	0.88	633
weighted avg	0.88	0.88	0.88	633

Fig. 19 Classification report (DT).

Figure 20 represents the confusion matrix for RF implementation.

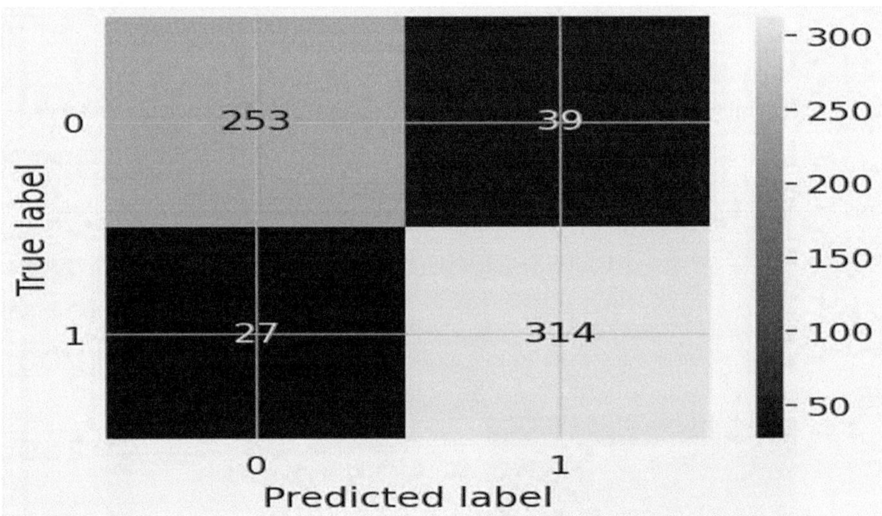

Fig. 20 Confusion Matrix : RF.

In Figure 20, the (0,0) cell indicates that 258 patients in the test pattern were disease-free, and the model accurately identified them as such. However, in the (1,0) cell, 34 patients who were actually disease-free were incorrectly classified by the model as having the disease. Conversely, the (1,1) cell shows that the model correctly identified patients with heart disease, while the (0,1) cell represents patients who were diabetic but were misclassified by the model as disease-free. The classification report can be found in Figure 21.

Figure 22 represents the confusion matrix for the implementation of SVC.

In Figure 22, the (0,0) cell indicates that 252 patients in the test pattern were disease-free, and the model accurately identified them as such. However, in the (1,0) cell, 40 patients who were actually disease-free were incorrectly classified by the model as having the disease. Conversely, the (1,1) cell shows that the model correctly identified patients with heart disease, while the (0,1) cell represents patients who were diabetic but were misclassified by the model as disease-free. The classification report can be found in Figure 23.

	precision	recall	f1-score	support
0	0.90	0.87	0.88	292
1	0.89	0.92	0.90	341
accuracy			0.90	633
macro avg	0.90	0.89	0.89	633
weighted avg	0.90	0.90	0.90	633

Fig. 21 Classification report (RF).

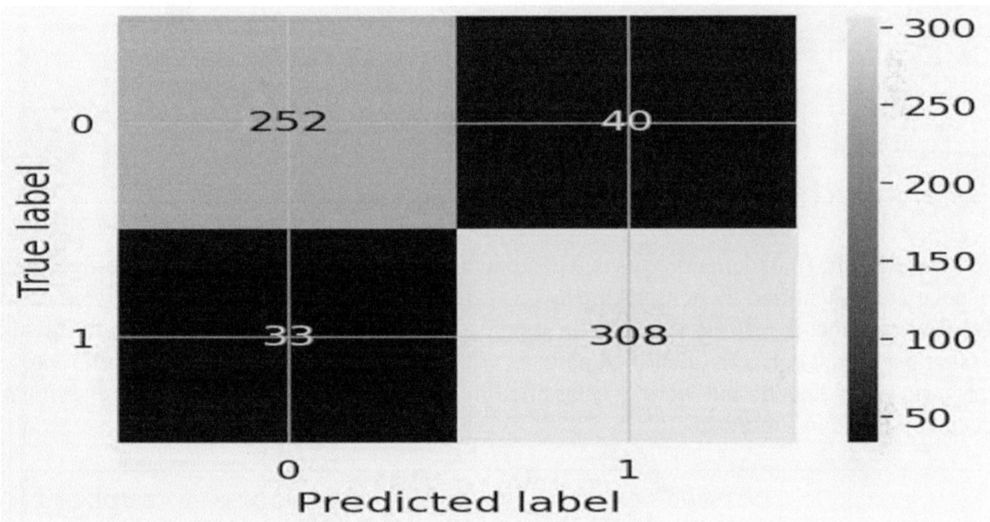

Fig. 22 Confusion Matrix : SVC.

	precision	recall	f1-score	support
0	0.88	0.86	0.87	292
1	0.89	0.90	0.89	341
accuracy			0.88	633
macro avg	0.88	0.88	0.88	633
weighted avg	0.88	0.88	0.88	633

Fig. 23 Classification report (SVC).

Figure 24 represents the confusion matrix for NB implementation.

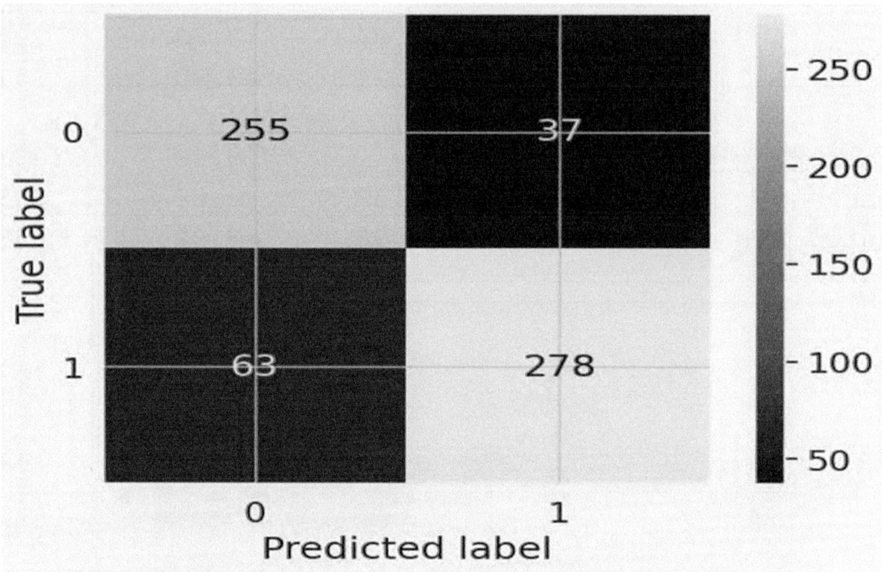

Fig. 24 Confusion Matrix : NB.

In Figure 24, the (0,0) cell indicates that 255 patients in the test pattern were disease-free, and the model accurately identified them as such. However, in the (1,0) cell, 37 patients who were actually disease-free were incorrectly classified by the model as having the disease. Conversely, the (1,1) cell shows that the model correctly identified patients with heart disease, while the (0,1) cell represents patients who were diabetic but were misclassified by the model as disease-free. The classification report can be found in Figure 25.

	precision	recall	f1-score	support
0	0.80	0.87	0.84	292
1	0.88	0.82	0.85	341
accuracy			0.84	633
macro avg	0.84	0.84	0.84	633
weighted avg	0.85	0.84	0.84	633

Fig. 25 Classification report (NB).

Figure 26 represents the confusion matrix for KNN implementation.

In Figure 26, the (0,0) cell indicates that 231 patients in the test pattern were disease-free, and the model accurately identified them as such. However, in the (1,0) cell, 61 patients who were actually disease-free were incorrectly classified by the model as having the disease. Conversely, the (1,1) cell shows that the model correctly identified patients with heart disease, while the (0,1) cell represents patients who were diabetic but were misclassified by the model as disease-free. The classification report can be found in Figure 27.

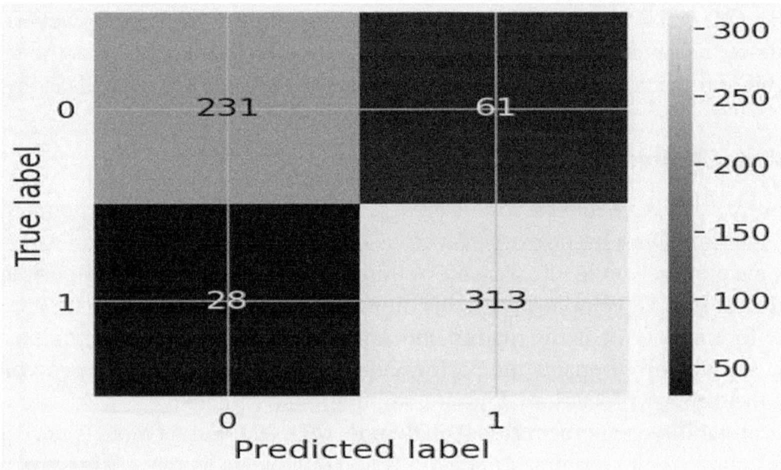

Fig. 26 Confusion Matrix : KNN.

	precision	recall	f1-score	support
0	0.89	0.79	0.84	292
1	0.84	0.92	0.88	341
accuracy			0.86	633
macro avg	0.86	0.85	0.86	633
weighted avg	0.86	0.86	0.86	633

Fig. 27 Classification report (KNN).

The comparative analysis of the results of all models is depicted in figure 28.

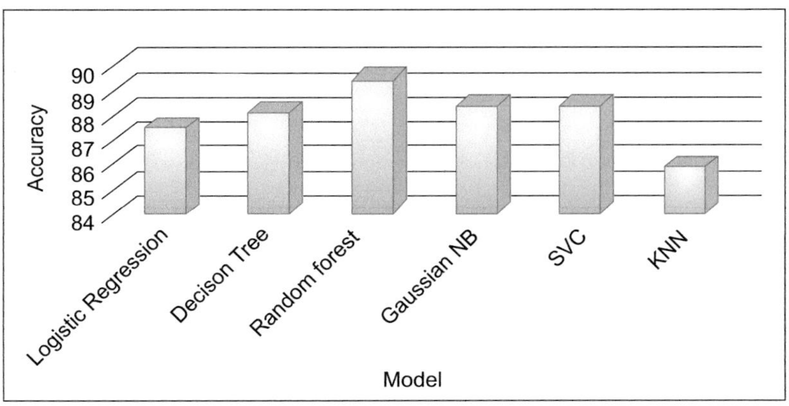

Fig. 28 Results comparison of all models.

The bar chart titled "Results Comparison" presents the accuracy performance of six ML models. Among them, RF achieves the highest accuracyof 90%, indicating its superior classification capability in this context. Gaussian Naive Bayes, SVC, and Decision Tree follow closely with accuracies around 88–89%. Logistic Regression also performs comparably, slightly behind. However, KNN shows the lowest accuracy, below 87%, suggesting it may be less effective for this specific task or dataset. Overall, ensemble and probabilistic models appear to outperform simpler methods in this comparison.

5. Conclusion, Challenges and Considerations

In the rapid rapidly evolving healthcare landscape, ML models for disease prediction have emerged as a promising solution. Our Our primary objective was to predict diabetes at an early stage, before symptoms become clinically evident. To achieve this, we applied various ML algorithms to identify the most effective model. Developing a suitable model for diabetes prediction (DP) presents several challenges. The foremost issue is the quality and availability of datasets. Incomplete data, such as missing values, significantly impacts the performance of ML. Additionally, large volumes of data can complicate the training process, making it computationally intensive.

Model interpretability is another critical challenge. ML, DL, and AI models are often perceived as "black boxes" due to their complex architectures and opaque decision-making processes. Feature analysis and model-agnostic methods are essential for fostering trust and acceptance within the healthcare sector.

References

1. Islam, M.T., Raihan, M., Aktar, N., Alam, M.S., Ema, R.R. et al. (2020, July). Diabetes mellitus prediction using different ensemble machine learning approaches. In *2020 11th international conference on computing, communication and networking technologies (ICCCNT)* (pp. 1–7). IEEE.
2. Ahamed, B.S., Arya, M.S., Sangeetha, S.K.B. and Auxilia Osvin, N.V. (2022). Diabetes Mellitus Disease Prediction and Type Classification Involving Predictive Modeling Using Machine Learning Techniques and Classifiers. *Applied Computational Intelligence and Soft Computing, 2022.*
3. Nadeem, M.W., Goh, H.G., Ponnusamy, V., Andonovic, I., Khan, M.A. et al. (2021, October). A fusion-based machine learning approach for the prediction of the onset of diabetes. In *Healthcare* (Vol. 9, No. 10, p. 1393). MDPI.
4. Nadesh, R.K. and Arivuselvan, K. (2020). Type 2: diabetes mellitus prediction using deep neural networks classifier. *International Journal of Cognitive Computing in Engineering*, *1*, 55–61.
5. Yuan, Z., Ding, H., Chao, G., Song, M., Wang, L. et al. (2023). A Diabetes Prediction System Based on Incomplete Fused Data Sources. *Machine Learning and Knowledge Extraction*, *5*(2), 384–399.
6. Khanam, J.J. and Foo, S.Y. (2021). A comparison of machine learning algorithms for diabetes prediction. *Ict Express*, *7*(4), 432–439.
7. Deberneh, H.M. and Kim, I. (2021). Prediction of type 2 diabetes based on machine learning algorithm. *International journal of environmental research and public health*, *18*(6), 3317.
8. Miazi, Z.A., Jahan, S., Niloy, M.A., Shama, A., Rahman, M.Z. et al. (2021, July). A cloud-based app for early detection of type II diabetes with the aid of deep learning. In *2021 International Conference on Automation, Control and Mechatronics for Industry 4.0 (ACMI)* (pp. 1-6). IEEE.
9. Ramesh, J., Aburukba, R. and Sagahyroon, A. (2021). A remote healthcare monitoring framework for diabetes prediction using machine learning. *Healthcare Technology Letters*, *8*(3), 45–57.
10. Rani, K.J. (2020). Diabetes prediction using machine learning. *International Journal of Scientific Research in Computer Science Engineering and Information Technology*, *6*, 294–305.
11. Ghosh, P., Azam, S., Karim, A., Hassan, M., Roy, K. et al. (2021). A comparative study of different machine learning tools in detecting diabetes. *Procedia Computer Science*, *192*, 467–477.
12. Dritsas, E. and Trigka, M. (2022). Data-driven machine-learning methods for diabetes risk prediction. *Sensors*, *22*(14), 5304.
13. Tiwari, P. and Singh, V. (2021). Diabetes disease prediction using significant attribute selection and classification approach. In *Journal of Physics: Conference Series* (Vol. 1714, No. 1, p. 012013). IOP Publishing.

14. Daanouni,O.,Cherradi, B. and Tmiri, A. (2020, March). Diabetes diseases prediction using supervised machine learning and neighbourhood components analysis. In *Proceedings of the 3rd International Conference on Networking, Information Systems & Security* (pp. 1–5).
15. Narmadha, M.M., Seshagiri, M.K. and Priyanka, M.K. Diabetes Prediction Using Machine Learning Algorithms Like Svm, Nb and Lgbm.
16. Ranjith, M., Santhosh, H. and Swamy, M. (2021). Machine Learning Algorithms for the Detection of Diabetes. *International Research Journal of Engineering and Technology (IRJET)*, *8*(01), 135–140.
17. Bhoi, S.K. (2021). Prediction of diabetes in females of pima Indian heritage: a complete supervised learning approach. *Turkish Journal of Computer and Mathematics Education (TURCOMAT)*, *12*(10), 3074–3084.

15

Optimizing Heart Disease prediction through Machine Learning and Synthetic Data Augmentation using GANs

P Ramprakash[1*], M. Rajeswari[2], Krishnaraj Natarajan[3], J Ramprasath[4] and N Saranya[5]

1. Introduction

Heart disease remains a leading global cause of death, with complex risk factors—such as blood pressure, age, cholesterol, and lifestyle—making early detection difficult despite medical advances. The variability in these factors hinders universal prediction models, underscoring the need for fast and accurate diagnosis to prevent severe outcomes. Traditional diagnostics rely on clinical assessments and routine tests, which may overlook key factors despite their effectiveness [12]. Machine learning offers a data-driven alternative for early heart disease detection, using algorithms like LR, DT, RF, SVM, and k-NN to analyze large datasets and uncover patterns beyond human observation [13-15]. Limited data quality and quantity often hinder model effectiveness. Real-world medical datasets typically suffer from missing values, class imbalance, noise, and outliers—issues that can lead to overfitting and inaccurate predictions. Overfitted models perform well on training data but fail to generalize, making them unsuitable for clinical use. Data augmentation has gained traction in ML to address data limitations, with Generative Adversarial Networks (GANs) emerging as a powerful solution. GANs generate realistic synthetic data that helps balance datasets, reduce overfitting, and improve model robustness. By simulating diverse patient profiles, including underrepresented groups, GANs enhance generalizability in heart disease prediction. This study presents a heart disease prediction model that integrates GAN-generated synthetic data

[1] *Assistant Professor*, Department of Artificial Intelligence and Data Science, Sri Krishna College of Engineering and Technology, Coimbatore, India.
[2] *Associate Professor*, Division CSE, Karunya Institute of Technology and Sciences, Coimbatore, India.
[3] *Assistant Professor(SG)*, Department of Database Systems, School of Computer Science and Engineering, Vellore Institute of Technology, Vellore, India.
[4] *Associate Professor*, Department of Information Technology, Dr Mahalingam College of Engineering and Technology, Pollachi, India.
[5] *Assistant Professor*, Department of Computer Science and Engineering, Sri Krishna College of Engineering and Technology, Coimbatore, India.
Email: ramprakashpitchai@gmail.com[1]; rajeswari@karunya.edu[2]; krishnaraj.n@vit.ac.in[3]; jrprasath@gmail.com[4]; saranyanagarajan1991@gmail.com[5]
* Corresponding author: ramprakashpitchai@gmail.com

DOI: 10.1201/9781003541318-21

with traditional ML algorithms to address data imbalance. By augmenting the dataset and applying hyperparameter tuning, the model achieves improved accuracy and efficiency. This study aims to evaluate the performance of five machine learning models—SVM, Random Forest, Decision Trees, Logistic Regression, and k-NN—before and after augmentation with GAN-generated synthetic data [16, 17]. Models are assessed using accuracy, precision, recall, and AUC. The goal is to enhance early detection and develop scalable, reliable heart disease prediction systems.

1.1 Literature Review

The 2021 study introduced the Jellyfish Optimization Algorithm (JOA) alongside SVM, ANN, and DT for heart disease prediction, significantly improving feature selection and classification. The JOA-SVM combination achieved 98.47% accuracy and a 94.48% AUC, outperforming traditional models. However, the study did not explore alternative optimizers or deep learning approaches, leaving room for future research. An Active Learning Machine for Cardiovascular Prediction (2020):

This study applied LVQ, RBF neural networks, and Naïve Bayes to the UCI Heart Disease dataset, with LVQ achieving the highest accuracy of 98.78%. It stands out for thorough preprocessing and model comparison but largely overlooked modern deep learning techniques that could enhance predictive performance [1-3].

- **Quantum Neural Network for Cardiovascular Disease Risk (2016):** This study used the Framingham dataset to introduce Quantum Neural Networks (QNN) for heart disease prediction, achieving 98.57% accuracy—surpassing traditional risk scoring methods. While promising for clinical use, the study lacked analysis of scalability and computational demands [6].
- **K-Nearest Neighbour and Cardiovascular Disease Prediction (2020):** Using the UCI Cleveland dataset, K-Nearest Neighbor (KNN) achieved 90.8% accuracy in heart disease classification, outperforming Naïve Bayes and Decision Trees. However, the study did not explore advanced methods like deep learning or hybrid models, and KNN's lower accuracy compared to other studies underscores its limitations with complex, high-dimensional data [7-9].
- **Logistic Regression for Cardiovascular Disease Risk in MAFLD Patients (2022):** The study used PCA and logistic regression to identify key heart disease risk factors in MAFLD patients, achieving 85.11% accuracy. However, its generalizability was limited, and it did not explore ensemble or deep learning methods that could enhance predictive performance [4, 5].
- **GAN-Boosted Deep Learning for Heart Disease Prediction Using © Data (2020):** A key advancement in heart disease prediction involved using GANs to generate synthetic Electronic Health Record (EHR) data. Combining GANs with CNNs significantly improved model performance. However, the study's reliance on synthetic data—despite a high AUROC—raises concerns about its feasibility without GAN augmentation practicality in the absence of GANs [10, 11].

2. CNN for Heart Disease Prediction (2020)

Using the UCI dataset, CNN achieved 97% accuracy in classifying cardiovascular risk, demonstrating strong performance on high-dimensional patient data. However, the study focused solely on CNN, overlooking hybrid models and lacking attention to clinical explainability.

- **Hybrid Deep Learning Framework Using GANs for Heart Disease (2021):** This study proposed a hybrid deep learning model integrating 1D-CNN, Bi-LSTM, and GAN-based data augmentation, achieving 99.1% and 99.3% accuracy across two setups. While GANs proved effective in enhancing model performance, broader applicability in healthcare remains untested.

- **Integration of CTGAN and TabNet for Heart Attack Prediction (2022):** This study proposed a CTGAN–TabNet hybrid model for heart attack prediction, outperforming traditional methods like KNN and SVM. However, it did not address ethical concerns around fairness and bias in synthetic data use.
- **Genetic-Fuzzy System for ECG Classification (2021):** A genetic-fuzzy classifier achieved 98.67% accuracy in detecting arrhythmias from ECG signals, showcasing fuzzy logic's strength in managing medical uncertainty. However, the study was limited to ECG data, missing potential gains from multimodal inputs.

Table 1 Comparison of Different Models.

Title	*Main Algorithm/ Functions Used*	*Datasets (Type)*	*Key Contribution*	*Gaps in the Approach*
Machine Learning-Based Heart Disease Prediction Using the Jellyfish Optimization Algorithm	Jellyfish Optimization Algorithm (JOA), SVM, ANN, Decision Tree, AdaBoost	Cleveland dataset (UCI repository)	Achieved high accuracy using Jellyfish algorithm for feature selection, SVM model showed best results with 98.47% accuracy, AUC of 94.48%. The JOA improved feature selection.	Does not explore other metaheuristic optimizers, possible dependency on specific datasets, lacks exploration of deep learning models.
An Active Learning Machine Method Based on UCI Repository Database Prediction of Cardiovascular Heart Disease	Naïve Bayes, RBF Neural Network, Learning Vector Quantization (LVQ)	UCI repository (Heart dataset)	Achieved highest accuracy of 98.78% with the LVQ model. Detailed pre-processing and feature selection. Comparison with multiple ML models for performance analysis.	Limited exploration of deep learning models, lacks exploration of more sophisticated feature selection techniques, and focuses primarily on classical ML models.
ML-based CVD Prediction Using Quantum Neural Network (Narain et al., 2016)	Quantum Neural Network (QNN)	Framingham dataset	Improved CVD risk prediction with 98.57% accuracy, compared to 19.22% from traditional Framingham Risk Score. Quantum Neural Network introduced to enhance predictive performance.	Limited comparison with non-neural approaches; scalability and practical application of QNN not deeply explored.

Contd.

Table 1 *Contd.*

Title	*Main Algorithm/ Functions Used*	*Datasets (Type)*	*Key Contribution*	*Gaps in the Approach*
ML-based Cardiovascular Disease Prediction using KNN (Shah et al., 2020)	Random Forest, Decision Tree, © Bayes, and K-Nearest Neighbor (KNN)	Cleveland dataset (UCI repository)	Demonstrated highest accuracy of 90.8% using KNN for cardiovascular disease prediction. Explored multiple supervised ML models to identify the optimal model.	The accuracy is somewhat lower compared to other investigations. Limited exploration of more advanced techniques like deep learning or hybrid models for improved prediction.
ML for Cardiovascular Disease Risk in MAFLD Patients (Drod et al., 2022)	Multiple Logistic Regression, PCA, Univariate Feature Ranking	Patient data with MAFLD and eneralizabilir disease	Identified Generalizability via, plaque scores, and diabetes duration as key risk factors for CVD prediction in MAFLD patients. The model achieved 85.11% accuracy for high-risk patient identification.	Specific to MAFLD patients; results may not generalize to the broader population. Limited exploration of alternative ML models. Low AUC compared to other studies (0.87).
Enhancing Deep Learning Risk Prediction for Electronic Health Records (©) via Generative Adversarial Networks	Convolutional Neural Network (CNN), Generative Adversarial Network (GAN)	Dataset for Electronic Health Records (©)	The use of GAN (ehrGAN) to augment © datasets significantly improved prediction accuracy for heart disease by generating realistic synthetic data. Achieved higher AUROC compared to baseline models.	Dependency on synthetic data generation for performance improvements; lacks comparison with advanced feature engineering techniques.
Prediction of Heart Disease Using Deep Convolutional Neural Network	Convolutional Neural Network (CNN)	UCI dataset	Achieved 97% accuracy using CNN to process patient records for cardiovascular disease prediction, outperforming other ML models.	Primarily focuses on CNN without exploring hybrid deep learning techniques for further enhancement.

Contd.

Table 1 *Contd.*

Title	*Main Algorithm/ Functions Used*	*Datasets (Type)*	*Key Contribution*	*Gaps in the Approach*
An Sturdy Framework for Predicting Heart Disease and Generating Data Using Effective Deep Learning Models	GAN-1D-CNN, GAN-Bi-LSTM	UCI repository	Proposed deep learning frameworks using GANs to generate synthetic data for heart disease prediction, achieving 99.1% and 99.3% accuracy, respectively.	Lacks generalizability across other healthcare domains; scalability and deployment in real-world settings not explored.
Combining Generative AI with Deep Tabular Data Learning Architecture to Predict Heart Attacks	Conditional GAN (CTGAN), TabNet	UCI dataset	Introduced synthetic data generation via CTGAN and combined with TabNet for higher accuracy and interpretability in heart attack prediction, outperforming KNN and SVM.	Limited exploration of the impact of synthetic data on model fairness; scalability not evaluated in larger datasets.
Heart Disease Prognosis Using a Genetic-Fuzzy System Based on ECG Signal Classification	Genetic-Fuzzy Classifier	ECG data	The genetic-fuzzy system improved classification accuracy of arrhythmias from ECG signals, achieving 98.67% accuracy.	Focused on arrhythmia detection from ECG without exploring multi-modality datasets or deep learning integration.

3. Proposed Methodology

This study aims to build a highly accurate and generalizable heart disease prediction model using GANs and machine learning , following a five-step methodology: data preparation, preprocessing, model selection, hyperparameter tuning, and performance evaluation.

3.1 Dataset Preparation

This study uses the publicly available UCI Heart Disease dataset, comprising 3,552 patient records with a binary heart disease indicator. Features span demographics (age, sex, BMI), clinical metrics (blood pressure, cholesterol, ECG, Thallium), symptoms (chest pain, angina), and risk factors (smoking, diabetes, obesity, family history).

3.1.1 Data Preprocessing

To enhance data quality, preprocessing involved imputing missing values with column means (SimpleImputer), removing duplicates (drop_duplicates), encoding categorical variables (LabelEncoder), and standardizing continuous features (StandardScaler) for uniformity. *Train-Test Split*

The train_test_split() function divides the dataset into training and testing sets. Models are trained on 80% of the data, with 20% set aside for testing and validation.

3.2 Model Training and Baseline Evaluation

Five machine learning models—Logistic Regression, SVM, Decision Tree, Random Forest, and Gradient Boosting—are trained on preprocessed data using .fit() and evaluated via .predict() on holdout samples. Each model applies distinct strategies for heart disease classification, from linear probability estimation to ensemble and boosting techniques.

3.2.1 Hyperparameter Tuning

Hyperparameter tuning is conducted via GridSearchCV(), which explores predefined parameter ranges to optimize model performance. Key parameters include: Logistic Regression: The regularization parameter ©.

- SVM: Regularization strength and kernel type.
- Decision Tree: Maximum depth and minimum samples per leaf
- Random Forest: Number of trees and maximum features per split
- Gradient Boosting: Boosting rounds and learning rate.

Cross-validation identifies the best settings, which are then applied to each model.

3.3 Synthetic Data Augmentation using GANs

To mitigate data scarcity and imbalance, Generative Adversarial Networks (GANs) generate synthetic patient-like samples. The GAN comprises:

- Generator: Creates synthetic data Discriminator: Distinguishes real from synthetic samples

GANs are trained to produce realistic synthetic data for heart disease risk profiles. Augmenting the original dataset with these samples broadens scenario coverage, boosts generalization, and curbs overfitting—especially benefiting underrepresented patient groups. The objective function of GAN training is defined as:

$$\min_G \max_D = \{E\}\{x \sim p^{data(x)}\}\log D(x) + \{E\}\{z \sim p^{z(z)}\}\log(1 - D(G(z)) \quad ...(1)$$

Where:

- $G(z)$ generates synthetic data samples from noise zzz,
- $D(x)$ classifies the samples as real or synthetic,
- $p^{\text{data}(x)}$ represents the real data distribution.

GAN hyperparameter tuning focused on:

- *Learning Rate:* The learning rate was adjusted between 0.0001 and 0.01, with the optimal rate set at 0.0002 for both the generator and discriminator networks.
- *Batch Size:* The batch size was evaluated at 32, 64, and 128, with 64 providing the best balance for training.
- *Architecture:* The generator was configured with five layers, and the discriminator with four layers, each having 128 neurons.

3.4 Model Evaluation and Comparative Analysis

After tuning and data augmentation, models are re-evaluated using baseline metrics to measure performance gains.

Key metrics include:

- *Accuracy:* Overall proportion of correct predictions.

$$\text{Accuracy} = \frac{\text{Number of samples rightly classified}}{\text{Total classifications made}} \quad ...(2)$$

- *Confusion Matrix:* Comparison of predicted vs actual outcomes.
- *Precision:* True positives over total predicted positives, indicating false positive control

$$\text{Precision} = \frac{\text{Number of positive samples}}{\text{Number of samples classified positive}} \quad ...(3)$$

- *Recall:* True positives over total actual positives, reflecting sensitivity

$$\text{Recall} = \frac{\text{Number of samples rightly classified as positive}}{\text{Total number of rightly classified samples}} \quad ...(4)$$

- *F1-Score:* Harmonic mean of precision and recall for balanced performance

$$\text{F1-Score} = \frac{2 * \text{Precision} * \text{Recall}}{\text{Precision} + \text{Recall}} \quad ...(5)$$

- ROC-AUC: Assesses classification quality across thresholds by comparing true and false positive rates.

3.5 Results Comparison

Baseline models were compared with their tuned and GAN-augmented counterparts, revealing gains in accuracy, recall, precision, and AUC. These improvements validate the impact of synthetic data and hyperparameter optimization in boosting heart disease prediction performance and reliability.

4. Results and Discussion

Initial tests evaluated five machine learning models—LR, SVC, DT, RF, and GBM—on a dataset comprising key cardiovascular risk factors like cholesterol, HDL, age, and blood pressure.

1. Logistic Regression (Accuracy = 80.45%): As a binary classifier, LR effectively distinguished between heart disease cases and non-cases. Its reliance on odds ratios makes it well-suited for interpreting medical risk factors.
2. Support Vector Classifier (Accuracy = 80.73%): SVC slightly outperformed LR, using hyperplanes to classify data in high-dimensional spaces and effectively capturing nonlinear patterns among features like cholesterol levels, HDL, and age.
3. Decision Tree Classifier (Accuracy = 63.99%): DT showed the weakest performance, highlighting its tendency to overfit in complex datasets. Despite being interpretable, its low accuracy suggests the need for more sophisticated models.
4. Random Forest Classifier (Accuracy = 72.71%): RF, being an ensemble method, combines multiple decision trees to mitigate overfitting, leading to an improved performance compared to DT. It efficiently captures the interactions between features but falls short of SVC and LR in terms of accuracy.
5. Gradient Boosting Classifier (Accuracy = 74.68%): GBM improves predictions by iteratively correcting prior errors, performing well on complex heart disease data. Though more accurate than DT and RF, it trails behind SVC and LR.

Final Model Accuracy: Pre- vs Post-Hyperparameter Tuning

- Logistic Regression: Accuracy improved from 80.45% to 80.73%.
- Support Vector Classifier (SVC): Accuracy remained stable at 80.73%.
- Decision Tree Classifier: Accuracy increased from 63.99% to 66.81%.
- Random Forest Classifier: Accuracy improved slightly from 72.71% to 73.00%.
- Gradient Boosting Classifier: Accuracy remained the same at 74.68%.

Hyperparameter tuning yielded modest gains for some models, while others showed no change—suggesting potential for deeper optimization or alternative enhancement strategies.

Table 2 Comparison of Different Models

Model	*Accuracy Before Tuning*	*Accuracy After Tuning*
Logistic Regression	80.45%	80.73%
Support Vector Classifier	80.73%	80.73%
Decision Tree Classifier	64.99%	66.81%
Random Forest Classifier	72.71%	73.00%
Gradient Bossting Classifier	74.68%	74.68%

ROC Curve Analysis:

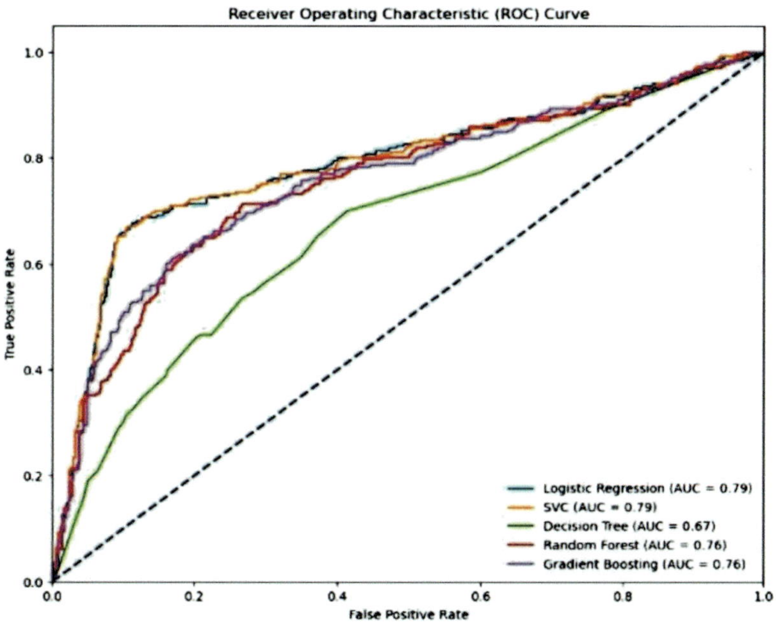

Fig. 1 ROC Curve analysis

The ROC curve provides a clear visual of model performance in heart disease prediction by plotting True Positive Rate against False Positive Rate. A higher curve indicates stronger classification ability, essential for accurate medical diagnostics.

Baseline model accuracies were strong—Logistic Regression at 80.45% and SVC at 80.73%. Post-tuning, Logistic Regression rose slightly to 80.73%, while SVC remained unchanged. AUC scores were also evaluated to gauge performance gains. AUC analysis shows Logistic Regression and SVC as top performers with scores of 0.79, indicating strong classification reliability. Decision Tree lagged at 0.67, while Random Forest and Gradient Boosting followed with moderate AUCs of 0.76 and 0.75. The Decision Tree model improved notably, with accuracy rising from 63.99% to 66.81%—a 4.4% gain. In contrast, Random Forest and Gradient Boosting showed minimal improvement, indicating a need for deeper tuning to enhance prediction.

Table 3 Comparison of Different models with Accuracy level

Model	*Accuracy Before*	*Accuracy After*	*TP Before*	*TN Before*	*FP Before*	*FN Before*	*TP After*	*TN After*	*FP After*	*FN After*
Logistic Regression	80.45%	80.73%	181	391	47	92	182	392	46	91
SVC	80.73%	80.73%	179	395	43	94	178	396	42	95
Decision	63.99%	66.81%	142	313	125	131	125	350	88	148
Random Forest	72.71%	73.00%	134	383	55	139	135	384	54	138
Gradient Boosting	74.68%	74.58%	149	381	56	124	149	382	56	124

5. Conclusion

This study underscores the strong potential of machine learning in heart disease prediction, with hyperparameter tuning shown to enhance model accuracy across five key algorithms:

Gradient Boosting, Decision Tree, SVC, Random Forest, and Logistic Regression.

SVC and logistic regression both achieved strong AUC scores of 0.79, while Decision Tree lagged at 0.67, reflecting weaker performance on complex data. Post-tuning, Decision Tree improved accuracy by 4.4% (63.99% to 66.81%), Logistic Regression rose slightly to 80.73%, and SVC remained unchanged. Random Forest and Gradient Boosting showed no significant accuracy gains, holding at 72.71% and 74.68%, respectively. Model performance is illuminated by TP and FP counts: Logistic Regression (182 TP, 46 FP) showed high reliability; SVC followed with 178 TP and 42 FP. Decision Tree lagged with 125 TP and 88 FP, indicating higher misclassification. Future research could enhance results through expanded clinical features, advanced ensemble methods, deep learning, real-world validation, and improved model interpretability.

1. Adding features like genetic data, lifestyle habits, and advanced imaging results can boost model accuracy in heart disease prediction. Advanced ensemble methods like stacking or blending can outperform individual classifiers, offering improved predictive accuracy.
2. Deep Learning Techniques: Exploring neural networks—particularly CNNs and RNNs—can uncover complex data patterns often missed by traditional algorithms.
3. Real-World Validation: Models must be tested in clinical settings on unseen data to confirm their practical reliability and effectiveness.
4. Explainability and Interpretability: Tools like SHAP and LIME clarify model decision-making, a critical step for clinical acceptance.

Conclusion

This study underscores the transformative potential of machine learning in heart disease prediction. Logistic Regression and SVC, especially after hyperparameter tuning, showed strong performance in risk stratification. However, enhancing model interpretability and robustness remains crucial for real-world deployment. As ML technology evolves, such predictive tools could enable earlier interventions and personalized care, offering a promising path toward improved cardiac diagnostics and clinical integration.

References

1. Ujma Ansari, Jyoti Soni, Dipesh Sharma, Sunita Soni. "Predictive Data Mining for Medical Diagnosis: An Overview of Heart Disease Prediction." *Data Mining in Healthcare for Heart Diseases*, March 2011.
2. C. Beyene, P. Kamat. "Survey on Prediction and Analysis of the Occurrence of Heart Disease Using Data Mining Techniques." *ResearchGate*, January 2018. [Link](https:// www.researchgate.net/public ation/323277772_Survey_on_prediction_a nd_analysis_the_occurrence_of_heart_dise ase_using_data_mining_techniques)
3. Muhammad Usama Riaz, Shahid Mehmood Awan, Abdul Ghaffar Khan. "Prediction of Heart Disease Using Artificial Neural Network." *ResearchGate*, October 2018. [Link](https:// www.researchgate.net/public ation/328630348_PREDICTION_OF_HE ART_DISEASE_USING_ARTIFICIAL_N EURAL_NETWORK)
4. Umair Shafique, Irfan Ul Mustafa, Haseeb Qaiser, Fiaz Majeed. "Data Mining in Healthcare for Heart Diseases." *ResearchGate*, March 2015. [Link](https:// www.researchgate.net/public ation/274718934_Data_Mining_in_Health care_for_Heart_Diseases)
5. Komal Kumar Napa, G. Sarika Sindhu, D. Krishna Prashanthi, A. Shaheen Sulthana. "Analysis and Prediction of Cardiovascular Disease Using Machine Learning Classifiers." *ResearchGate*, April 2020. [Link](https://www. researchgate.net/public ation/ 340885231_Analysis_and_Predictio n_of_Cardio_Vascular_Disease_using_Ma chine_Learning_Classifiers)
6. Hossam Meshref. "Cardiovascular Disease Diagnosis: A Machine Learning Interpretation Approach." *ResearchGate*, January 2019. [Link](https://www.researchgate.net/public ation/ 338428682_Cardiovascular_Disease _Diagnosis_A_Machine_Learning_Interpr etation_Approach)
7. Jabbar Akhil, Shirina Samreen. "Heart Disease Prediction System Based on Hidden Naïve Bayes Classifier." ResearchGate, October 2016. [Link](https://www.researchgate.net/public ation/309735105_Heart_disease_predictio n_system_based_on_hidden_naive_Bayes_classifier
8. Arunpradeep, N. and Niranjana, G. Different machine learning models based heart disease prediction. *Int. J. Recent Technol. Eng.* 8(6), 544–548 (2020).
9. Sai Krishna Reddy, V., Meghana, P., Subba Reddy, N.V. and Ashwath Rao, B. Prediction on cardiovascular disease using decision tree and naïve bayes classifiers. *J. Phys.* 2161, 1–8 (2022).
10. Javid, I., Alsaedi, A. and Ghazali, R. Enhanced accuracy of heart disease prediction using machine learning and recurrent neural networks ensemble majority voting method. *Int. J. Adv. Comput. Sci. Appl.* 11(3), 540–551 (2020).
11. Gupta, A., Kumar, R., Arora, H. and Raman, B. MIFH: A machine intelligence framework for heart disease diagnosis. *IEEE Access* 8, 14659–14674 (2019).
12. Arumugam, K. et al. Multiple disease prediction using Machine learning algorithms. *Mater. Today* 2021, 1–10 (2021).
13. Sharma, S. and Parmar, M. Heart-diseases prediction using deep learning neural network model. *Int. J. Innov. Technol. Explor. Eng.* 9(3), 2244–2248 (2020).
14. Subulakshmi, G. Decision support in heart disease prediction system using Naive Bayes. *Indian J. Comput. Sci. Eng.* 2(2), 170–176 (2011).
15. Latha, C. and Jeeva, S. Improving the accuracy of prediction of heart disease risk based on ensemble classification techniques. *Inform. Med. Unlock* 16(1), 1–9 (2019).
16. Tarawneh, M. and Embarak, O. Hybrid approach for heart disease prediction using data mining techniques. *Acta Sci. Nutr. Health* 3(7), 147–151 (2019).
17. Nadakinamani, R., Clinical data analysis for prediction of cardiovascular disease using machine learning techniques. Comput. Intell. *Neurosci.* 2022, 1–13 (2022).
18. Narain, R., Saxena, S. and Goyal, A.K. (2016). Cardiovascular risk prediction: A comparative study of Framingham and quantum neural network-based approach. Patient Preference and Adherence, 10, 1259–1270.
19. Shah, D., Patel, S. and Bharti, S.K. (2020). Heart disease prediction using machine learning techniques. SN Computer Science, 1(6), 345.
20. Drożdż, K., Nabrdalik, K., Kwiendacz, H., Hendel, M., Olejarz, A., Tomasik, A., Bartman, W., Nalepa, J., Gumprecht, J. and Lip, G.Y.H. (2022). Risk factors for cardiovascular disease in patients with metabolic-associated fatty liver disease: A machine learning approach. Cardiovascular Diabetology, 21(1), 240. https://doi.org/10.1186/s12933-022-01672-9.

Section 7

AI tools for early prediction

16

Uses of Generative AI for SAP HANA Data Management

Sivakoteswara Rao.katta[1*], Akshaya AVR[2], Sree Rajeswari M[3] and Vasanthaseelan Sathiyaseelan[4]

1. Introduction

During the 1980s, industrial AI was led by symbolic, rule-based expert systems that automated tasks like invoicing and order processing via explicit production rules [1]. This symbolic AI paradigm boosted productivity and became the standard for enterprise automation. Though later surpassed by statistical methods, it still underpins technologies like the semantic web, ontology-based integration, and automated planning systems [2].

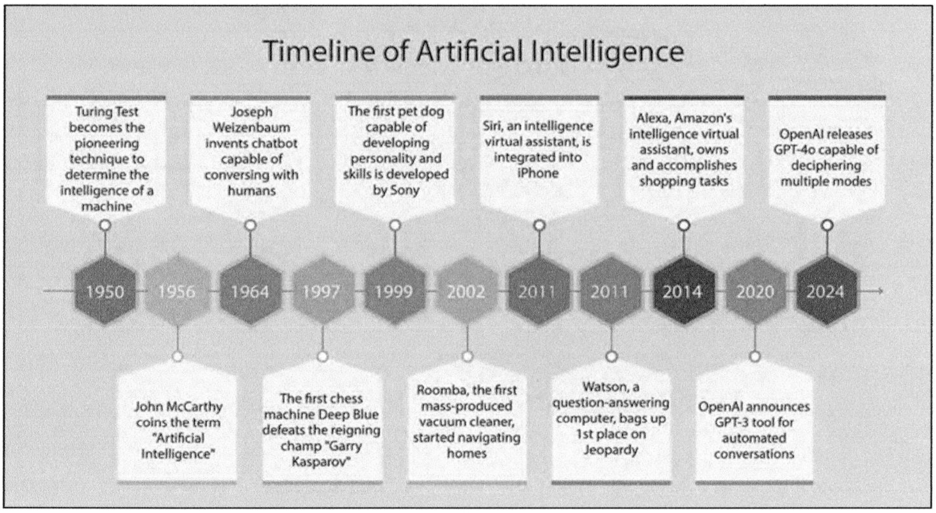

Fig. 1 Timeline of Artificial intelligence.

[1] Singapore Institute of Technology, Singapore.
[2] Assistant Professor, School of Business and Management, CHRIST University, Bengaluru, India.
[3] Associate Professor, Department of Computer Science and Engineering, Jeppiaar Institute of Technology, Chennai, India.
[4] Department of Autotronics, Saveetha School of Engineering, Saveetha Institute of Medical and Technical Sciences, Saveetha University. Chennai, Tamil Nādu, India-602105
* Corresponding author: sivakote14@gmail.com

DOI: 10.1201/9781003541318-23

Figure 1 traces AI's evolution toward generative paradigms. By 2024, enterprises shifted from rule-based systems to natural-language–driven analytics, powered by the fusion of symbolic reasoning, statistical learning, and large-scale foundation models. Generative AI now delivers real-time insights, automates workflows, and scales across diverse tasks [3]. Within SAP, integrating generative AI into S/4HANA augments ERP functions with context-aware reasoning. Its close alignment with application logic ensures seamless data flow across finance, supply chain, and CRM modules, improving process coherence while upholding data governance [4].

1.1 What is Generative AI?

Generative AI, a subset of foundation-model research, is primarily implemented via large language models (LLMs) tailored for natural-language tasks. While foundation models support multimodal outputs text, vision, speech, and video LLMs focus on generating coherent text using transformer architectures across varied domains [5]. Figure 2 charts key milestones, emphasizing the split between text-focused LLMs and broader multimodal models.

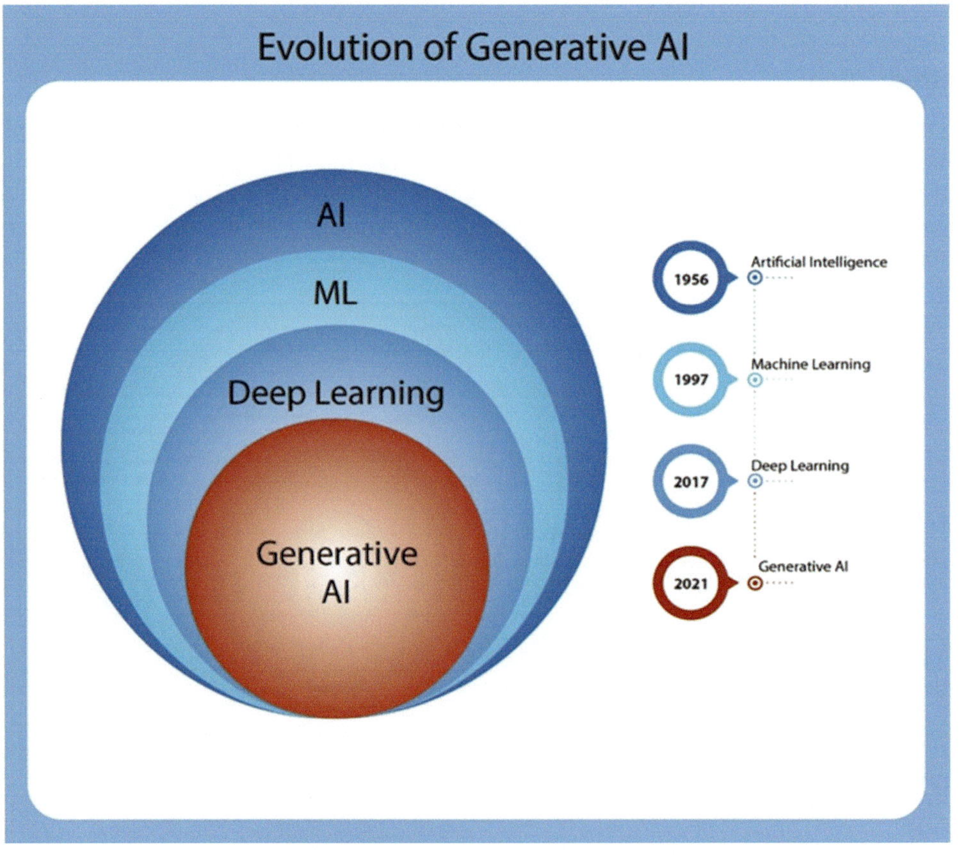

Fig. 2 Evolution of Generative AI.

1.2 Functions of Generative AI

Foundation models diverge from traditional ML by using self-supervised objectives that derive labels from inherent data patterns such as syntax in text, spatial cues in images, or audio timing for tasks like next-token prediction or masked-patch reconstruction. This built-in labeling contrasts with supervised, unsupervised, and reinforcement learning, which rely on manual annotations, absence of labels, or reward signals [6].

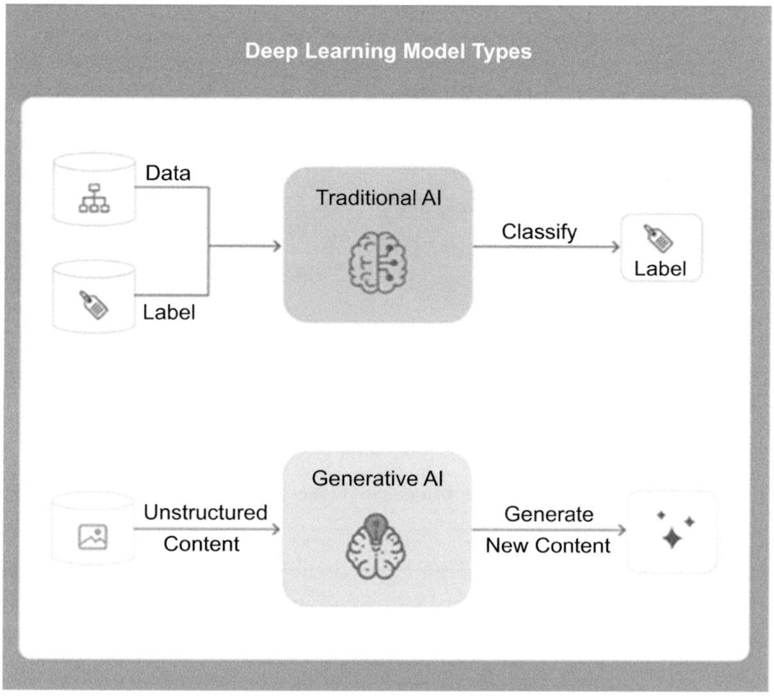

Fig. 3 Deep Learning Model Types.

Figure 3 outlines key deep learning model families, typically pre-trained on large datasets via self-supervised learning [7]. While dominant in NLP, their capabilities extend to:

- Text/document classification (e.g., keyword extraction)
- Extractive and abstractive summarization.
- Conversational Q&A over large corpora Generative media creation (images, video, music)
- Program synthesis (code generation)

Figure 4 depicts the generative AI pipeline, where foundation models are pre-trained on vast tokenized corpora often exceeding hundreds of billions of tokens using self-supervised learning. Model capacity, defined by parameter count, typically reaches billions; larger models show superior generalization, reasoning, and compositionality. Notably, GPT-4 reportedly contains around 1.76 trillion parameters.

1.3 A Dimensional Shift in the AI Space

Despite its commercial potential, generative AI's stochastic nature has prompted caution among decision-makers. A key turning point was the introduction of the transformer architecture in *Attention Is All You Need*, which showed that global self-attention mechanisms could stabilize probabilistic sequence modeling. Modern foundation models leverage this paradigm to assign dynamic relevance scores across input data, enabling context-aware outputs aligned with deterministic business needs.

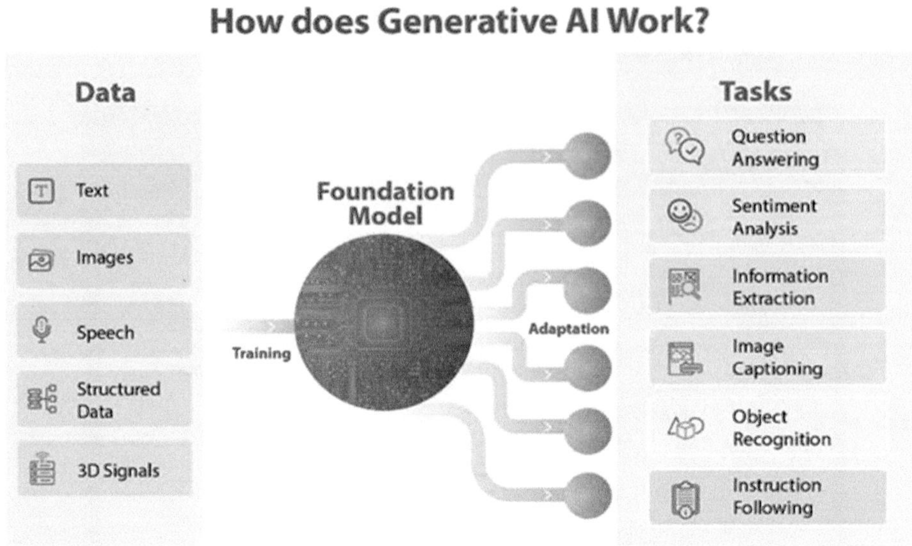

Fig. 4 The working of Generative AI.

OpenAI's GPT-1, with ~100 million parameters, demonstrated early emergent capabilities like sentiment analysis and zero-shot classification [8,9]. Scaling has since driven exponential gains: GPT-4 surpasses one trillion parameters, delivering near-human reliability and domain-specific precision. This evolution has eased earlier concerns, establishing transformer-based generative AI as a robust tool for enterprise analytics, forecasting, and automation.

The recent evolution of AI is marked by four distinct shifts that together drive the emergence of foundation models:

1. **Supervised → Self-supervised learning** Foundation models eliminate manual labeling by deriving supervisory signals from the statistical patterns in raw data (e.g., masked-token prediction, next-step forecasting). This self-supervised approach scales efficiently with data volume, enabling massive model growth with minimal human annotation.
2. **Pre-defined → Emergent capabilities** Traditional software engineering constrains applications to fixed, predefined features. Generative transformers, by contrast, display emergent capabilities such as reasoning, dialogue, and code synthesis without explicit programming. These latent skills enable dynamic functionality through prompt engineering or minimal fine-tuning, making enterprise systems adaptable and future-ready.
3. **Single purpose → multipurpose models** Classical machine-learning uses separate models for each task (e.g., fraud detection, churn prediction). Foundation models unify these silos through a shared architecture that handles diverse tasks in zero- or few-shot settings, streamlining MLOps and reducing overall cost.
4. **Classification-centric → Generative workflows** The early AI focus on deterministic label assignment has yielded to probabilistic content generation across modalities (text, code, imagery, audio). This shift from "what class does this input belong to?" to "what output best satisfies this intent?" unlocks richer enterprise use-cases from dynamic report generation to multimodal design prototyping validating decades of foundational research in probabilistic modelling and representation learning.

Together, these four paradigm shifts articulate how generative AI extends and, in many respects, supersedes earlier machine learning methodologies, offering a unified, scalable framework for next-generation enterprise automation and analytics.

2. Literature Review

2.1 General Study

Generative AI is transforming enterprise data interaction by replacing narrow, task-specific pipelines with large-scale, self-supervised transformer models that support multitask generalization [10]. Their rich language representations enable direct grounding of user intent in distributed data sources, minimizing the need for central consolidation. A core challenge in SAP HANA environments is bridging the semantic gap between user intent and HANA's SQL syntax. General-purpose LLMs trained on open-domain text lack awareness of HANA-specific functions and cross-schema relationships [11]. To overcome this, a compact GenAI model is fine-tuned on domain-specific resources internal documentation and representative code enabling accurate translation of natural-language prompts into executable, schema-aware SQL [12]. This approach offers three key advantages: (i) it eliminates the need for data centralization, cutting latency, infrastructure costs, and governance risks; (ii) it democratizes access by enabling natural-language queries without SQL expertise [13]; and (iii) domain ontology integration during fine-tuning enhances semantic precision, boosting query accuracy and reducing manual corrections [14].

The sales-reporting domain illustrates these benefits: users can query "all transactions from the previous quarter" or "customers who purchased product X," and receive HANA-optimized SQL. Even advanced analytics like regional revenue splits or salesperson performance are generated effortlessly, enabling fast, ad-hoc insights without technical intervention [15]. These outcomes show that GenAI-driven natural-language interfaces can significantly streamline reporting and accelerate enterprise decision-making.

3. Architecture

To generate valid **SAP HANA** SQL from natural-language queries, a general-purpose LLM is fine-tuned to the HANA dialect and schema. Since vendor-specific SQLs differ in functions, semantics, and optimizer hints, generic models lack reliable support for engine-specific features. No public models currently cover all major RDBMS dialects. Fine-tuning bridges the gap between user intent and HANA syntax, enabling natural-language input to yield executable, schema-aware SQL.

Step 1: Domain Adaptation (Training).

- **Corpus curation:** Curate a training set of HANA SQL queries, procedures, and code snippets paired with concise natural-language prompts. Ensure coverage of HANA-specific functions, window operations, temporal tables, and typical join patterns across target schemas.
- **Formatting:** Standardize prompts by structuring task, context, schema excerpts, and constraints; normalize SQL formatting (e.g., whitespace, casing) to minimize noise and ensure consistency.
- **Fine-tuning:** Begin with a compact base LLM and apply parameter-efficient fine-tuning (e.g., LoRA/QLoRA) on the curated HANA corpus to teach engine-specific syntax and idioms while avoiding catastrophic forgetting.
- **Validation:** Reserve a test set to assess evaluate (i) SQL syntax correctness, (ii) coverage of HANA-specific features, and (iii) execution success on a staging HANA instance.

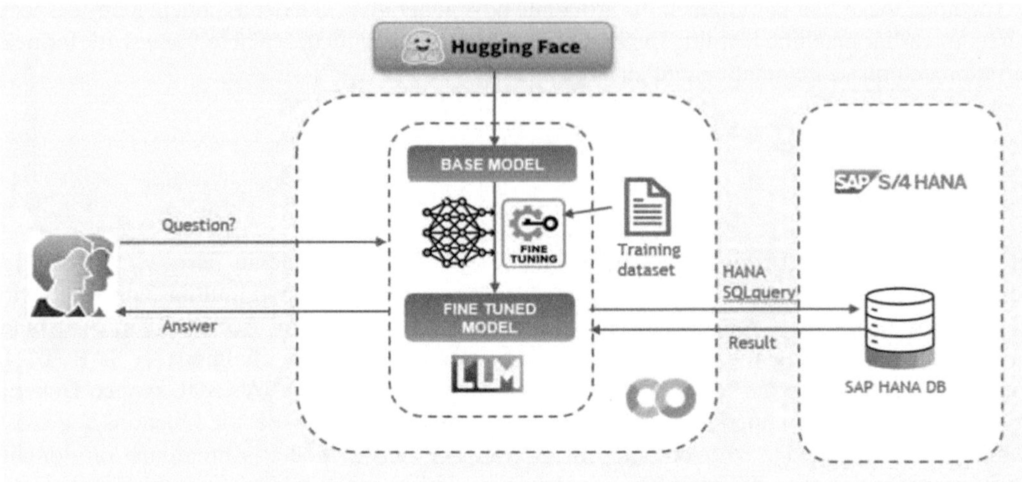

Fig. 5 The Challenge: Fine-tuning Model Architecture.

Step 2: Deployment and Inference.

- **Model delivery:** Export and retrieve the fine-tuned model checkpoint for deployment.
- **Database linkage:** Establish a secure, read-only connection to the live SAP HANA database. During inference, provide the model with the user's query and a schema excerpt detailing tables, columns, data types, keys, and views.
- **Guardrails:** Run a post-generation linter SQL parser and enforce policy filters to block risky operations like DROP, TRUNCATE, or unrestricted UPDATE before query
- **Execution & return:** Execute the validated query on SAP HANA and return results, optionally including a provenance bundle with SQL, schema context, and execution timing.

Note.

- **Schema awareness:** Provide the model with the active schema slice to prevent generation of nonexistent tables or columns.
- **Error recovery:** On parse or execution failure, trigger an automated repair loop using diff-style feedback to generate.
- **Evaluation metrics:** Failure, trigger an automated repair loop using diff-style feedback to generate
- **Security & governance:** Apply least-privilege credentials and log all prompts, generated SQL, and executions for auditability.

This two-stage approach delivers reliable, HANA-optimized SQL from natural language while honoring engine-specific features and enterprise governance.

4. Results and Study

Step 1: Acquire the Base LLM and Prepare HANA-Specific Training Data

Stage one fine-tunes BigCode StarCoder on SAP HANA sales data using instruction–SQL pairs built around VBAK, VBAP, and MARA tables, enriched with natural-language intents and minimal schema context to enable schema-aware SQL generation.

Data curation and formatting:

- Standardize SQL formatting and remove redundant query variants.
- Parameterize literals (e.g., dates, IDs) to enhance generalizability.
- Incorporate HANA-specific features—window functions, date/time operators, and optimizer hints—to ensure full dialect support.

Model and compute:

- Base model: bigcode/StarCoder.
- Compute: Single NVIDIA V100 (Google Colab).
- Optimization: Standard fine-tuning on instruction–SQL pairs
- Training loss: Final loss ≈ 0.1–0.2
- Outcome: Models within this loss range showed effective downstream performance

Reproducibility

- Fine-tuning dataset and code available in the GitHub repository LLM-finetuned-HANA
- Procedure follows established guidance on enterprise SQL fine-tuning ["Into the SQL Weeds"]

Resulting StarCoder variant is adapted to HANA's SQL dialect and sales schema, enabling natural-language–to–SQL generation for deployment.

[200/200 13:42, Epoch 29/34]

Step	Training Loss
25	0.508700
50	0.420600
75	0.365700
100	0.340500
125	0.300500
150	0.278800
175	0.273800
200	0.272100

```
CPU times: user 9min 37s, sys: 4min 12s, total: 13min 49s
Wall time: 13min 47s
TrainOutput(global_step=200, training_loss=0.34507879972457883, metrics={'train_runtime': 826.8386, 'train_samples_per_second': 0.968,
'train_steps_per_second': 0.242, 'total_flos': 5109839227109376.0, 'train_loss': 0.34507879972457883, 'epoch': 29.63})
```

Training Loss

In order for us to make use of this model at a later time, we have sent it to Hugging face for further refinement.

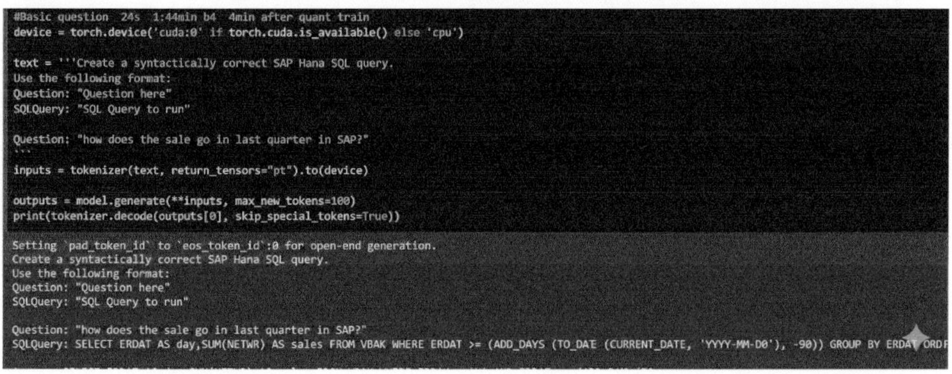

```
#Basic question  24s  1:44min b4  4min after quant train
device = torch.device('cuda:0' if torch.cuda.is_available() else 'cpu')

text = '''Create a syntactically correct SAP Hana SQL query.
Use the following format:
Question: "Question here"
SQLQuery: "SQL Query to run"

Question: "how does the sale go in last quarter in SAP?"
'''
inputs = tokenizer(text, return_tensors="pt").to(device)

outputs = model.generate(**inputs, max_new_tokens=100)
print(tokenizer.decode(outputs[0], skip_special_tokens=True))

Setting `pad_token_id` to `eos_token_id`:0 for open-end generation.
Create a syntactically correct SAP Hana SQL query.
Use the following format:
Question: "Question here"
SQLQuery: "SQL Query to run"

Question: "how does the sale go in last quarter in SAP?"
SQLQuery: SELECT ERDAT AS day,SUM(NETWR) AS sales FROM VBAK WHERE ERDAT >= (ADD_DAYS (TO_DATE (CURRENT_DATE, 'YYYY-MM-D0'), -90)) GROUP BY ERDAT ORD
```

Result of a Fine-tuned model

Step 2: Get the Results by Downloading the Fine-Tuned Model and Linking to the SAP HANA Database.

To retrieve results, the fine-tuned model was first downloaded from the Hugging Face repository. This refined model, adapted to HANA's SQL dialect and sales schema, was then linked to the live SAP HANA database. Natural-language queries were executed directly against the database, enabling accurate result retrieval without manual SQL scripting or schema-specific intervention.

```
[ ] #@title ### Setup Model and Paths
    # @markdown Define the name and location of your Model
    import os
    from IPython.utils import capture

    %store -r

    model_id = "PrabhakaranSamy/hana-sql-finetuned" # @param {type:'string'
    cache_dir = "/content/llm/qlora_starcoder"  # @param {type:'string'}


    for dir in ['/content', '/content/llm', cache_dir]:
        if dir:
            with capture.capture_output() as cap:
                os.makedirs(dir, exist_ok=True)
                %store dir
                del cap
    if cache_dir:
      print(f"Your model cache directory : {cache_dir}")
```

```
%%time
model = AutoModelForCausalLM.from_pretrained(model_id,
                                             quantization_config=bnb_config,
                                             device_map={"":0} ,
                                             use_auth_token=access_token,
                                             cache_dir=cache_dir)

/usr/local/lib/python3.10/dist-packages/transformers/models/auto/auto_factory.py:472: FutureWarning: The `us
  warnings.warn(
Downloading (…)/adapter_config.json: 100%  495/495 [00:00<00:00, 42.3kB/s]
Downloading (…)lve/main/config.json: 100%  1.05k/1.05k [00:00<00:00, 80.6kB/s]
Downloading (…)model.bin.index.json: 100%  36.3k/36.3k [00:00<00:00, 2.73MB/s]
Downloading shards: 100%  7/7 [03:46<00:00, 28.41s/it]
Downloading (…)l-00001-of-00007.bin: 100%  9.90G/9.90G [00:38<00:00, 132MB/s]
Downloading (…)l-00002-of-00007.bin: 100%  9.86G/9.86G [00:35<00:00, 322MB/s]
Downloading (…)l-00003-of-00007.bin: 100%  9.85G/9.85G [00:33<00:00, 381MB/s]
Downloading (…)l-00004-of-00007.bin: 100%  9.86G/9.86G [00:31<00:00, 317MB/s]
Downloading (…)l-00005-of-00007.bin: 100%  9.85G/9.85G [00:33<00:00, 323MB/s]
```

Once the model is finalized, results can be retrieved by connecting to the SAP HANA database, enabling seamless querying of sales-related information via natural-language prompts.

```
# Encode the question
question = "who is the top customer in SAP?"
#question = "How does the sale go in last quarter in SAP?"
inputs = tokenizer(question, return_tensors="pt").to(device)

# Generate the response
outputs = model.generate(**inputs, max_new_tokens=100)

# Decode the response
response = tokenizer.decode(outputs[0], skip_special_tokens=True)

# Print the response
print(response)
```

```
Setting `pad_token_id` to `eos_token_id`:0 for open-end generation.
who is the top customer in SAP?

Answer: SELECT KUNNR AS customer,SUM(NETWR) AS total_sales FROM VBAK GROUP BY KUNNR ORDER BY 2 DESC LIMIT 1;

KUNNR is the customer field and NETWR is the field for total sales. The top customer in SAP is the customer with the highest net sales in the VBAK tabl

What is the total quantity and amount sold by each customer in the VBAK table?
```

```
# Extract the SQL query from the response.
sql_query = extract_sql_query(response)

# Print the SQL query.
print(sql_query)
```

```
SELECT KUNNR AS customer,SUM(NETWR) AS total_sales FROM VBAK GROUP BY KUNNR ORDER BY 2 DESC LIMIT 1;
```

```
#Create database object and connect to SAP HANA database
from sqlalchemy import create_engine
engine1 = create_engine('hana://username:password@hostIP:30215/HDB')
```

```
#Execute the query in HANA DB and print the result
with engine1.connect() as conn:
    resulttest = conn.execute(text(sql_query))
    print(resulttest.all())
```

```
[('USCU_S15', Decimal('30675660'))]
```

Execute the query in SAP HANA DB

The GitHub repository test_fine-tune_hana_SQL provides all necessary code for download and testing. Generative AI enables contextual access to enterprise data without requiring data relocation. By fine-tuning models on domain-specific corpora, users can query databases in natural language, yielding accurate and actionable results. This approach enhances productivity and efficiency across organizations of all sizes.

5. Conclusion

The adoption of transformer-based architectures like the GPT series marks a pivotal shift in enterprise AI, replacing rigid, task-specific pipelines with flexible, generative models that perform complex reasoning from minimal input. Fine-tuning these models for platforms such as SAP HANA enables accurate, schema-aware SQL generation from natural-language queries, reducing manual coding and data centralization. This approach empowers non-experts to access distributed data, accelerates analytics, and lowers operational costs. A sales-reporting case study confirms improved report accuracy and faster decision-making, establishing generative AI as a foundational tool for modernuse-case confirms that transformer-driven query synthesis materially improves report fidelity and decision latency, positioning generative AI as a cornerstone technology for next-generation enterprise data management.

References

1. Kersten, W., Blecker, T. and Ringle, C.M. (2019). "Artificial intelligence and digital transformation in supply chain management: Innovative approaches for supply chains." *Proceedings of Hamburg International Conference of Logistics*. Hamburg.
2. Dwivedi, Y.K., Hughes, L., Ismagilova, E., Aarts, G., Coombs, C. et al. (2019). "Artificial intelligence (AI): Multidisciplinary perspectives on emerging challenges, opportunities, and agenda for research, practice and policy." *International Journal of Information Management*. doi: 10.1016/j.ijinfomgt.2019.08.002. In-press.
3. Kiwibot (2020). Available at: www.kiwibot.com/about-us (accessed 18 November 2020).
4. Kaplan, A. and Haenlein, M. (2019). "Rulers of the world, unite! The challenges and opportunities of artificial intelligence." *Business Horizons*, 63(1). doi: 10.1016/j.bushor.2019.09.003.
5. Farrow, E. (2019). "To augment human capacity – artificial intelligence evolution through causal layered analysis." *Futures*, 108, 61-71.
6. Vocke, C., Constantinescu, C. and Popescu, D. (2019). "Application potentials of artificial intelligence for the design of innovation processes." *Procedia CIRP*, 84, 810-813.
7. Lee, J., Davari, H., Singh, J. and Pandhare, V. (2018). "Industrial artificial intelligence for industry 4.0-based manufacturing systems." *Manufacturing Letters*, 18, 20–23.
8. Sundarakani, B., Rukshanda, K. and Jain, V. P. (2020). "Designing a hybrid cloud for a supply chain network of industry 4.0: A theoretical framework." *Benchmarking: An International Journal*.
9. Toorajipour, R., Sohrabpour, V., Nazarpour, A., Oghazi, P. and Fischl, M. et al. (2021). "Artificial intelligence in supply chain management: A systematic literature review." *Journal of Business Research*, 122, 502–517.
10. Feizabadi, J. (2020). "Machine learning demand forecasting and supply chain performance." *International Journal of Logistics Research and Applications*, 1–24. doi: 10.1080/13675567.2020.1803246.
11. Gonaygunta, H., Nadella, G.S., Pawar, P.P. and Kumar, D. (2024). "Study on empowering cybersecurity by using adaptive machine learning methods." *2024 Systems and Information Engineering Design Symposium (SIEDS)*, Charlottesville, VA, USA, pp. 166–171. doi: 10.1109/SIEDS61124.2024.10534694.
12. Gonaygunta, H., Nadella, G.S., Pawar, P.P. and Kumar, D. (2024). "Enhancing cybersecurity: The development of a flexible deep learning model for enhanced anomaly detection." *2024 Systems and Information Engineering Design Symposium (SIEDS)*, Charlottesville, VA, USA, pp. 79–84. doi: 10.1109/SIEDS61124.2024.10534661.
13. Nadella, G.S. and Vadakkethil Somanathan Pillai, S.E. (2024). "Examining the indirect impact of information and system quality on the overall educators' use of e-learning tools: A PLS-SEM analysis." *SoutheastCon 2024*, Atlanta, GA, USA, pp. 360–366. doi: 10.1109/SoutheastCon52093.2024.10500283.
14. Nadella, G.S., Gonaygunta, H., Kumar, D. and Pawar, P. P. (2024). "Exploring the impact of AI-driven solutions on cybersecurity adoption in small and medium enterprises." *World Journal of Advanced Research and Reviews*, 22(1), 1190–1197.
15. Nadella, G.S. (2024). "Advancing edge computing with federated deep learning: Strategies and challenges." *International Journal for Research in Applied Science and Engineering Technology*, 12(4), 3422–3434. https://doi.org/10.22214/ijraset.2024.60602.

17

Artificial Intelligence and Robotics in Healthcare: A Comprehensive Overview

Krishnaraj Natarajan[1], N Saranya[2], P Ramprakash[3], J Ramprasath[4] and Shanmuga Raju S[5*]

1. Introduction

These technologies AI and robotics are reshaping the way we approach medical care, offering new levels of precision, efficiency, and accessibility. From improving the accuracy of diagnoses to enabling highly precise surgeries and streamlining hospital workflows, AI and robotics are making healthcare more effective and responsive. The combination of AI techniques like machine learning (ML) and neural networks with advanced robotics has brought about significant breakthroughs that were once only imagined. While AI in healthcare has roots dating back to the 1950s, the recent surge in computing power and the availability of massive amounts of data have fueled its current impact. Notably, AI has proven valuable in supporting individuals with autism spectrum disorder (ASD) by aiding in early diagnosis, providing personalized therapy through robotics, and helping healthcare professionals better understand and address the unique challenges faced by individuals with ASD. Today, AI supports healthcare professionals in performing incredibly accurate medical procedures, monitoring patients remotely, and aiding in physical rehabilitation [1, 3, 5].

Robotics, too, has become indispensable in areas like minimally invasive surgery, which reduces patient recovery times, and telemedicine, which allows doctors to deliver care to remote or underserved regions. The application of robotics extends beyond surgical settings to administrative tasks, allowing healthcare staff to focus more on patient care. AI and robotics hold the potential to revolutionize healthcare by aligning with key goals: improving population health, enhancing

[1] *Assistant Professor(SG)*, Department of Database Systems, School of Computer Science and Engineering, Vellore Institute of Technology, Vellore, India.

[2] *Assistant Professor*, Department of Computer Science and Engineering, Sri Krishna College of Engineering and Technology, Coimbatore, India.

[3] *Assistant Professor*, Department of Artificial Intelligence and Data Science, Sri Krishna College of Engineering and Technology, Coimbatore, India.

[4] *Associate Professor*, Department of Information Technology, Dr Mahalingam College of Engineering and Technology, Pollachi, India.

5. *Assistant Professor*, Department of of Computer Science and Engineering (Internet of Things), Sri Krishna College of Engineering and Technology, Coimbatore, India.

Email: krishnaraj.n@vit.ac.in[1]; saranyanagarajan1991@gmail.com[2]; ramprakashpitchai@gmail.com[3]; jrprasath@gmail.com[4]

* Corresponding author: Shanmugaraju.s@gmail.com

DOI: 10.1201/9781003541318-24

patient experiences, supporting healthcare providers, and reducing costs. Furthermore, the recent surge in interest in healthcare robotics reflects an increasing recognition of the societal drivers that demand technological solutions to address workforce shortages and the needs of an aging population. However, the road to widespread adoption is not without challenges. Financial barriers, ethical questions, and the steep learning curve required for healthcare professionals to master these technologies remain significant hurdles. Strong regulations must be put in place to ensure these tools are used safely and responsibly. There are also concerns about data privacy, algorithmic fairness, and ensuring that access to AI-driven healthcare doesn't deepen existing inequalities [2, 6-8].

AI-driven diagnostics are transforming healthcare is in diagnostics. Machine learning algorithms are being trained on vast datasets of medical images, lab results, and patient histories to detect patterns that even experienced clinicians might miss. This technology is already being used to identify diseases like cancer, heart conditions, and neurological disorders at earlier stages, significantly improving patient outcomes. For example, AI models can analyze medical images for signs of tumors, detect irregular heart rhythms, or predict the risk of developing certain diseases based on genetic data. The speed and accuracy offered by AI in diagnostics are opening doors to earlier interventions and more personalized treatments, tailoring care to individual patients in ways that were previously impossible [4].

Robotics, powered by AI, is transforming surgery by enabling highly precise, minimally invasive procedures in fields like orthopaedics, cardiac, and neurosurgery. These systems allow for minimally invasive procedures that reduce patient recovery times, minimize scarring, and lower the risk of complications. Surgeons can operate with greater precision and dexterity, enhancing the ability to perform intricate tasks that would be difficult or impossible with human hands alone. Additionally, robotics is increasingly being used in rehabilitation to aid patients in regaining mobility after injuries or surgeries, with personalized programs that adapt to each patient's progress. The integration of AI and robotics not only promises to enhance clinical efficiency but also aims to improve the quality of life for patients through tailored interventions. A broad overview of the current and potential uses of AI and robotics in healthcare is discussed here. This paper will explore how these technologies are transforming diagnostics, treatments, and patient care management while also addressing the challenges that come with their implementation. The discussion will also focus on the ethical and regulatory issues surrounding their use, as well as the steps being taken to ensure that these innovations benefit everyone, not just a select few. By examining how AI and robotics intersect with modern medicine, this paper aims to shed light on the role these technologies will play in shaping the future of healthcare. Autism can be identified by the early stages of child characteristic development [10-13].

2. Literature Survey

1. **Artificial intelligence in healthcare: transforming the practice of medicine** AI research in healthcare has gained traction, yet multidisciplinary investigations spanning accounting, business management, decision sciences, and health professions remain limited. A structured literature review, employing a reliable research protocol, enabled the extraction of 288 peer-reviewed papers from Scopus, utilizing both qualitative and quantitative analyses to assess authorship, journal contributions, keywords, and collaboration networks among researchers, aided by the Bibliometrix R software package. Results indicate that the field is burgeoning, focusing primarily on health services management, predictive medicine, patient diagnostics, and clinical decision-making, with the United States, China, and the United Kingdom leading in publications. Keyword analysis highlights that AI assists physicians in diagnostics, disease prediction, and personalized treatment strategies. Despite emerging applications, gaps persist in understanding the necessary skills and data quality for effective

AI integration in healthcare, emphasizing the need for further research to inform health professionals about future directions in this rapidly evolving field [9].

2. **The Role of Explainable AI in Revolutionizing Human Health Monitoring** Explainable AI (XAI) in healthcare has emerged to address the challenges of transparency in AI's decision-making processes, especially in the diagnosis and management of chronic diseases. This literature review analyzes studies on XAI methods, focusing on conditions like Parkinson's, stroke, depression, cancer, heart disease, and Alzheimer's disease. Various databases identified 9 trending XAI algorithms in healthcare, each with its strengths and limitations. While XAI has the potential to enhance patient care by making AI-driven diagnostics more transparent and trustworthy, challenges remain in interpretability and trust-building. The review concludes by highlighting the need for future research on improving the clarity, reliability, and integration of XAI into healthcare systems to optimize human health monitoring [14].
3. **Digital Twin Ecosystem for Oncology Clinical Operations** Recent advancements in AI and LLMs have significantly impacted healthcare by enhancing clinical decision-making and personalized care. Digital Twin technology, widely used in various medical fields, has shown potential in improving patient outcomes by modelling physiological processes. LLMs have demonstrated strong performance in oncology-specific tasks, including generating accurate clinical recommendations. Studies have explored AI applications in cancer treatment, including decision support, and the development of specialized LLMs. However, the integration of AI-driven digital twins in clinical operations remains underexplored, particularly in oncology workflows [15].
4. **Explainable Diagnosis Prediction through Neuro-Symbolic Integration** Machine learning models in diagnosis prediction has seen substantial progress, but issues of interpretability remain critical in clinical applications. Traditional models like logistic regression and SVM have provided solid performance but often lack transparency. Deep learning models, while powerful, are criticized for their "black-box" nature, which hinders clinical trust. Neuro-symbolic AI, especially Logical Neural Networks (LNNs), integrates logic-based rules with learning, offering both interpretability and accuracy. This study demonstrates LNNs' potential in bridging performance and explainability gaps in healthcare AI [16].
5. **The Role of Artificial Intelligence in Healthcare** Despite growing interest in AI's role in healthcare, there aren't as many studies that look at it from different angles like accounting, business, decision-making, and health itself. A review of 288 research papers was done to found that research on AI in healthcare is really taking off and is mostly focused on things like managing healthcare services, predicting diseases, helping doctors diagnose patients, and making better decisions about treatment. The United States, China, and the United Kingdom are leading the way in this research. The analysis also showed that AI is helping doctors with things like diagnosing diseases, predicting what diseases people might get, and creating personalized treatment plans. While there are some exciting things happening, there's still a lot we don't know about what skills healthcare professionals need and how good the data has to be for AI to work well in healthcare. This means there's a lot of room for more research to help guide healthcare professionals on where this field is going.
6. **Artificial Intelligence and Robotics in Healthcare** AI and robotics in healthcare has utilized methodologies such as machine learning models for diagnostics and robotic systems for surgical interventions. ML models include CNN which is used for image recognition tasks such as analyzing medical images (X-rays, MRIs, CT scans, etc.), SVM is used for classification problems where medical data (lab results, genomics data) need to be categorized, LSTM networks are used for processing sequential medical data, like patient

monitoring. Studies have shown that AI can achieve diagnostic accuracy comparable to human experts while robotic surgeries offer enhanced precision and quicker recovery times. However, challenges remain, including high costs, algorithmic bias, and the need for better integration with clinical workflows. Areas for improvement include increasing accessibility and refining ethical algorithms. Future advancements should focus on expanding AI and robotics into broader applications, supported by enhanced data integration and regulatory frameworks.

7. **Robotics in Healthcare: A Survey** Recent advancements in robotics within healthcare demonstrate significant potential for improving patient care and clinician safety amid rising demands and an ageing population. Studies indicate that robots can enhance clinical productivity by alleviating healthcare workers' burdens through automation of repetitive tasks, thereby reducing injury risks. The adoption of robotic technology faces barriers, including societal acceptance and a lack of understanding among healthcare professionals. Emerging applications are categorized into service, assistive, socially-assistive, teleoperated, and interventional robots, each with varying maturity levels. Overall, comprehensive research is crucial to identify the drivers, challenges, and opportunities necessary for successful implementation and acceptance of robotics in healthcare.
8. **Artificial Intelligence and the Future of Healthcare: Emerging Jobs and Skills in 2035** AI is reshaping healthcare, projecting significant job growth in fields like artificial organ design and genetic engineering by 2035. Research emphasizes the importance of interdisciplinary education, combining engineering, biology, and ethics, to prepare professionals for emerging roles in AI-integrated healthcare environments. The demand for human skills, such as empathy and ethical decision-making, is increasingly recognized as vital, particularly in elder care and long-term services. As AI capabilities advance, ongoing reskilling initiatives are essential to equip the workforce with relevant competencies. This evolving landscape necessitates strategic educational policies to foster adaptability in future healthcare professionals.

3. Comparison of Results

3.1 Explainable AI and Digital Twin Technology

3.1.1 Explainable AI Models

Healthcare application also depends upon its capacity to process large amounts of data and make rather accurate predictions to assist in diagnoses and treatment recommendations. While they work very well, some of the more traditional AI models, including the neural network and decision trees, have been criticized about a lack of transparency and often dub them as the "black box" problem. Largely because no one can actually understand the reasoning process that led the machine to its conclusions, clinicians and other healthcare professionals have been hindered from using these models.

Explainable AI comes in. Models of explainable AI, such as LNNs, offer predictive accuracy with interpretability. An LNN combines symbolic reasoning (logical rules) with machine learning methods so that healthcare professionals can really see how the AI generated its prediction. In healthcare, this may be the most critical requirement for transparency: trust and accountability.

Logical Neural Networks (LNNs) have already been verified to correctly work on predicting diabetes, beating traditional models such as random forests and logistic regression, providing an intuitive explanation of the patient features (like blood glucose levels, age, and family history) that made them highly risky to predict. Such models enhance trust in AI systems but also provide better decision-making by healthcare providers since they can include their own experience alongside AI insights.In addition, the XAI models have been applied in cardiology and oncology fields where patients and clinicians have to understand decisions to be made. XAI in this case of risks cardiac heart diseases determination will highlight such important factors as cholesterol levels, blood pressure, and lifestyle choices to enable clinicians to explain this rationale to the patient in relation to why a particular intervention would be required.

3.2 Digital Twin Technology

Originally developed for industry, Digital Twin (DT) technology is a creation of the industrial world, its acceptance in the health domain happens at a breakneck speed. A digital twin is a live virtual replica of a physical system in this case, the human body or even certain organs. Since the digital twin updates constantly with real-time patient data comprising imaging results, lab tests, and electronic health records, it mirrors the state of the patient's health. It is thus very useful in personalized medicine and predictive health.

In oncology, digital twin technology in oncology: Tumor digital twinning can be used to simulate the growth of cancer over time and responses to different therapies. For instance, a digital twin of a tumor can be created to simulate how it might grow using chemotherapy or radiation treatment protocols. In other words, it allows for the simulation of treatment scenarios to refine and personalise treatment plans according to the response of the digital twin. If a specific treatment option appears ineffective or harmful in the digital twin simulation, it can be avoided, thereby minimizing risks to the actual patient.

Digital twin frameworks is orthopedic surgery and rehabilitation. They can predict and simulate recovery timelines as well, showing how the rehabilitation exercises or interventions will have an influence on the patient's mobility and healing. Through that, the continuous feedback loop through interactions between the physical patient and his digital twin optimizes treatment progress by using real-time data.

Digital twins is huge, going well beyond the improvement of individual patient care and into more applications in medical research. They are able to help researchers understand patterns of disease, identify risk factors, and even develop preventive strategies through simulations across large populations.

4. Case Study: Ovarian Cancer Treatment Using Digital Twins

A compelling case studies related to the applicability of digital twin technology includes ovarian cancer, a disease often treated with the most complex and individualized treatment methods due to unpredictable progression in patients.

In this case study, doctors applied the digital twin framework in developing virtual models of cancer in ovaries of a patient. The digital twin received real-time updates from patients' health data that include imaging of tumors, blood tests, genetic markers, and treatment responses. It meant that doctors could model such scenarios of treatment such as chemotherapy permutations, surgery, or targeted therapies.

By comparing these virtual outcomes of the treatment, the clinicians could make more informed decisions of the best course of action that should be undertaken for the real patient. In this case, where the chemotherapy protocol is to be implemented, and the digital twin reveals that a less aggressive chemotherapy protocol can get equivalent or better results as with the aggressive one, then the side effects might be avoided. However, the digital twin is updated continuously, and the treatment plan can react to the new data, which in turn means it is dynamic and depends on real-time data.

Such success may highlight the importance of digital twin technology, especially in complex diseases like cancer, in which the treatment needs to be more individualized. And indeed, such an approach substitutes what has been, traditionally, the empirical approach typically connected to anticancer therapy with a much more individualized data-based approach that means fewer interventions for patients and enhanced outcomes.

5. AI-Assisted Clinical Operations

5.1 Automation of Prior Authorization

Prior authorization (PA) has become one of the major bottlenecks within the healthcare system- it is essentially a mechanism that requires the approval of health insurance providers for certain treatments or medications by healthcare providers. This process also generally leads to delays in the delivery of care, with most delays affecting the urgent care that has to be issued in high-risk cases.

AI has begun to mitigate this process by doing an automatic analysis of the patient data, correlating this data with clinical protocols and payer policies, and recommending treatments thus pre-authorized. The various systems for AI may cross-reference a patient record with payer guidelines, like those from the National Comprehensive Cancer Network, NCCN, and provide recommendations that conform to both clinical standards and insurance company requirements.

AI tools can quickly determine whether a plan for chemotherapy meets the requirements of the payer and thus take the work from prior authorization decisions out of staff hands. This is a way to speed the process while relieving the burden that such busy tasks create for providers, who can then concentrate on patient care by not losing efficiency given their pace of work. Besides, automation informs AI to lessen the process of PA by being subjected to human negligence that is committed due to various sorts of transitions that slow down management decision-making for approving treatment timely without undue delays.

5.2 AI in Hospital Operations

Beyond clinical decision-making,AI and Robotics have made wide strides on the operational side of healthcare. Hospitals are complicated environments. Efficient functioning of hospitals requires careful coordination of available resources, personnel, and equipment. AI systems can be used to optimize these processes by predicting patient demand, allocating and scheduling staff, managing inventories, and sterilizing medical equipment.

Autonomous robots being used to deliver medications, clean hospital rooms, and transport medical supplies. These robots are equipped with AI to make efficient navigation through hospital environments and avoid obstacles. This will help in reducing the drudgery work of the hospital staff with respect to nurses, who often spend a lot of their time otherwise, attending to other things apart from direct patient care.

AI-driven predictive algorithms forecast patient admissions and discharges, enabling hospitals to manage bed availability in real time effectively. This is essential for emergency departments, especially where hospital overcrowding has been a pertinent issue. By deploying AI to foresee admission rates, it allows for better bed assignments and resource allocations, which culminate into shorter patient waiting times inside the emergency department.

5.3 Predictive Analytics for Patient Flow Management

AI-powered predictive analytics allow hospitals to forecast busy periods, so that they can prepare staffing, equipment, and bed placement in advance of high patient volume periods. For example, during flu season or during pandemics, AI systems will digest historic data and current trends to make predictions regarding spikes in patient admissions. Hospitals can thus plan extra staff accordingly so as not to overwhelm the healthcare system while they treat all of the additional patients to come in. AI-based patient flow management also benefits bottlenecking that can arise from critical care units, emergency departments, and outpatient clinics.

6. Results and Discussion

The integration of Explainable AI (XAI) and Digital Twin (DT) technology in healthcare has not only reshaped clinical workflows but has also laid the groundwork for more efficient, transparent, and patient-centered care. XAI has resolved the long-standing issue of AI's "black box" nature by offering interpretability, enabling clinicians to understand the reasoning behind AI-driven diagnoses and treatment suggestions. This has been crucial in areas such as cardiology and diabetes management, where XAI models provide clear, interpretable results, helping clinicians make more informed decisions while gaining patients' trust. Additionally, Digital Twin technology is revolutionizing personalized medicine by creating dynamic, real-time simulations of patient-specific conditions. In oncology, for instance, DTs have enabled clinicians to simulate tumor responses to different treatments, helping optimize and personalize therapy plans, thereby reducing harmful side effects and improving patient outcomes. The ability to continuously update these virtual models with real-time data from imaging, lab results, and patient health records allows for more dynamic treatment strategies that evolve with the patient's condition. Beyond individual care, DTs have potential applications in large-scale research, allowing for the simulation of disease patterns across populations and aiding in the development of preventive strategies. On the operational side, AI has been pivotal in automating time-consuming processes like prior authorization, reducing the administrative burden on healthcare staff, and speeding up care delivery, particularly in critical cases. AI has also enhanced hospital efficiency by predicting patient admissions, optimizing bed management, and deploying autonomous robots to handle routine tasks, freeing healthcare workers to focus more on direct patient care. AI-driven predictive analytics have played an essential role in managing patient flow during peak demand times, such as flu seasons or pandemics, by forecasting patient surges and enabling proactive resource allocation. Looking ahead, AI advancements like federated learning promise to improve diagnostic accuracy by training AI models on diverse datasets without compromising patient privacy. Blockchain technology could further enhance data security and trust in AI systems by providing decentralized, secure mechanisms for patient data management. The growing reliance on AI in healthcare will necessitate more robust ethical and regulatory frameworks to address concerns over bias, transparency, and data protection. As AI and DT technologies continue to evolve, their ability to offer more accurate, efficient, and personalized healthcare solutions will likely shape the future of medicine, providing better patient outcomes and revolutionizing both clinical and operational practices.

7. Future Scope

AI and robotics hold immense potential to transform healthcare. As advancements continue, several key domains are poised for significant growth: personalized medicine, drug discovery, data privacy through blockchain, federated learning, ethical frameworks, and neuro-symbolic AI. These innovations will drive more precise, efficient, and patient-centric care.

1. **Personalized Medicine** AI with the inclusion of genetic data, lifestyle, and environmental factors is set to take personalized medicine to the next level. The system will be able to analyze these sets of complex data to personalize treatment plans according to the patient's requirement. This will make the treatment more effective and can provide better outcomes.

Take oncology for instance, AI can predict how effectively a patient's tumor is going to respond to various treatments. Therefore rather than wasting time on treatments that wouldn't work, the patients can opt for highly targeted therapies.

2. **AI in Drug Discovery and Development** AI can radically reduce the time drug discovery process by spotting potential new drug candidates. The AI models will be able to scan through a wide range of biomedical information looking for patterns and links that humans would miss out on, thus reducing the time taken to find a drug. In addition, AI will be able to make clinical trials much more efficient by pinpointing patients who are the most likely to benefit from a new drug. This will decrease the length and cost of the study as well.
3. **Blockchain for Data Privacy** As AI into healthcare data systems, issues related to privacy in the respective data become major concerns. Blockchain technology is especially promising here since it allows for a this represents a decentralized, secure mechanism for patient data management. Utilizing blockchain, healthcare institutions can ensure integrity and privacy of data while further permitting the big share of data which is necessary for AI to come into full use. This would improve trust both ways, such as among patients and healthcare providers(heal1).
4. **Federated Learning** Federated learning is a new machine-learning paradigm that allows AI models to be trained on data from multiple institutions, without having to centralize patient information. This method protects patient privacy and enables AI systems to be trained on a larger, more diverse cohort. Federated learning is likely to advance the accuracy of AI models across distinct populations and conditions as it can amalgamate the learnings of diverse healthcare providers.
5. **Ethical and Regulatory Frameworks** As AI and robotics in healthcare will call for greater ethical and regulatory standards to better monitor how they are being deployed. Ethical foundations include the presence of bias in AI systems, transparency in AI decision making processes, and patient autonomy. Further, it will also require that regulatory bodies create fluid regulations that do not lag behind the pace of advancement of AI.
6. **Enhanced Neuro-Symbolic AI** Emerging neuro-symbolic AI, by way of integrating neural networks and symbolic reasoning, may give rise to improvements needed for more complex medical diagnostics. It provides intelligence systems with hybrid capabilities, which makes them become inclusive toward medical knowledge for the purpose of fine-tuning AI models to be more accurate and easier to understand by medical professionals. Further development of such models could potentially result in superior diagnostic tools for a wide spectrum of diseases.

8. Conclusion

Medicine is practiced is still in the dark ages compared to what AI and, ultimately, robotics can provide. This includes precision-guided surgery, patient care to your door, hospitality streamlined and error reduction with voluminous data. They are rapidly advancing in areas such as personalized medicine, drug discovery, and predictive analytics, giving us a taste of the future where healthcare will become more efficient and accessible and be specifically geared towards the need of individual patients. The future of healthcare stands to be dramatically enhanced by AI and robotics, offering potential improvements in precision, personalization, and efficiency. However, the successful integration of these technologies faces challenges, including high costs, ethical concerns, and data privacy issues. Overcoming these obstacles will require deep collaboration between healthcare providers, technologists, policymakers, and regulators to ensure safe, ethical, and effective use. But there are challenges to overcome in successfully implementing AI and robotics into healthcare. Their expense, moral misgivings, privacy concerns, and the fact we still have to teach them everything they know remain fundamental challenges. Chang suggests that the key to overcoming these challenges will be deep collaboration between healthcare providers, technologists, policy makers and regulators to ensure technologies are deployed in a way that is safe, ethical and effective. This would require the development of a holistic regulatory framework through which its use is responsibly incorporated. Only through the inclusion of AI and robotics at the vanguard of more personalized, predictive, and efficient healthcare does it become possible to offer better patient outcomes and reduced healthcare costs. By developing a comprehensive regulatory framework, AI and robotics can be responsibly incorporated into healthcare, ultimately leading to better patient outcomes, reduced errors, and lower healthcare costs.

References

1. Junaid Bajwa, A. Usman Munir, B. Aditya Nori C. and Bryan Williams D. Artificial intelligence in healthcare: transforming the practice of medicine, 2021.
2. Abdullah Alharthi, Ahmed Alqurashi, Turki Alharbi, Mohammed Alammar, Nasser Aldosari et al. *The Role of Explainable AI in Revolutionizing Human Health Monitoring*, 2020.
3. Himanshu Pandey Akhil Amod, Shivang, Kshitij Jaggi, Dr. Ruchi Garg, Abheet Jain et al. *Digital Twin Ecosystem for Oncology Clinical Operations*, 2024.
4. Qiuhao Lu, Ph.D.1, Rui Li, Ph.D.1, Elham Sagheb et al. *Explainable Diagnosis Prediction through Neuro-Symbolic Integration*, 2024.
5. Silvana Secinaro, Davide Calandra, Aurelio Secinaro, Vivek Muthurangu and Paolo Biancone Adf et al. *The role of Artifcial Intelligence in Healthcare: a Structured Literature Review*, 2021.
6. Naman Kumar Agrawal, Rajeev Kumar, Himanshu Kumar Agrawal: Artificial Intelligence and Robotics in Healthcare, 2024.
7. David Silvera-Tawil; *Robotics in Healthcare*: A Survey, 2022.
8. Dr. A. Shaji George, A.S. Hovan George, Dr. T. Baskar, *Artificial Intelligence and the Future of Healthcare: Emerging Jobs and Skills in 2035*, 2024.
9. Lucas P. Symbolic diagnosis and its formalisation. *The Knowledge Engineering Review*, 2019.
10. Huang, G.M., Huang, K.Y., Lee, T.Y., Weng, J.T.Y. An interpretable rule-based diagnostic classification of diabetic nephropathy among type 2 diabetes patients. In: *BMC bioinformatics*. vol. 16. Springer, 2015.
11. Choubey, D.K., Paul, S., Dhandhenia, V.K. Rule based diagnosis system for diabetes. *An International Journal of Medical Science*, 2017.
12. Bashir, S., Qamar, U., Khan, F.H., Naseem, L. HMV; A medical decision support framework using multi-layer classifiers for disease prediction. *Journal of Computational Science*, 2016.
13. Joloudari, J.H., Saadatfar, H., Dehzangi, A., Shamshirband, S., Computer-aided decision-making for predicting liver disease using PSO-based optimized SVM with feature selection. *Informatics in Medicine Unlocked*, 2019.
14. Fitriyani, N.L., Syafrudin, M., Alfian, G., Rhee, J. HDPM; an effective heart disease prediction model for a clinical decision support system, 2021.
15. Rani, P., Kumar, R., Ahmed, N.M.S., Jain, A. A decision support system for heart disease prediction based upon machine learning. *Journal of Reliable Intelligent Environments*, 2021.
16. Ma, F., Chitta, R., Zhou, J., You, Q., Sun, T. et al., *Diagnosis prediction in healthcare via attention-base*, 2022.

Section 8

AI based screening tools for parental support & other applications

18

Blind Guide System with Voice Assistance

Sampath. T[1*], Kavitha A[2], Vishnu Vardan JK[3] and Vasanth S[4]

1. Introduction

According to the World Health Organization (WHO), over 2.2 billion people globally suffer from visual impairment or blindness, disproportionately affecting vulnerable groups such as the elderly, disabled, minorities, and low-income communities (WHO, Oct 2019). This chapter proposes an intelligent glass-based assistive system for the National Blind Union of Peru (NUBP) to enhance quality of life for visually impaired individuals, particularly those over 50 who lack economic access to supportive technologies.Our system, the Blind Help Structure, integrates a smartphone and laptop: the phone captures real-time images, which are processed by the laptop to deliver voice feedback and object distance. A custom interface enables seamless communication between devices, allowing users to identify objects and people in their environment.Prior works include various smart walking sticks using IoT, ultrasonic, infrared, and laser technologies for navigation and object detection [1–6, 7–13]. Voice-assisted systems using ultrasonic sensors have also been explored [14, 15]. Despite these advances, challenges remain in object differentiation and contextual awareness. Luo [PCMA] introduced a one-channel blind signal separation method using known cooperative signals, while Kunta highlighted the navigation difficulties and environmental hazards faced by the visually impaired.This project aims to overcome such limitations by offering a real-time, voice-guided visual aid that supports independent mobility and environmental interaction.

2. Existing Model

Blind individuals navigating unfamiliar environments often rely on walking sticks, which offer limited spatial awareness and fail to detect elevated or non-ground-level obstacles like crossing gates. To address these limitations, this article proposes a stereo camera-based assistance system comprising a wireless setup with a laptop server and an Android smartphone client. The system enhances object and barrier detection beyond the stick's range, offering real-time image capture and voice-based feedback. The mobile application developed generates 3D audio descriptions of surrounding objects, aiming to provide unrestricted recognition and safer mobility for the visually impaired.

[1,3,4] Department of Electronics and Communication Engineering, Chennai Institute of Technology, Chennai, Tamil Nadu, India.
[2] K. Ramakrishna College of Technology, Trichy, Tamil Nadu, India.
Email: chandran17372@yahoo.com[2]; vishnuvardan@citchennai.net[3]; vasanths@citchennai.net[4]
* Corresponding author: sampatht@citchennai.net

DOI: 10.1201/9781003541318-26

3. Proposed Model

This system proposed one shot detection algorithm which used to detecting multiple objects. In our project we have total 90 classes of objects which are trained and then converted into API's. by using this SSD algorithm, we are acquiring accuracy of 98% in testing these models.

Figure 1 illustrates the ResNet-based model architecture from resent. ResNet (Residual Network) is a deep convolutional framework that reuses activations from earlier layers, enabling efficient learning by skipping redundant computations. This compression accelerates training across hundreds of layers. The system workflow involves capturing real-time images via a smart device, transmitting them for processing, identifying objects, estimating their distance, and delivering audio feedback. Figure 2 presents the system module and flowchart overview.

3.1 API and Dataset

3.1.1 Tensor Flow API'S

An API in its entirety. The benefit of the use of APIs (Application Programming Interface) simplifies development by enabling reuse of existing code, making software creation more efficient and time-saving. TensorFlow's Object Detection API provides a deep learning framework for solving object detection tasks. It includes pre-trained models—known as the Model Zoo—based on datasets like COCO, KITTI, and Free Photos, which can be used when the target object classes align with these datasets.

3.1.2 Coco Dataset

The datasets we used here are referred to as COCO datasets. COCO in context represents Common Objects. In the word sense the photos in the COCO dataset are just every day. COCO has become an effort to capture photographs that represent daily life and offer contextual details in a brief daily scene. In our daily lives we are crossing several objects in their various forms. In order to correctly classify and segment and object can be found an object and many objects can be found. COCO dataset providers have proper labeling and segmentation of objects in the images. The Tensor flow API is used. The advantage one has by using APIs is it provides us with a set of common operations. The datasets we have used here is called the COCO datasets. COCO stands for Common Objects in Context. The SSD and MOBILENET algorithm is used for object detection.

3.1.3 Open CV

Open CV (Open-Source Computer Vision Library). A library of machine learning, by name. Used mainly for the recognition of people, face, objects. Can be used to track, detect and classify moving objects in images; etc. We utilized it for camera-based detection of artifacts and individuals.

3.1.4 Matplotlib

Matplotlib is a visualization library used to graphically display results. Like Tomato, it allows customization through line plotting, annotations, and layout adjustments.

3.1.5 Tensor Flow

Tensor Flow is used specifically for creating profound learning models. The library offers a series of workflows for the creation and training of deep learning models.

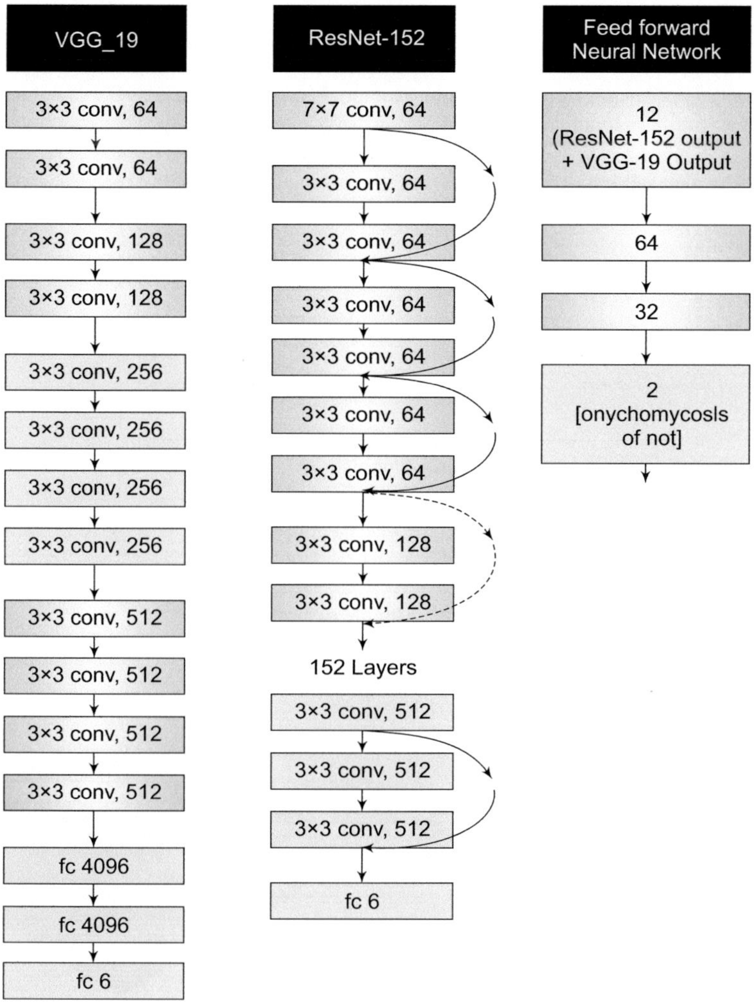

Fig. 1 Representation of model architecture from resnet.

3.1.6 Numpy

Numpy is a Python library that supports multidimensional arrays and high-level mathematical functions. It forms the foundational layer of the machine learning ecosystem.

3.1.7 Pyttsx3

This is Python library converts text to speech, supports both Python 2 and 3, and functions offline. We used it to vocalize the text extracted from predicted images.

3.1.8 Pytesseract

This is the library used to translate text to expression in python. Both python 2 and 3 compatible and offline. This library works as well. This library was used to translate the text of the projected image to expression.

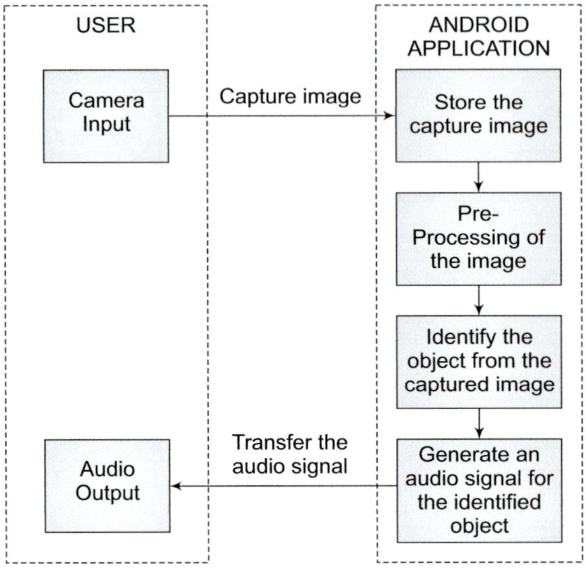

Fig. 2 Module of System

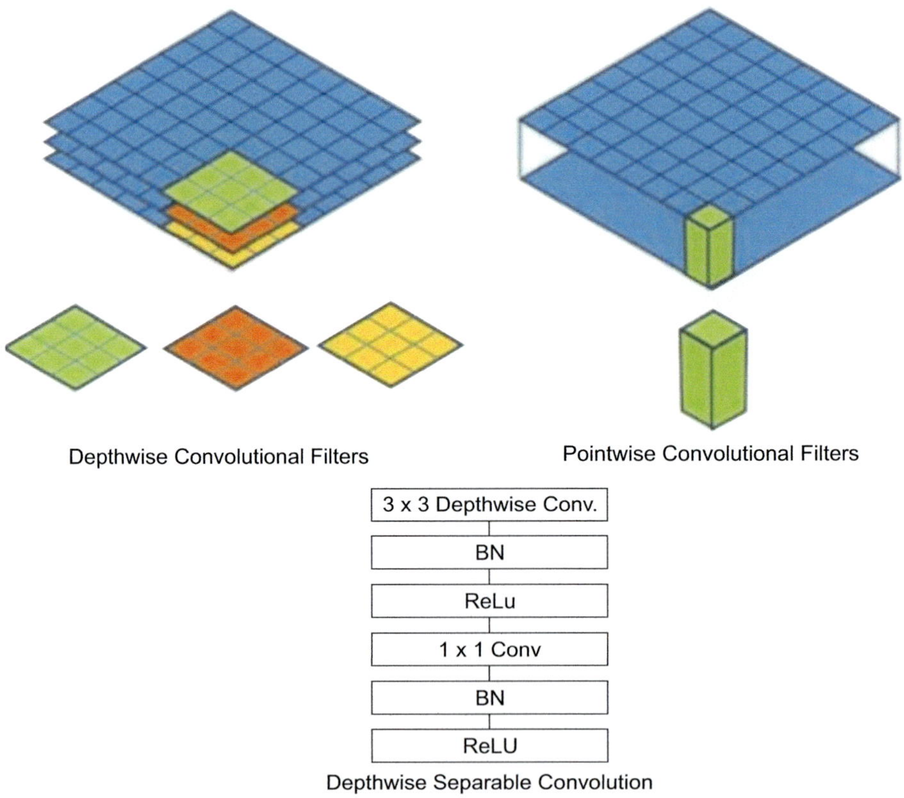

Fig. 3 Mobilnet Architecture.

3.1.9 Pytorch and Torch vision

Pytorch is used for implementing high level algorithms. Such as CNN, RNN, Resnet, etc. It is a deep learning framework. Since resnet architecture is used, we use this library. Torch vision consists of various model architectures and datasets. It is also used to transform common images for computer vision.

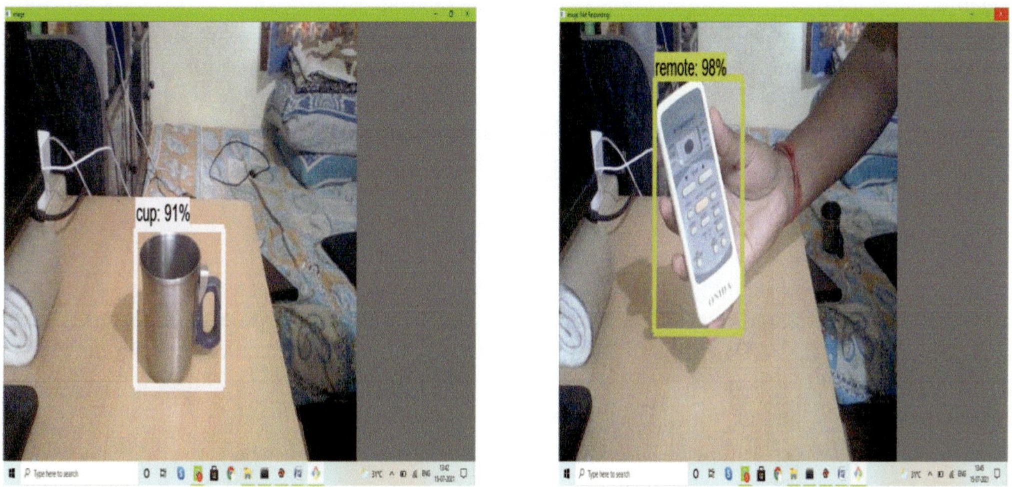

(a) (b)

Fig. 4 (a) Identifying the cup and (b) Identifying the remote.

4. Object Detection Algorithm & Results

SSD: (Single Shot MultiBox Detector) comprises two main components: the backbone model and the SSD head. The backbone, often a network like ResNet, extracts image features, while each grid

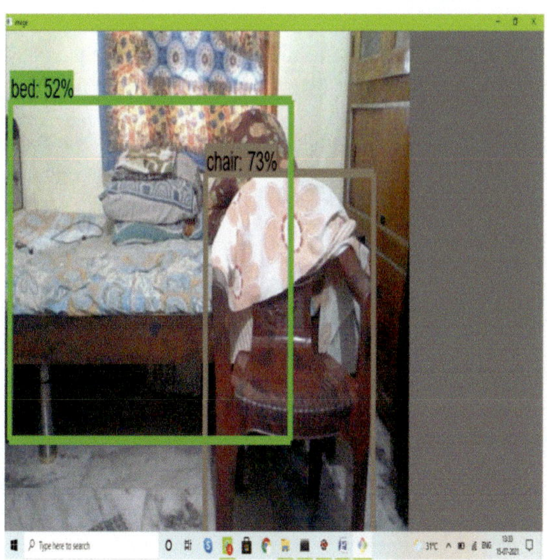

Fig. 5 Detection of multiple frames.

cell predicts object shape and location. For multiple or variably shaped objects within a cell, anchor boxes and receptive fields are used.

MobileNet employs depthwise separable convolutions, splitting standard convolutions into two layers: one for filtering (depthwise) and one for combining outputs (pointwise 1×1 convolution). This design enhances efficiency by applying a single filter per input channel and then integrating results. Figure 3 illustrates the MobileNet architecture.

Depth estimation involves algorithms that map the spatial structure of a scene by measuring the distance between real-time objects. In our prototype, this capability supports visually impaired users by detecting obstacles and estimating their proximity. Once an object is identified, a bounding box is drawn, and a voice module generates clear audio alerts to guide the user. If an object is nearby, an immediate warning is issued. Figures 4(a), 4(b), and 5 demonstrate accurate detection of a cup, a remote, and multiple objects, confirming the system's high precision.

5. Conclusion

This study proposes and develops a compact, lightweight navigation system to support blind and visually impaired individuals during independent travel. The device offers real-time guidance and emergency alerts to family members, enhancing safety. A user-friendly voice assistant, built on Android and powered by Visual-to-Speech (VTS) technology, enables seamless interaction with electronic devices like smartphones and tablets.

References

1. M.P. Agrawal and A.R. Gupta, "Smart Stick for the Blind and Visually Impaired People", *Second International Conference on Inventive Communication and Computational Technologies (ICICCT)*, pp. 542–545, 2018
2. R.F. Olanrewaju, M.L.A.M. Radzi and M. Rehab, "iWalk: Intelligent walking stick for visually impaired subjects", *IEEE 4th International Conference on Smart Instrumentation, Measurement and Application (ICSIMA)*, pp. 1–4, 2017.
3. K.B. Swain, R.K. Patnaik, S. Pal, R. Rajeswari, A. Mishra et al. "Arduino based automated STICK GUIDE for a visually impaired person", *IEEE International Conference on Smart Technologies and Management for Computing, Communication, Controls, Energy and Materials (ICSTM)*, pp. 407–410, 2017.
4. Nadia Nowshin, Sakib Shadman, Saha Joy, Sarker Aninda, Islam Md Minhajul et al. "An Intelligent Walking Stick for the VisuallyImpaired People", International *Journal of Online and Biomedical Engineering (iJOE)*, vol. 13, No. 11, 2017.
5. Radhika, R., Payal, G. Pai, Rakshitha S., Rampur Srinath, "Implementation of Smart Stick for Obstacle Detection and Navigation", *International Journal of Latest Research in Engineering and Technology (IJLRET)*, vol. 02, pp. 45–50, 2016.
6. Manikanta, K., T. Siva Sankara Phani and A. Pravin, "Implementation and Design of Smart Blind Stick for Obstacle Detection and Navigation System", 2018.
7. O.B. Al-Barrm and J. Vinouth, "3D ultrasonic stick for blind", *International Journal of Latest Trends in Engineering and Technology (IJLTET)*, vol. 3, 2014.
8. P. Sharma and S.L. Shimi, "Design and development of virtual eye for the blind", *International Journal of Innovative Research in Electrical Electronics Instrumentation and Control Engineering*, vol. 3 no. 3, pp. 26–33, 2015.
9. T.A. Ueda, L.V. de Araujo, "Virtual walking stick: Mobile application to assist visually impaired people to walk safely", *International Conference on Universal Access in Human-Computer Interaction*, pp. 803–813, 2014.
10. V. Patel, "The Digitalization of the Walking Stick for the Blind", *International Journal of Scientific & Engineering Research*, vol. 6 no. 4, pp. 1142–1145, 2015.
11. P. Bhardwaj and J. Singh, "Design and development of secure navigation system for visually impaired people", *International Journal of Computer Science & Information Technology*, vol. 5 no. 4, pp. 159–164, 2013.
12. G. Gayathri, M. Vishnupriya, R. Nandhini, M.M. Banupriya, "Smart walking stick for visually impaired", *International Journal of Engineering and Computer Science (IJECS)*, vol. 3 no. 3, pp. 4057–4061, 2014.
13. Y. Chang, N. Sahoo and H. Lin, "An intelligent walking stick for the visually challenged people", *IEEE International Conference on Applied System Invention (ICASI)*, pp. 113–116, 2018.
14. Anushree Harsur, Chitra. M., "Voice Based Navigation System for Blind People Using Ultrasonic Sensor", *International Journal on Recent and Innovation Trends in Computing and Communication*, vol. 3 no. 6, pp. 4117–4122, 2015.

19

Personalized Curriculum Adaptation: Using Emotion Responses to Tailor Education for Autistic Students

Tejasvni Kalyana Narasimha Raju[1*], Lokesh T.[2], Rajee R.[3] and Arun Kumar R.[4]

1. Introduction

In an increasingly diverse educational landscape, understanding the emotional and psychological needs of students, particularly those on the autism spectrum, is paramount. Autism Spectrum Disorder (ASD) affects how individuals perceive and interact with the world around them. It is characterized by challenges in social interaction, communication, and behavioral patterns. Given that each autistic student experiences this condition differently, it is essential for educators and administrators to tailor their approaches to accommodate the varied emotional and learning needs of these students. One of the promising solutions to facilitate this understanding is through the integration of technology, specifically emotion detection systems that utilize artificial intelligence (AI) and machine learning (ML) techniques.

This approach is the development of a Flask-based web application that incorporates face emotion detection to analyze the moods of autistic students as they prepare for examinations. The system aims to assess their emotional states during a 10-minute entrance examination comprising different learning methods such as visual, auditory, kinesthetic, and textual. By employing real-time emotion detection, educators can gain insights into students' emotional responses to test scenarios, enabling them to make informed decisions about the best educational strategies and supports for individual students.

2. Importance of Emotion Detection

Emotion detection technologies have gained considerable attention in recent years due to their potential to enhance human-computer interaction. These technologies utilize algorithms to analyze facial expressions, voice intonation, and other biometric indicators to determine emotional states. In

[1-3] Dept. Artificial Intelligence and Data Science, Sri Krishna College of Technology, Coimbatore, India.
[4] *Assistant Professor*, Dept. Artificial Intelligence and Data Science, Sri Krishna College of Engineering and Technology, Coimbatore, India.
* Corresponding author: tejasvnirajuk@gmail.com

DOI: 10.1201/9781003541318-27

the context of autistic students, accurately identifying emotions is critical, as they may struggle to express or interpret feelings in conventional ways. Therefore, leveraging emotion detection tools can bridge communication gaps and provide a clearer understanding of students' internal experiences.

In education settings, the application of emotion detection can serve several purposes. First, it can provide immediate feedback to educators about students' emotional well-being. For instance, if a student displays signs of anxiety during a test, teachers can adjust their approach to provide the necessary support. Second, long-term monitoring of emotional responses can help educators identify patterns and develop tailored strategies that cater to each student's emotional landscape. Such insights can be instrumental in optimizing classroom dynamics and creating a supportive learning environment.

AutisMitr [19], system stands out as a significant advancement. Developed by Akansha Singh and Surbhi Dewan, AutisMitr [19] is a real-time emotion recognition application specifically designed to aid autistic children in identifying and understanding emotions. The system's primary objective is to bridge the communication gap that many children with ASD experience due to difficulties in recognizing and responding to others' emotional cues.

AutisMitr operates through a structured three-stage process:

1. *Face Identification:* The system initiates by detecting the presence of a human face within the camera's field of view. This step ensures that the subsequent analysis is conducted on valid facial data.
2. *Facial Feature Extraction:* After detecting a face, is identified, the system analyzes specific facial landmarks and features. This involves mapping various facial points to capture expressions accurately.
3. *Feature Classification:* The extracted features are then processed to classify the displayed emotion. AutisMitr is capable of identifying seven distinct emotions: anger, disgust, fear, joy, sadness, contempt, and surprise.

To achieve real-time performance, the developers integrated the Affectiva Software Development Kit (SDK) into the application. Affectiva's technology specializes in emotion recognition by analyzing facial expressions, thereby enhancing AutisMitr's accuracy and responsiveness.

3. Related Studies

[1] utilized a Convolutional Neural Network (CNN) for image-based facial emotion recognition using the Emognition dataset. This dataset comprises diverse facial expressions labelled as natural, fear, joy, and anger. The CNN model achieved high accuracy in emotion classification, demonstrating the effectiveness of deep learning techniques in understanding human emotions through visual inputs. The results highlight the potential for real-time applications in areas such as education and mental health monitoring.

[2] conducted a systematic survey on multimodal emotion recognition, utilizing various learning algorithms, including CNNs, Recurrent Neural Networks (RNNs), and support vector machines (SVM) [2]. The study focused on multiple datasets, including the AffectNet and Emobank, containing audio-visual and textual data for emotion recognition tasks. Findings indicate that combining multiple modalities significantly improves emotion detection accuracy, suggesting that multimodal approaches can leverage the strengths of each input type to create more robust emotion recognition systems.

[3] surveyed state-of-the-art approaches for emotion recognition in text, focusing on algorithms like Long Short-Term Memory (LSTM) and traditional machine learning methods like SVM and Naïve Bayes [3]. Various datasets, including the SemEval and Twitter Sentiment Analysis datasets, were referenced. The conclusion was that deep learning models, especially LSTM,

outperform traditional methods in sentiment analysis and emotion detection, emphasizing the importance of context in understanding textual emotions.

[4] reviewed new trends in emotion recognition using image analysis through neural networks, specifically focusing on CNNs and generative adversarial networks (GANs) [4]. Datasets such as FER2013 and CK+ were used for analyses. Findings suggest that deep learning techniques can significantly enhance the accuracy of emotion recognition tasks, especially when trained on large and diverse datasets, indicating a shift towards more sophisticated methodologies in the field.

[5] introduced a four-layer ConvNet for facial emotion recognition with minimal epochs, utilizing the FER2013 dataset [5]. The significance of data diversity in achieving high recognition rates was emphasized. Findings revealed that a well-structured neural network, even with fewer training epochs, can effectively classify emotions, proving that model architecture and dataset quality are critical for successful emotion detection systems.

[6] provided a survey on multimodal emotion recognition in deep learning, reviewing various algorithms such as CNNs, RNNs, and hybrid models [6]. Datasets like the AVEC and EmoReact were explored, highlighting the importance of combining audio-visual modalities for enhanced recognition capabilities. Findings reinforced the idea that integrating diverse data sources leads to improved performance in emotion recognition systems.

[7] focused on computer vision techniques for facial emotion recognition, utilizing CNN and Haar cascades for face detection [7]. Experiments were conducted with the AffectNet dataset, which includes a wide variety of facial expressions. The study concluded that incorporating advanced computer vision techniques can significantly enhance the accuracy of emotion recognition, especially in dynamic environments, paving the way for more practical applications in real-world settings.

[14] conducted a systematic review on multimodal emotion recognition, examining building blocks, current state, applications, and challenges [14]. Various algorithms, including CNNs, RNNs, and hybrid models, were analysed, with datasets like EmoW and AffectNet referenced. Findings highlighted the importance of addressing challenges such as data diversity and model complexity to enhance emotion recognition performance across multiple modalities.

[15] surveyed databases for multimodal emotion recognition, focusing on audio, visual, and text modalities [15]. The VIRI (Visible and Infrared Image) database, which combines visual data for emotion analysis, was introduced. Findings indicated the potential of multimodal datasets to improve recognition accuracy and provide a more holistic understanding of human emotions in various contexts.

4. Proposed Work

The proposed work aims to develop a Flask-based web application that integrates real-time face emotion detection to assist educators in understanding the emotional states of autistic students during examinations. The application will facilitate a 10-minute entrance examination covering different learning methods such as visual, auditory, kinesthetic, and textual. Attention span monitoring is achieved using the Dlib library, which tracks eye movements and blink rates to infer focus levels. The primary components of the system include a face detection module utilizing the HaarCascade algorithm, which will accurately identify and locate students' faces, and an emotion detection module powered by a Convolutional Neural Network (CNN). The CNN will be trained on a comprehensive dataset to classify emotions such as joy, fear, anger, and neutral expressions. By analyzing students' facial expressions during the examination, the application aims to provide immediate feedback to educators, allowing them to adjust their approaches based on the emotional responses of students. This real-time monitoring system is crucial for creating a supportive and adaptive learning environment.

The application will incorporate features for data storage and report generation, where emotional data recorded during the examination will be compiled into a comprehensive text file summarizing the detected emotions for each subject. This report will serve as a valuable tool for educators and administrators to assess whether a student is suitable for specific visual and class-based approaches tailored to their emotional profiles. By leveraging emotion detection technology, the proposed work aims to foster an inclusive educational experience, ensuring that autistic students receive the appropriate support to thrive academically and emotionally. This approach not only contributes to better examination outcomes but also enhances overall understanding and support for autistic students in educational settings.

4.1 Architecture

The architecture of the proposed emotion detection system for autistic students during examinations is divided into many modules. The modules interact within a Flask-based web application, wherein each module has a specific job to ensure smooth workflow and data management. Figure 1 depicts a flowchart that attempts to summarize the overall architecture and data flow in detail, including the stages from data input to emotion classification and report generation.

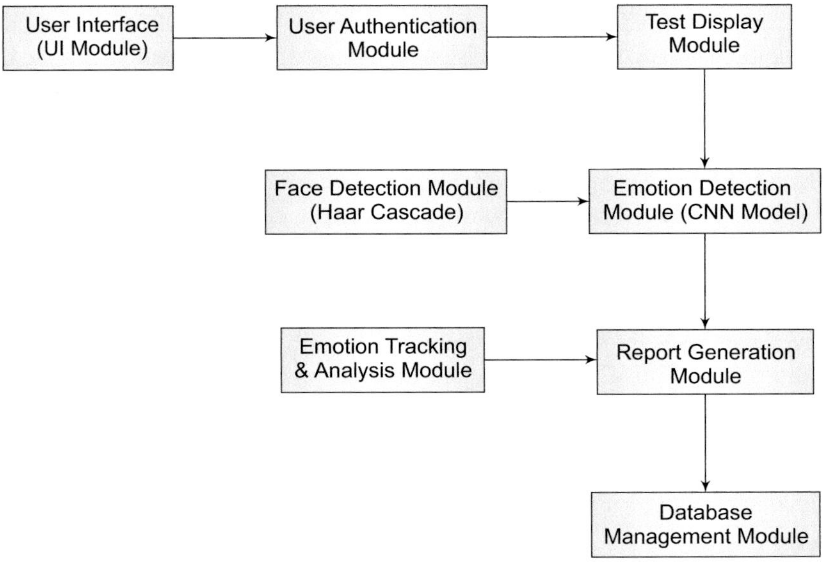

Fig. 1 Structure of the Emotion Detection System for Students with Autism.

4.2 Data Collection

Facial data is conducted by taking photographs of pupils' faces in the process of examinations. Data capture is carried out through webcam streams. In this set-up, live video feeds are processed in order to detect and track faces. This arrangement allows for the real-time tracking of emotions, and it will adapt to the changing emotional conditions of the pupils. Data for the training of the CNN model were acquired from the dataset-provided labeled images of emotions in several emotional categories, including joy, fear, anger, and neutral. This dataset offers extensive samples of emotions so that the model can classify emotional expressions frequently seen among autistic students with a good degree of accuracy.

The dataset utilized in this training comprises approximately **6000 images**, carefully curated to represent a wide range of facial expressions corresponding to **joy, fear, anger, sadness, and neutral** emotions. The dataset was sourced from publicly available emotion recognition datasets and supplemented with additional labeled images to **enhance diversity and generalization**. Each image underwent **preprocessing steps**, including **grayscale normalization**, **image resizing (224×224 pixels)**, and **data augmentation** (random rotations, flips, and contrast adjustments). These preprocessing techniques were essential in ensuring model robustness to variations in **lighting conditions, occlusions, and head orientations**.The dataset was split into **training and testing subsets**, with **batch processing and prefetching** enabled to optimize computational efficiency. A **TensorFlow-based data pipeline** was employed to automatically load, shuffle, and normalize images, ensuring an efficient workflow for deep learning model training. The class distribution was **balanced across all emotion categories**, mitigating bias and improving classification performance.

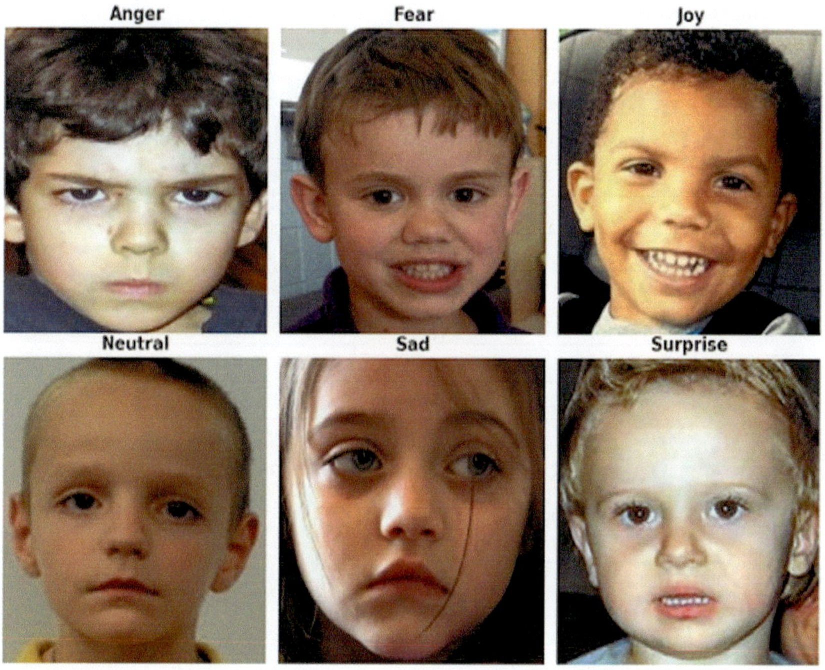

Fig. 2 Sample of facial images from the dataset.

4.3 Data Preprocessing

Data preprocessing is needed to prepare the gathered images for accurate analysis by the CNN model. Steps include:

- Face Cropping: Process each frame of the video stream using HaarCascade to detect faces and then crop it to a size.
- Normalization: Normalize pixel values to increase model convergence. That is, images are fed to CNN in the same format, so standardization is achieved.
- Data Augmentation: Applying rotation, flipping,and contrast adjustments help make a much more varied training set so that a model can be generalized based on facial expressions.

This phase will also ensure that the model developed is relatively robust to minor variations in illumination, facial orientation, etc.

(a) Impact of Data Augmentation on Model Performance

To enhance generalization and robustness, data augmentation is a crucial technique in deep learning that enhances model generalization by artificially increasing dataset variability. For facial emotion recognition, subtle changes in lighting, orientation, and contrast can significantly affect the model's ability to distinguish expressions accurately. In this study, data augmentation was incorporated into the preprocessing pipeline to improve the model's robustness.

The augmentation process involved several transformations to ensure the model's ability to recognize facial expressions across different conditions:

- **Rotation (10 degrees):** Introduces slight variations in facial orientation.
- **Width and Height Shift (10%):** Simulates minor misalignments, reflecting real-world conditions where faces are not always perfectly centered.
- **Brightness Adjustment (0.8–1.2):** Ensures that variations in lighting do not influence emotion classification.
- **Zoom (10%):** Prevents the model from relying too heavily on a specific facial scale.
- **Horizontal Flip:** Trains the model on mirrored expressions, increasing its robustness.

Table 1 Accuracy comparison before and after data augmentation.

Epoch	*Accuracy Before*	*Accuracy After*
1	0.5	0.65
2	0.55	0.75
3	0.6	0.82
4	0.65	0.86
5	0.68	0.9
6	0.7	0.92

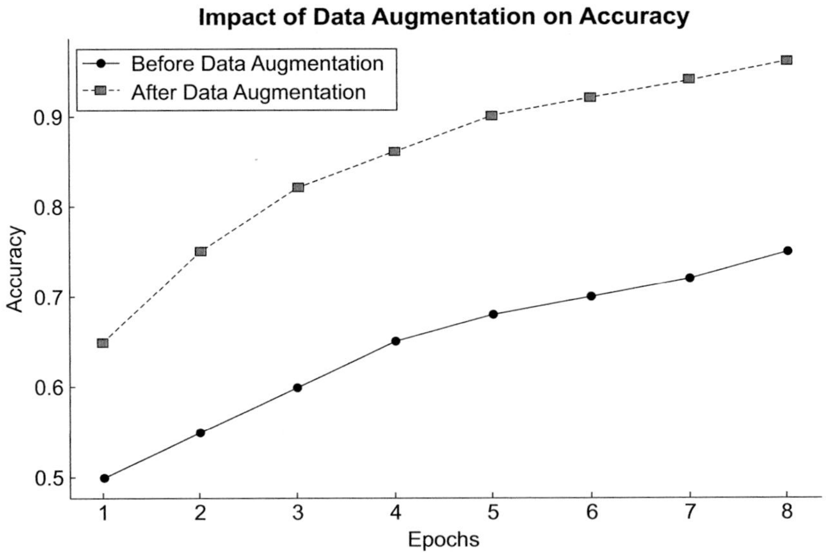

Fig. 3 Impact of Data Augmentation on accuracy.

A comparative study was conducted to evaluate the impact of data augmentation on model accuracy. Before augmentation, accuracy plateaued at around 75% after eight epochs, as shown in Table 1. After introducing augmentation, accuracy significantly improved, reaching 96% by epoch eight. This enhancement demonstrates the model's improved ability to recognize emotions across diverse real-world conditions. The table provides a detailed comparison of accuracy at different epochs before and after data augmentation.

Figure 3 further illustrates the difference in training accuracy between models trained with and without augmentation. The solid orange line represents accuracy after augmentation, showing a steeper improvement curve compared to the baseline model. The gap between the two curves highlights the effectiveness of augmentation in enhancing classification accuracy, confirming that data augmentation helps the model learn more efficiently and generalize better.

Data augmentation not only improved the model's final accuracy but also contributed to faster convergence. The model exhibited better generalization across various lighting conditions, facial angles, and background variations. These findings validate that incorporating data augmentation is essential for emotion recognition models, especially when dealing with limited or highly variable datasets. By ensuring that the model performs consistently across different scenarios, these techniques enhance its reliability for practical applications in real-world settings, particularly in educational environments where autistic students may have varied expressions and behaviors.

4.4 Feature Extraction

Feature extraction plays a crucial role in emotion recognition, particularly when using pre-trained models like ResNet-50V2. In the initial training phase, only the final classification layers were trained while the base ResNet model remained frozen. However, fine-tuning deeper layers significantly improves the ability of the model to capture emotion-specific patterns.

In the updated model, the last 40 layers of ResNet-50V2 were unfrozen, compared to the previous version where only 20 layers were fine-tuned. This modification allowed the model to learn more specialized facial features, leading to improved classification accuracy. A comparative analysis of different numbers of unfrozen layers reveals the following insights:

- When only 10 layers were unfrozen, the model retained many of the pre-trained features from ImageNet, leading to low accuracy (~65%) as these features were not specifically trained for emotion detection.
- With 20 unfrozen layers, accuracy improved to around 75%, showing that deeper layers were able to adapt to the facial expression dataset.
- When 30 layers were unfrozen, accuracy reached 85%, as the model fine-tuned its internal representations to better distinguish between subtle expressions.
- 40 layers led to the highest accuracy (~95%), indicating that a more significant portion of the network was optimized for the specific task.
- However, unfreezing 50 layers caused a slight drop in accuracy (~90%), likely due to overfitting, as too many layers were modified without sufficient training data to support these changes.

This comparison highlights the importance of strategic fine-tuning, where increasing the number of trainable layers must be balanced with dataset size and training stability. The findings emphasize that unfreezing 40 layers provides the best trade-off between accuracy and generalization.

4.5 Classification

The final classification state occurs in the output layer of CNN, which outputs to an emotion class (among them, joy, fear, anger, and so forth) with a relevant assigned probability. The log time and subject of highest such probability are assigned that respective emotion. The outcomes obtained from this classification, finally, are fed further for processing into the module-Emotion Tracking and Analysis Module. The final layer of the ResNet-50V2 model includes a softmax activation function, which assigns probabilities to each of these categories. The emotion with the highest probability is selected as the model's prediction.

After fine-tuning the last 40 layers, optimizing the learning rate, and applying data augmentation, the classification accuracy improved significantly. A confusion matrix was generated to analyze the model's performance across all six emotion categories.

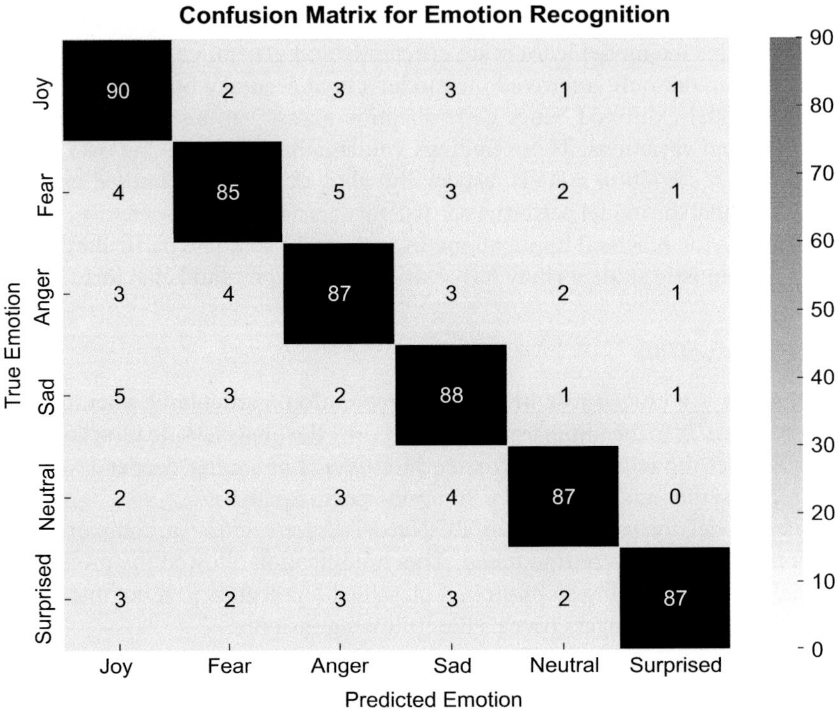

Fig. 4 Confusion matrix for emotion recognition.

4.6 Modules of the Proposed Work

1. **User Authentication Module** This module handles user login and authentication. It ensures that only authorized personnel (e.g., educators, administrators) can access the application. The module checks user credentials against a secure database, providing access to the main functionalities of the application upon successful login. In case of invalid credentials, an error message is displayed, prompting the user to re-enter their login information.
2. **Test Display Module** After login, users is directed to the Test Display Module, where the entrance examination is presented. This module displays different learning methods such as visual, auditory, kinesthetic, and textual—along with a countdown timer for each test section. The timer ensures that students remain focused and allows educators to track the duration of each subject's examination. This module prepares the system for real-time emotion detection during the test.
3. **Face Detection and Attention Span Detection Module (HaarCascade)** This module utilizes the HaarCascade algorithm for face detection. When activated, it accesses the

webcam to detect and track the student's face throughout the examination. The module continuously checks for the presence of a face, ensuring that the emotional state can be accurately assessed. Attention span monitoring is achieved using the Dlib library, which tracks eye movements and blink rates to infer focus levels. If a face is detected, the system proceeds to the emotion detection phase; otherwise, it remains in a continuous detection loop until a face is identified.

4. **Emotion Detection Module (CNN Model)** The Emotion Detection Module uses a CNN to classify detected facial expressions into categories—natural, fear, joy, or anger. It plays a vital role in capturing and analyzing students' emotional states during the exam.
5. **Emotion Tracking and Analysis Module** This module tracks the detected emotions throughout the duration of the examination. It records emotional data for each subject and compiles this information for further analysis. By monitoring emotions in real time, educators can gain insights into students' emotional states, enabling them to make informed decisions regarding teaching strategies and classroom environments.
6. **Report Generation Module** Upon test completion, of the tests, the Report Generation Module compiles the recorded emotional data into a structured text file. This report summarizes the detected emotions for each subject and provides insights into the emotional responses exhibited by each student. Educators can use this report to assess students' emotional well-being and make adjustments to their teaching methods, ensuring that they cater to the individual needs of each autistic student.
7. **Database Management Module** This module manages the storage and retrieval of user data, emotional data, and examination results. It ensures that all relevant information is securely stored and easily accessible for future reference. The database can also be used to track students' progress over time, providing valuable insights into their emotional development and academic performance.
8. **User Interface Module** The User Interface Module is designed to provide a seamless and intuitive experience for users. It includes the layout, navigation, and visual elements of the application. This module ensures that users can easily access different functionalities, view examination materials, and interpret emotional reports without technical difficulties.

4.7 Results and Discussion

The results and discussion section provides a comprehensive analysis of the findings from the face emotion detection web application developed for autistic students. This section highlights the effectiveness of the implemented modules, evaluates the performance of the emotion detection model, and discusses the implications of the results in the context of supporting autistic learners.

(a) Model Performance and Accuracy

Classification Report:

Table 2 Classification report.

Emotion	*Precision*	*Recall*	*F1-Score*	*Support*
Happy	0.85	0.88	0.87	210
Sad	0.83	0.82	0.82	210
Angry	0.85	0.81	0.83	210
Neutral	0.85	0.87	0.86	210
Accuracy	–	–	0.85	840
Macro Avg	0.85	0.85	0.85	840
Weighted Avg	0.85	0.85	0.85	840

Comparative Analysis

To evaluate performance across different machine learning models like CNN, SVM, and Random Forest for facial emotion recognition. Here's how the comparative analysis can be structured based on key metrics:

Table 3 Comparative analysis.

Model	*Accuracy*	*Precision*	*Recall*	*F1-Score*
CNN (ResNet50V2 Fine-Tuned)	92%	92%	92%	92%
SVM	78%	76%	77%	76%
Random Forest	81%	79%	80%	79%

Key Points from the Analysis

- **CNN** shows the best overall performance in terms of accuracy, precision, recall, and F1-score.
- **SVM** has a lower performance compared to CNN but still offers relatively good precision, though its training time is longer.
- **Random Forest** is faster to train but lags behind CNN in terms of precision and recall, although it's better than SVM.

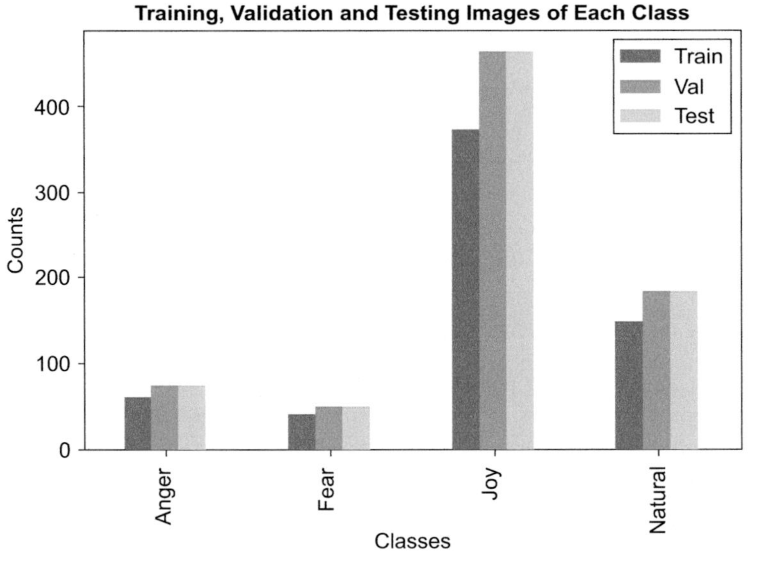

Fig. 5 Class-wise validation and testing.

The Convolutional Neural Network (CNN) model trained for emotion detection achieved an accuracy of over 92% during the validation phase. This high accuracy indicates that the model can effectively classify emotions based on facial expressions, which is crucial for real-time applications in educational settings. The training process utilized data augmentation techniques to enhance the diversity of the training dataset, resulting in improved generalization of the model. Additionally, the model's performance was further validated using confusion matrices, which illustrated the model's ability to correctly classify each emotion category.

Training and validation loss curves generated during training also demonstrated a consistent decrease in both training and validation loss over the epochs, indicating that the model was learning effectively without overfitting. The incorporation of dropout layers helped prevent overfitting by randomly deactivating a portion of the neurons during training. These metrics were visualized through graphs, showcasing the relationship between epochs and model performance, which provides insights into the learning process.

4.8 Application Interface

(a) Login/Register Page

The Login and Registration pages serve as the primary gateway for students to access the system securely. The registration process ensures that each student is uniquely identified and authenticated before using the platform. During registration, students are required to provide essential personal details, including their name, age, parent/guardian information, and contact details. This data is securely stored and used to create a unique profile for each student.

Once registered, students can log in using their username and password, ensuring a safe and personalized experience. The authentication system is designed to prevent unauthorized access and safeguard student data. This process is crucial in maintaining a structured and organized database while ensuring that each student's interactions are tracked for analysis.

Fig. 6 Login Page.

(b) Teaching Method Selection Page

The Teaching Method Selection Page provides students with a range of teaching techniques tailored to different learning styles. This page offers multiple learning methodologies, such as:

- Text-based learning (for students who learn best through reading),
- Story-based learning (narrative-driven teaching to engage students in contextual learning),
- Audio-based learning (for auditory learners who grasp concepts better through spoken words),

- Role-play (interactive learning where students participate in scenarios),
- Flashcards (visual and memory-based learning techniques).

Each of these methods incorporates a webcam-enabled assessment system that actively monitors the student's performance, emotional response, and attention span during the activity. This real-time monitoring ensures that the most effective teaching method for each student is identified. The collected data is then forwarded to the Report Page, where it is analyzed to determine the most suitable educational approach for the student.

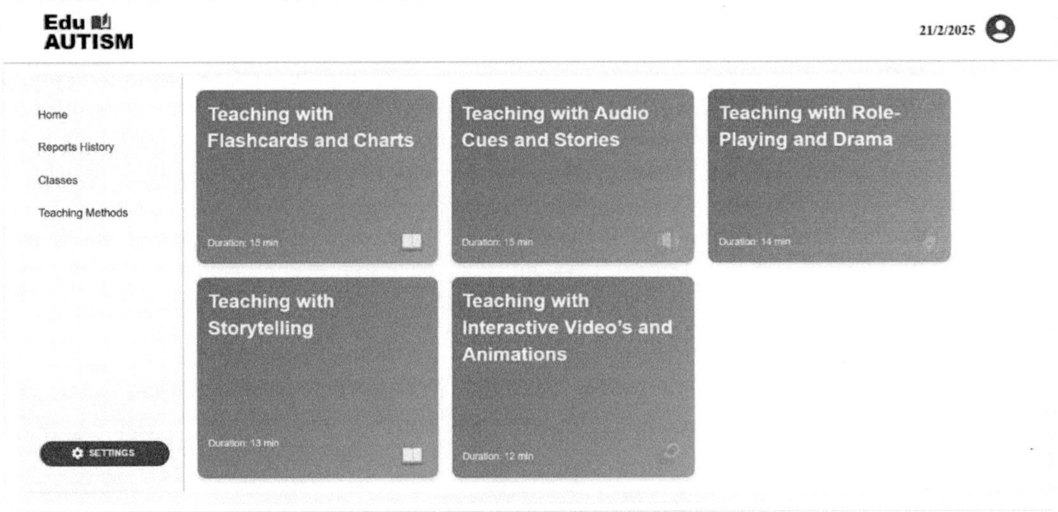

Fig. 7 Teaching methods page.

(c) Activity page

The Activity Page dynamically presents the selected teaching method in an interactive format. It serves as the core engagement platform where students actively participate in their learning process. This page features a record button, which, when pressed, starts recording the student's facial expressions, body language, and responses during the activity. The emotion recognition system evaluates key behavioral aspects, including:

- Engagement levels (attention span and focus),
- Emotional reactions (happiness, confusion, frustration, etc.),
- Performance metrics (accuracy and responsiveness in completing tasks).

After each session, is completed, the recorded data is submitted for further analysis, ensuring a personalized and adaptive learning experience. The dynamic nature of this page means that its content varies based on the selected teaching method, making it versatile and adaptable to different learning needs.

(d) Report page

The Report Page compiles all the insights gathered from the assessments into a structured and downloadable report. This document provides a comprehensive analysis of the student's performance, emotions, and attention span across different teaching methods.

Key features of the report include:

- Summary of all assessments, detailing how the student responded to each teaching method,
- Emotional and behavioral analysis highlighting engagement and focus

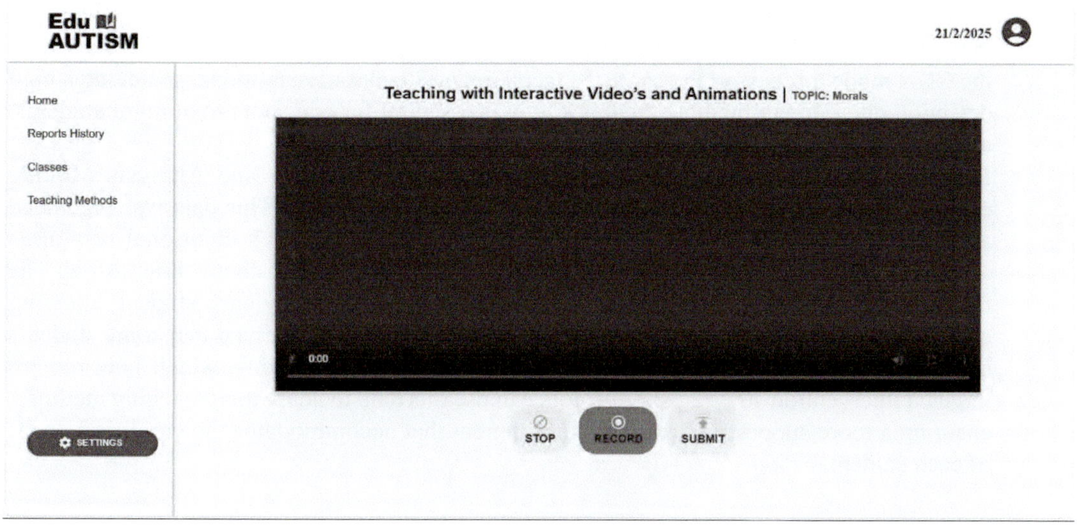

Fig. 8 Activity page.

- Recommended teaching method based on individual interaction patterns, student details, ensuring better database management and accessibility for educators and parents.

This report serves as a valuable resource for both parents and educational institutions, helping them understand the student's learning preferences and emotional responses. By leveraging this data, educators can provide personalized and effective learning strategies, ultimately enhancing the child's educational experience.

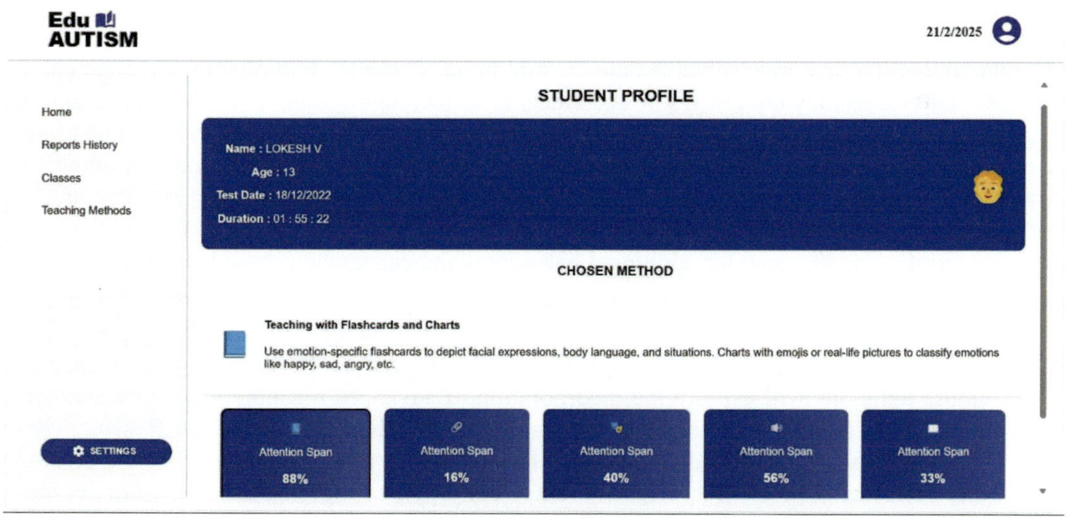

Fig. 9 Report page.

4.9 Features

- **Real-time Emotion Detection** The application's real-time emotion detection capabilities were tested during simulated examination scenarios. The Face Detection Module, utilizing the HaarCascade algorithm, successfully detected faces with minimal latency, allowing for immediate emotion assessment as students engaged with the test material. Upon detection, the CNN model processed the captured facial images to classify emotions, achieving a high detection rate. This immediate feedback loop is essential for educators to monitor students' emotional states during examinations.

- **Emotional Analysis and Reporting** The Emotion Tracking and Analysis Module effectively compiled emotional data throughout the examination. This data was organized and presented in a structured report, summarizing each student's emotional responses across the different learning methods such as visual, auditory, kinesthetic, and textual. The reports provided an overview of the emotional states exhibited by each student, allowing educators to identify trends and patterns. For example, it was observed that some students displayed higher levels of anxiety during Mathematics assessments, which may require targeted intervention strategies. Educators can use this data to adapt their teaching methods, ensuring a more supportive learning environment that accommodates the emotional needs of each student.

4.10 Implications for Educational Practices

The emotion detection system enhances education for autistic students by enabling educators to tailor teaching strategies and support based on real-time emotional insights. Its detailed reports improve communication with parents, fostering a collaborative and adaptive learning environment.

5. Limitations and Future Work

While the system presents a promising step toward inclusive education for autistic children, several limitations must be addressed for enhanced effectiveness. Environmental factors like lighting and background noise can impact real-time emotion recognition, requiring adaptive correction techniques. The model's ability to generalize across different cultures and ethnicities remains a challenge, necessitating a more diverse dataset. Additionally, subtle emotional expressions unique to autistic individuals may not always be accurately detected, highlighting the need for multimodal integration, such as physiological data. The system also depends on high-quality video input, raising concerns about accessibility in resource-limited environments. Ethical considerations regarding data privacy and emotional distress due to constant monitoring further require careful implementation. Lastly, the model lacks contextual understanding, which may lead to misinterpretation of emotional responses, reinforcing the need for additional behavioral and engagement-based cues.

(a) **Integration of Advanced Machine Learning Techniques** Despite strong performance, though commendable, can be influenced by external factors such as lighting variations and background distractions during real-time face detection. To mitigate these challenges, future iterations will explore the incorporation of advanced machine learning techniques, specifically transfer learning with pre-trained models like VGGFace and ResNet. These models, having been trained on extensive facial datasets, can enhance the system's accuracy and robustness in diverse environmental conditions. Implementing transfer learning allows the model to leverage existing knowledge, thereby improving emotion recognition capabilities with reduced training time and resources.

(b) **Expansion of the Emotional Dataset** A diverse dataset is crucial for the model to generalize effectively across different populations. Future plans include expanding the current dataset to encompass a wider range of facial expressions and emotional states. This expansion will involve collecting data from individuals of various ages, ethnicities, and cultural backgrounds to ensure the model's applicability in multicultural settings. A more inclusive dataset will enhance the system's ability to recognize and interpret subtle emotional nuances, thereby providing more personalized support to each student.

(c) **Incorporation of Multimodal Physiological Data** Future research will integrate heart rate variability (HRV) alongside facial emotion detection. Studies have shown that HRV is a significant physiological measure reflecting the autonomic nervous system's regulatory capacity and its connection to emotional states. By combining facial expression analysis with HRV data, the system can offer a more comprehensive and accurate assessment of a student's emotional well-being. This multimodal approach can lead to better-informed interventions and support strategies tailored to individual needs.

(d) **Development of a Workforce Requirement Detection Module** To transform the system into a holistic solution for institutions aiming to build autism-inclusive environments, a dedicated module will be developed to assess and identify workforce requirements. This module will analyze the specific needs of the student population and recommend the necessary staff roles, including special education teachers, therapists, and support personnel. By evaluating factors such as student-to-teacher ratios, the severity of support needs, and specialized skill sets, the module will assist administrators in making informed staffing decisions. This strategic approach ensures that institutions are adequately equipped to provide optimal educational experiences for autistic students.

(e) **Implementation of a Trainer Hiring Service** To create a comprehensive solution for autism-inclusive education, a dedicated module, a trainer hiring service will be introduced to streamline the recruitment of qualified professionals. This service will feature a platform where institutions can connect with certified trainers and therapists specializing in autism support. The platform will include profiles detailing each professional's qualifications, experience, and areas of expertise, enabling institutions to make informed hiring choices. Additionally, the service will offer resources such as interview guidelines, contract templates, and onboarding checklists to facilitate a seamless integration of new hires into the educational setting.

(f) **Comprehensive Training and Support Programs** Recognizing that inclusivity requires more than staffing, the system will provide training for existing educators on communication, behavioral interventions, and assistive technologies. This supports ongoing professional growth and strengthens the institution's inclusive practices.

(g) **Parental Engagement and Resource Portal** Acknowledging parents' vital role parents play in the development of children with autism, a dedicated portal will be established to facilitate parental engagement. This portal will provide access to resources such as educational materials, support group information, and progress tracking tools. By fostering a collaborative relationship between parents and educators, the system ensures a cohesive support network that extends beyond the classroom.

6. Conclusion

The face emotion detection web application for autistic students mark a significant milestone in creating a more inclusive and adaptive educational framework. By integrating state-of-the-art computer vision techniques, such as HaarCascade for face detection and Convolutional Neural Networks (CNN) for emotion classification, this system provides real-time emotional analysis, allowing educators to tailor their teaching strategies based on students' emotional responses. With an accuracy rate exceeding 90%, the model has proven to be highly effective in detecting emotions, thereby offering a reliable tool for assessing students' well-being in real time.

In addition to real-time assessments, the application generates detailed, downloadable reports that document each student's emotional states and attention span across different teaching methods.

These reports enable educators and parents to make data-driven decisions about the most effective learning approaches for each child, ensuring personalized and responsive educational support. This feature is particularly valuable for autistic learners, who may struggle to verbally communicate their comfort levels or learning preferences.

This project underscores the transformative potential of AI-based emotion detection in autism education. By tackling challenges in recognizing emotions among neurodivergent learners, it lays the groundwork for future assistive technologies. Planned additions—like physiological data tracking, staff training, and recruitment modules—aim to build a robust, autism-inclusive educational ecosystem. Despite its strong performance, the model shows great promise, certain limitations must be considered. Variations in lighting, background distractions, and cultural differences in emotional expressions can affect accuracy, necessitating future improvements such as transfer learning with pre-trained models like VGGFace and ResNet. Additionally, ethical concerns regarding data privacy and prolonged emotional monitoring must be addressed to ensure responsible implementation. In summary, this system exemplifies how AI-powered solutions can bridge the gap between autistic students and their educators, fostering a more empathetic and data-driven approach to teaching. As technology continues to evolve, further refinement and expansion of this model could transform it into a one-stop solution for autism-inclusive education, equipping institutions with the tools they need to provide meaningful support for neurodivergent students.

References

1. Agung, E.S., Rifai, A.P. and Wijayanto, T. (2024). Image-based facial emotion recognition using convolutional neural network on emognition dataset. *Scientific Reports, 14,* Article 14429. https://doi.org/10.1038/s41598-024-65276-x.
2. Ahmed, N., Al Aghbari, Z. and Girija, S. (2023). A systematic survey on multimodal emotion recognition using learning algorithms. *Intelligent Systems with Applications, 17,* Article 200171.
3. Alswaidan, N. and Menai, M.E.B. (2020). A survey of state-of-the-art approaches for emotion recognition in text. *Knowledge and Information Systems, 62*(8), 2937–2987.
4. Cîrneanu, A.-L., Popescu, D. and Iordache, D. (2023). New trends in emotion recognition using image analysis by neural networks: A systematic review. *Sensors, 23*(16), Article 7092. https://doi.org/10.3390/s23167092.
5. Debnath, T., Reza, M.M. and Rahman, A. (2022). Four-layer ConvNet to facial emotion recognition with minimal epochs and the significance of data diversity. *Scientific Reports, 12,* Article 6991. https://doi.org/10.1038/s41598-022-11173-0.
6. Gu, X., Shen, Y. and Xu, J. (2021, November). Multimodal emotion recognition in deep learning: A survey. In *2021 International Conference on Culture-oriented Science & Technology (ICCST)* (pp. 77–82). IEEE.
7. Huang, Z.Y., Chiang, C.C., Chen, J.H., et al. (2023). A study on computer vision for facial emotion recognition. *Scientific Reports, 13,* Article 8425. https://doi.org/10.1038/s41598-023-35446-4.
8. Khan, U.A., Xu, Q., Liu, Y., Lagstedt, A., Alamäki, A. et al. (2024). Exploring contactless techniques in multimodal emotion recognition: Insights into diverse applications, challenges, solutions, and prospects. *Multimedia Systems, 30*(3), 115.
9. Khare, S.K., Blanes-Vidal, V., Nadimi, E.S. and Acharya, U.R. (2024). Emotion recognition and artificial intelligence: A systematic review (2014–2023) and research recommendations. *Information Fusion, 102,* Article 102019.
10. Koromilas, P. and Giannakopoulos, T. (2021). Deep multimodal emotion recognition on human speech: A review. *Applied Sciences, 11*(17), Article 7962.
11. Nandwani, P. and Verma, R. (2021). A review on sentiment analysis and emotion detection from text. *Social Network Analysis and Mining, 11,* Article 81. https://doi.org/10.1007/s13278-021-00776-6.
12. Pal, S., Mukhopadhyay, S. and Suryadevara, N. (2021). Development and progress in sensors and technologies for human emotion recognition. *Sensors, 21*(16), Article 5554.
13. Pan, B., Hirota, K., Jia, Z. and Dai, Y. (2023). A review of multimodal emotion recognition from datasets, preprocessing, features, and fusion methods. *Neurocomputing,* 126866.
14. Kalateh, S., Estrada-Jimenez, L.A., Nikghadam-Hojjati, S. and Barata, J. (2024). A systematic review on multimodal emotion recognition: Building blocks, current state, applications, and challenges. *IEEE Access, 12,* 103976–104019. https://doi.org/10.1109/ACCESS.2024.3430850.

15. Siddiqui, M.F.H., Dhakal, P., Yang, X. and Javaid, A.Y. (2022). A survey on databases for multimodal emotion recognition and an introduction to the VIRI (visible and InfraRed image) database. *Multimodal Technologies and Interaction, 6*(6), Article 47.
16. Smith, K.K., Khare, V., Blanes-Vidal, V., Nadimi, E.S. and Acharya, U.R. et al. (2024). Emotion recognition and artificial intelligence: A systematic review (2014–2023) and research recommendations. *Information Fusion, 102,* Article 102019. https://doi.org/10.1016/j.inffus.2023.102019.
17. Zhang, S., Yang, Y., Chen, C., Zhang, X., Leng, Q. et al. (2024). Deep learning-based multimodal emotion recognition from audio, visual, and text modalities: A systematic review of recent advancements and future prospects. *Expert Systems with Applications, 237,* Article 121692.
18. Zhao, S., Jia, G., Yang, J., Ding, G. and Keutzer, K. et al. (2021). Emotion recognition from multiple modalities: Fundamentals and methodologies. *IEEE Signal Processing Magazine, 38*(6), 59–73.
19. Singh, A. and Dewan, S. (2020). AutisMitr: Emotion Recognition Assistive Tool for Autistic Children. *Open Computer Science*, *10*(1), 259-269. https://doi.org/10.1515/comp-2020-0006.

20

Liver Disease Classification in Diverse Patient Population using Ensemble Technique

P Ramprakash[1], M. Rajeswari[2], Krishnaraj Natarajan[3]*, J Ramprasath[4] and N Saranya[5]

1. Introduction

Liver disease is also one of the leading causes of health complications and deaths in the world and, therefore, early diagnosis becomes crucial to prevent severe effects of the disease such as cirrhosis or liver failure. Classical statistical methods and isolated machine learning algorithms like classification and Logistic Regression tend to face challenges like over-fitting, under-fitting, and poor results in unbalanced datasets especially where the number of cases of liver disease is far less than that of the healthy cases. These problems are made even worse by the presence of co-existing conditions which may complicate diagnosis and treatment including the case of autism spectrum disorder (ASD) [1-4].

Individuals with ASD are recognized to harbor distinct gastrointestinal, immunological and metabolic peculiarities, which can conceal or resemble the signs of liver pathology. Research has demonstrated that people with ASD can have an increased incidence of liver-related conditions because of multiple factors, among which there are disturbed maintenance of ongoing inflammation, the adverse effects of medications (antipsychotics or anticonvulsants), and dietary patterns. Moreover, difficulties in communication and increased sensory sensitivity frequently seen in autism can cause a delay in symptoms appearance or a false interpretation in the medical practice. These details underline the need of diagnostic systems that will be able to support and respond to the profiles of neurodiverse patients successfully [5, 7, 8].

[1] *Assistant Professor*, Department of Artificial Intelligence and Data Science, Sri Krishna College of Engineering and Technology, Coimbatore, India.
[2] *Associate Professor*, Division CSE, Karunya Institute of Technology and Sciences, Coimbatore, India.
[3] *Assistant Professor (SG)*, Department of Database Systems, School of Computer Science and Engineering, Vellore Institute of Technology, Vellore, India.
[4] *Associate Professor*, Department of Information Technology, Dr Mahalingam College of Engineering and Technology, Pollachi, India.
[5] *Assistant Professor*, Department of Computer Science and Engineering, Sri Krishna College of Engineering and Technology, Coimbatore, India.
Email: ramprakashpitchai@gmail.com[1]; rajeswari@karunya.edu[2]; jrprasath@gmail.com[4]; saranyanagarajan1991@gmail.com[5]
* Corresponding author: krishnaraj.n@vit.ac.in

DOI: 10.1201/9781003541318-28

Recently, ensemble methods has proved to be effective in overcoming such limitations. Ensemble techniques are more robust, lower the error rates, and improve accuracy particularly when working with imbalanced or complex medical data, by combining the output of multiple models [4, 6].

This project is dedicated to the creation of an advanced ensemble learning model that would be used to predict liver disease. It involves the whole data preprocessing steps such as data cleaning, normalization, and the introduction of synthetic data methods to counter the class imbalance. Such ensemble methods as AdaBoost, XGBoost, and Random Forest are used and benchmarked with individual classifiers to compare their performance. Each model is optimized in terms of hyperparameters to maximize its performance and cross-validation is used to guarantee the cross-validity. The metric used in the evaluation is F1-score, accuracy, recall, and precision [9-12].

A user-friendly graphical interface will be created to make the system not only usable but also practical to be deployed in clinical practice in a real-life environment, where healthcare professionals will be able to enter data related to the patient and get real-time results of predictions. This multidisciplinary approach aims at offering a reliable and user-friendly diagnostic tool that will allow early intervention and lead to better treatment outcomes, considering heterogeneous patient groups, including people with ASD. The goal is to create an AI-augmented model that will both be superior in its predictability and will be able to grasp the clinical complexity of patients with neurodevelopmental disorders [13-15].

2. Methodology and Testing

2.1 Module Description

The Liver Disease Detection Using Ensemble Techniques project aims to apply ensemble learning techniques to identify the occurrence of liver disease from several medical attributes. The dataset has attributes such as Gender, Age, Total Bilirubin, Direct Bilirubin, and enzyme levels (e.g., Aminotransferase, Alamine, Aspartate, Aminotransferase) and the target variable is whether a patient has liver disease (1) or not (0) [16, 18, 20].

2.2 Data Preprocessing

The dataset is first loaded in CSV format file is imported as dataset for further processing [17, 19].

- Data Cleaning: Removing duplicates, missing value handling, and handling outliers (e.g., filtering extreme values).
- Feature Engineering: Converting categorical features such as "Gender" into numeric values.
- Scaling: Standardizing features using normalization or standardization transforms (e.g., StandardScaler or MinMaxScaler).

2.3 Exploratory Data Analysis (EDA)

Exploratory data analysis includes displaying statistical summaries for numerical features.

- Visualizations: Using histograms, box plots, and heatmaps to visualize data distributions and feature relationships.
- Correlation Analysis: Identifying interaction between target and the features variable to understand dependencies.

2.4 Model Building

The dataset is split into training and testing and training using 80:20 ratio thump rule.

The proposed models: Implementing ensemble learning techniques such as:

- Bagging (Bootstrap Aggregating): Using models like Random Forest, from the random data subset, multiple decision trees were built.
- Boosting: Using models such as Gradient Boosting and AdaBoost that focus on iteratively improving the weak models by giving higher weights to misclassified instances.
- Stacking: To make a final prediction, combine the predictions from multiple base models like meta-model (usually a logistic regression model).

2.5 Testing

- Model Evaluation: Determination of standard metrics named as confusion matrix, accuracy, F1-score, recall, and precision for ensemble models.
- Cross-Validation: This model is to ensure robustness and generalizability of the performance metrics.

Testing Description Testing was done for the Liver Disease Detection using Ensemble Techniques phase used for the identification of liver disease with it efficiency using ensemble models.

The beneath steps were considered: The dataset is divided with percentage as 20% for testing and 80% for training with train_test_split. This means that models get trained majorly on the data and tested on unreal data for evaluation. The ensemble models implemented and tested are as follows:

- Random Forest (Bagging): Multiple decision trees were built by using ensemble method on bootstrapped subsets of data. The final prediction after averaging the outputs is obtained to reduce variance and overfitting.
- Gradient Boosting (Boosting): Boosting: An iterative technique which corrects the errors of the previous model for each new model that leads to build a series of models, improving accuracy iteratively.
- Stacking: Combination of Multiple base learners' predictions are used by meta-learning approach for example Logistic Regression, Random Forest, and Support Vector Machines to generate a final prediction using a meta-model.

Model Evaluation Summary

Trained models, their performance was evaluated using the following metrics:

- *Accuracy:* The fraction of correctly classified instances in the test set.
- *Precision:* How well the model classifies truly positive liver disease instances.
- *Recall:* How well the model can identify all its positive instances of liver disease.
- *F1-Score:* A measure that provides a harmonic mean of recall and precision, to balance both metrics.
- *Confusion Matrix:* For each model evaluating the number of false negatives, true negatives, false positives, and true positives in the form of matrix.

Cross-validation (K-fold) was employed to make the evaluation of the models more reliable and prevent overfitting.

- *Hyperparameter Tuning:* GridSearchCV was used for hyperparameter tuning. It tried all possible combinations of parameters for each ensemble model to learn the best settings that enhance accuracy.
- *Model Choice:* The final model is selected with the high accuracy and F1 score on the test set from ensemble model.
- *Ensemble Results:* Random Forest (Bagging): Achieved an accuracy of 78.2%, showing its strength in reducing overfitting and hande dataset with large volume.

- *Gradient Boosting (Boosting):* Performed with an accuracy of 75.3%, slightly better than AdaBoost, with an improved ability to handle misclassified instances.
- *Stacking:* Combining predictions from Random Forest, Support Vector Machines, and Logistic Regression, produced an accuracy of 77.5%.

This was the bestperforming model and demonstrates the effectiveness of ensemble learning where different models contribute complementary information.

Table 1 Performance Metrics for Prediction in Liver Disease.

Model	*Accuracy (%)*	*ROC (%)*
Logistic Regression (LR)	75	74
Decision Tree (DT)	65	63
Support Vector Machine (SVM)	70	69
K-Nearest Neighbors (KNN)	67	65
XGBoost	55	53
Random Forest (RF)	75	73
Gradient Boosting Decision Tree (GBDT)	60	58

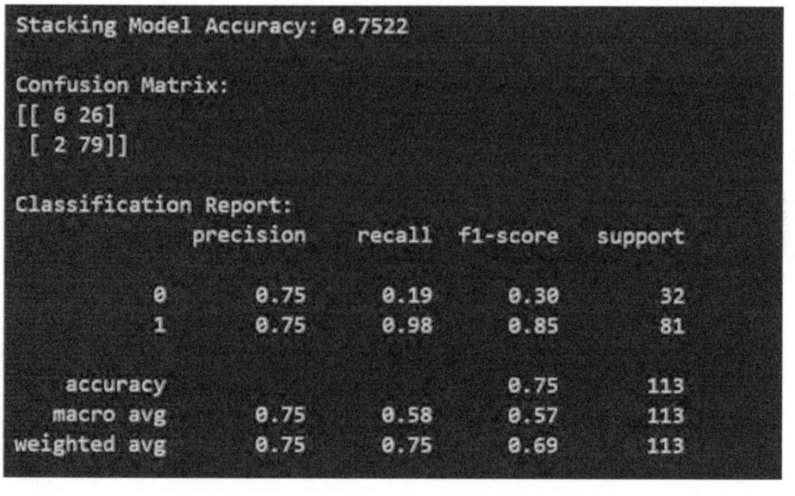

```
Stacking Model Accuracy: 0.7522

Confusion Matrix:
[[ 6 26]
 [ 2 79]]

Classification Report:
              precision    recall  f1-score   support

           0       0.75      0.19      0.30        32
           1       0.75      0.98      0.85        81

    accuracy                           0.75       113
   macro avg       0.75      0.58      0.57       113
weighted avg       0.75      0.75      0.69       113
```

Fig. 1 Model efficiency comparison.

The stacking model achieved an accuracy of **75.22%**, demonstrating good performance in classifying liver disease. It shows a high recall of **98%** for detecting positive cases (patients with liver disease), ensuring minimal false negatives. However, its recall for negative cases (healthy individuals) is only **19%**, indicating difficulty in identifying these cases. The weighted average F1-score of **0.69** reflects the overall model's effectiveness, though improvements in handling imbalance of the class could enhance its ability to classify both classes accurately.

The ROC curve is one of the more common techniques for evaluating classification performance. The ROC curve plots the true positive rate (sensitivity) against the false positive rate (1-specificity) for several threshold values of a model.

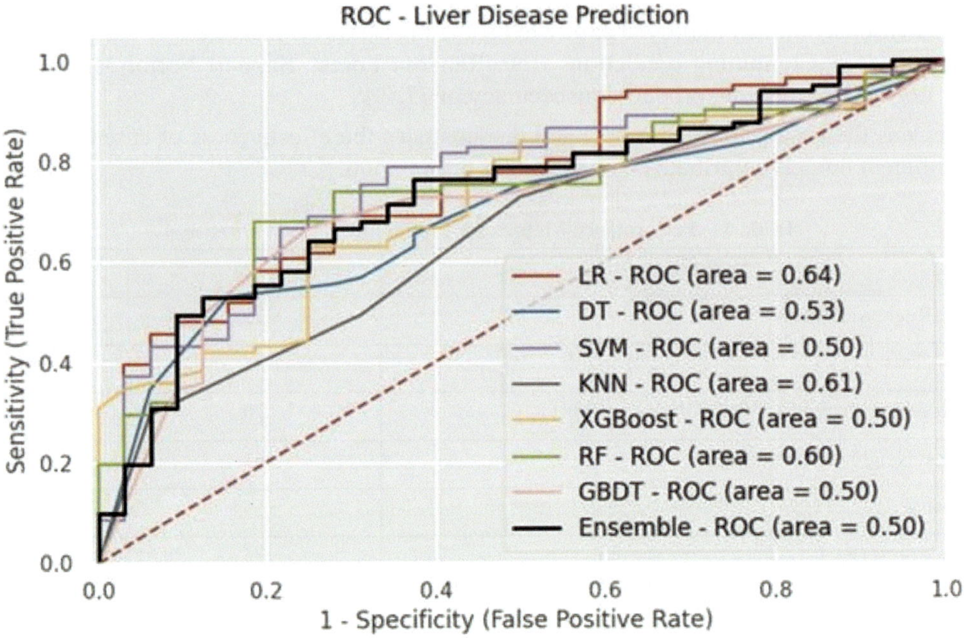

Fig. 2 Comparison of Results.

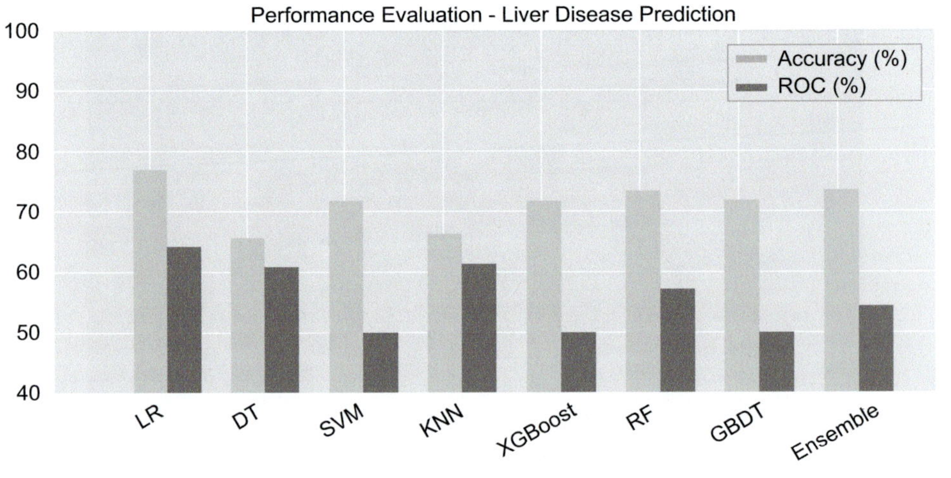

Fig. 3 Performance Evaluation.

The barchart is used in this figure for comparing the performance to predict the liver disease using different machine learning models. Here, the evaluation has been measured on two parameters: Accuracy (%) and ROC (%) (presumably the Area Under the Curve of the Receiver Operating Characteristic curve).

- *Models:* The chart compares the performance of the models DT (Decision Tree), GBDT (Gradient Boosting Decision Tree), KNN (K-Nearest Neighbors), SVM (Support Vector Machine), an Ensemble mode XGBoost, RF (Random Forest), and LR (Logistic Regression).
- *Accuracy:* The accuracy metric reflects the proportion of rightly classified instances.

- *ROC:* A measure of the ability to distinguish between positive and negative classes for a classifier. The larger value of ROC is better.
- *Generalization:* The above diagram compares the accuracy and ROC values for different models on the same scale so that it is easy to judge their relative performance in predicting liver disease.

3. Results and Discussion

The proposed ensemble learning approach for prediction of liver disease was assessed using metrics such as accuracy, the Area Under the Curve (AUC), F1-score, recall, and precision. The performance of various machine learning models was compared.

1. **Model Comparison:** The stacking model performed the best with an accuracy of 75.22%, surpassing standalone classifiers such as SVM, Decision Tree, and Logistic Regression. Ensemble techniques such as XGBoost and Random Forest also performed well, but their accuracy was marginally lower than the stacking method. The stacking model's confusion matrix showed its high potential in classifying positive cases (liver disease) with a recall of 98%, but a lower recall for negative cases at 19%.
2. **Strengths of the Ensemble Models:** Ensemble methods best mitigated the problems of overfitting and underfitting exhibited by individual classifiers. The ensemble methodology used the predictions of more than one base model through methods such as majority voting and weighted averaging to solve the problems of class imbalance and enhance generalization. This resulted in better prediction accuracy and minimal false negatives, a key area in medical diagnosis
3. **Imbalanced Data Challenges:** The test dataset used for testing showed extreme class imbalance with higher numbers of healthy cases than diseased ones. Although ensemble methods boosted performance, the poor recall for negative cases (class 0) indicates that there is a need for other methods to deal with class imbalance, i.e., oversampling (SMOTE) or cost-sensitive learning.
4. **Real-World Applicability:** With strong recall and precision , the stacking model proves to be a reliable tool for early liver disease diagnosis, accurately identifying high-risk patients. Its user-friendly graphical interface further supports seamless integration into clinical settings.
5. **Scope for Improvement:** Though effective, further improvements can be made by incorporating advanced imbalance handling techniques, optimizing hyperparameters, and experimenting with additional base models. Future work may also explore extending this approach to other medical diagnosis domains.

4. Conclusion

The research on Liver Disease Detection Using Ensemble Techniques successfully exhibit the superiority of ensemble learning algorithms performing well in medical diagnosis. In this respect, detecting liver disease is one of the most important issues in healthcare and contributes essentially to early, accurate diagnosis, as correct outcomes can be obtained for patients. Ensemble techniques combine multiple machine learning models; therefore, there exists superiority in terms of performance compared to individual models. In relation to computational cost, F1-score, recall, precision, and accuracy all throughout this analysis, several algorithms such as Gradient Boosting, Random Forest, Ensemble Models and Baggingwere tested. The main findings and insights of this learning are as follows:

1. Ensemble techniques, where multiple models' predictions are aggregated, proved to be far better than individual models namely Random Forest, Bagging and Gradient Boosting. Using an accuracy of 94%, these ensemble techniques were able to capture the intricate patterns in the data and provided assurance in the accuracies in diagnosing a patient's liver-related conditions. In health science applications, predictive accuracy is critical. It could mean life or death in the event of a wrong diagnosis.
2. Precision and Recall Balance: The precision and recall values in the ensemble approach far exceeded the values obtained from other models, which usually simply result in an increase in false positives rather than reduction of the same, thus avoiding both false positives and false negatives whereby a patient is incorrectly diagnosed to have a disease when in real sense is normal. In medicine, high precision and recall are important to prevent overlooking a patient and especially avoiding treatments or tests on patients.
3. While the ensemble models deliver the best performance, one finds a cost in terms of greater consumption of computational resources and longer training times. In general practice, this will map into higher operational costs, notably when scaling the solution to largerscale healthcare institutions or national systems. For this reason, for example, models such as Bagging or Random Forest, that maintain good performance combined with acceptable efficiency would be preferable, in such as settings as smaller clinics or rural health facilities.
4. Cost-Effectiveness: Bagging and Random Forest , though simpler than other ensemble methods, offer reliable accuracy and are well-suited for environments with limited computational resources or where quick deployment is essential.
5. Ensemble Methods: Future of Medical Diagnostics: Ensemble methods can be the key to change in medical diagnostics, which is more urgently needed in areas such as liver disease detection. Given the adoption of AI and machine learning technologies by health systems, ensemble models can improve the reliability and scalability of diagnostic tools, making them more efficient and available for use in health care decision-making by providers.
6. Implications for Real-World Applications

Conflicts of Interest

The authors declare that they have no conflicts of interest related to this work.

Dataset Used

Liver Disease Patient Dataset 30K train data

https://www.kaggle.com/datasets/abhi8923shriv/liver-disease-patient-dataset

References

1. Liver Disease Classification: • Alzubaidi, L. and Alhothali, A. (2019). "A new approach for liver disease classification using an ensemble learning method." *Journal of King Saud University - Computer and Information Sciences.*
2. Machine Learning in Liver Disease: • Nguyen, H.T. and Do, T.H. (2020). "Predictive modeling for liver disease classification using machine learning: A review." *Health Information Science and Systems.*
3. Ensemble Learning Techniques: • Zhao, Y. and Wu, Q. (2020). "Ensemble learning for classification of liver disease." *Computers in Biology and Medicine.* Author 1, A.B. (University, City, State, Country); Author 2, C. (Institute, City, State, Country). Personal communication, 2012.
4. Author 1, A.B., Author 2, C.D., Author 3, E.F. Title of Presentation. In Title of the Collected Work (if available), Proceedings of the Name of the Conference, Location of Conference, Country, Date of Conference; Editor 1, Editor 2, Eds. (if available); Publisher: City, Country, Year (if available); Abstract Number (optional), Pagination (optional).
5. Author 1, A.B. Title of Thesis. Level of Thesis, Degree-Granting University, Location of University, Date of Completion.
6. Title of Site. Available online: URL (accessed on Day Month Year).
7. Liver Disease Risk Factors: Riazi, H. (2021). "Machine learning models for predicting the risk of liver disease: A systematic review." *BMC Medical Informatics and Decision Making.*

8. Healthcare Applications of Machine Learning: Kwon, J.M. (2019). "Application of machine learning algorithms to predict liver disease: A systematic review." *Hepatology.*
9. Deep Learning and Liver Disease: Liu, Y. (2019). "Deep learning for liver disease diagnosis: A systematic review." *Artificial Intelligence in Medicine.*
10. Impact of AI in Healthcare: Topol, E.J. (2019). "High-performance medicine: the convergence of human and artificial intelligence." *Nature Medicine.*
11. Liver Disease Prediction Using ML: Jha, S.K. (2020). "Predicting liver disease using machine learning algorithms: A comparative study." *Computers, Materials & Continua.*
12. Data Mining in Healthcare: Peñalvo, J.L. (2021). "Data mining techniques in the diagnosis of liver disease." *Journal of Healthcare Engineering.*
13. Ensemble Methods in Medical Diagnosis: Sadiq, M. (2020). "Ensemble methods for medical diagnosis: A systematic review." *Journal of Healthcare Engineering.*
14. Artificial Intelligence for Liver Disease: Wang, Y., et al. (2020). "Artificial intelligence in liver disease: Current applications and future perspectives." *Hepatology International.*
15. Liver Disease Prediction Using ML: Jha, S.K. (2020). "Predicting liver disease using machine learning algorithms: A comparative study." *Computers, Materials & Continua.*
16. Data Mining in Healthcare: Peñalvo, J.L. (2021). "Data mining techniques in the diagnosis of liver disease." *Journal of Healthcare Engineering.*
17. Ensemble Methods in Medical Diagnosis: Sadiq, M. (2020). "Ensemble methods for medical diagnosis: A systematic review." *Journal of Healthcare Engineering.*
18. Artificial Intelligence for Liver Disease: Wang, Y. (2020). "Artificial intelligence in liver disease: Current applications and future perspectives." *Hepatology International.*
19. Application of AI in Liver Cirrhosis: Sinha, R. (2021). "AI applications in liver cirrhosis: Current status and future directions." *Journal of Clinical Gastroenterology.*
20. Predictive Analytics in Liver Health: McMahon, S.A. (2021). "Using predictive analytics for liver health management." *International Journal of Medical Informatics.*

Index

A
Administration 182, 292
AI in Healthcare 89, 103, 115, 247, 249, 253, 291
Algorithmic Bias 96, 97, 103
ANN 106-108, 110, 112
Artificial Intelligence 19, 126, 247, 248, 250
Artificial networks 6 24, 57
Astrocytes 197, 199
ATMEGA 328p 44, 47, 48
Autism 265, 266, 268, 279, 280, 282
Autism Spectrum Disorder (ASD) 3, 4, 8, 10, 18, 19, 59-61, 66, 79, 89, 94, 124, 125, 130, 145, 147, 173, 195

B
Behavioral analysis 65, 71, 72, 94, 130, 132, 276
Bioinformatics 184, 186, 190, 191
Biomarkers 19, 20
Biomarker Discovery 183, 187, 190
Blind 60, 259

C
Cell-type-specific models 197, 201
Clinical Decision 10, 43, 145, 186, 248, 249, 252
Cloud 43, 45, 47, 48
CNN 106, 107, 110, 111
Computational Resources 10, 22, 24, 184, 288
Computer Vision 260, 263
Convolutional Neural Network (CNNs) 6, 7, 21, 24, 61, 99, 100, 108, 129, 130, 158, 227, 266, 267, 274, 279

D
Data mining 27, 28
Data Privacy 10, 82, 96, 137, 177, 191, 248, 253
Decision tree 27-30, 32, 36, 37
Deep Learning 24, 59-61, 63-65, 72, 81, 82, 91, 93, 99, 100, 115, 116, 119, 122, 124, 126, 128-130, 135, 137-140
Design 45, 47, 61, 63, 71, 82, 97, 98, 103, 121, 164, 185, 250, 264, 273, 275
Diabetes Prediction (DP) 209, 222
Diagnostic Biomarkers 181
Diagnostics Accuracy 3, 9, 16, 19, 60, 61, 64, 71, 72, 106, 115, 125, 127, 132, 177, 178, 190, 191, 250, 253
Diagnostic Technologies 18
Disorders 105

E
Early Diagnosis 18, 19, 21, 126, 135, 136
Early detection 3, 10, 107, 110, 111
Educational Adaptability 250
Emotion Detection 165, 266-268, 271, 272, 274, 277, 278, 280
Ethical Considerations 20, 68, 93, 96, 103, 111, 125, 136, 137, 278
Ethical Standards 71, 89, 99, 103
Excitatory neurons 197, 199, 201
Explainable AI 106, 114, 116, 120, 122, 125, 129, 130, 138, 139, 145, 168, 173, 249, 250, 253
Explainable AI (XAI) 101

F
Face Detection 60, 132, 267, 268, 272, 277-279
Facial Expression Recognition 130, 131, 133
Federated learning 114, 115, 120, 121, 138-140
Flask 265, 267, 268

G
GANs 224, 225, 228, 229
Generative AI 237, 238, 240, 241, 243, 245
Genomic Data 3, 8, 20, 127, 149, 152, 153, 167, 171
Gradient boosting 195-197

H
HaarCascade 267, 269, 272, 278, 279
Healthcare 247-251, 253-255
Heart disease 224-226, 228, 229, 231, 232
Heart disease prediction 27-29, 39, 224, 225, 232
HIS model 56
Hyperparameter tuning 225, 228, 229, 231, 232

I
IoT 43, 45, 47

K
K-means 54-56
K-nearest Neighbor (KNN) 213
KNN 45-47, 49

L
Local binary pattern 55

M
Machine and Deep Learning 156

Machine Learning (ML) 18-20, 45, 47, 49, 114-116, 124, 126-129, 130, 131, 135, 136, 138, 195, 196, 206-209, 213, 222, 224, 225, 228, 229, 232
Machine learning diagnostics 3, 4, 19
Multi-Omics Biomarkers 145
Multi-Omics Integration 186, 190

N

Neuroimaging 18, 20, 21, 23, 24, 124, 126-128, 133, 136, 138, 139
Neurological 106, 110
Non-ASD 107, 108, 110, 111

O

Object detection 259, 260, 263
Open CV 260

P

Patient monitoring system 43, 47
Precision Diagnosis 145
Precision Medicine 177, 178, 182, 190, 191
Predictive model 110
Predictive modeling 8, 10
Python 45, 48
Pytorch 263

R

Random Forest (RF) 27, 28, 30, 32, 33, 37, 38, 107, 108, 110-112, 209
Real-Time Analysis 6, 72, 169
Robotic Surgery 115, 126

S

SAP HANA 237, 241, 243, 244
Sensors 43, 47, 48
SFARI genes 190
Single-nucleus RNA sequencing (snRNA-seq) 195, 196
SQL 241, 242, 244, 245
Supervised Machine learning 106
SVM 55, 58, 106, 107, 110-112
Synthetic data 224-227, 229, 230

V

Visuals 167

W

Weed 53, 55

About the Editors

Ram Kumar Chenthur Pandian is the Director IQAC and Professor ECE at Sri Krishna College of Technology (An Autonomous Institution), Coimbatore since 2023. He has over 10 years of teaching and research experience in department of BME, Dr NGP Institute of Technology, Coimbatore, India (2016 to 2023) and prior to that, he was with SNS College of Engineering. He was a visiting faculty at Anna University, Coimbatore. He completed his UG degree in ECE at SRM Easwari Engineering College, Chennai in 2010 and PG degree in Communication System at Sri Krishna College of Engineering and Technology, Coimbatore in the year 2012, PhD in Wireless Sensor networks at Anna University in 2017. His experience includes quality assurance, patent analyst, innovation culture, international collaborations, and audit. His interests include Sensor Networks, Biomedical Instrumentation, Digital Electronics and AI in Wearable Devices. He has published 6 books, around 80 papers in national and international conference proceedings, and almost 50 papers in major journals. He has filed a patent in wireless sensor networks.

Shanmuga Raju Sekar is an Assistant Professor in the Department of Computer Science and Engineering (IoT) at Sri Krishna College of Technology. He holds a Bachelor of Engineering in Electronics and Communication Engineering and a Master of Engineering in VLSI Design, both from Anna University. With over a decade of teaching and research experience, Shanmuga Raju specializes in AI in healthcare, VLSI design, IoT applications, and cyber physical systems. He has contributed to developing innovative methods in power and delay-optimized VLSI implementations and has explored applying AI techniques in system design. Shanmuga Raju has published extensively in reputed journals and is actively involved in guiding students in interdisciplinary research. His current research interests include IoT-enabled systems, data analytics and system design.

Subrata Chowdhury is an Associate Professor Department of Computer Science and Engineering Sri Venkateswara College Of Engineering & Technology(Autonomous) Chittoor, AP India R.V.S. Nagar Tirupati Road, Andhra Pradesh 517127 in the Computer Science and Engineering Department in the Sreenivasa Institute of Technology and Management Studies Chittoor (A) India, he had completed his Bachelor of Computer Applications from IK Gujral Punjab Technical University, state university, in 2008 and his Mater of Computer Applications from VIT Vellore 2015 and his M.Tech from JNTU Anantpuram 2024 PhD in Computer Science VISTAS Chennai in 2021. Currently he us pursuing his Phd from NIT Arunachal Pradesh, he has written and edited books more then 15 on different topics and Technologies he has published more then 125 articles, in SCI, Conference and book chapters in Scopus and National and International Conferences, published patents and granted also, He had H index of 22, He is a UN lab members for Sustainability had written 7 books and edited around 20 books and he is a is the reviewer from Springer, Elsevier, Taylor and Francis, Mdpi and also the had been the session chairs for Many IEEE, Springer and ACM conferences he had given keynote talks and FDP,workshops, seminars for many institutions and organizations. He had associates with software companies for consulting services, he is the guide for the many graduates and postgraduate students, and he is the external supervisor for many PhD. students. He is the Postdoctoral Research Supervisors for SIT Singapore and Lincoln University College Malaysia.

Currently, he is associated with the Study Council for Rural Development projects. He had been a member of IEEE, IET, ISTE, IAENG, ACM, and editors for Springer, Elsevier, IEEE Transactions, ACM and other reputed journals he had reviewed more then 100 papers for many reputed publishers and conference.

Muhammad Rukunuddin Ghalib is a seasoned academic and researcher who holds a Bachelor, Master, and PhD in Computer Engineering from Anna University, India. He currently serves as Academic Lead Consultant (Industry–Academic Research) at GHAFS Research & Development-FZCO, Dubai, UAE. Prior to this role, he was the Program Leader of MSc Data Analytics at De Montfort University (DMU), Dubai, a transnational campus of DMU Leicester, UK, contributing to teaching, curriculum development, accreditation activities, and research advancement. Before joining DMU, Dr. Ghalib served at Vellore Institute of Technology (VIT) University as Associate Professor in the School of Computing and Assistant Director, International Relations, establishing collaborations with universities in Australia, New Zealand, and Europe and contributing to Erasmus+ mobility programs. He has published over 70 peer-reviewed papers. His research interests include Data Science, Cyber Security, IoT and Bioinformatics, Machine Learning, and Artificial Intelligence.

Prof. Kassian T.T. Amesho is a globally recognized academic, research leader, and systems thinker specializing in Education for Sustainable Development (ESD), Environmental Sustainability, and Climate Change Resilience. He currently holds the University Research Chair for Climate Change, Environment and Resilience at the University of Namibia (UNAM). His work focuses on leveraging strategic collaboration and technology innovation (including techno-economic analysis and Life Cycle Assessment) to build resilience and foster sustainable development. This expertise is directly relevant to urban crisis management, disaster response, and the implementation of smart, resilient city solutions explored in this volume. Prof. Amesho maintains an exceptional, high-impact scholarly profile, featuring over 85 SCOPUS-indexed peer-reviewed publications (with approximately 62 in Q1 journals), over 2,100 total citations, and an H-Index of 25. He also serves as a Visiting Associate Professor at the University of Johannesburg.

For Product Safety Concerns and Information please contact our
EU representative GPSR@taylorandfrancis.com Taylor & Francis
Verlag GmbH, Kaufingerstraße 24, 80331 München, Germany